HANDBOOK OF DENOMINATIONS

In Memory
of
Frank S. Mead (1898–1982)

HANDBOOK OF DENOMINATIONS

IN THE UNITED STATES

New Eighth Edition

Frank S. Mead

Revised by

Samuel S. Hill

Abingdon Press
NASHVILLE

HANDBOOK OF DENOMINATIONS IN THE UNITED STATES

New Eighth Edition

Fifth Printing 1988

This book is printed on acid-free paper.

Library of Congress Cataloging in Publication Data

MEAD, FRANK SPENCER, 1898–1982
Handbook of denominations in the United States.
Bibliography: p. Includes index.
1. Christian sects—United States. 2. Sects—United States.
I. Hill, Samuel S. II. Title.
BR516.5.M38 1985 291'.0973 84-24342

ISBN 0-687-16571-7

MANUFACTURED BY THE PARTHENON PRESS AT
NASHVILLE, TENNESSEE, UNITED STATES OF AMERICA

PREFACE
to the Eighth Edition

Obtaining information about America's religious groups can be difficult; providing it to others is a king-sized undertaking. For one thing, there are so many. For another, finding a way to make contact with them to gather facts and figures, especially from the smaller, less highly organized ones, can be a mystery. And then there is the question of which ones to include in a reference book of this kind. Finally, classifying them—that is, under which heading, if any, to place them and how to list them by title—sometimes requires a judgment call or even a bold venture.

Since the Seventh Edition was issued in 1980, five years ago, the decision has been made to remove a few bodies from this listing; also to add a few. A group was excluded if it obviously was very small and attempts to make contact proved fruitless. Some quite small groups do retain a place in the *Handbook* owing to their historic importance or to their position of some significance on the recent American scene.

The twin facts of few deletions and few additions reveal something about the status and patterns of religion in America. The interpretive essay in the back of this book seeks to develop this phenomenon. American religion continues to grow and adapt, but the changes have little to do with the appearance of new religious bodies. The manner in which older groups diminish and disappear also affords clues to the patterns of American religion.

Users of this *Handbook* are reminded that it also includes a glossary—terms employed by the religious bodies themselves in their faith, worship, and organization—and a listing of the addresses of the headquarters of the various denominations.

Finding the material about a certain group treated here can sometimes be a challenge. The reader is referred to the index as well as to the table of contents for help. In the event a group is not included here, one may turn to J. Gordon Melton, *Encyclopedia of American Religions*, or to Arthur C. Piepkorn's multivolume *Profiles in Belief*.

The denominations are arranged alphabetically. In the case of a large family—Baptist, Methodist, Pentecostal, or Judaism, for example—the various bodies that belong to each are listed alphabetically under those headings, irrespective of size. Some classifications may puzzle the user. "Plymouth Brethren" is in the P section, not as a unit in the "Brethren" family. The reason is that *Brethren* means one thing in the case of that family of German Protestantism, but quite something else to the nineteenth-century English group that is only coincidentally—and not always necessarily—called Plymouth Brethren. Mormons may be found under L, since they are actually Latter Day Saints. The various Eastern Christian bodies are treated as "Orthodox."

Finally, I must pay tribute to the late Frank S. Mead, the true author of the *Handbook of Denominations in the United States*. He thought it up, worked it up, and followed it up, from its inception in 1951 through the Seventh Edition of 1980. I am proud to have my name associated with his in this Eighth Edition.

Samuel S. Hill
Gainesville, Florida
December 1984

CONTENTS

ADVENTIST

Adventism in general is a Christian faith based upon the conviction that the second advent of Christ is the sole hope of the world. It holds that the nature of the human race is fallen because of sin and that on the basis of neglect or rejection of God's plan of salvation, those rebellious against the government of God will be ultimately destroyed, while believers, by God's grace, will be saved. After this cataclysmic event Jesus Christ will reign in triumph through the thousand-year period, or millennium, of Rev. 20:1-6. The whole Adventist thesis rests heavily upon the prophetic and apocalyptic texts of Daniel and Revelation.

As a religious movement, it began with a widespread "awakening" on the question of the advent, that developed spontaneously in both the Old World and the New in the early decades of the nineteenth century. It became strongest and most clearly defined in the United States, at first under the leadership of William Miller (1782–1849) of Low Hampton, New York, a veteran of the War of 1812 respected as a diligent student of the Bible, though he did not have formal college or seminary training.

The movement under Miller was at first an interchurch (or more accurately, *intra*church) development, with many Methodists, Christians, Baptists, Presbyterians, and Congregationalists among its adherents. It was thus a movement within existing churches, and in the days of its beginnings there was no intention or attempt to organize a separate denomination. So influential was William Miller that for years his followers were known as Millerites. Miller himself became a Baptist in 1816 and at once began a careful study of the Scriptures, concentrating on the prophecies of Daniel and Revelation. Using only the Bible, its marginal references, and Cruden's *Concordance*, he came to the same conclusion that many Old and New World biblical scholars had already reached—that the symbolic "day" of Bible prophecy represents a year. He also concluded that the 2,300 "days" of Dan. 8:14 started concurrently with the "seventy weeks of years" of Dan. 9, or from 457 B.C., the year of the command to rebuild and restore Jerusalem; and he believed that the longer of the two periods would end in or about the year 1843, as calculated by Jewish reckoning. Miller thought that the "sanctuary" mentioned in Dan. 8:14 was the earth (or the church) that would be cleansed by fire at the second advent. He came to believe that this cleansing would occur sometime between March 21, 1843, and March 21, 1844.

When the advent expectation failed to materialize by the spring of 1844, many left the movement. Miller's associates, on the basis of meticulous study of Old Testament types, set a second date, October 22, 1844, as the great antitypical Day of Atonement, confident that the "day of the Lord is near, even at the door." By 1844 there were between 50,000 and 100,000 Adventists in North America. Some disposed of their property as the day of expectation approached, gave away their goods, settled all their accounts, and waited prayerfully for the Lord to come. When October 22 passed with no second coming, vast numbers lost all interest in Adventism and went back to their former churches or abandoned the Christian faith altogether.

Those who continued as Adventists formed several smaller bodies. At first a loosely knit organization came into being at a conference in Albany, New York, in 1845. This group held generally to Miller's positions and theology, emphasizing the personal and premillennial character of the second advent of Christ, the resurrection of the dead—the faithful to be raised at Christ's coming, the rest a thousand years later—and the renewal of the earth as the eternal abode of the redeemed. Known at first as the American Millennial Association, a portion later came to be called Evangelical Adventist, a church that has dwindled with the passing of the years to the point of obscurity. Another and larger group in 1861 became known as the Advent Christian Church.

While the general expectation of the advent had united the disparate groups, the disappointment brought all their differences to light again. Nearly all Adventists were, at first, agreed that the second advent of Christ would be premillennial—that is, that his return would *precede* the thousand-year period foretold in Rev. 20. Today, however, many, including the Advent Christian group, hold the amillennial position.

In other areas there was wide difference of viewpoint also. Just what is the state of the dead—conscious or unconscious—as they await the resurrection? Who are to arise—the righteous *and* the wicked, or only the righteous? Is there to be eternal punishment for the wicked or ultimate annihilation? What is the nature of immortality? Does the cleansing of the sanctuary of Dan. 8 refer to a sanctuary in heaven, or on earth? When should the Sabbath be celebrated—on the first day, or on the seventh; on Sunday, or on Saturday? Over these questions the Adventists, as organized bodies, became divided into the three major groups we find them today.

Advent Christian Church

While William Miller was never active in the founding of the Advent Christian Church, his teachings concerning the imminent return of Christ were strongly influential. More important were the teachings of such men as Charles F. Hudson and George Storrs concerning the nature and mortality of the human race. Dissatisfied with what they felt was a purely Platonic doctrine of the immortality of the human soul, they rejected it completely and sought a more biblical emphasis. They preached a new doctrine of "conditional immortality," which declared the unconscious state of all the dead until the resurrection at Christ's return, the establishment of a divine tribunal for the determination of rewards and punishments, the ultimate extinction of all evil, and the inauguration of the everlasting kingdom of God upon this earth as a restored paradise.

The first Advent Christian Association was established at Salem, Massachusetts, in 1860, and its members—still Adventists, though cut off in their new doctrine from other Adventist churches—publicly disclaimed any intent to form a separate denominational group. They founded two colleges—Aurora College at Aurora, Illinois, and the Boston Bible School (now Berkshire Christian College) at Lenox, Massachusetts. Missionary work began in 1891; today there are mission stations in Malaysia, Japan, India, and the Philippines. The church maintains two homes for the aged, an orphanage, and a publishing department that issues four denominational periodicals.

Congregational in polity, 29,838 members in 364 local churches are grouped in 5 regional districts of the United States and Canada. These conferences, together with various institutions and cooperating societies, are associated under the Advent Christian General Conference of America, which meets in triennial session. The only creedal statement is a declaration of principles adopted by the general conference of 1900, with revisions in 1934, 1964, and 1972. Two sacraments are observed—baptism by immersion and the Lord's Supper. Worship is held on the first day of the week.

In 1964 this church merged with the Life and Advent Union, an Adventist group with 3 churches and 300 members, organized by John T. Walsh in 1848.

Church of God General Conference

This church is the outgrowth of several independent local groups of similar faith; some of them were in existence as early as 1800, and others date their beginnings from the arrival of British immigrants in this country around 1847. Many were organized originally under the name Church of God in Christ Jesus, and also carried the name Church of God of the Abrahamic Faith for many years. The corporate name today is the Church of God General Conference, Oregon, Illinois.

State and district conferences of these groups were formed as an expression of mutual cooperation. A national organization instituted at Philadelphia in 1888 met again in 1889; however, because of strong convictions on questions of congregational rights and authority, it ceased to function until 1921, when the present general conference was formed at Waterloo, Iowa.

The Bible is accepted as the supreme standard of faith. Adventist in viewpoint, the second (premillennial) coming of Christ is strongly emphasized. The church teaches that the kingdom of God will be literal, beginning at Jerusalem at the time of the return of Christ and extending to all nations. Emphasis is placed on the oneness of God and the Sonship of Christ; it is taught that Jesus did not exist prior to his birth in Bethlehem and that the Holy Ghost is the power and influence of God. Members believe in the restoration of Israel, the times of restitution, the mortality of humans (asleep in death until the resurrection), the literal resurrection of the dead, the reward of the righteous on earth, and the complete destruction of the wicked in a second death. Membership is dependent upon acceptance of doctrinal faith, repentance, and baptism (for the remission of sins) by immersion.

Delegates from each church meet each year to determine church plans and policies and to elect officers who serve as a board of directors. A general conference supports Oregon Bible College for the training of ministers; the Oregon Bible College Development Foundation, an endowment fund for the college; a Publishing Department that produces church literature and curriculum; and an Outreach and Church Development Department, which promotes youth work, Sunday School activity, mission, and evangelism. The work of the general conference is carried on under the direction of the board of directors, which meets as necessary throughout the year. The executive officer is an executive director who adminsters the work as a whole. The conference is incorporated as the Church of God, General Conference. Because of the congregational nature of the church's government the general conference exists primarily as a means of mutual cooperation and for the development of yearly projects and enterprises. There are 7,620 members in 95 churches, divided into 13 state and district conferences. The church periodical, *The Restitution Herald,* is published monthly. Mission stations are located in India, Mexico, the Philippine Islands, Nigeria, and Ghana.

Seventh-day Adventist

By far the largest single Adventist body in point of numbers, both in the United States and particularly throughout the world, is the Seventh-day Adventist Church, which traces its beginnings back to the 1840s. It arose in the aftermath of what has been termed the Great Disappointment, the failure of the Millerites' prediction that Christ would return on October 22, 1844.

By April of 1845, the Adventists who had unified during the Millerite Movement were becoming divided over interpretations of the relevance of that movement's past. The majority group abandoned its earlier belief that a significant event had occurred in 1844 and concluded that the 2,300-year prophecy of Dan. 8 would end sometime in the future.

Members of a smaller group, who would later become the Seventh-day Adventists, continued to study the Scriptures, searching for explanations of their past. They concluded that an event had indeed occurred in October of 1844 that had relevance to their past experience. They believed that the event corresponded with a change in Christ's ministry in heaven from the Holy to the Most Holy Place. As Adventists looked toward the Most Holy Place, the theology of what they termed the Third Angel's Message (Rev. 14) began to form. The group focused on the commandments of God and the faith of Jesus, seeking to show the interrelationship between the law and the gospel. It was thus that the Sabbath of the fourth commandment came to hold great relevance for the group.

As early as 1844, a small group of these Adventists near Washington, New Hampshire, had begun observing the Sabbath on the seventh day. A pamphlet written by Joseph Bates in 1846 gave the question wide publicity and created great interest. Shortly thereafter, Bates, together with James White, Ellen Harmon (later Mrs. James White, whose writings Seventh-day Adventists hold "in highest esteem. . . . [they] accept them as inspired counsels from the Lord"), Hiram Edson, Frederick Wheeler, and S. W. Rhodes, with the aid of regular publications, set out to champion the seventh-day Sabbath, along with the imminence of the Advent. Hence the name—Seventh-day Adventist.

The growth of the group around these leaders was slow at first, owing to the general derision in which Adventists were held. By 1855, however, it was prosperous and numerically strong enough to set up headquarters at Battle Creek, Michigan, with a publishing house, the Seventh-day Adventist Publishing Association. In 1860 the name Seventh-day Adventists was officially adopted, and in 1903 the headquarters was moved to its present location in Washington, D.C.

Doctrinally, the Seventh-day Adventists are evangelical conservatives with a sound Protestant recognition of the authoritative nature of the revelation of God through the inspired writings encompassed in the entire Bible. Their standard statement, appearing annually in their yearbook, states that they believe in the transcendent, personal, communicating God as revealed in the Father, the Son, and the Holy Spirit, each equally and uniquely divine, personal, and eternal. They believe in creation by divine fiat and recognize the fall of of the human race. Humans are by nature mortal, but may receive immortality through divine grace and the redemption offered through the total atoning work of Jesus Christ.

The church holds that the great principles of God's law are embodied in the Ten Commandments and exemplified in the life of Jesus Christ. Their observance of the seventh day as the Sabbath is based on the fourth commandment: "Six days shalt thou labour . . . but the seventh day is the sabbath of the Lord thy God."

The tithe provides the entire support of the ministry of the church. Beyond their tithes, Seventh-day Adventists give generously toward missions, local church expenses, and other church enterprises. In 1982 their total per capita giving was $778.66 in North America, and $194.32 in the world field.

The members believe in the gift of prophecy in the church; that the dead awaiting the resurrection are in an unconscious state; that the whole person will be resurrected on the last day, with immortality for the righteous and destruction by fire for the wicked. They seek religious liberty for all and advocate the complete separation of church and state. They consider the body of man to be the temple of the Holy Spirit and, in consequence, rigidly abstain from the use of alcoholic beverages, tobacco, and the promiscuous use of drugs. Likewise, they advocate sound principles of healthful living through diet, exercise, and philanthropic outlook. The church teaches the premillennial, personal, visible return of Christ "at a time unknown but close at hand" and in a new earth to be created out of the ruins of the old as the final abode of the redeemed. Immersion is practiced as the biblical form of baptism and foot washing as a preparatory service for Communion.

The overall administrative body of the church is the executive committee of the general conference, chosen by delegates from the various church groups in the quinquennial sessions. Working under this general conference are three lesser governmental units: (1) the 13 division organizations, administering church affairs on different continents; (2) 85 "union conferences," which make up the divisional organizations; and (3) 413 "local conferences," or missions, the smallest administrative units.

Each unit has a large amount of autonomy in a highly representative form of government. Local congregations elect lay elders, deacons, and other officers; the local conference office supervises all local pastoral and evangelistic work and pays all pastors and other workers in its territory from a central fund.

The evangelism, publishing, educational, health and welfare work are outstanding and highly successful. Regarding itself not as just another church, but as a movement established in the fulfillment of Bible prophecy to prepare humankind for the second advent and to revive and restore neglected truths of the Reformation and of the Apostolic church, it carries forward its work in 604 languages and dialects, 182 with publications and 422 orally. Fifty publishing houses are distributed over the world, with 4 in the United States.

In North America there are 10 liberal arts colleges; 3 universities; a theological seminary; and medical, dental, and physical therapy schools. In the United States and abroad the church supports 442 medical units and 51 nurses' training schools, 926 colleges and secondary schools, and 4,105 elementary schools. There are 4,646 weekly radio and television broadcasts in 80 languages; more than 6 million students are enrolled in Bible correspondence schools. An international broadcast, "The Voice of Prophecy," goes out over 1,043 stations weekly, and a weekly TV program, "Faith for Today," is viewed on 92 outlets. Still another, "It Is Written," is seen on 100 outlets each week.

Inasmuch as Seventh-day Adventists practice adult (age of accountabil-

18,087 – husban
+ w
1,500 – child

19,587

To

KEY PRINTING

1112 KEOKUK STREET
LINCOLN, ILLINOIS 62656
PHONE: 217-732-9879
Fax: 217-732-9866

Date ____________ Time ____________

Taken by ____________

M ____________

of ____________

Phone ____________ Ext. ____________

❑ Telephoned ❑ Called to see you ❑ Wants to see you
❑ Please Call ❑ Will Call Again ❑ Urgent

Message ____________

____

____

____

ity) baptism, no infants or children are reported in their total membership, listed at 3,897,814 in 23,382 churches; membership is limited to those who uphold church standards, including abstinence from liquor and tobacco. There are 622,961 Seventh-day Adventists in the United States and Canada, organized into 4,166 churches.

AFRICAN ORTHODOX CHURCH, THE

Believing that black Episcopalians should have churches of their own, a Protestant Episcopal rector, George Alexander McGuire, withdrew from that church in 1919 to establish independent black churches in the United States, Cuba, and Canada. He called them Independent Episcopal churches, but in 1921 the first general synod of the new body changed its name to The African Orthodox Church and elected McGuire as its first bishop. He was consecrated by Archbishop Vilatte, who took his episcopal orders from the West Syrian Church of Antioch. This placed McGuire in the traditional apostolic succession, which he valued highly.

The church lays strong emphasis upon the apostolic succession and upon historic sacraments and rituals. It celebrates the original seven sacraments of the Roman Catholic Church; its worship is a blend of Western and Eastern liturgy, creeds, and symbols. The liturgy is usually Western, a mingling of Anglican, Greek, and Roman patterns. Three creeds—Apostles', Nicene, and Athanasian—are used.

The denomination maintains the position that no priest may marry the guilty party in a divorce and that innocent parties are remarried only after special pemission by a bishop. The government is, of course, episcopal; bishops are in charge of dioceses, or jurisdictions, and groups of dioceses form a province, each led by an archbishop and a primate. The primate, in turn, presides over the provincial synod. At the head stands a primate archbishop metropolitan, general overseer of all the work of the church, which now extends over the United States into Canada, Latin America, and the Union of South Africa. Membership, as in the Roman Catholic Church, is counted not by communicants but by the number of persons baptized; in the United States there were 24 churches and 6,000 members in 1957.

AMANA CHURCH SOCIETY

Officially named the Amana Church Society (from the Aramaic *to remain faithful*), this group stems from the Pietistic movement in early eighteenth-century Germany. In 1714 a small company under the leadership of Johann Friedrich Rock and Eberhardt Ludwig Gruber stirred the German people with their pronouncements that the days of true and direct inspiration from God had not ended. These leaders and others had the divine gift of inspiration. They established new churches in the province of Hessen, Germany, but were persecuted until 1842, when approximately 800 of them came to America, and settled near Buffalo, New York. There they organized a Christian communal group called the Ebenezer Society.

All property was held and shared collectively; each person did the work for which he or she was fitted and shared equally in the rewards. Each of the six Ebenezer villages had a common school, a meetinghouse, and a store, and the settlers farmed the land around them, which had been purchased from the Seneca Indians through an American land syndicate. In 1854 and thereafter, they moved to Iowa, where the villages of Amana (East, South, Middle, High, West) and Homestead were established. Here the church became a nonprofit religious corporation, taking the name "Amana Society" in 1859.

In 1932 many communal practices were abandoned, and the Amana business society, with its own board of directors, and the Amana Church Society, with a separate board of 13 trustees, were organized. The Amana Church Society remains nonprofit while the Amana business society operates under a cooperative plan as a pecuniary corporation. The business society conducts many different enterprises and farms 25,000 acres of land, with the stockholders voting for directors in the multimillion dollar corporation. Employees draw salaries or wages.

The purpose of the Amana Church Society is purely religious; it is based upon the salvation of souls in the service of God. The members believe that God can inspire people now, as well as of old, but no one has been inspired since the historic leaders and the two early Americans, Christian Metz and Barbara Landmann, who died in the latter part of the nineteenth century. The Amana Church Society accepts the teachings of a holy universal church, the remission of sins, the communion of saints, the resurrection of the body, the punishment of the wicked, and life everlasting. It acknowledges baptism by fire and the Holy Spirit. Young members are confirmed at age 15 and admitted to the church at 21; children attend both church-sponsored Sunday schools and public schools. There is no ordained ministry; the church services consist of hymnsinging, prayer, readings from the testimonies of Rock, Gruber, Metz, and Landmann, and sermons preached by the elders. The church is separate from the temporal affairs of the community but is still a dominant influence. There is a church in each of the villages, and in 1979 there were 1,500 members.

AMERICAN ETHICAL UNION

The Ethical Movement in the United States builds its thought and program upon moral philosophy and the ethical traditions of the great religions of humankind; its main emphasis is upon ethics rather than creed or ceremony; members include both theists and nontheists. A statement of principles declares that

> the search for ethical values and their progressive realization are inherently a religious enterprise . . . All human beings, however different in their abilities or backgrounds, have an equal right to such fulfillment as encourages the fulfillment of their fellowmen. Such a goal requires diversity in beliefs and practices, and therefore freedom of conscience, thought, and expression. . . . Our attitude toward that which is beyond present knowledge, including questions about cosmic matters, is one of free and cooperative exploration, and respect for individual experience.

Stress is laid upon the development of conscience and a sense of responsibility.

There are 25 active Ethical Culture societies in the Ethical Union, the first of which was founded by Felix Adler in 1876. The Union is a founding member of the International Humanist and Ethical Union, which has organizations in some 34 countries around the world. Meetings feature inspirational music, meditation, readings from Scripture or other inspired poetry or prose, and an address upon some social, political, philosophic, religious, or ethical subject. Ethical Culture leaders serve as counselors, officiate at weddings and funerals, name children, and perform in general the functions of a minister. There are Sunday schools, young people's groups, and study groups; very effective work is done in educational, philanthropic, and social projects. The New York Society must be given credit for starting settlement work in the cities of this country; at the present time societies in New York, Chicago, and Philadelphia sponsor still such programs. Free kindergartens, visiting nurses, the Child Study Movement, the abolition of child labor and capital punishment, model tenements, the inauguration of free legal aid societies, civil liberties, and interracial adoption practices—all constitute Ethical Culture drives.

Outstanding Ethical Culture schools have been developed at Central Park West and Riverdale in New York City and in Washington, D.C., attracting many who are not otherwise identified with the movement. There are approximately 4,000 members.

AMERICAN EVANGELICAL CHRISTIAN CHURCHES

Launched in 1944 and first incorporated in Illinois, the A.E.C.C. is described as "an ecclesiastical body or denomination of interdoctrinal character." It seeks to compromise between Calvinistic and Arminian beliefs. Local churches established under its charter are known as American Evangelical Churches and often as American Bible Churches or simply as Community Churches. Each church is sovereign in its management but is obliged to cooperate with the national headquarters if it is to retain membership in the body.

Ministerial applicants must subscribe to seven articles of faith: (1) the Bible as the written Word of God; (2) the Virgin birth; (3) the deity of Jesus Christ; (4) salvation through the atonement of Christ; (5) the guidance of life through prayer; (6) the return of Christ; (7) the establishment of the kingdom of God on earth. Upon completion of training, ministerial students are granted licenses enabling them to perform all the functions and offices of the ministry, with the exception of officiating at marriages. Full ordination is withheld until the licentiate has become pastor of a regular congregation or is engaged in full-time evangelistic or missionary work. The present ministerial membership is reported at 200, of whom about half are engaged as full-time pastors.

All ordinations must be performed under the supervision of either regional or national officers; five regional offices in the United States and one in Canada supervise the work of the organization. A training school and missionary home are operated in Pineland, Florida. The American Bible School in Florida specializes in home study courses. There are 35 churches operating in the British Isles.

AMERICAN RESCUE WORKERS

Incorporated in 1884 as the Salvation Army and in 1896 as the American Salvation Army, with its name amended to the organizational charter in 1913, the American Rescue Workers organization engages in typical rescue mission work. It offers emergency aid (lodging, clothing, food), half-way houses and rehabilitation centers for alcoholics and drug addicts, workshops and social service programs for the socially and physically handicapped, and evangelism, yet has the status of a full-fledged nonsectarian church. The rites of baptism and Communion are administered by the officers and ministers in charge of local corps, and regular church and Sunday school services are held in the chapels and mission halls. Ministers are ordained at annual councils after approval by an ordination committee.

The articles of religion include subscription to the Trinity, the inspiration of the Scriptures and their use as the divine rule of faith and practice, the fall of the human race, redemption through the atoning sacrifice of Christ, restoration through repentance and belief in Christ, regeneration through the work of the Holy Spirit, and immortality of the soul.

Government is by a board of managers elected by the members of the corporation. Organization is on a military pattern, with Paul E. Martin as commander in chief and territorial commanders in charge. A periodical, *The Rescue Herald,* is published in Williamsport, Pennsylvania. There are approximately 2,000 members in 14 churches.

ANGLICAN ORTHODOX CHURCH

The Rev. James Parker Dees resigned from the priesthood of the Protestant Episcopal Church in 1963 to protest what he believed to be "its failure to proclaim firmly the Biblical doctrine, and on account of its emphasis on the social gospel and pro-communist program." With a group of other former members, he organized the Anglican Orthodox Church to preserve the traditional tenets of Anglicanism—belief in the fundamental (King James) Bible truths and morality, the (1928) Book of Common Prayer, the 39 Articles of Religion, the homilies, the doctrines of the Anglican Reformers, and the basic Anglican traditions and church government. Dr. Dees was consecrated bishop by Bishop Wasyl Sawyna of the Holy Ukranian Autocephalic Orthodox Church and by Bishop Orlando J. Woodward of the Old Catholic succession.

The fundamentalist doctrines of the Virgin birth, the atoning sacrifice of the cross, the Trinity, the resurrection, the second coming, salvation by faith alone, and the divinity of Christ are emphasized. There are 2,630 members in 37 established churches and five missions in the United States and the missionary congregations in Canada, Europe, and Asia; and 250,000 members are claimed in branches in South India, Madagascar, Pakistan, Nigeria, Rhodesia, Fiji Islands, Colombia, Kenya, the Philippines, Liberia, and England. The ministers of the church are trained at Cranmer Seminary in Statesville, North Carolina.

APOSTOLIC CHRISTIAN CHURCH (NAZAREAN)

The Apostolic Christian Church (Nazarean) began in this country with the arrival of a Swiss, S. H. Froelich, about the year 1850. Froelich went to work immediately among Swiss and German immigrants, and founded a number of small churches in the Midwest.

The theology is conservative. The church consists of members who have been converted to Christ, reborn, baptized, and who strive for sanctification; "and of such friends of the truth who sincerely and earnestly strive to attain adoption to sonship in Christ." Members are required to live "according to the Gospel of Christ, subject to the authorities, strive to be at peace with their fellow men, and fulfill their obligations as good citizens." They refuse to take up arms, since this denies the biblical command to love one's enemies; but they will engage in noncombatant service.

The local churches are independent in polity but united in fundamental organization. Each church is served by elders who are authorized to baptize, lay on hands, serve the Lord's Supper, and conduct meetings for the exercising of church discipline.

Nearly half the membership is found in Illinois and Ohio; small bodies are located in nearly all the northern states, from New England to the West Coast and Canada. With 46 churches and 2,684 members, there are missionaries in Brazil, Argentina, New Guinea, and Ghana. There is also a nonprofit service organization, known as the Apostolic Christian Church Foundation.

APOSTOLIC CHRISTIAN CHURCH OF AMERICA

Descending from a movement originated by S. H. Froelich in Switzerland in 1832, the Apostolic Christian Church of America was begun through the labors of Benedict Weyeneth, a Swiss who came to America about 1847 and organized a number of Swiss-German churches.

The doctrine is based largely upon the teaching of salvation by grace through faith in Jesus Christ, aimed "solely at the saving of souls, a change of heart through regeneration, and a life of godliness guided and directed by the Holy Spirit." Members are noted for their life of simplicity and obedience to the Bible but will support the government with any service that is "compatible with the teachings of Christ and the Apostles." Willful disobedience of church doctrine is punished by expulsion, but membership can be reinstated.

There are no educational institutions, and the ministers are not paid. Moreover, they are not expected to study or prepare their sermons but to depend entirely upon the inspiration and revelation of the Holy Spirit. There are more than 11,000 members and 80 congregations—2 in Japan, 1 in Canada, and the remainder in the United States.

APOSTOLIC FAITH

Organized in Portland, Oregon, in 1907 by the Reverend Mrs. Florence L. Crawford, "not to promote any new doctrine but rather to reestablish, maintain, and teach all the doctrines as taught by Christ and by his Apostles in the days of the early church," the Apostolic Faith is "Trinitarian, Fundamental and Evangelistic." Arminian in theology, it presents the usual doctrines of fundamentalism, stressing especially justification by faith (as taught by Luther), entire sanctification (as taught by Wesley), and the baptism of the Holy Ghost as evidenced at Pentecost. There are 55 churches and 6,000 members in the United States (mostly in the South and West). Branches exist in several foreign countries, with more members in Africa than in America.

Shunning "the swelling of numbers," there are baptismal records but no membership reports; a "born again" experience and subscription to the doctrines of the group are required for membership. It is "a church without a collection plate" (no offering is taken during services); worldly amusements (dancing, theater, card playing, drinking, smoking) are banned. Members are required to dress conservatively, and there is no marriage with unbelievers.

Governing bodies consist of a board of five trustees, of which the general overseer of the denomination is chairperson, and a board of 24 elders. The church was incorporated as Apostolic Faith Mission of Portland, Oregon, U.S.A. A headquarters church, a campground, and a publishing house that circulates evangelical literature in more than 60 languages and dialects are also located in Portland.

APOSTOLIC OVERCOMING HOLY CHURCH OF GOD

Bishop W. T. Phillips, a former member of The Methodist Church, became deeply concerned with the teaching of the doctrine of holiness and, in 1916, after four years of study and preaching on the doctrine, organized the Ethiopian Overcoming Holy Church of God. The word Ethiopian was later changed to Apostolic.

Active in 22 states and in the West Indies, Haiti, and Africa, the ministers, both men and women, are supported by tithes. Worship includes foot washing and divine healing. Services generally are free emotional affairs, with the participants speaking in tongues and engaging in ecstatic dances.

It is claimed that this church existed "even from the days of Enos," when Christianity was known to be in existence in Abyssinia. Marriage to the unsaved, the use of snuff, foolish talking, jesting, and use of slang are forbidden.

In doctrine, sanctification and holiness are stressed, with the tenet of the deity of Christ, the final resurrection of the dead, the evil to be punished at the time of this Last Death and Last Judgment at the second coming of Christ. A special Relief Fund provides for the needs of orphans, widows, the aged, and disabled members. A publishing facility is located in the headquarters building in Birmingham, Alabama. Bishop Jasper Roby is the executive bishop; he and 6 other bishops supervise the work of the church, which claims more than 100,000 members in 300 local churches.

ARMENIAN CHURCHES

Armenia claims to be the first Christian nation. The apostles Thaddeus and Bartholomew were believed to have traveled there during the time of Paul, and Christianity was adopted as the state religion in A.D. 301. St. Gregory the Illuminator, preaching in Armenia at that time, became the first head of this national church, with the title of Catholicos.

The story of the Christian church in Armenia is written in blood; it suffered in the inevitable conflict between the Byzantine Empire and Persia and in numerous persecutions by the Turks. Thousands escaped to America before and after World War I and functioned under the jurisdiction of the Etchmiadzin See from 1887 to 1933, when a dispute arose over the domination of the church in Soviet Armenia, insofar as it affects the American diocese. A split occurred: One group organized independently and is known as the Armenian Apostolic Church of America; in 1957 it came under the jurisdiction of the Holy See of Cilicia in Lebanon. The other is known as the Armenian Church of America and is under the See of Etchmiadzin.

Today, in spite of the division into two dioceses, the Armenian churches work in harmony where dogma and liturgy are concerned. Each elects its own primates. Deacons, priests, bishops, and archbishops are ordained and elevated by the hierarchical authorities of the respective jurisdictions. Both the Armenian Church of America (including the diocese of California) and the Armenian Apostolic Church of America claim to be the true American branch of the ancient church of Armenia. The former group has a membership of 450,000 in 66 churches; the latter has 125,000 members in 29 churches.

In government, both churches are democratic in that the officials are elected. Each province and diocese has a constitution adapted to its particular needs but which must be approved by the Catholicos of its respective jurisdiction.

Doctrine is based on the historic writings and declarations of the early church fathers. The saints and the Virgin Mary are venerated; the Assumption of the Virgin is celebrated but not accepted as a dogma. A translation of the Scriptures by St. Sahak and St. Mesrob and their students is accepted as the only authoritative Armenian version of the Bible. There are seven sacraments: Baptism by immersion eight days after birth, confirmation immediately following baptism, Holy Communion even for infants, penance, marriage, ordination, and extreme unction. The principal service is the Holy Sacrifice of the Divine Liturgy; various orders of "hour" services and celebrations of feasts are observed. The Bible is read in Armenian at these services. Language schools, Sunday schools, cultural programs, and libraries help to keep the native tongue alive.

BAHA'I

The Baha'i faith aims at a universal community of the human race, the unity of all religions, and peace for the whole world. Its founder, Baha'u'llah, said, "The religion of God is for the sake of love and union; make it not the cause of enmity and conflict." His followers see in his teachings the same spirit that spoke in Moses and Jesus, Krishna and Buddha, Zoroaster and Muhammad; to them he is the "return" of all previous prophets and religious leaders, the Promised One of the world's great religions.

Actually, the Baha'i faith originated with the teachings of Mirza Ali Muhammad, called the Bab (Arabic: *gate* or *door*), who suffered persecution and was martyred in 1850. It is estimated that 20,000 followers of the faith, then known as Babi, were slain during that persecution. Bab's successor, Mirza Husayn Ali, who was given the title Baha'u'llah (The Glory of God), died in 1892, leaving a vast accumulation of writings that are still treasured as the sacred scriptures of Baha'i belief. His eldest son, Abbas Effendi, later known as Abdul-Baha, spent some forty years in captivity; released in 1908 at the time of the revolution of the Young Turks, he toured Egypt, Europe, and the United States. In 1912 at Wilmette, Illinois, he laid the cornerstone of the first Baha'i house of worship in the West. This is now the seat of Baha'i national administrative offices in the United States.

The Wilmette temple is a unique structure in which the numeral nine, the Baha'i symbol of unity, is repeatedly emphasized: There are nine concrete piers, nine pillars, and nine arches; it is set in a park with nine sides, nine avenues, gateways, and fountains. The building was dedicated in 1953 to "the unity of God, the unity of his prophets, the unity of mankind." Services of worship are conducted weekly in the auditorium with *a capella* music and readings from the sacred scriptures of the world's religions. A Baha'i home for the aged was built in Wilmette in 1958.

Coordination and direction of international activities are now vested in the Baha'i Universal House of Justice, a body of nine members elected for terms of 5 years, located at the World Center in Haifa, Israel. In addition to administrative and judicial functions, this body legislates matters not expressly revealed in Baha'i writings. Another international institution, the International Teaching Center, functions with boards of counselors assigned to each continent. Local groups are organized as Spiritual Assemblies, supervised by a National Spiritual Assembly that consists of 9 members. Since 1963 there has been marked growth: There are more than 24,000 local assemblies and 133 national assemblies; followers of the faith now reside in 7,400 localities in the United States and 115,000 worldwide. Within this world fellowship are people of all races, nationalities, and creeds—black, yellow, brown, red, and white; Europeans, Asiatics, Africans, Americans; former Moslems, Hindus, Christians, and Jews—perfect integration in recognition of the truth of their founder's statement, "Ye are the fruits of one tree and the leaves of one Branch."

There are central Baha'i temples at Frankfurt, Germany; Sydney, Australia; Kampala, Uganda; Panama City, Panama; Delhi, India; and Samoa. Publishing trusts have been established at Wilmette, London, Buenos Aires, Rio de Janeiro, New Delhi, Teheran, Kampala, Frankfurt, Brussels, and 13 other locations. The writings of the Baha'i faith have been translated into more than 700 languages.

There is no ritual and no clergy, in the belief that each seeker may act upon truth and the Spirit without ecclesiastical aid. Unpaid teachers and "pioneers" give assistance to students. Marriage and funeral services are simple and flexible. Meetings vary from public lectures, study classes, and discussion groups for inquirers to meetings for the Baha'i community, conventions, and summer and winter schools and institutes. Schools are located in Maine, California, and Michigan. Events within the communities are scheduled by a special calendar of 19 months of 19 days each, with the New Year at the vernal equinox. The Baha'i day starts and ends at sunset.

The chief purpose of the Baha'i faith is to unite the world in one religion and one social order; hence, its chief principle is "the oneness and the wholeness of the human race." Among other dominant principles are the following:

(1) independent investigation of the truth; (2) the essential harmony of science and religion; (3) recognition of the divine foundation of all religions; (4) universal compulsory education; (5) the equality of all men and women; (6) the spiritual solution of economic problems; (7) the need for a universal auxiliary language; (8) universal peace based upon a world federation of nations; (9) the elimination of all prejudice; (10) recognition of the essential unity of mankind.

In its effort to develop spiritual qualities of character, Baha'i prescribes monogamy; discourages divorce; emphasizes strict obedience to one's government; condemns idleness; exalts any work performed in the spirit of service; prohibits slavery, asceticism, monasticism, and the use of alcohol and narcotics except for medicinal purposes; insists upon prayer and fasting as means of elevating the soul.

BAPTIST

Baptists constitute one of the major Protestant forces in the United States. Twenty-seven Baptist denominations reported an approximate membership of 29 million in 1983; there are about 95,000 local Baptist churches, each independent of the others. Members also are completely independent of one another, yet bound together by an amazingly strong "rope of sand" in a great common allegiance to certain principles and doctrines based generally upon the competency of each individual in matters of faith.

It is often heard among them that they have no founder but Christ and that Baptists have been preaching and practicing from the days of John the Baptist. That is true in a limited sense; there were certainly men and women then holding what have come to be considered distinctly Baptist principles. But as a church, or organized churches, they began in Holland and England.

With the Reformation early in the sixteenth century, scattered groups began to advocate the convictions of faith that are today the warp and woof of Baptist theology and ideology. We find the name in various forms in Germany and Switzerland: Pedobaptists, who baptized infants and children; Anti-Pedobaptists, who opposed infant baptism; and Anabaptists, who rebaptized adults once baptized as children. The Anabaptists were the left wing of the Reformation and held to a literal application of the Word of God in social matters; they were communistic and pacifistic, opposing capital punishment, oaths in court, the holding of public office, and payment of taxes and interest; and they rejected infant baptism as unscriptural. They insisted upon the separation of church and state, and defended this belief heroically, to the point of fanaticism and martyrdom. Under persecution they spread all over Europe. Some fled to Norway, others to Italy, Poland, Holland, and England.

In Holland a group of Mennonites, followers of the former Anabaptist leader Menno Simons (see Mennonites), were teaching Anabaptist principles: that the Scriptures were the sole authority for man's faith and practice, that baptism was a believer's privilege, that church and state should be completely and forever separated, and that church discipline should be rigidly enforced in business, family, and personal affairs. These Mennonites met a little group of British Separatists who had taken refuge in Amsterdam from the religious persecutions under James I. Many lived in Mennonite homes, and one of their leaders, John Smyth, was completely captured by the Mennonite argument. He rebaptized himself and his followers in the Anabaptist, or Baptist, faith and organized the first English Baptist church in 1609. When he tried to make Mennonites of his people, however, he went too far. Baptist they would be, but not Mennonite, for that meant a threat to their British heritage, and they were still good Englishmen and proposed to remain so. Smyth was excommunicated and died in 1612, leaving behind him in a "confession" his convictions that

> the magistrate, by virtue of his office, is not to meddle with religion, or matters of conscience, nor to compel men to this or that form of religion or doctrine, but to leave the Christian religion to the free conscience of every one, and to meddle only with political matters.

Smyth's people drifted back across the channel and, with persecution waning, established yet another Baptist church in London.

These first two churches were General Baptist churches, believing in a general atonement for all. In the course of time there arose a Particular Baptist Church, holding to the predestinarian teachings of John Calvin and preaching a limited atonement. The first Particular (British) church dates back to 1638. A third body, known as Immersion Baptist, broke away and in 1644 wrote a confession of faith which is still held by many modern Baptists. It was this confession that stamped these people popularly for the first time as Baptist.

Those early British Baptists wielded a tremendous influence in their time and upon the future; it is claimed that "more than any king or Parliament, they set the heart and mind of England free." John Smyth's teaching that "the magistrate . . . is not to meddle with religion, or matters of conscience" has become one of humankind's great spiritual principles. William Carey was sent to India in 1793 and became the pioneer of modern missions. More than a century earlier, in 1631, Roger Williams had come to America; he was to be the first great champion of freedom for faith and conscience on this side of the Atlantic.

Williams was not a Baptist, but a Separatist minister when he arrived. His story is well known: preaching "new and dangerous opinions against the authority of magistrates," he organized a Baptist church at Providence, Rhode Island. John Clarke established another Baptist church at Newport at about the same time. The Baptists are still arguing as to which was first; many scholars put the Providence church in 1639, the Newport church in 1641.

These were Particular, or Calvinistic, Baptist churches. Their strength was challenged by the rise of interest in Arminian theology during the preaching of George Whitefield, but their Calvinism prevailed; it is the theological standard of many, if not most Baptists in this country today. Their progress was slow; bitter persecution of their church ennobled them and left one of the darkest blots on colonial history.

Following the tour of Whitefield through the colonies, a dispute arose among Baptists, dividing them into Old Lights, or Regulars, who distrusted revivals and emotionalism, and New Lights, or Separates, who demanded a reborn membership in their churches. Separate Baptists were outstanding in the fight for religious freedom in the new land. The friction died down with the signing of the Constitution, however, and new unity was found in a foreign missions crusade. The first Protestant missionary board in America was the American Board, made up of Baptist, Reformed, Congregational, and Presbyterian church members.

In 1814 the Baptists organized their own separate General Missionary Convention of the Baptist Denomination in the United States of America for Foreign Missions. This convention, representing a national Baptist fellowship, marked the first real denominational consciousness. It was followed eventually by other organizations which welded them firmly together: a general Baptist convention; a general tract society—later called the American Baptist Publication Society; various missionary societies for work at home and abroad; an education society; and the Baptist Young People's Union.

These organizations were on a national scale. Their unity was disrupted first by a feeling that home missions agencies within the body had failed to evangelize southern territory and, later, by the question of slavery and the Civil War. The great division occurred in 1845, when southerners "seceded" to form their own Southern Baptist Convention in order to carry on the work of their churches more effectively. From this point forward there were to be Northern and Southern Baptist conventions.

Various other Baptist groups, following to the logical end their love of independence, established themselves from East to West. While they differ in certain minor details, they are generally agreed upon the following principles of faith: the inspiration and trustworthiness of the Bible as the sole rule of life; the Lordship of Jesus Christ; the inherent freedom of individuals to approach God for themselves; the granting of salvation through faith by way of grace and contact with the Holy Spirit; two ordinances—the Lord's Supper and baptism of believers by immersion; the independence of the local church; the church as a group of regenerated believers baptized upon confession of faith; infant baptism as unscriptural and not to be practiced; complete separation of church and state; the immortality of the soul; the unity of humankind; the royal law of God; the need of redemption from sin; and the ultimate triumph of God's kingdom.

These overall doctrines have never been written into any official Baptist creed for all the churches, but they have been incorporated into two important confessions of faith. The Baptist churches of London wrote a Philadelphia Confession in the year 1689, and this was enlarged by the Philadelphia Association in 1742. The New Hampshire State Baptist Convention drew up another confession in 1832. The Philadelphia Confession is strongly Calvinistic in statement; the New Hampshire Confession only moderately so.

Baptists have insisted upon freedom of thought and expression in pulpit and pew. This has made them one of the most democratic religious bodies in America—and one in which liberal or conservative doctrine is preached freely. They have insisted, too, upon the absolute autonomy of the local congregation; each church arranges its own worship, examines and baptizes it own members. There is no age limit set on membership, but the candidate is usually of an age to understand and accept the teachings of Christ. Candidates for the ministry are licensed by local churches and ordained upon recommendation of a group of sister churches.

Baptist churches are commonly found grouped into associations, local and state, for purposes of fellowship. National conventions are established among many of them to carry on educational and missionary work and to make pension plans. Most state and regional conventions meet annually with delegates representing all Baptist churches in a given area. These conventions receive reports, make recommendations, and help to raise the national mission budgets, but they have no authority to enforce their decisions. (Some regional regrouping has taken place in the North among American Baptists.)

In Washington, D.C., there is a Baptist Joint Committee on Public Affairs for American and Southern conventions and other Baptist groups; this committee serves mainly to spread the Baptist conviction on public morals and to safeguard their principle of separation of church and state.

Finally, there is the growing Baptist World Alliance, organized in 1905, which now includes more than 34 million Baptists. The alliance meets every five years and is a purely advisory body, discussing common themes and problems. Headquarters of the Alliance is now located in Washington, D.C.

American Baptist Association

Sometimes called Landmarkers because of their historic belief that there is no universal Church or ecclesiastical authority higher than a local congregation, members of the American Baptist Association claim that those Baptists organized in conventions are not faithful to Bible missions methods. Maintaining that their own is the true New Testament form, they hold themselves separate from all other religious groups. They "strongly protest the trend of many Baptist groups to identify themselves with Protestantism, believing that their [Baptist] faith preceded the Protestant Reformation."

Organized in 1905 as the Baptist General Association, the church adopted its present name in 1924. Teaching that the great commission of Christ (Matt. 28:18-20) was given to a local congregation, members believe that the local church is the only unit authorized to administer the ordinances and that it is an independent and autonomous body responsible only to Christ. Thus every church is equal "with every other like church"; they have been called Church-Equality Baptists.

Their doctrine is strictly fundamentalist. They stand for the verbal inspiration of the Bible, the Triune God, the Virgin birth and deity of Christ, the suffering and death of Christ as substitutionary, the bodily resurrection of Christ and all his saints. The second coming of Jesus, "physical and personal," is to be the crowning event of the "gospel age"; this second advent will be premillennial. There is eternal punishment for the wicked; salvation is solely by grace through faith and not by law or works. There must be absolute separation of church and state and absolute religious freedom. They denounce abortion on demand, homosexuality, and premarital sex as being contrary to biblical teachings.

Government of both the local congregation and the annual messenger meeting of the association is congregational in nature. Missionary work is conducted on county, state, interstate, and foreign levels, the program originating in the local church and the missionaries being supported by the cooperating churches. Educational work is pursued through the Sunday schools, 5 seminaries, 3 colleges, and 16 Baptist institutes.

The greater strength of this group is found in the South, Southwest, West, and Southeast; but much new work has begun in recent years in the East and North. Their 1983 statistics show 2,800 churches with a total combined membership of 378,000 and 2,500 ordained clergy with charges. The membership continues to shift from rural to urban.

A comprehensive publishing program includes 14 monthly and semimonthly periodicals, Sunday school literature designed to cover the entire Bible in a 10-year period, and literature for young people and vacation Bible schools. National and state youth encampments are held annually, as well as annual pastors' and missionary conferences on a regional and national level.

American Baptist Churches in the U.S.A.

Until the Revolutionary War, Baptist work in the northern states was in the hands of the local churches, some of which formed themselves into associations such as the Philadelphia Association and the Warren Association of Rhode Island. Beyond these associations, which were limited to Virginia, New Jersey, Pennsylvania, and Rhode Island, there was no central administrative body to bind the churches together. The association did well, building churches, colleges, schools, and libraries; by the time of the split with the Southern Baptists about 1845, plans for a national coordinating body were underway.

In the early years of the nineteenth century there were three mutually maintained organizations in the North: the American Baptist Home Mission Society; the American Baptist Missionary Union, later known as the American Baptist Foreign Mission Society; and the American Baptist Publication Society. The defection of the Southern Baptists served to intensify the efforts of these three bodies; they were separate corporations, but they often called annual meetings at the same time and place.

The women of the northern churches formed their own home and foreign missionary societies in the 1870s. Separate appeals for funds to support all these competing societies created confusion and dissatisfaction and led eventually to the formation of the Northern Baptist Convention in 1907. This convention, actually a corporation with restricted powers in conducting religious work, receiving and expending money, and affiliating itself with other bodies, changed its name in 1950 to the American Baptist Convention. In 1955 the two women's missionary societies joined administratively with their counterparts, the older foreign and home mission societies. Consequently, the two foreign societies and the two home societies, respectively, function now under identical officers, boards of managers, and administrative staffs, though each society maintains its own corporate identity. In 1968 the Women's Foreign Society was legally merged into the American Foreign Missionary Society. These societies, with the American Baptist Historical Society, the Ministers and Missionaries Benefit Board, and the American Baptist Board of Education and Publication were known as cooperating organizations of the convention.

State conventions and city mission societies were drawn into closer unity by grouping them into affiliated organizations through which they raised and distributed funds under a cooperative plan with a unified budget. The Division of World Mission Support supervised the collection of money for this unified budget. Numerous other councils and committees carried on the work of the convention under the supervision of the general council, which functioned between the annual gatherings. In 1950 the first general secretary was elected.

In 1972 the Convention adopted its third and present name and restructured to strengthen the representational principle and to develop a much fuller integration of the national program agencies into the structure of the American Baptist convention. A larger (200-member) general board, representative of election districts, is the policy making body. A national staff council of executives of national program boards and regional, state, and city units serves to coordinate the corporate affairs of the denomination under the leadership of the general secretary.

The local church, however, is still the basic and independent unit of American Baptist government and administration. There are 5,817 churches and 1,607,541 members, 27 regional and state conventions, and 9 Baptist city societies. The church is at work in 14 children's homes, 48 homes for the aged, 7 hospitals, 10 theological seminaries, 6 academies, 27 senior colleges and universities, 4 junior colleges, and a school for nursing education. The Board of National Ministries has workers in 35 states; it supports Bacone College for Native Americans in Oklahoma and carries on widespread work among blacks, Native Americans, and oriental residents in the United States. The Board of International Ministries supports missionaries in Burma, Assam, India, Bengal, Thailand, Japan, Okinawa, Hong Kong, the Philippines, and Central America and maintains a cooperative relationship in ten European countries. American Baptists also financially support the work of the Burma Baptist Convention.

In matters of faith, each Baptist church speaks for itself, but there are certain doctrines held in common. The Bible is the foundation of their belief; the individual conscience, the interpreter of the Bible. There is the usual Baptist insistence upon the inspiration and validity of the Scriptures, the lordship of Christ, immortality and the future life, the unity of humankind, and the need of humanity's redemption from sin. The ordinances of baptism and the Lord's Supper are considered as aids, more than as necessities for a Christian life.

Generally it may be said that Northern Baptists represented in the American Baptist Churches in the U.S.A. are less conservative in thought and theology than those in the Southern Baptist Convention, but this doctrinal difference is not the major cause of the continuing separation. Divergent views on the questions of race, and open Communion, and especially the Protestant trend toward ecumenicity are now the major hurdles. American Baptists are represented in the National Council of the Churches of Christ in the U.S.A. and in the World Council of Churches; Southern Baptists are represented in neither. American Baptists have made gestures toward union with the General Baptists, the Southern Baptists, the National Baptist Convention, the Seventh Day Baptists, the Disciples of Christ, and the Church of the Brethren, and have welcomed Free Baptists into full fellowship. Unless and until these varying attitudes are changed or reconciled, there does not seem to be any real possibility for reunion of the two larger Baptist bodies in the United States.

Baptist Bible Fellowship, International

The Baptist Bible Fellowship is one of the "evangelical independent" groups—perhaps the largest and fastest growing body of independent Baptists in the United States—loosely affiliated with one another in the preaching and teaching of ultraconservative Baptist doctrine. They teach that Jesus was a Baptist in his thinking and work. They are biblical literalists, denouncing all modernists and liberals. They recognize only baptism by immersion, participate in Communion only with members of their own church, and are adamant in opposing dancing, drinking, smoking, movies, gambling, and sexual promiscuity. No formal membership statistics are kept, but membership probably stands near 1 million.

Baptist Bible College in Springfield, Missouri, is the principal institution supported by these independent Baptists, but Liberty Baptist College in Lynchburg, Virginia, also trains many in its membership.

Baptist General Conference

The history of what is now known as the Baptist General Conference began at Rock Island, Illinois, in the summer of 1852. Gustaf Palmquist, a schoolteacher and lay preacher, had arrived from Sweden the previous year to become the spiritual leader of a group of Swedish immigrants who had been influenced by the pietistic movement within the state church (Lutheran) of Sweden. At Galesburg, Illinois, he came in contact with the Baptists and early in 1852 was baptized and ordained a Baptist minister. Visiting his countrymen at Rock Island, he won his first converts to the Baptist faith and baptized three in the Mississippi River on August 8, 1852. From this humble beginning has come a denomination of 138,000 members, 803 churches, and 16 state or district conferences. In 1879 a national conference—the Swedish Baptist General Conference of America—was organized.

For several decades the American Baptist Home Mission Society and the American Baptist Publication Society of the American (then the Northern) Baptist Convention aided the new work among the immigrant Swedes, but gradually the church became self-supporting. A theological seminary was founded in Chicago in 1871, and the first denominational paper was launched the same year. From 1888 to 1944 foreign missionary activities were channeled through the American Baptist Foreign Mission Society; after a separation in 1944, caused largely by a desire to become completely independent, the Swedish Conference set up its own foreign board and today has more than 110 missionaries in India, Japan, the Philippine Islands, Ethiopia, Mexico, Argentina, Brazil, and the Ivory Coast.

Following the First World War, with its intensified nationalistic conflicts, the transition from Swedish to English in church services was greatly accelerated and practically completed in three decades. In 1945 the word Swedish was dropped from the name of the conference; it had already been dropped by most of the local churches. With the language barrier removed, the growth of the conference has been rapid and far-reaching. Although its greatest strength lies in the North Central and Pacific Northwest sections of the United States, home missionaries are at work in all the northern states, in some of the southern states, and in Canada. One of its most effective organizations is the Evangelism Corps, made up of young lay volunteers who spend a year in concentrated home missions work.

The conference owns and controls Bethel College and Seminary at St. Paul, Minnesota (a four-year college and a three-year theological school with 2,200 students). Affiliated are two children's homes, seven homes for the aged, and a Hebrew mission. Six periodicals, including *The Standard*, the official denominational organ, are issued by the Board of Trustees. Harvest Publications offers Bibles, books, and Sunday school materials.

Basically the church's doctrine is theologically conservative, "with unqualified acceptance of the Word of God," and holds the usual Baptist tenets. It is a strong fellowship of churches, insistent upon the major beliefs of conservative Christianity but with respect for individual differences on minor points.

The conference tends to become more and more inclusive and to appeal to people of all nationalities. About 50 percent of the pastors are not even of Swedish descent, and a large number of the churches contain very few members of that descent. The transition has been rapid because of the lack of Swedish immigrants and also because of the people's quick assimilation into the American way of life.

Baptist Missionary Association of America

Organized at Little Rock, Arkansas, in May 1950 as the North American Baptist Association, this group changed its name to the Baptist Missionary Association in 1968. It concentrates on fostering and encouraging missionary cooperation and has had startling growth, enrolling 1,390 churches and 228,381 members in 25 states. There are workers in the home missions field and in missionary work abroad—Mexico, Japan, Brazil, Taiwan, Portugal, Cape Verde Islands, Uruguay, Guatemala, Costa Rica, Nicaragua, Australia, Italy, France, Africa, India, Bolivia, and the Philippines. A strong publications department issues literature for Sunday school and training classes, pamphlets, books, tracts, and magazines in both English and Spanish. The church also owns and operates a printing business in Brazil, where literature is printed in Portugese for use in Africa and Europe. A worldwide radio ministry is also maintained.

The members are militant fundamentalists, claiming to hold the historic Baptist faith and placing strong emphasis upon the verbal inspiration and accuracy of the Scriptures, direct creation, the Virgin birth and deity of Jesus, his blood atonement, justification by faith, salvation by grace alone, and the imminent, personal return of Christ to earth. They brand as unscriptural open Communion, alien baptism, pulpit affiliation with heretical ministers, unionism, modernism, modern conventionism, one-church dictatorship, and "all the kindred evils arising from these practices." The Lord's Supper and baptism are accepted as ordinances; baptism is considered "alien" unless administered to believers and by "divine authority as given to the Missionary Baptist churches."

This body carries on the Landmark Baptist movement, holding to the historic succession of independent Baptist churches from the time of Christ. It shares this conviction with the American Baptist Association; before 1950 these two present-day bodies were one.

Churches are completely autonomous in the Baptist tradition and, regardless of size, have an equal voice in the cooperative missionary, publication, evangelical, and educational efforts of the association. Member churches must, however, conform to the doctrinal standards of the association and deny alien baptism and modernism in all its forms.

There are three junior colleges, maintained on a state level, and several orphans' homes. A theological seminary is located at Jacksonville, Texas.

Bethel Ministerial Association

Founded as the Evangelistic Ministerial Alliance at Evansville, Indiana, in May of 1934, this body was incorporated as the Bethel Baptist Assembly on March 16, 1960. There are 5,000 members in 25 churches, 49 ordained clergy, and five Sabbath schools with an enrollment of 530. Details on doctrine, organization, and so on, are available from the organization.

Black Baptist

The first black Baptist church in America was organized at Silver Bluff, across the Savannah River from Augusta, Georgia, in 1773. Other churches followed: in Petersburg, Virginia, in 1776; Richmond, Virginia, in 1780; Williamsburg, Virginia, in 1785; Savannah, Georgia, in 1785; and Lexington, Kentucky, in 1790. It is interesting that Andrew Bryan, a slave, was the first pastor of the First African Baptist Church in Savannah and that its organization came about through the efforts of Abraham Marshall (white) and Jesse Peter (black).

As early as 1700, white slaveholders in the South were providing religious teaching and places of worship for their slaves—at least most of them did little to prevent such activity. Usually, however, slaves sat in the gallery of the white churches, identified with the faith of their owners. White ministers, sometimes assisted by black helpers, moved from one plantation to another, holding services more or less regularly. Occasionally a black minister was liberated to give full time to religious work among blacks, and these ministers had great influence. They were consulted by whites as the respected leaders of their people and were a real power up to the time of the slave rebellion of 1831, led by Nat Turner. For a period following this disturbance it was illegal in some sections of the South for blacks to become Christians or to build meetinghouses.

The great majority of blacks in pre–Civil War days were either Baptists or Methodists. When Bull Run was fought in 1861, there were 200,000 black members of the Methodist Episcopal Church, South, and 150,000 black Baptists. In 1793 there were 73,471 Baptists in the United States, one-fourth of them black; in 1806 one-third of the Baptists of North Carolina were black. The lack of formality in the Baptist churches, together with the absence of ritual and the freedom and democracy of the local congregation, appealed to blacks more than did the episcopal structure of the Methodist. This was accented at the end of the Civil War; a revival spirit swept the blacks, creating thousands of new churches. Aided by the Freedman's Aid Society and various Baptist organizations, nearly 1,000,000 black Baptists worshiped in their own churches within 15 years.

The first black Baptist association, the Providence Baptist Association of Ohio, was formed in 1836; the first attempt at national organization occurred in 1880 with the creation of the Foreign Mission Baptist Convention at Montgomery, Alabama. In 1886 the American National Baptist Convention was organized at St. Louis, and in 1893 the Baptist National Educational Convention was organized in the District of Columbia. All three conventions were merged into the National Baptist Convention of America at Atlanta in 1895.

In 1915 a division arose over the adoption of a charter and the ownership of a publishing house. The group rejecting the charter continued to function as the National Baptist Convention of America, while the group accepting the charter became known as the National Baptist Convention of the U.S.A., Inc. (incorporated, that is, under the laws of the District of Columbia). The former is frequently referred to as the "unincorporated" and the latter as the "incorporated" convention, but both trace their beginnings to the Foreign Mission Baptist Convention of 1880.

About 87 percent of black Christians in the United States were either Baptist or Methodist in 1965, with Baptists comprising 65 percent of that total. Although comprehensive figures are not presently available, it is likely that the growth of Pentecostal bodies has reduced that percentage somewhat. Members are grouped into a large number of denominations, some of them quite small. The two oldest and largest, the National Baptist Convention in the U.S.A., Inc., and the National Baptist Convention of America, the "unincorporated" body, number about 6 million and 2.5 million, respectively.

Black Baptist doctrine runs quite parallel to that of white Baptist churches, but is slightly more Calvinistic. The polity of the two larger white conventions prevails; local churches unite in associations, usually along state lines, for the purposes of fellowship and consultation. There are also state conventions concerned with missionary work, often extending beyond state boundaries.

Foreign missionary work is especially strong in Africa, and home missionary efforts are generally expended in the direction of helping needy churches and schools, and family support and relief. The National Baptist Convention, Inc., has several missionary stations in the Bahamas; the convention has a total of five colleges, one theological seminary, and one training school for women and girls. The convention has stations in Jamaica, Panama, and Africa and gives support to 10 colleges in these countries.

The old enmities between the two conventions are disappearing, but no reunion is expected for some time to come. Dialogue has begun, however, toward the union of the National Baptist Convention of the U.S.A, Inc., and the American Baptist Churches.

As the outcome of a vigorous dispute in the National Baptist Convention of the U.S.A, Inc., over procedures in the election of convention officers, a new Progressive National Baptist Convention, Inc., was organized in 1961. Its membership now stands at 550,000.

Central Baptist Association

This association was formed in 1956 and is composed of 41 churches in Virginia, Tennessee, Kentucky, Indiana, Michigan, and South Carolina. Present membership is approximately 4,000. Following usual Baptist doctrine and polity, its officers have no jurisdiction over the member churches. A tabernacle, a children's home, and a youth camp are located at Jasper, Virginia.

Its heritage is in the Primitive Baptist faith. The name is meant to indicate acceptance of the Holy Scriptures in their entirety, varying neither to the right nor to the left. One distinctive doctrine specifies two resurrections of the dead—one of the just and another of the unjust.

Conservative Baptist Association of America

The Conservative Baptist Association is officially described as a

> voluntary fellowship of sovereign, autonomous, independent and Bible-believing Baptist churches. . . . The Association is wholly separated from all other organizations. . . . The several churches are held together . . . by a common abiding love for the work and person of Jesus Christ, and the Word of God, as well as love for and confidence in one another.

The founders of this association were active in an earlier organization known as the Fundamentalist Fellowship, founded in 1920 within the American (then the Northern) Baptist Convention. This group of conservative church people opposed what they considered to be the infiltration of liberal and modernistic tendencies and teachings within that convention. The basic disagreement was doctrinal, having to do with fundamentally different views and interpretations of the Scriptures and of Baptist theology. The dispute was aggravated by the "inclusive" policy of the American Baptist Foreign Mission Society, under which missionaries of conservative and liberal theologies were sent to home and foreign fields.

The Conservative Baptist Association was formally organized on May 17, 1947, at Atlantic City, New Jersey, as an *association* of local conservative Baptist churches. As an association, it is distinguished from the Conservative Baptist *movement* in the United States. Several conservative Baptist institutions—such as the Conservative Baptist Foreign Mission Society, the Conservative Baptist Home Mission Society, and a number of schools and colleges—function as part of the movement but are separate and autonomous.

The work of the association includes building a fellowship of churches; providing resources and personnel in areas of Christian education, leadership training, new church planting, financial services to pastors and staff, stewardship ministries, women's ministries, and retirement advisory services; serving in pastoral placement; printing and distributing literature, books, and Sunday School material; endorsing chaplains for the United States armed forces; and providing a national magazine, the *Conservative Baptist*.

Doctrinally, it stands for the infallibility of the Scriptures; God as Father, perfect in holiness, infinite in wisdom, measureless in power; Christ as the eternal and only begotten Son of God—his sinlessness, Virgin birth, atonement, resurrection, and ascension; the Holy Spirit as coming forth from God to convince the world of sin, of righteousness, and of judgment; the sinfulness of all people and the possibility of their regeneration, sanctification, and comfort through Christ and the Holy Spirit; the church as the living body, with Christ as head; the local church as free from interference by any ecclesiastical or political authority; the responsibility of every human being to God alone; and the ordinances of baptism and the Lord's Supper.

Associational and regional officers are elected at annual meetings; a board of directors is made up of the associational officials and 18 regional representatives, elected for three-year terms. The membership totals 225,000 in 1,111 churches. It supports five schools, including seminaries in Portland, Oregon, and in Denver.

Duck River (and Kindred) Associations of Baptists (Baptist Church of Christ)

Confined to five southern states, the Duck River Baptists originated in 1825 from a protest movement within the old Elk River Association, which was strongly Calvinistic. In 1843 the ranks of the dissenters were broken by a dispute over the legitimacy of missions and the support of a publication society and a denominational school. Those who withdrew became known as Missionary Baptists and, in a few instances, as Separate Baptists or the Baptist Churches of Christ. The division persists; there are today two Duck River associations.

Doctrinally the members are liberally Calvinistic; they hold that "Christ tasted death for every man"; that God will save those who come to him on gospel terms; that sinners are justified by faith; that the saints will "persevere in grace." They stand for believer's baptism by immersion and celebrate the Lord's Supper and foot washing as scriptural ordinances. They admit their close gospel ties with Regular, United, and Separate Baptists.

The churches are congregational in government, with 8 separate Associations and 1 independent church that meet annually for fellowship in a General Association: Duck River, Mt. Zion, Mt. Pleasant No. 1, Mt. Pleasant No. 2, New Liberty, Original East Union, East Union, and Union. The Mt. Pleasant Associations are located in Alabama, Tennessee, Mississippi, and Georgia. The others are located in Tennessee.

There is a "correspondence" relationship with other associations in Alabama, Tennessee, Mississippi, and Georgia. Membership is by vote of the local congregation; the ministers are ordained by a vote of two or more ministers.

There are, as of 1982, 10,972 members in 103 churches.

Free Will Baptist

The rise of the Free Will Baptists can be traced to the influence of Arminian-minded Baptists who migrated to the colonies from England. The denomination organized on two fronts at almost the same time. The southern line, or Palmer movement, began in 1727 when Paul Palmer established a church at Chowan, North Carolina. The northern line, or Randall movement, began with a congregation organized by Benjamin Randall in 1780 in New Durham, New Hampshire. Both groups taught the doctrines of free grace, free salvation, and free will. There were gestures toward union of the northern and southern groups, but the outbreak of the Civil War prevented that. The northern body extended more rapidly into the West and Southwest. In 1910 this line of Free Will Baptists merged with the Northern Baptist denomination, taking along 857 of its 1,100 churches, all its denominational property, and several colleges. In 1916 representatives of remnant churches from the Randall movement reorganized into the Cooperative General Association of Free Will Baptists.

By 1921 the southern churches had organized into new associations and conferences, and finally into a General Conference. The division continued until November 5, 1935, when the two groups merged into the National Association of Free Will Baptists, at Nashville, Tennessee.

Doctrinally, it holds that Christ gave himself as a ransom for all, not just the elect; that God calls all of us to repentance; and that whosoever will, may be saved. Baptism is by immersion. This is one of the few Baptist groups that practices open Communion. It also practices foot washing. Government is strictly congregational. There are 2 Bible colleges, 2 liberal arts colleges, and 243,000 members in 40 states, with 2,500 churches. Some 160,000 of these members reside in 7 southern states.

General Association of Regular Baptist Churches

Twenty-two Baptist churches of the American Baptist Convention left that convention in May of 1932 to found the General Association of

Regular Baptist Churches. Their protest was against what they considered the modernist tendencies and teachings, the denial of the historic Baptist principle of independence and autonomy of the local congregation, the inequality of representation in the assemblies of the convention, the control of missionary work by convention assessment and budget, and the whole convention principle in general.

Any Baptist church coming into the General Association is required to "withdraw all fellowship and cooperation from any convention or group which permits modernists or modernism within its ranks." Dual fellowship or membership is not permitted. Participation in union evangelical campaigns, or Thanksgiving services, or membership in local ministerial associations where modernists are involved or present is considered unscriptural.

Missionary work is conducted through six approved Baptist agencies, completely independent of any convention, and completely orthodox; a close watch is maintained upon these agencies before annual approval is granted. Likewise, only nine schools are approved; these, too, are guarded against any defection from approved practice or doctrine.

The association subscribes to the New Hampshire Confession of Faith with a premillennial interpretation of the final article of that confession. It holds to the infallibility of the Bible, the Trinity, the personality of Satan as the author of all evil, humankind as the creation of God, and humankind born in sin. There are doctrines dealing with the Virgin birth, the deity of Jesus, and faith in Christ as the way of salvation through grace. The saved are in everlasting felicity; the lost are consigned to endless punishment. There is a bodily resurrection; Christ rose and ascended and will return premillennially to reign in the millennium. Civil government is by divine appointment. There are only two approved ordinances: baptism by immersion and the Lord's Supper.

Church government is strictly congregational. Associated churches have the privilege of sending six voting messengers to an annual convention; thus a church with 50 members has the same power as a church with 2,500 members. A Council of Eighteen is elected—nine each year—to serve for two years. It makes recommendations to the association for the furtherance of its work and implements and puts into operation all actions and policies of the association. Its authority depends completely upon the will and direction of the association.

In 1983 there were 1,593 churches in the fellowship, with 260,000 members. The 9 approved schools had a total student body of more than 6,000, and 2,149 missionaries were at work in the 5 missionary agencies. State and regional associations have been established across the country. These are supplied with literature published by the Regular Baptist Press, including *The Baptist Bulletin*, a monthly magazine.

General Baptist

The General Baptist church claims its name and origin in John Smyth and Thomas Helwys and the group of Baptists organized in England and

Holland in 1611 (see general article on Baptist). Roger Williams is held to be its first minister in the American colonies.

General Baptists in the colonies along the Atlantic coast were at first overwhelmed by the influence of Calvinism (General Baptists have always been Arminian), but their work was reopened by Benoni Stinson with the establishment of the Liberty Baptist Church in what is now Evansville, Indiana, in 1823. They spread into Illinois and Kentucky, and a general association of General Baptists was organized in 1870. Since that time it has grown steadily; today it is strong in Kentucky, Tennessee, Indiana, Michigan, Illinois, Missouri and Arkansas and has located churches in Oklahoma, Nebraska, Kansas, Iowa, Arizona, California, Florida, Ohio, and Mississippi.

The confession of faith is similar to that of Free Will Baptist: that Christ died for all; that failure to achieve salvation lies completely with the individual; that humankind is depraved and fallen and unable to save itself; that regeneration is necessary for salvation except in the case of infants and idiots, who are not responsible for sin; that salvation comes by repentance and faith in Christ; that the Christian who perseveres to the end is saved; that the wicked are punished eternally; that the dead, just and unjust, will be raised at the judgment. The Lord's Supper and believer's baptism by immersion are the only authorized Christian ordinances and should be open to all believers. Some of the General Baptist churches practice foot washing.

Church polity is about the same as that found in all Baptist churches. The denomination is congregational in church government. Churches of a common area are organized into local associations, which are in turn organized into a general association. Both local and general associations are representative bodies and advisory in power. A peculiar feature of the General Baptist church lies in the use of a presbytery, into which the ordained members of local associations are grouped; they examine candidates for the ministry and for the diaconate. Ministers and deacons are responsible to this presbytery, which exists only on the local level.

Current statistics show 870 churches, with a total membership of 74,844. At Oakland City, Indiana, the church maintains a liberal arts college with a theological department. A publishing house is operated at Poplar Bluff, Missouri, where the monthly paper, *General Baptist Messenger,* is issued, together with Sunday school literature.

Foreign missionary work is supported in Guam, Saipan, Jamaica, and the Philippines, and home missionary work is actively carried out in various states.

General Conference of the Evangelical Baptist Church, Inc.

The Evangelical Baptist church was organized by the members of several Free Will Baptist Churches in 1935; it was formerly known as the Church of the Full Gospel, Inc.

The doctrine of their members is Arminian, Wesleyan, and premillennial; organization is similar to that of the Free Will Baptists, with whom they are still in close fellowship. They exchange pastors regularly with the Wilmington Conference of the Free Will Baptist Church. As of 1952, there were about 2,200 members in 31 churches.

Landmark Baptist

"Landmarkism" among Baptists is a position held by some concerning the nature of the church and certain details of church practice. The name originated with the writings of James Madison Pendleton and James Robinson Graves in Kentucky and Tennessee in the latter part of the nineteenth century, though Landmarkers insist that their concepts go back to the apostolic period.

There are four distinguishing tenets of Landmarkism:

1. The church is always vocal and visible. The expression "the church" is used only when speaking of the institution. All saved people make up "the family of God," not "the church." While members of Protestant churches may be saved, they are not members of true churches.
2. The "commission" was given to the church; consequently, all matters covered by it must be administered under church authority. Ministers of other denominations are not accepted in Landmark Baptist pulpits.
3. Baptism, to be valid, must be administered by the authority of a New Testament (Baptist) church. Baptisms administered by any other authority are not accepted.
4. There is a direct historic "succession" of Baptist churches from New Testament times; that is, Baptist churches have existed in practice, thought not by name, in every century.

These principles are held primarily by the churches of the American Baptist Association, though there are an estimated 1,500,000 members of different Baptist churches that hold to the Landmark position and doctrine. The largest concentration is in the South and Southwest. More than 15 Bible institutes and seminaries are supported by these churches.

National Baptist Evangelical Life and Soul Saving Assembly of the U.S.A.

This assembly was founded in 1920 at Kansas City, Missouri—not as another denomination, but as an evangelical group working within the National Baptist Convention (unincorporated). It had the endorsement of the parent body for 17 years, but became an independent group in 1937.

No new doctrine is set forth by this group; it has no doctrine except the "Bible doctrine as announced by the Founder of the Church, Jesus Christ." Concentration is mainly upon evangelical and relief efforts. The assembly maintains an "automatic" correspondence school, offering courses in evangelology, deaconology, missionology, pastorology, and laymanology; degrees are granted in 60, 90, and 120 days.

In 1951, there were 57,674 members and 264 churches reported.

National Primitive Baptist Convention of the U.S.A.

The black population of the South, all through the years of slavery and Civil War, worshiped with the white population in their various churches. This was true of this group, formerly the Colored Primitive Baptists. They attended white Primitive Baptist churches until the time of the emancipation, when their white brethren helped them establish their own churches, granting them letters of fellowship and character, ordaining their deacons and ministers, and assisting in other ways.

The doctrine and polity are quite the same as those of the white Primitive Baptist organization except that the members are "opposed to all forms of church organization"; yet there are local associations and a national convention, organized in 1907. Each church is independent, receiving and controlling its own membership; there is no appeal from a decision of the officers of the local church.

There is a membership of 250,000 in 606 churches. Unlike the white Primitive Baptist church, since 1900 this group has been establishing aid societies, conventions, and Sunday schools, over the opposition of the older and more orthodox members.

North American Baptist Conference

The churches in this conference began as German Baptist churches, established on our soil by German immigrants more than a century ago. They first settled in New Jersey and Pennsylvania—where Penn's Quakers offered them the perfect religious freedom they sought. The scattered churches later became the North American Baptist General Conference and organized the first local churches from 1840 through 1851.

The prosperity of these German Baptist churches followed the rise and fall of German immigration. By 1851 there were 8 churches and 405 members, and in that year they organized an Eastern Conference, for fellowship and mutual consideration of common problems.

The local conference idea was enlarged as the churches increased. As the membership moved across the nation, a total of 9 such conferences were established following geographical lines. In 1865 a joint meeting of Eastern and Western Conferences was held and called a General Conference. The Triennial Conference is now the chief administrative unit.

Twenty associations meet annually, elect their own officers and missionary committees, and guide their own work. The general conference meets triennially and is made up of cleric and lay representatives from all the churches. It superintends the work of publication, education, missions, and homes for the aged. A general council acts for the conference between sessions.

The German Baptists participated in the development of what is now Colgate-Rochester Divinity School in Rochester, New York. In 1935 they established a seminary of their own, the North American Baptist Seminary, which relocated from Rochester to Sioux Falls, South Dakota, in 1949. The North American Baptist College is in Edmonton, Alberta, Canada. There are ten homes for the aged and a very strong emphasis on missions. Home missions are conducted among Spanish Americans in the United States; foreign missionaries are located in Japan, Brazil, and Nigeria and the United Republic of Cameroon, West Africa.

Theologically, there is little variance from the usual Baptist position. In general, North American Baptists follow the New Hampshire Confession, stressing the authority of the Scriptures, the revelation of God in Christ, regeneration, immersion, separation of church and state, the congregational form of government. There are 59,370 members in 366 churches, concentrated in the Midwest.

Primitive Baptist

Primitive Baptists have the reputation of being the most strictly orthodox and exclusive of all Baptists. Unique in that they have never been organized as a denomination and have no administrative bodies of any kind (they believe that each church should "govern itself according to the laws of Christ as found in the New Testament, and that no minister, association, or convention has any authority over the churches"), they represent a nineteenth-century protest against "money-based" missions and benevolent societies, and against "assessing" churches to support missions, missionaries, and Sunday schools. The position taken was that there were no missionary societies in the days of the apostles, and therefore there should be none now.

Apart from this, there was objection to the centralization of authority in these societies. Sunday schools also were unauthorized by Scripture; these Baptists believed in the religious training of children but not in Sunday schools. They stood for evangelism as a missionary effort, but on individual responsibility and at individual expense, not under the sponsorship of a money-based society.

Spearheading this protest, in 1827 the Kehukee Association in North Carolina condemned all money-based and authoritarian societies as being contrary to Christ's teachings. Within a decade, several other Baptist associations across the country made similar statements and withdrew from other Baptist churches.

The various associations adopted the custom of printing in their annual minutes statements of their articles of faith, their constitution, and their rules of order. These statements were examined by all the other associations, and if they were approved, there was fellowship and exchange of messengers and correspondence among them; any association not so approved was dropped from the fellowship.

Added to this was the difficulty of communication in many parts of the South. The result was confusion; there was no chance under such conditions for growth as a denomination and little chance even for fellowship or quasi unity. This is apparent in the variety of names, some friendly and some derisive, that have been applied to them—Primitive, Old School, Regular, Anti-mission, and Hard Shell. In general, the term Primitive has been widely accepted and used.

A strong Calvinism runs through the Primitive doctrine. In general the members believe that by Adam's fall all posterity became sinners; that human nature is completely corrupt; that humankind cannot by its own efforts regain favor with God. God elected his own people in Christ before the world began, and none of these saints will be finally lost. The two biblically authorized ordinances are the Lord's Supper and baptism of believers by immersion. All church societies are human inventions and are to be denied fellowship; Christ will come a second time to raise the dead, judge all people, punish the wicked forever and reward the righteous forever; the Old and New Testaments are verbally and infallibly inspired.

Ministers must be called by God, come under the laying on of hands, and be in fellowship with the local church of which they are members before they can administer the two ordinances; they are to deny to any other clergyman lacking these qualifications the right to administer such ordinances. No theological training is demanded of ministers among Primitive Baptists; while there is no opposition to such education, the position is that the Lord will call an educated person if he wants one, but that lack of education should not bar a person from the ministry. Some Primitive Baptists still practice foot washing, but not all. In spite of their opposition to money-based missionary societies, they are intensely evangelistic, and their preachers travel widely and serve without charge, except when their hearers wish to contribute to their support.

Membership is granted only after careful examination and vote of the congregation. Factionalism, divisiveness, and politics prevent an accurate report on membership, which is concentrated in the South; it is estimated at 72,000 in 1,000 churches, but the figure is probably larger.

Reformed Baptist

This group is a fellowship of churches, rather than a denomination, and is made up of some 150 to 200 congregations, not all of which use the name Reformed. Some do not wish to be called Baptist. The bond that unites them is a strict adherence to "five-point Calvinism": belief in the Calvinistic tenets of total depravity, unconditional election, limited and definite atonement, irresistible (or invincible) calling, and the perseverence of all true saints. They also advocate the doctrines of the Synod of Dordt, "the Anabaptist doctrines of a called-out church," and the Philadelphia Confession.

These Baptists differ from other Calvinistic Baptists who may, variously, deny the necessity of preaching to all, or hold to a "Baptist succession" concept of the church. The churches involved are completely autonomous, independently supporting an unlisted number of missionaries and the publishing of church literature. No report on membership is available.

Separate Baptists in Christ (General Association of Separate Baptists)

The first Separate Baptists arrived in the United States in 1695 as one refugee section of the separatist movement in England. They were especially active during the days of the blazing preaching of Whitefield in the early eighteenth century and in the conflict between the Old Light and New Light sects. Separate Baptist churches of this period were marked by their milder Calvinism.

In 1787 Separate and Regular Baptist churches merged in Virginia in the United Baptist Churches of Christ in Virginia. There were other mergers and gestures toward union in New England and other states, but a few churches maintained their independence. In 1982 there were 100 Separate Baptist churches, 8,984 members, and 161 ordained ministers.

All creeds and confessions of faith are rejected by Separate Baptists; however, there is an annual statement of articles of belief by the several associations and the general association. These include statements of faith in the infallibility of the Scriptures and in the Trinity; three ordinances—baptism of believers by immersion only, the Lord's Supper, and foot washing; regeneration, justification, and sanctification through faith in Christ; the appearance of Christ on Judgment Day to deal with the just and the unjust. The "election, reprobation, and fatality" of Calvinism are rejected. Separate Baptists do not claim to be Protestants: "We have never protested against what we hold to be the faith once delivered to the saints."

They are congregational in government, with associations for advisory purposes only. The associations carry on a limited home missions work; there is a full-time missionary stationed in Africa, and individual members and churches support foreign mission programs in India, and those of other denominations. Recently the General Association has incorporated a mission program called Separate Baptist Missions. The churches are found in the Midwest and the South.

Seventh Day Baptist General Conference

Differing from other groups of Baptists in their adherence to the seventh day as the Sabbath, Seventh Day Baptists (or Sabbatarian Baptists, as they were called in England) first organized themselves as a separate body on this side of the Atlantic in 1672 at Newport, Rhode Island. Stephen Mumford, a member of the Bell Lane Seventh Day Baptist Church in London, had come here knowing well the perils of religious nonconformity and had entered into covenant relation with those who withdrew from "Doctor John Clarke's (Baptist) Church" under the Sabbath persuasion. Other churches were organized in Philadelphia and in New Jersey. From these three centers Seventh Day Baptists went west with the frontier; they now have 5,156 members in 60 churches and fellowships.

Belief in salvation through faith in Christ, believer's baptism by immersion, insistence upon intellectual and civil liberty and the right of every person to interpret the Bible "for himself under God" have characterized these churches. They hold only baptism and the Lord's Supper as ordinances and practice open Communion.

Local churches enjoy complete independence, although all support the united benevolence of the denomination, Our World Mission. For fellowship and service the churches are organized into eight regional associations, and these often assist local church councils in the ordination of deacons and ministerial candidates. The highest administrative body is the General Conference, which meets annually and delegates interim responsibilites to its president, executive secretary, and general council. The conference promotes World Mission giving and channels it through mission, publishing, and educational agencies. It also accredits ministers certified to it by ordaining councils and local churches.

The denomination participates in the ecumenical movement at local, regional, national, and world levels. The Seventh Day Baptist World Federation, an organization of Seventh Day Baptist conferences, includes those in Brazil, Burma, Central Africa (Malawi), England, Germany, Guyana, India, Jamaica, Mexico, Holland, New Zealand, and the Philippines, as well as those in the United States.

Southern Baptist Convention

It was inevitable that Northern and Southern Baptists should split over the slavery question, even before the outbreak of the Civil War. The friction between the two began a quarter of a century before Bull Run. The headquarters of the acting Baptist board of foreign missions was in Boston, where it was naturally strongly influenced by the abolition movement. There was bitter debate among the board members, and in the early 1840s it became evident that this board would not accept slaveholders as missionaries. The question of missionaries and missionary money was the immediate cause of the split. The "brethren of the North" first suggested separation; a month later, in May 1845, the Southern Baptist Convention was organized and at once established its own boards for foreign and home missions.

Southern historians now recognize that in addition to the slavery issue there had been a long-standing disagreement between Baptists in the North and those in the South over the nature of denominational organization. Certainly the slave issue precipitated the break, but there was a very significant consequence. Baptists in the United States under northern leadership heretofore had no central denominational organization, but there were separate and independent organizations (usually designated as "societies") for various phases of cooperative effort such as foreign and home missions and publication. Southerners had desired instead to have one organization controlling these varied activities. From the beginning the Southern Baptist Convention was such an organization. Northern Baptists, on the other hand, waited until 1907 to form a convention uniting their societies. Southern Baptists believe this cohesion of centralized organization and cooperative societies has had much to do with their growth.

In Maryland, Virginia, North Carolina, South Carolina, Georgia, Louisiana, Kentucky, and Alabama, 300 churches entered the new organization. Until the outbreak of the Civil War this convention had met biennially; since 1869 it usually has met annually.

A hard struggle for existence lay immediately ahead for the new convention. It suffered badly in point of churches, membership, and finances during the war. Homes, schools, the livelihood of citizens, the very pattern of southern society was destroyed, with devastating effect on all churches. An antimissionary movement decimated Baptist ranks, and membership—not finances and leadership—was affected when black Baptists withdrew to form their own convention. The recovery of the Southern Baptist Convention was amazing, however. In 1845 there had been 351,951 members, of whom 130,000 were black; by 1890 there were 1,235,908 members, all white; in 1983 there were 14,185,454 members in 36,531 churches, including an estimated 300,000 black members.

As previously noted, Southern Baptists generally hold to a more conservative theology than their northern relatives, but the basic tenets of belief are quite the same. The Southern Baptist faith is more definitely Calvinistic, and it is one of the ironies of Baptist history that the Southern Baptist Convention adheres more firmly to the New Hampshire Confession of Faith than does the American Baptist. Church polity and government are the same in both conventions; membership and ministry are exchanged in harmony and understanding.

Twenty denominational agencies work with 37 state conventions in home and foreign missions, Sunday schools, educational institutions, and ministerial retirement. The Home Mission Board operates throughout the United States and its territories, with more than 3,700 missionaries active in the field. An additional 2,500 summer missionaries are appointed each year. It cooperates with black Baptists; works among migrants in the South, Native Americans in the West and Southwest, 82 language groups, and the deaf; and provides loans for the erection of new church buildings.

Foreign missionaries are at work in 103 countries, on 5 continents, in 12,170 churches, of which 9,000 are self-supporting. In 1982, 140,000 baptisms were reported. There are 6,173 students in seminaries and 6,467 in correspondence courses; a total of 137,000 students are enrolled in 594 schools in 75 countries. Ninety-eight missionaries work in 24 publication centers; 26 million books, periodicals, curriculum pieces, and tracts were produced in 1982.

The Foreign Mission Board helps to operate 20 hospitals and 114 clinics and dispensaries overseas. At the end of 1983 there were 54 missionary physicians, 57 missionary nurses, and 61 other missionary personnel engaged in medical, dental, and health-care ministries. Half of the Southern Baptist Convention's Cooperative Program allocation budget of distribution funds ($59 million out of $118 million in 1984–85) goes to overseas missions.

The Sunday School Board provides the literature for and supervises the work of 7,839,855 students in 35,865 Sunday schools. The first chair of Sunday school pedagogy was established in 1915 at the Southern Baptist Theological Seminary. There are 6 theological seminaries in the Southern Baptist Convention, with 13,094 students, 46 senior colleges and universities, 6 junior colleges, 9 academies, and 3 Bible schools.

Southern Baptists are said to be the fastest growing large religious group in the United States; new churches are being established not only in the southern but in northern, eastern, and western states as well. The annual convention is being held increasingly in northern and western cities for two reasons: There are few southern cities with hotel accommodations adequate to care for the up to 22,000 messengers attending conventions; there are so many Southern Baptists living in northern territory that northern cities, from sheer force of numbers, are entitled to national conventions within their own region. State and territorial lines are being crossed, and it is more and more evident that the word *Southern* in the name is a misnomer. The denomination has become a *national* Baptist body in every meaning of the word.

Two-Seed-in-the-Spirit Predestinarian Baptist

Tracing their thought back to the Waldenses, the Two-Seed-in-the-Spirit Predestinarian Baptist Church in this country began in the late eighteenth century with Elder Daniel Parker's protest against missions and Sunday schools. Parker opposed the Arminian doctrine of the Methodists and based his dislike of the missionary effort and church schools on what he called his Two-Seed Doctrine. That, briefly, is the conviction that two seeds entered the life stream of humanity in the garden of Eden. One seed was good, planted by God; the other was evil, from the devil. The two seeds have been in conflict in humanity ever since. Every baby is predestined, born with one seed or the other. Nothing can be done for a child, one way or the other. Inasmuch as nothing can be done, mission is useless; it is, moreover, an institution that "usurps the privileges of God."

The seed is in the spirit, not the flesh; this is the cardinal point in the theology of the group. Other points include belief in the resurrection of the Body of Christ, the church, and salvation by grace alone. The church observes the Lord's Supper and practices foot washing. There is no paid ministry, "inasmuch as Christ came to save sinners, and He finished his work." Government is congregational; there are associations for fellowship only. There are no home missions or benevolences. The membership is decreasing; there were 201 members and 16 churches in 1945.

United Baptist

The United Baptist denomination represents a merging of several groups of Separate and Regular Baptists, mainly in the states of Virginia, Kentucky, and the Carolinas. While both Arminian and Calvinist theologies were held by the various bodies in those groups, they maintained a perfect freedom in preaching and polity after their union. As the years passed, many members found their way into either the Northern or Southern Baptist conventions; but the United Baptist is still recognized as a separate denomination, with 63,641 members in 568 churches. The first organization was in Richmond, Virginia, in 1787; a second group organized in Kentucky in 1801, when two associations—Salem and Elkhorn (Regular Baptists) and South Kentucky (Separate Baptists)—joined. Doctrinally there are still traces of Arminianism and Calvinism. Generally they hold that salvation is by grace rather than by works and conditional upon gospel requirements. Humankind is in a state of general depravity and is commanded to repent; people are led either to repentance, through the goodness of God, or to rebellion, by the devil. It is a matter of individual choice.

There are 26 associations for fellowship and counsel that are quite independent of one another yet work together closely. Closed Communion is practiced in some associations and churches, open Communion in others. There are three ordinances—baptism, the Lord's Supper, and (in most churches) foot washing.

United Free Will Baptist Church

While they trace their history back to the same original sources in the white Free Will Baptist Church, the United Free Will Baptist (Colored) has been independent since its official organization in 1901. Members are found largely in North Carolina, Georgia, Florida, Mississippi, Louisiana, and Texas.

Although in general agreement with the congregational polity of other Baptist bodies, this church grants a rather limited autonomy to the local church. There is a system of quarterly, annual, and general conferences, with graded authority. Doctrinal disputes may be carried up to the general conferences; district conferences may exclude members from fellowship.

Doctrinally they are in agreement with white churches of the same faith. There is one institution of higher learning—Kinston College at Kinston, North Carolina. There were 100,000 members in 836 churches in 1952.

BEREAN FUNDAMENTAL CHURCH

The Berean Fundamental Church had its origin in the work of Dr. Ivan E. Olsen in a small independent church in North Platte, Nebraska, in 1936. This became the mother church of a Berean Fellowship, and in 1947 the Berean Church Council, Inc., was formed. Since that time, it has established 52 churches in nine states: California, Colorado, Kansas, Minnesota, Missouri, South Dakota, Oregon, Wyoming, and Nebraska. Membership numbers 3,350.

The church stresses the standard fundamental doctrines of inerrancy of the Bible in all matters of faith and morals, Virgin birth, literal bodily resurrection, reality of heaven and hell, and so on. Strongly Bible-centered, it is active in evangelistic efforts. Unaffiliated with any denomination, it has no Sunday school curriculum or church literature; the churches are left free to choose for themselves from the publications of other (fundamentalist) churches. It maintains a Bible camp near North Platte, Nebraska, but has no Bible training schools or seminaries.

BIBLE FELLOWSHIP CHURCH

This body, strongly evangelical in purpose and effort, was founded in 1858 and today consists of 43 congregations in Pennsylvania, New Jersey, and New York. Its doctrinal emphases include salvation through the death and resurrection of Christ, transformed life through new birth by the Holy Spirit, the authority and trustworthiness of the Bible as the Word of God, the culmination of history in the second coming of Jesus, and "a shared-life in the church of believers, with every-member responsibility for the propagation of the Gospel by evangelism and missions."

The churches support missions on five continents, the Pinebrook Junior College, the Victory Valley Camp for children and youths, the Home for the Aging, and Pinebrook-in-the-Pines, a conference and retreat center in Pennsylvania.

BIBLE PROTESTANT CHURCH

The churches in this body represent separation from the Eastern Conference of the Methodist Protestant Church in 1939, when some 50 delegates and pastors (approximately one-third of the conference) withdrew in protest of the union of the Methodist Protestant Church with the Methodist Episcopal Church and the Methodist Episcopal Church,

South, and what the withdrawing group considered to be modernistic tendencies of those churches. While the church operates under its original corporate charter of the Eastern Conference, the name was subsequently changed to The Bible Protestant Church.

Doctrine is conservative; this church is a member of the fundamentalist American Council of Christian Churches. Cardinal points in its belief emphasize the verbal inspiration of the Bible; the Trinity; the deity, Virgin birth, resurrection, and ascension of Jesus Christ; salvation by faith in his blood and sacrifice, death and resurrection. There is a strong faith in premillennialism, with eternal punishment for the wicked and eternal joy for the righteous believer. Baptism and the Lord's Supper are practiced as divine institutions.

The churches are confined to New Jersey, New York, Pennsylvania, Virginia, and Michigan. Actually it is a fellowship of self-governing churches, organized in a conference that meets annually with lay and clerical representation. The chief officer is the president, who holds office for not more than three years. All local churches own and control their own property; all contributions to the conference are voluntary and not by assessment; local churches call their own ministers from the conference roll of ministers or from other churches approved by the Committee on Ministerial Qualifications; formal assignment of the pastor is by the Pastoral Relations Committee of the conference. Candidates for ordination must be graduates of high school and an approved seminary or Bible school. Missionary work is conducted by Bible Protestant Missions, Inc., in Japan and among migrant workers in America; Bible Protestant missionaries also serve in Mexico and Germany under the mission boards of other churches. There are 30 churches, with 2,126 members.

BIBLE WAY CHURCH, WORLDWIDE

At a ministerial conference of black Pentecostal ministers in September, 1957, some 70 churches withdrew from the Church of Our Lord of the Apostolic Faith to form the Bible Way Church, Worldwide. Its doctrine and teaching remain quite the same as those of the parent body. A phenomenal growth is reported—from 70 to 350 churches with 30,000 members in the United States, and more abroad. A general conference is held annually in July; a publishing house at Washington, D.C., circulates periodicals, religious pamphlets, and recordings.

BLACK MUSLIM

The Black Muslim movement in the United States began with the founding of a Moorish Science Temple in Newark, New Jersey, by

Timothy Drew. Drew took the name Noble Drew Ali and preached that the American blacks were actually Moors whose forefathers had lived in Morocco. His followers divided into several groups when he died in 1920; one group was led by Wallace D. Fard in Detroit. Calling himself the reincarnation of Noble Drew Ali, he taught "The Religion of the Black Men of Asia and Africa," based at first on the Bible and the Koran. But Fard was soon attacking the Bible and announcing himself as a tool in the hands of Allah. Black people, he said, were gods; the white race was the serpent devil and would ultimately be destroyed. Fard disappeared mysteriously in 1933, and soon his followers were claiming that he had been Allah personified—God, the Son of Man, the Savior. He was succeeded by the late Elijah Poole, known as Elijah Muhammad, who traced black ancestry back to people living on the moon 66 trillion years ago.

Elijah Muhammad continued to preach Fard's gospel of black revolution that would rid blacks of white domination and give them their rightful place (as an independent nation) within the United States. Building on the desparate conditions of poverty in the black ghetto areas, the movement spread across the country and increased to a militant membership that became of national interest—religiously, politically, socially, and economically.

Elijah Muhammad was imprisoned because of his advice to younger followers that they resist the draft; there he converted Malcolm Little (Malcolm X) to his cause. Black Muslims spurn their "white-given, slave-masters names" and use X to represent their unknown true names. The flaming preaching of Malcolm X helped build the membership to more than 300,000, but disagreements developed between Malcolm X and Elijah Muhammad, and membership began to decline when Malcolm X was murdered in New York City in 1965.

Today membership claims vary from 100,000 to 750,000; some students of the movement think it is much less than 100,000. The followers—and nonregistered sympathizers—are generally (nearly 80 percent) young male blacks between 17 and 35 years of age living in city ghettos, ex-Christian or anti-Christian and anti-white, and completely devoted to Elijah Muhammad's idea of the establishment of a separate black state (The Black Nation of Islam) in this country. They are not recognized as a legitimate branch of Islam by the orthodox Middle East Muslims, much as they desire that, but they claim that they accept and practice Mohammedan principles and teachings in everything but their extreme racism. Allah is to them the one true God, and they use the Koran and traditional Moslem rituals in their temple services.

Although marred by violence, the movement has achieved some very definite accomplishments. It has established a chain of industries to relieve black poverty—barbershops, supermarkets, bakeries, restaurants, cleaning establishments, and farms. Black Muslims do not gamble, smoke, drink, overeat, or buy on credit. They arrange parole for convicts and offer postprison guidance. Their claim that they give black men self-respect has at least that element of truth; they have reached many whom the church has been unable to reach, and this may account for much of their popularity.

BRETHREN

The terms Brethren and Dunker have been the cause of much confusion; they call for careful definition. *Dunker* is a direct derivation of the German word *tunken*, "to dip or immerse," and is identified with the peculiar method of immersion employed by this group of churches—trine (triple) immersion—in which the believer is immersed not once but three times, in the name of the Father, Son, and Holy Ghost. Variously through their long history Dunkers have been called Tunkers, Täufers, or Dompelaars. They were first called Brethren when their organization was established at Schwarzenau, Germany, in 1708.

It might be said generally that these Dunker, or Brethren, bodies are former German Reformed that took their theology and much of their practice from the Pietists of the seventeenth and eighteenth centuries. The Pietists were mostly Lutherans who had become unhappy with the formalism of worship and ritual in their state church and with the general "barrenness" of German Protestantism. They took the New Testament literally and endeavored to put its teachings into practice even in the least detail of their living. They spurned the idea of apostolic succession, and at the heart of their practice was a love feast, or agape, the serving of the Lord's Supper preceded by a ceremony of foot washing. They saluted one another with a "kiss of peace," dressed in the plainest clothing, covered the heads of women at services, anointed their sick with oil for healing and consecration, refrained from worldly amusements, and refused to take oaths, go to war, or engage in lawsuits. These doctrines and practices, with certain modifications, are held today by many Brethren.

From those German Pietists came the Church of the Brethren (Conservative Dunkers), the Brethren Church (Progressive Dunkers), the Old German Baptist Brethren (Old Order Dunkers), the Church of God (New Dunkers, disbanded in August 1962), and the Felloship of Grace Brethren Churches.

There are other Brethren groups. One unrelated historically to these, known as the River Brethren, also took its ideology from the German Pietists. That group includes the Brethren in Christ, the Old Order (or Yorker) Brethren, and United Zion Church (formerly United Zion's Children). Another—the Plymouth Brethren—is totally unrelated to any of these, being British rather than German in origin (see Plymouth Brethren).

The Brethren bodies that began in Germany were known for years simply as German Baptist Brethren; that title has largely disappeared except in the case of the Old German Baptist Brethren.

DUNKERS

Brethren Church (Ashland)

In 1882, a sharp division within the Church of the Brethren resulted in the organization of the Brethren Church. It is referred to as Progressive, sometimes Progressive Dunker (because of baptism by immersion), and sometimes Progressive Brethren. This description refers to its opposition to some outmoded practices of Church of the Brethren, especially in education and dress.

The Ashland, Ohio, body is the Arminian wing of the Progressive Dunker movement. It has 15,082 members in 122 churches. It supports a college and a seminary in the headquarters city.

Church of the Brethren

The Church of the Brethren began in 1708 with a brotherhood of eight persons in Schwarzenau, Germany. Because of economic necessity and persecution in central Germany, one group, under the leadership of Peter Becker, came to America in 1719 from Krefeld to take up free lands offered by William Penn. The members settled in Germantown, near Philadelphia, where they were joined in 1729 by 59 families brought across the Atlantic by Alexander Mack. From Pennsylvania, they spread across the country.

The Brethren's German speech, their opposition to war, and their insistence that the inner Christian life is more important than church organization made them suspect from the start. Morally they opposed the Revolution; in the Civil War they opposed slavery. The suspicion and misunderstanding waned as time went on; today historians commend the contributions of the Brethren to American democracy. In our own day the work of Brethren pacifists in World War II and the church's oustanding efforts in relief to Europe following that war have earned it respect in American Protestantism. In the early days at Germantown, the first German Bible and the first religious magazine in America were circulated in 1743 and 1764, respectively, by Christopher Sauer I, a friend of the Brethren, and by Christopher Sauer II, a Brethren elder.

In 1728 a group under Conrad Beissel left the Brethren to found the famous Ephrata Community (Seventh Day Baptists, German); in 1848 another break resulted in the establishment of the Church of God (New Dunkers). In 1881 a third group withdrew to organize the Old German Baptist Brethren (Old Order Dunkers); and in 1882 there was another split when the Brethren Church (Progressive Brethren) was organized. In 1926, a smaller group of conservatives withdrew and formed the Dunkard Brethren Church. The original body is known today as Church of the Brethren and has approximately 170,000 members in 1,064 churches in the United States. Overseas churches begun as the result of missionary activity in Ecuador, Nigeria, and India are now identified with autonomous churches in those countries, but the church maintains a cooperative relationship with them. Christians in China resulting from

Brethren missionary activity there are members of the United Christian Church in China.

In doctrine this church follows the mainstream of Protestant theology, with considerable freedom of thought for its members and clergy, and great emphasis on practical biblical piety. Its practical teaching is summarized in the following divisions: (1) the doctrine of peace, including refusal to go to war and a positive peacemaking program that makes them more than war resisters; (2) the doctrine of temperance, under which total abstinence is taught and largely practiced; (3) the doctrine of the simple life, under which unwholesome amusements and luxuries are shunned, and a practical, wholesome, temperate, clean way of personal and family life is stressed—they seek to develop a "concerned stewardship of life rather than prohibition of amusements and overindulgence in luxuries"; (4) the doctrine of brotherhood, under which all class distinctions are opposed as unchristian; and (5) the doctrine that religion means loving and willing obedience to Christ, rather than to creeds and cults. Christian living, rather than form, is stressed. Baptism is by trine (triple) immersion; the love feast is observed, following the pattern of John 13:1-17.

Moderators, lay or clerical, men or women, resident or nonresident, are in charge of local congregations, which enjoy a great deal of autonomy. Pastors are chosen by ballot of the local congregation. Above the local groups stands one of the 24 districts and the annual conference (a legislative body composed of delegates from the churches and an "upper house" known as the Standing Committee, made up of delegates from the districts). The annual conference is an overall unifying body.

A general board, composed of 25 members elected by the annual conference, supervises the general church program carried on by an employed staff. The board administers the overseas church program, represents the church in the field of social education, social action, relief and rehabilitation, and carries on a worldwide program of peace and human welfare. The program includes a volunteer service in America and abroad for hundreds of young men and women, including conscientious objectors, and other older volunteers. It supervises church schools, weekday religious education, and summer camps, and supports several colleges such as Elizabethtown, Juniata, and McPherson. There is one theological seminary. The board provides leadership and education for the ministry by locating and supporting new churches and by evangelism. It carries responsiblity for the printing and merchandising interests of the denomination.

The Church of the Brethren cooperates fully with the World Council of Churches, the National Council of the Churches of Christ in the U.S.A., and local church councils. Its membership strength extends from Pennsylvania and Virginia west to Kansas.

Fellowship of Grace Brethren Churches

Born in the 1881–1883 split in the original Brethren body in the United States, the Brethren Church is based doctrinally on a statement of faith,

Message of the Brethren Ministry, adopted in 1921. The Message included declarations of belief in the infallibility of the Scriptures; the preexistence, deity, and incarnation by Virgin birth of Jesus Christ; the vicarious atonement of Christ and his resurrection; justification by personal faith in Christ; resurrection of the dead; judgment of the world; believer's baptism by trine (triple) immersion; the ordinances of baptism, the Lord's Supper, Communion of the bread and cup, foot washing, and anointing of the sick with oil.

In 1939 a crisis in the Brethren church divided it into bodies that came to be known as the Ashland group and the Grace group. The latter is commonly called the Fellowship of Grace Brethren Churches. Both groups still carry the name of The Brethren Church and operate under one charter, but each has its own annual conference—the Ashland body at Ashland, Ohio, and the Grace body (usually) at Winona Lake, Indiana. Each conference has its own executives and its own educational institutions and mission boards. The Grace group is more definitely congregational in government. Both groups claim adherence to the Message of the Brethren Ministry, but it is generally true that the Grace group represents more nearly the Calvinistic viewpoint in theology; the Ashland group, the Arminian viewpoint.

Churches are grouped geographically into districts, which hold annual conferences. The Grace group numbers 42,023 in 299 churches; the Ashland group, 16,357 in 119 churches.

Old German Baptist Brethren (Old Order Dunkers)

While the Brethren Church (Progressive Dunkers) left the Church of the Brethren (Conservative Dunkers) because the latter body seemed too conservative, the Old German Baptist Brethren (Old Order Dunkers) left it because it was considered not conservative enough. The dissenters stood literally for the old order and traditions. The salient point in their opposition lay in their suspicion of Sunday schools, salaried ministers, missions, higher education, and church societies. They withdrew in 1881.

The basic objections still hold, but with certain modifications. Children are not enrolled in Sunday schools, but are encouraged to attend the regular services of the church and to join the church at an early age—anywhere from 15 to 20, the decision being left entirely to the individual. Many congregations list a majority of members between 15 and 40 years of age. The church today is not completely opposed even to higher education; a few of the youths enter high school and take training in college or professional schools for various professions.

The church stands for a literal interpretation of the Scriptures in regard to the Lord's Supper, and it practices closed Communion, which excludes all but its own membership. While it advocates compliance with the ordinary demands of government, it opposes cooperation in war: "Any member who enters into military service will fall into the judgment of the Church." Noncooperation in political and secret societies is required; the dress is severely plain, and all worldly amusements are frowned upon. The group follows other Brethren bodies in that there are no salaried ministers, complete abstinence from alcoholic liquors is enforced, the members refuse to take oaths or engage in lawsuits, the sick are anointed with oil, the heads of the women are veiled at worship, and wedding ceremonies are not performed for divorced persons.

There are no Sunday schools, missions, or educational work. An annual conference that rules on matters "on which the Scriptures are silent" is held each year at Pentecost. There are 5,251 members in 54 churches, with strength in Ohio, Indiana, and Pennsylvania.

RIVER BRETHREN

A considerable number of post-Reformation Anabaptists and Pietists, fleeing Europe, settled in Lancaster County, Pennsylvania, during the eighteenth century. During the latter third of the century, in cooperation with other mainline denominations, they developed fellowship groups designated as the United Brethren in Christ. A group in a community near the Susquehanna River came into disagreement with the rest of the fellowship over requirements relative to the Christian ordinances, and as a result, The Brotherhood by the River withdrew from the larger fellowship late in the century and formed a new denomination. The name River Brethren was associated with this body for more than a hundred years.

Other disputes in the new organization brought about the establishment of two smaller bodies—the Old Order, or Yorker, Brethren in 1843, and the Brinsers, or United Zion's Children, in 1855. These three churches today number about 15,000 communicant members in the United States and Canada.

Brethren in Christ Church (formerly River Brethren)

With the outbreak of the Civil War the draft reached into the ranks of the Brethren, and it became necessary for it to obtain legal recognition as an established religious organization in order to protect the objectors. The denomination opposes war and most of its members will not participate. A council meeting in Lancaster County, Pennsylvania, in 1863 adopted the name Brethren in Christ Church; it was not incorporated until 1904.

The Brethren in Christ Church pledges loyalty to the following doctrines: the inspiration of the Holy Scriptures; the self-existent, Triune God—Father, Son, and Holy Spirit; the deity and Virgin birth of Christ; Christ's death as atonement for our sins, and his resurrection from the dead; the Holy Spirit who convicts the sinner, regenerates the penitent, and empowers the believer; justification as forgiveness for committed sins and sanctification as heart cleansing and empowerment by the Holy Spirit; observance of the ordinances of God's house; temperance and modesty of apparel as taught in the Scriptures; the personal, visible, and imminent return of Christ; the resurrection of the dead, with punishment for the unbeliever and reward for the believer; the supreme duty of the church as worldwide evangelism.

While the government of this church is largely in the hands of the local churches, there are six regional conferences and a general conference, which is the ultimate and final authority. There is also a board of administration; a board of directors amenable to the board of administration has oversight of the general conference and of general church property and financial transactions.

The church has two institutions of learning: Messiah College at Grantham, Pennsylvania, and Niagara Christian College at Fort Erie, Ontario, Canada. Missionaries are at work in Africa, India, Japan, Nicaragua, Venezuela, and Cuba, and are engaged in Mennonite Central Committee work around the world. There are 16,201 members in 167 churches in the United States.

Old Order (Yorker) Brethren

The Old Order, or Yorker, Brethren is the smallest of all River Brethren groups in the United States; at latest report, there were 80 members in 4 congregations. The primary reason for its existence as a separate body lay in the organizers' feeling that the Brethren in Christ had become lax in its enforcement of nonresistance and nonconformity to the world. The group left the original body in 1843. *Old Order* refers to the members' desire to keep the old traditions alive; *Yorker* resulted from the fact that most of them, at the time of withdrawal, lived in York County, Pennsylvania.

The doctrine is no longer identical to that of the Brethren in Christ Church. Members refuse to build or to meet in church edifices; lacking these, they usually meet in their homes.

United Zion Church

Bishop Matthias Brinser was expelled from the Brethren in Christ Church in 1855, together with about 50 other members, for building and holding services in a meetinghouse. They organized their own group, United Zion's Children; in 1954 the body incorporated under the name United Zion Church.

This church is essentially the same in doctrine as the Brethren in Christ. It baptizes by trine immersion and observes foot washing as an ordinance, along with the Lord's Supper. It encourages the veiling of women and is opposed to divorce and immodest attire.

Located almost exclusively in Dauphin, Lebanon, and Lancaster counties in Pennsylvania, it lists 933 members and 13 churches. Church officers are bishops, ministers, and deacons; the top administrative body is a general conference composed of a representation of the various district conferences; the basic unit of government is the district conference.

No foreign missionary work of its own is reported, but it supports two missionaries working under the Brethren in Christ church. One home for the aged is maintained, and a monthly magazine, *Zion's Herald*, is published.

UNITED BRETHREN

United Brethren in the United States are found in two churches—the Church of the United Brethren in Christ (Old Constitution) and the United Christian Church. The Evangelical United Brethren Church, now merged into The United Methodist Church, was until recently one branch of this body. Originally one group, they were the spiritual descendants of Philip William Otterbein and Martin Boehm (for their early historical background see p. 170). At a general conference of the parent body held at York, Pennsylvania, in 1889, a dispute arose over proposed changes in the church constitution, concerned mainly with permitting members to join lodges and secret societies. There was a division into two churches: The majority group in the United Brethren in Christ; the minority in the Church of the United Brethren in Christ (Old Constitution). The larger body merged in 1946 with the Evangelical Church, becoming the Evangelical United Brethren Church, now merged into The United Methodist Church.

Church of the United Brethren in Christ

This group, in existence since 1841, opposed constitutional changes in 1889; its dissent is still one of discipline rather than of doctrine. The United Brethren who favored the new constitution later merged (in 1968) to help form The United Methodist Church. United Brethren believe in the Trinity; they also believe in the deity, humanity, and atonement of Christ. Observance of strict scriptural living is required of all members, who are forbidden the use of alcoholic drinks, membership in secret societies, and participation in aggressive (but not defensive) war. Baptism and the Lord's Supper are observed as ordinances.

Local, annual, and general conferences are held; the general conference meets quadrennially and is composed of ministers, district superintendents (presiding elders), general church officials, bishops, and lay delegates. Both men and women are eligible for the ministry and are ordained only once as elders. Missionary societies administer evangelism and church aid in the United States and on foreign fields in Sierra Leone, West Africa, Jamaica, the Republic of Honduras in Central America,

Hong Kong, and Nicaragua. A college and Graduate School of Christian Ministries are located at Huntington, Indiana, with secondary schools in Jamaica and Sierra Leone. There are 28,035 members in 281 churches, mostly in the Midwest. Still insisting upon loyalty to the old constitution, the church belongs to the National Association of Evangelicals and works in harmony with evangelical groups in other denominations.

BUDDHIST CHURCHES OF AMERICA

Buddhism is found in real strength in this country in Colorado, Washington, Oregon, California, and Hawaii, and represents the transplanting of the Buddhism of the East. With the recent influx of Asian immigrants to the United States—Southeast Asian, Korean, Chinese, and so on—and the rapid expansion of Nichiren Soshu of America (a new denomination) which has thousands of non-Japanese-American followers, the majority of Buddhists in the United States are no longer of Japanese ancestry, although their membership remains strong.

The faith is built upon the teaching of the founder, Buddha—Siddartha Gautama, the Enlightened One (566 B.C.)—who attained his enlightenment in India and whose teachings have spread all over the Far East. Often challenged as a system of religious faith, it remains a most complex and involved pattern of thought and action. It is divided into two schools—Hinayana, or Theravada, Buddhism, the Lesser Vehicle; and Mahayana Buddhism, the Greater Vehicle. These offer, on the one hand, a path of deliverance from suffering and, on the other, a thorough preparation for entry upon that path. Hinayana seems devised for those among its disciples who are satisfied with a comparatively modest attainment of Buddhist virtue, while Mahayana is the way of deliverance through true and real awareness of wisdom and compassion in everyday living as the very ground for the perfection of life.

Buddha himself put the essence of his system in these words: "One thing only I teach: sorrow [or pain], the cause of sorrow, the cessation of sorrow, and the path which leads to the cessation of sorrow." These are the Four Truths of Buddhism, the fourth of which includes the actual means of arriving at these truths by way of the "noble eightfold path"—"right views, right intention, right speech, right action, right livelihood, right effort, right mindfulness, right concentration." This description of the eight paths covers the whole training of the disciple who seeks nirvana, which means literally *blown out* or *extinguished*. The disciple strives to extinguish all desire, hatred, and ignorance, and thus to attain a nobler life.

There are no theories of creation, no miracles, and no divine being in Buddhism. Supreme reality is neither affirmed nor denied; it is only said to be beyond the comprehension of the human mind. It is actually a system of self-education in the conquering, or forgetting, of pain, sorrow, and suffering. Recognizing that this is a long process, Buddha taught that a person has an indefinite number of lives, or reincarnations, in which to accomplish it.

The first Buddhist temple in the United States was consecrated in San Francisco in 1898. The Buddhist Mission of North America began at that time and was incorporated in 1942 as the Buddhist Churches of America. It is the administrative organization for Jodo Shinshu Buddhism in the continental United States. There are 75 ministers, 62 temples, 40 branches, and about 250,000 members.

Jodo Shinshu Buddhism is a faith based on "the anatman doctrine, supplemented by the idea of karma and nirvana, the holy ease or a blissful mental state of absolute freedom from evil." Each church is autonomous, holding complete control of its own property. Weekly services are held, and Japanese-language schools are maintained by many of the churches. The titular head of Jodo Shinshu Buddhism bears the title of bishop, is in charge of all religious activities, and is authorized to transfer or dismiss the clergy.

Author's Note: A movement known as Zen Buddhism has found some interest among non-Buddhists in this country; it seeks to transmit the spirit of Buddhism without demanding allegiance to all the teachings of Buddha. It makes use of a question-and-answer technique *(mondo)* to reveal truths that are not necessarily religious, but truths that are found within the seeker and that will bring enlightenment *(bodhi)* and improvement of the condition of humankind. Wisdom *(prajna)* and love *(karuna)* are major emphases. (Zen Buddhism is a recognized denomination of Buddhism, separate from Jodo Shinshu.)

CHRISTADELPHIAN

John Thomas came to the United States from England in 1844. He joined the Disciples of Christ, but later became convinced that their doctrine made them the apostate church predicted by Scripture and that many other more important Bible doctrines were being neglected. He left the Disciples to organize a number of societies, which, under his leadership, began to preach the need for a return to primitive Christianity. Loosely organized, those societies bore no name until the outbreak of the Civil War, when their doctrine of nonresistance forced them to adopt a name, and they chose Christadelphians, or Brethren of Christ.

Christadelphians are both Unitarian and Adventist in theology. They reject belief in a personal devil, maintaining the Scriptures teach that Christ is not God the Son, but the Son of God; not preexistent, but born of Mary by the Holy Spirit. Humankind is mortal by nature, with Christ as the only means of salvation. Eternal life comes only to the righteous. Strong millennarians, they believe that Christ will come shortly to reward those who are worthy with immortality and destroy the wicked; that he will take David's throne in Jerusalem, the faithful will be gathered, and the world will be ruled from Jerusalem for a thousand years.

The church is congregational in polity; local organizations are known not as churches but as ecclesias. Membership is by profession of faith and immersion. There are no paid or ordained ministers in the usual sense; each ecclesia elects serving brethren, among whom are managing brethren, presiding brethren, and lecturing brethren. Women take no part in public speech or prayer, though all vote equally in the affairs of the ecclesia. Christadelphians do not vote in civil elections or participate in war, and they refuse to accept public office. There are no associations or conventions, but there are fraternal gatherings for spiritual inspiration. Many meetings are held in rented halls, schoolhouses, or private homes, though a number of ecclesias have their own buildings.

Home missions work is local, usually in the form of lectures and instruction in Christadelphian doctrine and righteous living. There are some foreign missions, and ecclesias are found in several countries. There is no educational work, with the exception of summer Bible schools in several states. Found in 42 states from coast to coast, they reported 15,800 members in about 850 ecclesias in 1967. Larger numbers are located in Great Britain, New Zealand, Australia, Canada, Germany, and other countries.

CHRISTIAN AND MISSIONARY ALLIANCE, THE

The Christian and Missionary Alliance originated in 1881 under the leadership of A. B. Simpson, a Presbyterian minister in New York City who left that church to carry on independent evangelistic work among the unchurched. Organized in 1887, the group was originally two societies, the Christian Alliance for home missions work and the International Missionary Alliance for work abroad. The two bodies merged in 1897, forming the present Christian and Missionary Alliance. At the time of the founding of the Assemblies of God, about one-tenth of that constituency resulted from the departure of about one-tenth of the Christian and Missionary Alliance membership. The two groups have a closely interwoven history and are doctrinally similar.

Strongly evangelical, the Alliance stands for the literal inspiration of the Bible and its inerrancy, the atonement wrought by Christ, the reality of supernatural religious experience, separation from the world, the premillennial return of Jesus Christ, sanctification, and practical holiness. While there is no creed as such, there is a formula of belief built upon a fourfold gospel of Christ as Savior, Sanctifier, Healer, and coming Lord; there is also a statement of faith (1965).

The Christian and Missionary Alliance maintains ministries in 46 nations and territories. In the United States and Puerto Rico, work is carried on in 20 organized districts with 1,597 churches fully or partially organized. Each of these churches or groups is a self-administering and self-governing unit engaged in missionary and evangelical activities. There is an overall conference, the General Council, which meets annually in various parts of the United States and Canada.

Foreign missionary work is carried on in South America, Africa, the Near East, India, Thailand, Japan, Hong Kong and Taiwan, Indonesia including Irian Jaya, and the Philippines. In these areas there are 938 missionaries from the Alliance and 5,526 indigenous workers in 4,453 organized churches, with 332,443 members.

In addition to the organized church work in North America, missionary activity is carried on among Native Americans, as well as other ethnic and minority groups. The Alliance maintains colleges at Nyack, New York; St. Paul; and San Francisco. Alliance Theological Seminary was founded in 1981. In 1977 there were 195,042 members in North America in 1,436 churches. Thus the Alliance has a larger constituency abroad than at home.

CHRISTIAN CATHOLIC CHURCH

The Christian Catholic Movement (*catholic* in the sense of *universal*, a church home for all true Christians) began prior to 1896, when John Alexander Dowie, a Congregational preacher educated in Scotland and ordained in Australia, gave it formal organization. Dowie also founded Zion City, Illinois, and when the city was settled in 1901, it became headquarters for the new church. Businesses and industries were developed, all controlled and governed by a theocracy of which Dowie was general overseer. He had extensive plans for educational and cultural projects; he criticized the injustices of capitalism and the excesses of labor leaders, alcoholic beverages, tobacco, medicine and the medical profession, secret lodges, and the press. He was also a tireless advocate of racial equality and integration.

Theologically, "CCC" is rooted in evangelical orthodoxy; it describes itself as an evangelical Protestant church. The Scriptures are accepted as the rule of faith and practice. Other doctrines call for belief in the necessity for repentance of sin and personal trust in Christ for salvation, baptism by trine immersion, the second coming of Christ, and tithing as a practical method of Christian stewardship. Dowie emphasized the healing of disease through prayer, and his success in healing led to the establishment of a tabernacle and "divine healing rooms," first in Chicago and later in Zion City.

Several years after the organization of the church at Zion, Dowie claimed to be Elijah the Restorer and maintained leadership of the group until 1906, when he was deposed and followed successively by Wilbur Glen Voliva, Michael J. Mintern, Carl Q. Lee, and currently Roger W. Ottersen.

At first an exclusively religious community, Zion City still contains a strong Christian Catholic church, but independent businesses have been welcomed, and many other churches are at work there. Since 1900 the church has sponsored a Zion Conservatory of Music which today has an enrollment of 240 pupils. Begun in 1935, its famous annual Passion Play, with a cast of over 200, has attracted thousands of visitors. Branches of the church have been established in Michigan City (Ind.), Phoenix, and Toronto, Canada. Missionary work is conducted in Japan, Australia, Israel, the Philippines, Guyana, and South Africa. In addition, the church supports missionaries under Inter Varsity, Campus Crusade, The Navigators, T.E.A.M., the Africa Evangelical Fellowship, and Wycliffe. In Jamaica it cooperates with The Missionary Church. It is a member of the National Association of Evangelicals.

Two radio programs, "Songs of Zion" and "Chapel-Time," are broadcast weekly, and a monthly publication, *Leaves of Healing,* is published for worldwide circulation. With six places of worship in the United States, there is a membership of 2,500.

CHRISTIAN CHURCH (DISCIPLES OF CHRIST)

Among the dozen largest religious groups in the United States, the Christian Church (Disciples of Christ) might be called the most American; it was born on the nineteenth-century American frontier out of a deep concern for Christian unity. There were four pioneers: Barton Stone, Thomas and Alexander Campbell, and Walter Scott, all from Presbyterian backgrounds.

Barton Stone believed that Christians could and should unite in the basis of simple faith in Christ and that the divisive doctrines and practices of denominationalism should be abolished. His church at Cane Ridge, Kentucky, became the center of the famous Kentucky Revival; but Stone came out of that movement convinced that salvation had little to do with church affiliation and that "deeds are more important than creeds." Disciplinary action was brought against him and against his followers in the established churches; they withdrew from these churches, reorganized under the name Christian, and spread across Kentucky, Ohio, and the central states.

Thomas Campbell served as a clergyman in the Seceder branch of the Presbyterian church in northern Ireland; he settled in a church in western Pennsylvania in 1807, where he advocated closer relations with all

Christians, appealed to the Bible as the basis of faith, and practiced open Communion. Censured, he led in the formation of "the Christian Association of Washington County, Pa.," and published a "Declaration and Address" that was to become the Magna Charta of the Christian Church (Disciples of Christ). In that declaration he argued that "schism, or uncharitable divisions" in the church were "anti-Christian, anti-Scriptural, anti-natural" and "productive of confusion and every evil work." The church and church membership should be based solely upon the belief and practices of New Testament Christianity; the articles of faith and holiness "expressly revealed in the Word of God" were quite enough without the addition of human opinions or creedal inventions.

Thomas Campbell laid the cornerstone; his son Alexander Campbell gave the movement its formative theology. He left a Seceder church in Scotland to join his father in Pennsylvania in 1810 and enlarged on the concept that every church should be autonomous and completely independent—that creeds, clerical titles, authority, and privilege had no justification in Scripture; that the Lord's Supper should be served at every Sunday service; and that baptism should be by immersion for adult believers (those adult enough to understand the meaning of the ordinance). He argued eloquently for Christian union and freedom of individual faith, and he welcomed to his independent church at Brush Run, Pennsylvania, all who came with simple faith in Christ as the Son of God and the Messiah. He met the same opposition his father had met and, with his congregation, joined an association of Particular Baptists, only to be separated from that body in 1830. Barton Stone used the word *Christian* to designate his group, feeling that all God's children should be known so. Campbell used the word Disciples. In 1832 the Christians and the Disciples merged; both names are still used, but usually and officially the body is known today as the Christian Church (Disciples of Christ).

Early in the movement, Walter Scott popularized the term *restoration*, meaning the restoration of New Testament pattern and practice. Like Stone, Scott was suspicious of the values of the current revivalistic frenzies; he related faith more to the mind than to emotions—it was not a matter of emotional experience but of intellectual acceptance of the truth of Christ's messiahship. He stressed the importance of such faith, together with repentance of sin and baptism by immersion.

The first national convention of the Disciples and their first missionary society (the American Christian Missionary Society) were organized in 1849; state conventions and societies had begun to meet in 1839. They grew rapidly through and following the Civil War period, especially in Ohio, Indiana, Illinois, Tennessee, and Missouri, in spite of conflict within the church over any emphasis on denominationalism or ecclesiastical organization. The differences between conservatives and progressives became acute in such matters as the organization of missionary societies and instrumental music in the churches; the Churches of Christ separated from the Disciples during that debate.

In matters of belief, conservative and progressive attitudes were and still are important, and the church allows for variance of opinion and stands for complete freedom in interpretation, stemming from the historic conviction that there is no creed but Christ and no saving doctrines save those of the New Testament. It could be said that the Disciples are "God-centered, Christ-centered, and Bible-centered"; beyond that, faith is a matter of individual conviction, but there are areas of general agreement and acceptance. The Disciples are firm in their belief in immortality but do not accept the doctrine of original sin; they hold that all people are of a sinful nature until redeemed by the sacrifice of Christ; they are not concerned with speculation about the Trinity and the nature of a triune God. They have no catechism, no set orders of worship; faith in Christ as Lord is the only requirement.

For more than a century the Disciples were strictly congregational in polity—a loosely bound association of local churches. But increasingly it was felt that such an arrangement, with overlapping boards and agencies and no representative voice, needed a restructure in the interests of efficiency and economy. Following a seven-year study and discussion, led by a 130-member Commission on Brotherhood Restructure, a whole new design of governmental organization was adopted at Kansas City in 1968. Under the new plan, the whole church works under a polity of "representative government" on three levels—local, regional, and general.

The local church is still the basic unit. All congregations listed in the latest year book are accepted as congregations; each congregation manages its own affairs, has its own charters and by-laws, owns and controls its property, calls its ministers, establishes its own budgets and financial policies, and has voting representatives in regional and national assemblies.

The churches are grouped into 35 regions organized to provide help, counsel, and pastoral care to members, ministers, and congregations. Each region organizes its own boards, departments, and committees. Within policies developed by the general assembly, the regions certify the standing of ministers and provide help and counsel to ministers and congregations in such matters as ordination, licensing, location and installation of ministers, and the establishment or dissolution of pastoral relationships. Regions have regional ministers as their administrative leaders.

The general assembly is made up of voting and nonvoting representatives from the local churches and regions, plus ministers and a few ex-officio members, the chief officers of institutions and unit boards, and members of the general board. The assembly receives and acts upon proposed programs, policies, reports and resolutions sent up through the general board, elects the officers of the church and half the members of the general board. The regions elect the other half.

The general board meets annually, processes business going to the assembly, recommends policies, reviews the total program of the church, elects or confirms the governing bodies of the various administrative units, and elects the committees of the general assembly and the members of an administrative committee. General board members are lay people and one-third ministers.

The administrative committee of the general board is made up of 40 members elected by the board; officers of the church are ex-officio members. Meeting at least twice a year, it provides long-range planning, implements policies, and promotes the causes and units of the church.

Officers of the church are of two classes—voluntary (nonsalaried) officers of the general assembly and salaried officers. There is a volunteer moderator, two vice-moderators, and a salaried general minister and president.

Membership continues to be largest in the lower Midwest and the Southwest. There are now 1,156,458 members in 4,291 churches in the United States and 37 congregations with 4,948 members in Canada. There are 36 colleges, seminaries, undergraduate schools of religion, and foundations; 10 centers for children and the retarded; and 41 health and housing centers for older adults.

The Disciples are represented in the National Council of Churches, and the World Council of Churches, and the Consultation on Church Union. The headquarters of a World Convention of Churches of Christ is in Dallas.

CHRISTIAN CHURCH OF NORTH AMERICA, GENERAL COUNCIL

Originally known as the Italian Christian Church, this body was incorporated in 1948 at Pittsburgh, Pennsylvania. Its first general council was held in 1927, at Niagara Falls, New York. It is described as pentecostal but does not engage in "the excesses tolerated or practiced among some churches using the same name." At least 50 percent of its membership (7,500 in 106 churches) is of Italian nationality or descent.

The church recognizes two ordinances—baptism and the Lord's Supper—and in its moral code and teaching stands against gambling, drunkenness, the use of tobacco, theater-going, and dancing. Intermarriage with unbelievers is strictly forbidden, and a conservative position ("as outlined in Matthew 19") is held in regard to marriage and divorce. The governmental form, by and large, is congregational. However, the General Council reflects a Presbyterian emphasis.

Foreign missionary work is conducted in India, South America, Africa, Australia, the Philippines, Europe, and Barbados. The group functions in cooperative fellowship with the Italian Pentecostal Church of Canada and the Evangelical Christian Churches—Assemblies of God in

Italy—and is an affiliate member of the Pentecostal Fellowship of North America and of the National Association of Evangelicals.

CHRISTIAN CHURCHES AND CHURCHES OF CHRIST

The churches and members of these independent Christian churches do not make up a denomination, but a fellowship; there is no formal organization other than in the local congregations, and there are no denominational societies, officials, or boards. The churches in this group are identified usually with the Disciples of Christ, a few congregations of the Churches of Christ, and the smaller Christian Churches, which preach and teach a conservative, fundamentalist theology that they feel is being neglected, especially among the Disciples. All three movements belong to the historical Campbellite tradition.

Their doctrine in general agrees with that of the Disciples and the Churches of Christ. It stresses the divinity of Christ, the agency of the Holy Spirit in conversion, the Bible as the inspired Word of God, future rewards and punishments, and God as a prayer-answering deity. They maintain that "all ordinances should be observed as they were in the days of the apostles," and they observe the Lord's Supper in open Communion every Sunday. The music in worship services includes instruments, a feature setting them apart from the Churches of Christ.

Membership is strongest in the lower and eastern midwestern states and in Kentucky. No official membership survey has ever been taken, because of the unusual nature of the fellowship, but various estimates, questionable in accuracy, have been made. There are said to be 1,040,856 members in 5,436 congregations. Some of these churches withdrew their names from the yearbook of the Disciples in protest against the recent "restructuring" of that denomination.

The group supports at least 32 small Christian Bible colleges in different sections of the country; has over 450 missionaries at work in dispensaries, hospitals, and Bible colleges; and circulates huge quantities of evangelical literature. Their publishing house—the Standard Publishing Foundation—is located at Cincinnati. In Johnson City, Tennessee, a liberal arts college and a graduate school of theology offer training in behalf of this fellowship.

CHRISTIAN CONGREGATION

The philosophy and work of the Christian Congregation, formed in Indiana in 1887, revolve about the "new commandment" of John

13:34-35. The group is a fellowship of ministers, lay people, and congregations seeking a noncreedal, nondenominational basis for union. It is pacifistic and opposes all sectarian strife, insisting that according to the new commandment, "the household of faith is not founded upon doctrinal agreement, creeds, church claims, names or rites," but solely upon the relationship of the individual to God. The basis of Christian fellowship is love; the importance of the actual relations of Christians toward one another transcends all individual belief or personal opinion. Independent Bible study is encouraged.

Churches and pastorates are now located in every state in the union; the chruch still remains strongest, however, in the areas where Barton Stone preached and where the original Christian Congregation groups were located—Kentucky, the Carolinas, Virginia, Pennsylvania, Ohio, Indiana, and Texas. The greater part of the group's work is carried on in rural, mountain, and neglected areas; in many respects it is identical with that of the Stone movement and his original Christian Church, although these congregations were established and at work when the Christian Church was organized.

Polity is congregational. A general superintendent presides over a board of trustees; relations between the superintendent and the board and the people are purely advisory. There are 100,694 members in 1,435 churches or local congregations.

CHRISTIAN UNION

Christian Union represents an attempt to unite all Christians in a consciousness of unity on a scriptural basis and to offer a larger unity in thought and worship. Organized in 1864 at Columbus, Ohio, its announced purpose is "to promote fellowship among God's people, to put forth every effort to proclaim God's saving grace to the lost . . . and to declare the whole counsel of God for the edification of believers."

There is no one creed binding upon members of the Union, but seven principles are stressed: the oneness of the Church of Christ, Christ as the only head of the church, the Bible as the only rule of faith and practice, good fruits as the one condition of fellowship, Christian union without controversy, complete autonomy for the local church, and avoidance of all partisan political preaching. Both men and women are ordained ministers, and the ordinances include baptism—preferably by immersion—and the Lord's Supper.

While church government is congregational, a series of councils meet for fellowship and to conduct such business as concerns the entire church. State councils meet once a year, and a general council meets every 2 years with lay and ministerial delegates. Local missionary work is largely evangelistic and is conducted by state missionary boards; a general mission board oversees home and foreign missions. Missionaries are located in Africa, Japan, Alaska, the Philippines, Liberia, Colombia, Algeria, and Ethiopia. In June 1977, 20 churches and 3,500 members, now called The Christian Union of Etinan, Nigeria, West Africa, were received into the church.

A college, Christian Union School of the Bible, is located at Greenfield, Ohio; a Christian Union Extension School is administered through its staff. One periodical, *The Christian Union Witness,* is published monthly at Excelsior Springs. There are 108 churches, the majority in Ohio, with 5,463 members.

CHRIST'S SANCTIFIED HOLY CHURCH

This church began with the preaching of holiness and sanctification in the Colored Methodist Episcopal Church in Louisiana by a small body of white evangelists; it was organized in 1904 as the Colored Church South. Its central theme is sanctification by faith "as an experience distinct from justification by faith in Christ, which is not brought about by a growth in grace but is wrought instantaneously." There is emphasis on "one Lord, one faith, one baptism"; unequal persons—holy and unholy—should not marry; both men and women are ordained to the ministry; the strict observance of all church rules is required; no member may use or sell tobacco or alcoholic liquors; and members pledge that they will "expose all evil" to church officials.

The governing body is a five-member Board No. 1, which ordains all deacons, deaconesses, and ministers, and supervises boards of extension, investigation, managers, ministers and others. An annual conference meets in September, a district conference in June, and a Sunday school convention in March. Listing 600 members in 30 churches in 1957, the church is too small to maintain any sizable missionary, philanthropic, or educational work. A summer Bible school, organized in 1940, meets at headquarters during the month of July.

CHURCH OF CHRIST (HOLINESS) U.S.A.

A Baptist preacher in Alabama and Mississippi, C. P. Jones, sought a new church and faith that would make him "one of wisdom's true sons. . . like Abraham, a friend of God." In 1894 he founded the Church of Christ (Holiness) U.S.A., which today reports 9,289 members in 159 churches.

Doctrinally, this church emphasizes original sin, the Holy Ghost as an indispensable gift for every believer, and Christ's atonement and second coming. There are two sacraments or ordinances: baptism and the Lord's Supper. Foot washing and divine healing are employed—not as sacraments but as aids to the growth of spiritual life. The church is episcopal in government, with final authority vested in a biennial convention. There are seven dioceses, each under a bishop's charge; a district convention made up of elders, ministers, and local lay representatives meets semiannually.

Missionary work is conducted at home and in Liberia and Nigeria. The church supports the Christ Missionary and Industrial College at Jackson, Mississippi, and a national publishing house in Chicago.

CHURCH OF CHRIST, SCIENTIST

At Lynn, Massachusetts, in 1866, Mary Baker Eddy recovered almost instantly from a severe injury after reading the account of Christ's healing of the palsied man (Matt. 9:1-8). Profoundly religious and a lifelong student of mental and spiritual causation, she came to attribute causation to God and to regard him as divine Mind. From these roots came Christian Science and the Church of Christ, Scientist.

Generally described as "a religious teaching and practice based on the words and works of Christ Jesus," Christian Science was regarded by Mrs. Eddy as "the scientific system of divine healing," the "law of God, the law of good, interpreting and demonstrating the divine Principle and rule of universal harmony"; she believed "the Principle of all harmonious Mind-action to be God". Mrs. Eddy included most of these definitions and descriptions in *Science and Health with Key to the Scriptures,* a volume which, together with the Bible, has become the twofold textbook of Christan Science.

Like many other religious leaders and pioneers, Mrs. Eddy hoped to work through existing churches. She did not plan another denomination, but organization became necessary as interest in the movement spread, and under her direction the Church of Christ, Scientist, a local church, was established at Boston in 1879. In 1892 she formed the present worldwide organization, the First Church of Christ, Scientist, in Boston, and its branch churches and societies. That church in Boston is frequently referred to as the mother church.

Applied not only to the healing of sickness but to the problems of life generally, the tenets and doctrines of Christian Science are often confusing to non-Scientists and call for careful explanation. They begin with the conviction that God is the only might, or Mind; he is "All-in-all," the "divine Principle of all that really is," "the all-knowing, all-seeing, all-acting, all-wise, all-loving, and eternal; Principle; Mind; Soul; Spirit; Life; Truth; Love; all substance, intelligence." The inspired Word of the Bible is accepted as "sufficient guide to eternal Life." The tenets state: "We acknowledge and adore one supreme and infinite God. We acknowledge His Son, one Christ; the Holy Ghost or divine Comforter;

and man in God's image and likeness." Jesus is known to Christian Scientists as Master, or Way-shower. They accept his Virgin birth and his atoning mission "as the evidence of divine, efficacious Love unfolding man's unity with God through Christ Jesus the Way-shower." He was "endowed with the Christ, the divine spirit without measure." Humankind, made in the image of God, "is saved through Christ, through Truth, Life, and Love as demonstrated by the Galilean Prophet in healing the sick and overcoming sin and death." The crucifixion and resurrection of Jesus are held as serving "to uplift faith to understand eternal Life, even the allness of Soul, Spirit, and the nothingness of matter."

This "nothingness of matter" involves the basic teaching of Christian Science concerning what is real and unreal.

> All reality is in God and His creation, harmonious and eternal. That which He creates is good, and He makes all that is made. Therefore the only reality of sin, sickness, or death is the awful fact that unrealites seem real to human, erring belief, until God strips off their disguise. They are not true, because they are not of God.

God forgives sin through destroying it with "the spiritual understanding that casts out evil as unreal." The punishment for sin, however, lasts as long as the belief in sin endures.

It is a mistake to believe that the followers of Christian Science *ignore* that which they consider unreal; rather, they seek to forsake and overcome error and evil through Christian discipleship, prayer, and progressive spiritual comprehension of the reality of God's allness and goodness and of humankind as God's likeness. Error is "a supposition that pleasure and pain, that intelligence, substance, life, are existent in matter . . . It is that which seemeth to be and is not." As Mrs. Eddy has stated (and this point is fundamental to Christian Science beliefs):

> If we would open their prison doors for the sick, we must first learn to bind up the broken-hearted. If we would heal by the Spirit, we must not hide the talent of spiritual healing under the napkin of its form, nor bury the *morale* of Christian Science in the grave-clothes of its letter. The tender word and Christian encouragement of an invalid, pitiful patience with his fears and the removal of them are better than hecatombs of gushing theories, stereotyped borrowed speeches and the doling of arguments, which are but so many parodies on legitimate Christian Science, aflame with divine Love.

She further wrote, "Nothing aside from the spiritualization—yea, the highest Christianization—of thought and desire, can give the true perception of God and Christian Science, that results in health, happiness and holiness." Christian scientists normally rely wholly on the power of God for healing, rather than on medical treatment. There is no church pressure involved, however, nor does the church abandon those who choose a different way.

Certain terms are important in the exposition of Christian Science. *Animal magnetism* is the specific term for the hypnotic error of belief in a mind and power apart from God (typified by the dragon in the

Apocalypse; Jesus as the Lamb of God exemplifies the conquering of this sin in every form). Healing is not miraculous, but divinely natural; disease is understood to be basically a mental concept which can be dispelled by active Christian discipleship, spiritual regeneration, and application of the truths to which Jesus bore witness. Heaven is not a locality but "harmony; the reign of Spirit; government by divine Principle; spirituality; bliss, the atmosphere of Soul." Hell is "mortal belief; error; lust; remorse; hatred; revenge; sin; sickness; death; suffering and self-destruction; self-imposed agony; effects of sin; that which 'worketh abomination or maketh a lie.' " Mortal mind is "the flesh opposed to Spirit, the human mind and evil in contradistinction to the divine Mind." Prayer is "an absolute faith that all things are possible to God—a spiritual understanding of Him, an unselfed love." Baptism is not observed as a traditional ceremony, but is held to be a continuing individual spiritual experience, "a purification from all error."

The approximately 3,000 local Churches of Christ, Scientist, as branches of the mother church, are organized under the laws of the states or countries in which they exist. They enjoy their own forms of democratic government within the general framework of bylaws laid down by Mrs. Eddy in the *Manual of the Mother Church*, which also provides for the Christian Science college organizations. Reading rooms open to the general public are maintained by all churches. The affairs of the mother church are administered by the board of directors, which elects a president, first and second readers, a clerk, and a treasurer. The board of directors is a self-perpetuating body and elects all other officers of the church annually, with the exception of the readers, who are elected by the board for a term of three years.

Important in the Christian Science movement are the readers, teachers, and practitioners. There are two readers in each church, usually a man and a woman; in all services on Sunday and Thanksgiving Day, they read alternately from the Bible and from *Science and Health*. The lesson-sermon of the Sunday service is prepared by a committee and issued quarterly by the Christian Science Publishing Society. This system is followed by all Christian Science churches throughout the world. A midweek meeting, conducted by the first reader alone, features testimonies of healing from sin and sickness.

Practitioners devote their full time to healing and are authorized to practice by the board of directors. There is a board of education consisting of three members—a president, a vice-president, and a teacher of Christian Science. Under the supervision of this board a normal class is held once in three years. Teachers are duly authorized by certificates granted by the board of education to form classes of pupils in Christian Science. One class of not more than thirty pupils is instructed by each teacher annually.

There is a board of lectureship consisting of nearly thirty members, appointed annually by the board of directors. At the invitation of branch churches free lectures are given by these members all over the world. A committee on publication serves as an ecumenical and informational office, representing the denomination to the press and public. The Christian Science Publishing Society is one of the most effective units within the church; it publishes much well-written literature, including the *Christian Science Sentinel*, the *Christian Science Journal*, the *Christian Science Quarterly*, the *Herald of Christian Science* in twelve languages and braille, and the *Christian Science Monitor*. The *Monitor* is acknowledged by journalists to be one of the finest newspapers in the world. A number of nursing homes that rely wholly on spiritual means for healing are independently maintained throughout the world.

At a time when its members were frequently citing the rapid growth of their denomination, Mrs. Eddy established the rule that membership statistics should not be made available for publication, believing that number of members is no indication of true spiritual growth. The government census of 1936 reported 268,915 members in the United States. Today Christian Science churches have been established in some 57 countries, with the largest concentration in English- and German-speaking areas. Church membership appears to have declined in the last several decades, reflecting a trend among some other Protestant denominations, though there has been growth in Third World areas during that period. Also, as in the case with probably no other church in America, the number of people who are studying Christian Science and attending its services but are not yet admitted to full membership quite probably exceeds the number who have been admitted.

CHURCH OF GOD

At least 200 independent religious bodies in the United States bear the name Church of God in one form or another. Of these, several trace their roots to western North Carolina and eastern Tennessee during the years just before and after 1900. In particular, the Tomlinson family and Cleveland, a town in southeast Tennessee, are focal points for these several historically related Church of God bodies. Those treated here are the Church of God (Cleveland, Tennessee); the Church of God of Prophecy; The Church of God with headquarters in Huntsville, Alabama; and The (Original) Church of God, Inc. For all the bodies that grew out of this southern Appalachian Holiness revival, a great deal of weight is attached to the group's title: The restoration of the "Church of God" mentioned in the New Testament is the key concern. The more conservative of these bodies claim to embody that restoration, some quite openly. All of these are pentecostal—that is, practice speaking in tongues.

That same practice characterizes black bodies: Church of God in Christ and Church of God in Christ (International). But Church of God (Anderson, Indiana) subscribes to Holiness teaching without being pentecostal. Moreover, its history is totally unrelated to the southern Appalachian developments; it is a dominantly midwestern denomination. These illustrations reveal that the diversity is great and that careful attention must be paid to specific titles by anyone seeking information.

Church of God, The (Huntsville, Alabama)

This body is rooted in the early Holiness revival of the Appalachian South. It calls itself simply The Church of God, although "World Headquarters" is sometimes added, as is the headquarters location of Huntsville, Alabama.

When A. J. Tomlinson died in 1943, his Cleveland, Tennessee, group was divided between his two sons, Milton A. Tomlinson, who remained in Cleveland as head of Tomlinson Church of God, and Homer A. Tomlinson, who organized his followers under the name Church of God and established his headquarters in Queens Village, New York. Upon Bishop Homer's death in 1968, the headquarters was moved to Huntsville, a location much closer to the majority of the congregations. Its membership was reported at 75,890 in 1978.

The Huntsville group shares much of the doctrine as well as the history of the Tomlinson-Cleveland movement. It does place heavy emphasis on the fulfillment of Scripture "for the last days" and on preparation now for the return of Christ. This body continues to make much of A. J. Tomlinson's commission to his son, Bishop Homer, to plant the church's flag in all the nations of the world. This conviction has led to the establishment of a world headquarters in Jerusalem, because Israel is to be the center of the reestablished kingdom of God. Central to the body's mission is the belief that it holds the keys to bring that kingdom on earth. Saints are to be elected and placed in the governments of nations to bring in the kingdom. Its thisworldly theocratic program distinguishes it from the other groups in the movement, all of which are premillennial—that is, they view the kingdom as coming upon the return of Christ.

Church of God, Inc., The (Original)

This church was organized in Tennessee in 1886 under the name Church of God, after a difference of opinion in regard to doctrine and teaching brought about a split among the followers of Richard G. Spurling. The faction adhering to the original doctrines added the word Original and incorporated in 1922.

The church believes in the "whole Bible, rightly divided"; in repentance, justification, and regeneration as defined by Martin Luther; in sanctification as defined by John Wesley; in divine healing; in the second coming of Christ; in eternal life for the righteous and eternal punishment for the wicked. Christian fruits alone stand as evidence of faithful Christian living; creeds that bind the conscience are considered unscriptural. It believes in the "filling with the Holy Spirit, with the Bible evidence of speaking with tongues as the Spirit gives utterance."

Ordinances include baptism by immersion, the Lord's tithing, free-will offerings, the Lord's Supper, and foot washing.

Local churches, following the apostolic pattern, take local names such as the Church of God at Corinth. Each local church is self-governing. The church recognizes the New Testament orders of ministers, apostles, deacons, exhorters, evangelists, bishops, and teachers as given in Ephesians 4:11-14. A general convention meets annually; a general office, publishing house, and denominational headquarters are at Chattanooga. A correspondence Bible school, chartered in Tennessee as Ridgedale Theological Seminary, grants degrees up to master of theology and offers honorary degrees of doctor of divinity and doctor of sacred literature. There are 70 churches, with about 20,000 members.

Church of God (Anderson, Indiana)

The Church of God with headquarters at Anderson, Indiana, began in 1880 as a movement within existing churches. It prefers that its name be accepted in an inclusive rather than in a denominational sense and is actually a movement in the direction of Christian unity and reestablishment of the New Testament standard of faith and life. The founders believed that the church at large was too restricted and overburdened with organization and ecclesiasticism; it should be "more directly under the rule of God."

Doctrine in this church includes belief in the divine inspiration of the Scriptures; the forgiveness of sin through the atonement of Christ and repentance of the believer; the experience of holiness; the personal return of Christ, not connected with any millennial reign; the kingdom of God as established here and now; final judgment; resurrection of the dead; reward of the righteous and punishment of the wicked.

Baptism is by immersion. Members of this church also practice foot washing and observe the Lord's Supper, but not as conditions of fellowship. They believe the church to be the Body of Christ, made up of all Christians, and that all Christians are one in Christ. The confusion of sects and denominations, however, is an obstacle to this unity. God desires restoration of the New Testament ideal in his church; it is a restoration based upon spiritual experience, not on creedal agreement.

There are 184,685 members reported, with 170,079 adherents in home and foreign mission stations. They are governed by a congregational system; while they preach the idea that God governs his church, they agree that human instrumentality is quite necessary. Membership is not on the basis of "joining," and hence no formal records are kept. Ministers meet in voluntary state and regional conventions that are chiefly advisory. The general assembly meets in connection with the annual convention held at Anderson.

The Church of God (Anderson, Indiana) is not related historically to the several Church of God bodies rooted in the Holiness revival of Tennessee and the Carolinas in the late nineteenth century; although it shares their Holiness commitments, it is not pentecostal. It is largely a midwestern denomination with concentration in Indiana, Ohio, Michigan, and Illinois. It supports Anderson College and Seminary, two other liberal arts colleges, and one Bible College. Its growth overseas is rapid; in 1983, the church overseas had grown to the size of the church in the United States and Canada.

Church of God (Cleveland, Tennessee)

On August 19, 1886, in Monroe County, Tennessee, a new Christian fellowship came into being. First known as the Christian Union, it numbered eight members and was headed by Richard G. Spurling. A Baptist minister, Spurling had been led to the Bible to stem the tide of the churches' spiritual indifference, formality, and accommodation to modern culture. With the formation of the group, a major Holiness revival was born. In fact, the name The Holiness Church was adopted in 1902. The next year, A. J. Tomlinson, an American Bible Society colporteur from Indiana with Bible college training in Cincinnati, joined the church and in 1909 was elected general overseer.

The body grew and matured in the succeeding years, despite some objections to its noisy services, since the members spoke in tongues. A critical juncture in 1923 resulted from concern over the personal role of A. J. Tomlinson and, more important, the nature of the church's government and the leader's authority. Tomlinson's alleged misappropriation of funds created a stir, but the disruption centered on the issue of theocratic government. What was the relative authority of the overseer and other leaders of the church? The majority—those with whom the Church of God (Cleveland, Tennessee) is continuous—rejected Tomlinson's leadership and went on its way under F. J. Lee as overseer. The others continued to regard Tomlison as general overseer and formed the body known today as the Church of God of Prophecy. The larger body remains larger, with 1981 membership reported as 456,797 and a comparable constituency in other countries.

Its major doctrines blend many orthodox Protestant themes with those that are specifically pentecostal: justification by faith, sanctification, baptism of the Holy Spirit, tongue speaking, the need to be born again, fruitfulness in Christian living, and a strong interest in the premillennial second coming of Christ. It professes belief in reliance upon the Bible "as a whole rightly divided rather than upon any written creed." At the same time, it is thoroughly Arminian (believing in human free will): It stresses pentecostal and Holiness tenets; practices divine healing; condemns the use of alcohol, tobacco, and jewelry; opposes membership in secret societies; and accepts baptism, the Lord's Supper, and foot washing as ordinances.

The Cleveland church elects its own officers and holds state conventions and a biennial general assembly. It operates Lee College, the Church of God School of Theology, three Bible schools, and a preparatory school. Its foreign missions enterprise is extensive.

Church of God (Seventh Day)

The Church of God (Seventh Day) grew out of the Advent movement which developed in the first half of the nineteenth century. The church separated itself from other Sabathkeeping Adventists over the issue of the inspiration of E. G. White's visions, taking exception to endorsement of those visions. The church began simultaneously and independently in Iowa and in Michigan in 1860. Several denominational designations were used and refined in its early history—Church of Christ, Church of Jesus Christ, and Church of God. The present name was settled on in 1884.

In 1888, the united body of the Church of God established a central office in Stanberry, Missouri. In the intervening years since that date, the church has undergone several notable changes, including divisions, schisms, and mergers. In 1933, it divided into what were known as the Salem and Stanberry organizations, due in part to sharply disparate views on polity and administration among the ministry. A merger of the majority was effected in 1949, at which time the administrative offices were relocated in Denver, Colorado. A small body of members in disagreement with the merger's objectives and statements elected to retain identity with a Salem office and continued to use the name Church of God (Seventh Day).

Beliefs of the two bodies vary slightly. The Salem body embraces conviction in apostolic succession and places emphasis on "Biblical organization" in the context of the designation of "7, 12 and 70" as appropriate numbers in church organization. That position also presupposes identity of the physical Church of God (Seventh Day) as the "true church." Such adherence is not generally embraced by the other body, located in Denver.

Common to both bodies is belief in the infallibility of Scripture, prominence of The Ten Commandments in Christian practice, premillennialism, contra-Trinitarianism, conditionalism in reference to the soul, fundamentalism in Christian living, the prophetic return of Israel to Palestine, the annual observance of Communion (accompanied by foot washing), and related fundamentalist views. The Salem body claims a membership in excess of 1,000 in 7 churches; the Denver body lists a U.S./Canadian membership of a little more than 5,000 in 125 churches and claims a worldwide membership of more than 40,000. Doctrine and polity in the latter body are discussed and established by ministerial councils and by the general membership in session, respectively.

Membership requisites in the Church of God (Seventh Day) are based on baptism by immersion, on profession of faith, and consent to fellowship with the general membership.

Church of God and Saints of Christ

The Church of God and Saints of Christ was founded in Lawrence, Kansas, in 1896 by William S. Crowdy, a black Baptist deacon who claimed visions from God, a divine commission to bring the truth of God to the world, and a prophetic endowment. He became the first bishop of the church, which today has a membership of 38,127 in 217 churches in the United States, with additional churches in Africa and the West Indies.

Sometimes called Black Jews, members of this church celebrate such Jewish holy and feast days as they feel have biblical authority and support; they observe the Sabbath on the seventh day, the Day of Atonement, and the Jewish New Year. They believe that their church is built upon the Patriarchs, prophets, and apostles of the Jewish tradition, and "Jesus the Anointed" is their chief cornerstone. They differentiate between prophetic Judaism, "which seeks to follow the living insight into the spiritual idea to its fullest implication," as opposed to legalistic Judaism. They accept the Decalogue as the standard of conduct for all humankind.

An executive bishop stands at the head of the church and the Bishops' Council; there is a 12-member board of presbytery, the law making body, and an ecclesiastical council made up of all evangelists and ministers; under these officials work general and district officers, deacons, teachers, and missionaries. Local churches are headed by overseers and divided into districts; each district has an appointed evangelist who assists the bishop of that district. The district bishop calls and presides over annual district conferences. A denominational religious convocation called Passover and a national business assembly are held annually, both under the guidance of the executive bishop. The church maintains a home for the aged, an orphans' home, and a school for primary grades.

Church of God by Faith, Inc.

Organized in 1914 and chartered in 1923 at Alachua, Florida, this group consists of 96 churches scattered throughout Florida, Georgia, Alabama, South Carolina, Maryland, New Jersey, and New York. Doctrine contains items of belief in regeneration and sanctification; baptism of the Holy Ghost and with fire; speaking in tongues; the Word of God as the communion of the blood and body of Christ; one Lord, faith and baptism; and the isolation of willful sinners from God and the church. Officers consist of a bishop and an executive secretary. A general assembly meets three times a year. A school that was maintained in Ocala, Florida, for several years is now used as a training institution for farmers. Membership is reported as 4,500 in 105 churches.

Church of God in Christ

Ministers C. H. Mason and C. P. Jones, rejected by Baptist groups in Arkansas for what was considered overemphasis on holiness, founded the Church of God in Christ (Memphis) in 1897. The name was divinely revealed to Mason, who stressed entire sanctification and, in a revival, had received the baptism of the Holy Spirit together with "signs of speaking with tongues." His ardent preaching on these gifts and subjects aroused resentment and subsequent division among his followers.

The doctrine is trinitarian, stressing repentance, regeneration, justification, sanctification, speaking in tongues, and the gift of healing as evidence of the baptism of the Spirit. Holiness is considered a prerequisite to salvation; ordinances include baptism by immersion, the Lord's Supper, and foot washing.

Church organization is held to have its authority in Scripture; there are presiding, assistant presiding, and state bishops, district superintendents, pastors, evangelists, deacons, and departmental presidents. Missionaries are found in South Africa, Thailand, Jamaica, Haiti, Liberia, and on the West Coast in Africa. Saints Junior College is maintained at Lexington, Mississippi; there is a department of publications and a Sunday school publishing house to supply the denomination with literature. There are 3,709,661 members in 9,982 churches. It regards itself as the largest pentecostal denomination in the world today. The large increase in membership is attributed to rapid growth and the return of members from the Church of God in Christ, International.

Church of God in Christ (International)

Fourteen bishops of the Church of God in Christ (Memphis) withdrew from that church to organize the Church of God in Christ (International) in Kansas City, Missouri, in 1969. Their disagreement with the parent body was not doctrinal but one of polity and the authority of government. The theological background here is Wesleyan but emphasizes two works of grace, full baptism by the Holy Ghost and speaking with other tongues "as the Spirit gives utterance." Membership is reported at 200,000 in 300 churches.

Church of God of Prophecy

Sharing origins and early history with the Church of God (Cleveland, Tennessee), this body dates its distinctive organizational life from the disruption of 1923. The removal of A. J. Tomlinson from the office of general overseer is viewed quite differently by this body. In contrast with the Cleveland church's interpretation, it sees this action as an effort by some of his opponents to strip him of power in favor of their own positions. It also favored and still favors a more centralized polity; it contends that its polity is theocratic.

Thus Tomlinson continued with these Church of God adherents, some 8,000 of them, as general overseer. The body was called the Tomlinson Church of God until 1952 when Church of God of Prophecy was adopted. The members are convinced that theirs is indeed the Church of God prophesied by Christ and his followers. Milton A. Tomlinson succeeded his father as general overseer in 1943.

Its doctrines are much the same as those of the body bearing the Cleveland, Tennessee, title. Its headquarters, too, are located there. Membership stood at 72,977 in 1981. It supports Tomlinson College, the White Wing Publishing Company, a number of divisions and departments, and overseas missionary work.

CHURCH OF ILLUMINATION

Described as a "church at large rather than a church of congregations," this body was organized in 1908 under the inspiration of the late Swinburne Clymer. His son, Emerson M. Clymer, continued his father's work until his death in 1983, when the church came under the direction of Gerald E. Poesnecker. Its stated purpose is to harmonize the teachings of philosophy with the truths of religion, thus offering a spiritual, esoteric, and philosophical interpretation of basic Bible teachings to those in search of spiritual truth. Membership is by written request and does not require severance of membership in any other church.

Much is made of the "priesthood of Melchizedek," which dates from "beyond the year 4255 B.C. and includes all that small body of chosen seekers initiated into the mysteries of the divine law." This priesthood has come down from the days of Genesis through Jesus, the Gnostics, the early Egyptians, Greeks, Indians, and Persians to the present time, where it is to be found in the Church of Illumination.

The essence of religion here is found in the simple biblical statement that "whatsoever a man soweth, that shall he also reap." This is interpreted as being a matter of inevitable compensation rather than of reward and punishment at the hands of God. Furthermore:

> Religion teaches the Law—the way of Life—a way which makes man aware of the all-important truth that he is, in fact, a child of God, and that within him, buried by much debris, is a spark of the Divine. This Divine Spark is the *Christos*—the unconscious Soul—which may be awakened and brought into consciousness—a second or Rebirth. This is the "talent" entrusted to man and for which he is responsible to his Creator. Neglected, it remains just as it is—a tiny spark. Recognized, aroused, awakened and brought into consciousness, it becomes an inexhaustible source of wisdom and power, lifting man to the heights of Illumination and achievement. The process that makes all this possible is, in reality, the Second Birth. It is the process of Regeneration—mortality taking on immortality—the means whereby the son of man actually and literally becomes the Son of God.

Enlarging upon this, four great fundamentals are taught: (1) the law of action and reaction (sowing and reaping); (2) humankind's indebtedness to God for their talents and their obligation to use them well; (3) the practice of the Golden Rule; and (4) the practice of the law of honesty. All this is the means to the fulfillment of the destiny of humankind. It is also taught that we are now in a "manistic" age (*manisis*, the recognition of the equality of man and woman), which will last 2,000 years and in which Revelation will become the "unsealed book of the Bible"; that the world at present is the scene of the final battle of Armageddon. There is also some emphasis upon reincarnation, although belief in this is not required of adherents.

Yearly conferences of ministers and leaders are held in various parts of the country. Officially there are 14 established churches with 9,000 members, but the bulk of the membership is made up of those who are members only in correspondence, not of any specific church.

CHURCH OF JESUS CHRIST

At least twenty independent religious bodies in the United States bear the name *Church of Jesus Christ*. The largest of these, headquartered in Cleveland, Tennessee, became a chartered group in 1927 under the leadership of Bishop M. K. Lawson. There were several splits or divisions in this group from 1934 through the 1960s; the parent church today claims a membership of 37,500.

In spite of their divisions, these several groups hold in common doctrines of justification by faith; the freedom of the individual to accept or reject the plan of salvation; baptism by immersion (in the name of Christ only) and baptism of the Holy Ghost, being born again of water and the Spirit; and the premillennial second coming of Christ. They have two ordinances, baptism and the Lord's Supper (with foot-washing fellowship). They practice divine healing and condemn the use of alcohol and tobacco. They oppose the taking of oaths before magistrates but call for obedience to and respect for civil government, except in the use of armed force. Exclusion from church membership is imposed upon those who sin willfully. They use only the scriptural terms: bishop, elder, evangelist, deacon, and pastor. Members regard this body not as an organization, but an organism, with Christ as founder and head.

Foreign missions are found in Africa, India, Haiti, Australia, Jamaica, Israel, Mexico, Panama, the Dominican Republic, and England. Home missions work stresses evangelism. There is one Bible Institute and several academies, the largest located in Terrell, Texas.

CHURCH OF OUR LORD JESUS CHRIST OF THE APOSTOLIC FAITH, INC.

Confident that it is "a continuation of the great revival begun at Jerusalem on the day of Pentecost in A.D. 33," this church was organized at Columbus, Ohio, in 1919 by R. C. Lawson. Doctrine is stated to be that of the apostles and prophets, with Christ as the cornerstone. Perhaps the basic emphases are those laid upon Christ's resurrection and premillennial second coming, the resurrection and translation of the saints, the priesthood of all believers, and the final judgment of humankind. Baptism is by immersion, and baptism of the Holy Spirit is necessary for second birth. Foot washing is practiced, but not as an ordinance.

Found in 32 states, the British West Indies, Africa, the Philippines, Haiti, the Dominican Republic, and London, England, the church reports a membership of 45,000 in 155 churches. Twenty-two elementary schools, a Bible College, 18 extension schools, a clinic, and an orphanage are maintained. A national convocation meets every other year at the headquarters church, Refuge Temple in New York City. Officers of the denomination include five apostles, 32 bishops, 27 district elders, three secretaries, one treasurer, and a public information officer.

CHURCH OF THE NAZARENE

The theological and doctrinal foundations of the Church of the Nazarene lie in the preaching of the doctrines of holiness and sanctification as taught by John Wesley in the eighteenth-century revival in England. Its physical structure is the result of the merging of three independent Holiness groups already in existence in the United States. An eastern Holiness body, located principally in New York and New England and known as the Association of Pentecostal Churches in America, joined in 1907 with a western (California) body called the Church of the Nazarene; the two merging churches agreed on the name Pentecostal Church of the Nazarene. The southern group, known as the Holiness Church of Christ, united with this Pentecostal Church of the Nazarene in 1908. In 1919, Pentecostal was dropped from the name, leaving it as we know it today, Church of the Nazarene. This was primarily a move to disassociate in the public mind any connection with other pentecostal groups that taught or practiced speaking in tongues, a practice not endorsed by the Church of the Nazarene.

The background of the Nazarenes is definitely Methodist; they adhere closely to the original Wesleyan ideology. Most of the early Holiness groups in this country came out of the Methodist Episcopal Church; two of the original seven general superintendents of Church of the Nazarene were former Methodist ministers, and the Nazarene *Manual* has been called a "rewritten and modified Methodist *Discipline*."

The doctrine of the church is built around sanctification as a second definite work of grace subsequent to regeneration; all ministers and local church officials must have undergone this experience. Other doctrines include belief in the plenary inspiration of the Scriptures as containing all truths necessary to Christian faith and living; the atonement of Christ for the whole human race; the justification, regeneration, and adoption of all penitent believers in Christ; the second coming of Christ, the resurrection of the dead, and the final judgment. Members of this church believe in divine healing but never to the exclusion of medical agencies. The use of tobacco and alcoholic beverages is denounced. Two ordinances—baptism by sprinkling, pouring, or most often immersion and the Lord's Supper—are accepted as "instituted by Christ." Members are admitted on confession of faith and on agreement "to observe the rules and regulations . . . of the Church." It is a middle-of-the road church, neither extremely ritualistic nor extremely informal; one church historian calls it the "right wing of the holiness movement."

There are 4,902 local congregations grouped into 81 districts in the United States and Canada and an additional 124 districts, or Intercontinental Zones, and mission areas, totaling 205 districts throughout the world. Local pastors are elected by local churches; each district is supervised by a district superintendent who is elected for a four-year term by the members of the district assembly.

The general assembly also elects a general board consisting of an equal number of lay and ministerial members, which is in turn divided into eight administrative departments: world missions, home missions, evangelism, publication, pensions and benevolences, education and the ministry, church schools, and youth. Missionary work is conducted in 60 world areas by 553 missionaries. There is strong emphasis upon evangelism. Eight liberal arts colleges are maintained, two of which were opened in 1968. A theological seminary in Kansas City, Missouri and Bible colleges in the United States, Canada, and the British Isles are supported by the church.

The books and periodicals of the church are produced at the Nazarene publishing house in Kansas City. The annual volume of business exceeds $10,000,000. Membership in the United States is reported at 498,491; in Canada, 9,514; in Intercontinental Zones at overseas stations, 198,806—a total membership of 706,811. There are 7,547 churches at home and overseas.

CHURCHES OF CHRIST

The largest of the three principal bodies in the Campbellite movement, the Churches of Christ are located throughout the nation but concentrated in the South and Southwest. Because this is a brotherhood and not a denomination, centralized activities such as record keeping are opposed. Recent more scientific efforts show the membership to be about 1,250,000 in nearly 13,000 churches.

There is a distinctive plea for unity at the heart of the Churches of Christ—a unity that is Bible-based. It is believed that the Bible is "the beginning place" in and through which God-fearing people can achieve spiritual oneness—to "speak where the Bible speaks and to be silent where the Bible is silent" in all matters pertaining to faith and morals. Consequently, members recognize no other written creed or confession of faith. In all religious matters, there must be a "thus said the Lord."

In modern times the churches are related to the restoration movement—the work and thinking of James O'Kelly in Virginia, Abner Jones and Elias Smith in New England, Barton Stone in Kentucky, and Thomas and Alexander Campbell in West Virginia (see Christian Church [Disciples of Christ]). These four movements, all contending that "nothing should be bound upon Christians as a matter of doctrine which is not as old as the New Testament," and all once completely independent, eventually became one strong religious stream because of their common purpose and plea.

The leaders among the Churches of Christ in the nineteenth century were more conservative religiously than their counterparts among the Disciples of Christ. They contended for a strict adherence to the New Testament pattern of worship and church organization. Congregations refused to join any intercongregational organization, such as a missionary society. Their worship was simple, and they opposed the addition of instrumental music on the grounds that the New Testament did not authorize it and that the early church did not use it. Around the beginning of the twentieth century, a recognition of differences between the conservative and more liberal wings of the restoration movements became evident, and in the 1906 census of religious bodies, the Churches of Christ were listed separately for the first time. They deny being a denomination but claim to be nondenominational, with no headquarters, no governing bodies, and no clergy. They cooperate voluntarily in international radio programs sponsored by any one congregation.

Today one of the outstanding features of the Churches of Christ lies in their acceptance of the Bible as a true and completely adequate revelation. This basic concept has resulted in such characteristic practices as weekly observance of the Lord's Supper, baptism by immersion, *a cappella* song, a vigorous prayer life, support of church needs through voluntary giving, and a program of preaching and teaching the Bible. This concept also explains the autonomy of local churches, governed by elders and deacons appointed under New Testament qualifications; dignified worship services; enthusiastic mission campaigns; and far-flung benevolent programs, all financed by the local churches.

The great scriptural doctrines usually classified as consevative are received in the Churches of Christ, including the concept of the Father, the Son, and the Holy Ghost as members of one Godhead; the incarnation, Virgin birth, and bodily resurrection of Christ; the universality of sin after the age of accountability, its only remedy in the vicarious atonement of the Lord Jesus Christ. Strong emphasis is also laid on the church as the Body and bride of Christ. A figurative rather than a literal view is prevalent with reference to the book of Revelation. Membership is contingent upon an individual's faith in Jesus Christ as the only begotten Son of God, repentance, confession of faith, and baptism by immersion into Christ for the remission of sins. Church attendance is stressed.

While professing identity with the original church established by Christ and the apostles at Pentecost, the Churches of Christ maintain that the final judgment of all religious groups is reserved unto the Lord. Members believe they are "Christians only, but not the only Christians." This view, however, still allows for a vigorous evangelism that finds unacceptable the doctrines, practices, names, titles, and creeds that have been grafted into the original Christianity.

Ministers are ordained rather than licensed, and they hold tenure in their pulpits under mutual agreement with the elders of churches in which they preach. Their authority is moral rather than arbitrary, the actual government of the church being vested in its eldership.

A vigorous missionary program is carried on in 75 nations outside the United States, and in recent years a strong movement to extend the influence of the group in the northeastern United States has developed. Counting native workers in the foreign field and mission activities within the United States, there are more than 1,000 missionaries or evangelists supported by other than the group to whom they preach. A quota of chaplains is maintained in the the air force and in the army.

Properties owned by the group probably exceed $2,500,000,000 in value. There are 21 colleges, including 1 in Japan; 70 secondary and elementary schools; 40 homes for orphans or the aged; and 65 periodicals, newspapers, and magazines published throughout the country. The oldest publication, *The Gospel Advocate*, has been published continually since the 1860s. Since all official status in these institutions is lacking, none being authorized to speak for the entire church, their conformity in ideas and teachings is all the more remarkable.

Another medium of evangelism has been put to use in the publication of articles in a number of national magazines. Many churches offer correspondence courses. The "Herald of Truth" radio and television program has nationwide coverage; it is sponsored by the Highland Church of Christ in Abilene, Texas, and supported by hundreds of other churches and individuals throughout the country. The "Amazing Grace Bible Class," conducted by Dr. Ira North until his death and now by Jim Mankin, is sponsored by the Madison, Tennessee, Church of Christ, the largest of the 13,000 churches. The program is seen and heard by more than 100 television and radio stations and over the armed forces network.

CHURCHES OF CHRIST IN CHRISTIAN UNION

This church originated in a defection from the Christian Union churches (see Christian Union), at the 1909 meeting of that group at Marshall, Ohio. It was organized "to allow a complete freedom in the preaching of full salvation as stated doctrinally by John Wesley"—a teaching and a freedom the dissenters felt was being neglected in the parent body. Their first council was held at Jeffersonville, Ohio, in that year, and annual district councils have been held since that date. In 1945 legislation was enacted to provide for the organization of additional councils in other states; it now reaches into 17 states and several countries abroad.

The Churches of Christ in Christian Union are generally evangelistic in faith and work; camp meetings, revivals, and soul-winning campaigns are held regularly throughout the denomination. Worship follows simple forms, with little that is ritualistic or traditional. It is characteristic that emphasis is placed "on the blessing of God rather than on the ingenuity of man." A general council meets every two years at Circleville, Ohio, the body's headquarters. There is one college, Circleville Bible College, established to train ministers and lay workers.

The Reformed Methodist Church merged with this body in September 1952 and is now known as the North Eastern District of the Churches of Christ in Christian Union. There is a total of 251 churches, with 11,943 members.

CHURCHES OF GOD, GENERAL CONFERENCE

John Winebrenner (1797–1860), a member of the Reformed Church in Maryland, was active in the religious revival that swept this country in the early years of the nineteenth century. His ardent evangelism proved unpopular in the Reformed Church, and he severed relations with it in 1826 to form an independent "church of God" in Harrisburg, Pennsylvania. In 1830 Winebrenner and six other preachers organized the first eldership. The terms *eldership* and *conference* are used interchangeably today in this church. A general eldership was organized in 1845, distinguishing the national body from other local or area elderships organized since 1830. The words In North America were added in 1845, and Church became Churches in 1903. In 1975 the name was changed to Churches of God, General Conference.

Arminian in theology, these churches consider the Bible the sole rule of faith and practice. They believe in justification by faith, repentance and regeneration, the Triune God, the office and work of the Holy Spirit, practical piety, observance of the Lord's Day, and the resurrection of the just and unjust at the final judgment.

The churches were to be, according to Winebrenner, "spiritual, free, and independent churches consisting of believers only, without any human name or creed or ordinance or law." Each local church today is a Church of God. Sectarianism is held to be antiscriptural. Two ordinances are "perpetually obligatory"—baptism by immersion (the church does, however, accept on transfer the baptismal forms of members from other churches) and the Lord's Supper. The ordinance of foot washing is not obligatory. The Lord's Supper is called Communion in many of the churches and may be observed at any time, "as the time of observance is not of major importance nor is the posture of the communicant."

Organization consists of 16 elderships, or conferences, that meet annually in their respective states; there is also an Indian and Pakistan conference, and there is missionary work in Haiti. The General

Conference is composed of ministerial and lay delegates in equal numbers, with a proportionate number of youths from the annual conferences; it meets triennially and plans work in evangelism, education, and the other interests of the church. Local churches are presbyterian in government, but ministerial appointments follow a semi-itinerant system. There is a coeducational college (Findlay) and Winebrenner Theological Seminary at Findlay, Ohio. There are 360 churches and 36,000 members, with primary strength in Pennsylvania, and the midwest a secondary area.

CHURCHES OF GOD, HOLINESS

The Churches of God, Holiness, originated in Atlanta in 1914 with a group of eight people under the leadership of K. H. Burruss. Large churches were founded in Atlanta and in Norfolk, Virginia, in 1916; by 1922 there were 22 churches in 11 states, Cuba, the Canal Zone, and the British West Indies. At that time the churches were incorporated into what is currently known as the National Convention of the Churches of God, Holiness.

All doctrine within this group is tested strictly by New Testament standards; the Scriptures are accepted as inspired, and the New Testament "gives safe and clearly applied instructions on all methods of labor, sacred and secular," and on the conduct of the whole of life. The churches believe in the Trinity; in justification, entire sanctification, and regeneration; and that the gift of the Holy Spirit is an act subsequent to conversion. Perfection is both *present* and *ultimate*. One must believe in divine healing to be acceptable as a member, but medicines and doctors, not being expressly denounced by Scripture, are approved for those who desire them. Two ordinances, baptism and the Lord's Supper, are observed. The washing of feet is approved but not regularly practiced.

Pastors are assigned by the one bishop of the denomination and are assisted in the local congregation by deacons. In direct supervision over the pastors is a state overseer, also appointed by the bishop. State conventions are held annually. The highest administrative body is the national convention, a delegate body that elects the national president, or bishop. The church reports 25,600 members and 32 churches.

CHURCHES OF THE LIVING GOD

Two churches of common origin, similar in type but differing in detail, bear the title Church of the Living God. Both came out of an organization formed at Wrightsville, Arkansas, in 1889 by William Christian, who "by virtue of a divine call, created the office of chief." Christian held that "Freemason religion" is the true expression of religion and insisted that his "organism" be known as "operative Masonry and [that] its first three corporal degrees shall be baptism, Holy Supper, and foot washing." Both groups are organized along fraternal lines; members tithe their incomes in support of the church and call their churches temples.

The first body, the larger, is known as the Church of the Living God (Motto: Christian Workers for Fellowship). It claims 45,320 members in 276 churches; it stresses believer's baptism by immersion, and the use of water and unleavened bread in the celebration of the Lord's Supper. A chief bishop is the presiding officer; there is an annual assembly; a general assembly meets every four years to elect other officers and determine the laws for the church. Membership is biracial.

The second body, called the House of God, Which Is the Church of the Living God, the Pillar and Ground of the Truth, Inc., is also episcopal in polity and generally follows the form and thought of the Workers for Fellowship group. They have 2,350 members in 107 churches.

COMMUNITY CHURCHES, THE NATIONAL COUNCIL OF

Community Churches in the United States date from the mid-1800s. According to the most recently published history of the Community Church movement (Shotwell, *Unity Without Uniformity* [Community Church Press, 1984]), these churches are a result of the desire to eliminate overchurching in some communities and solve attendant economic and staffing problems; to replace the restrictiveness and divisiveness of denominationalism with self-determination and Christian unity; to refocus primary loyalty from organizations outside a community to the community itself and, by addressing specific needs there, to effect a more relevant religion.

Since each church is adjusted to the needs of a different communty, there is much variety among Community Churches in worship, work, and witness styles and methods. There are several general categories of churches. Federated and United Churches have resulted from mergers of congregations previously affiliated with certain denominations. Some of these have continued alignments with two or more denominations; others have become entirely independent. Some individual congregations also have severed denominational ties, while others have affiliated with the Community Church movement while continuing relationships with one or more denominations. The majority of Community Churches never have had denominational alignments.

Community Churches were first organized nationally in 1923. The current organization, The National Council of Community Churches, resulted from a 1950 merger of two previous councils, one composed of churches with predominantly black and the other of churches with predominantly white memberships. It is headquartered in Homewood, Illinois. A return to a former name, The International Council of Community Churches, is planned.

Currently The National Council provides services to more than 1,300 Community Churches, in all 50 states and several nations. Services include ecclesiastical endorsement, personnel placement, insurance, continuing education, direct and brokered consultation for help in various areas; and supportive networks for clergy and their spouses and children. Publications include *The Christian Community*, a monthly newspaper, and *The Pastor's Journal*, a quarterly for professionals.

The parent organization brings Community Churches into mutually beneficial relationships at national, regional, and area conferences. It endorses nonsectarian educational institutions and mission agencies that have demonstrated ability to meet human needs and further Christian unity. It is a member of the Consultation on Church Union, National Council of Churches, and World Council of Churches; however, representatives can neither speak for nor commit Community Churches. Financial support for The National Council's activities and for all institutions and agencies is provided voluntarily by churches and individuals. Membership stands at 190,000 in 185 churches.

Understanding of the Community Church movement is complicated by these facts: Many of the movement's churches do not have *Community* in their names; many churches that do include this word are purely denominational, are members of a national organization outside the historic movement, or are completely independent.

CONGREGATIONAL BIBLE HOLINESS CHURCH

A pentecostal movement, this body dates back to 1922. It was founded under its present name and organization in 1977, when the Light of the Way Open Door Church merged with the Independent Holiness Church.

It describes itself by such terms as Trinitarian, international, pentecostal, charismatic, evangelical, and missionary. It cooperates with a number of other conservative bodies, Baptists of several kinds, Assemblies of God, and Holiness and Pentecostal churches. Its Articles of Faith are the same as those of the Assemblies of God, and it works closely with the National Baptist Convention, U.S.A.

Reporting 100,000 members in 500 churches in the United States, this body also carries on overseas missionary work in Brazil, Guyana, Thailand, and elsewhere. At home it sponsors three Bible colleges. Its membership is strongest in Ohio, California, West Virginia, and Florida, with headquarters presently in New Bern, North Carolina.

CONGREGATIONAL CHRISTIAN CHURCHES (NATIONAL ASSOCIATION)

This association was organized in 1955 by a group of churches desiring to "preserve historic Congregational forms of freedom and fellowship (the Congregational Way)." With 419 churches and an estimated 100,000 members, it is the largest of several Congregational bodies that did not participate in the merger of the General Council of Congregational Churches and the Evangelical and Reformed Church into the United Church of Christ in 1957.

The National Association brings local churches together for counsel, inspiration, and fellowship, but still preserves the independence and autonomy of the local churches. Member churches are either established Congregational Christian churches or affiliated associations of local churches in sympathy with the purposes of the association. A moderator presides over an annual meeting of all the churches; an executive committee of 12, elected for 4 years, acts for the association between meetings. Eight commissions (Christian education, the ministry, publications, women's work, youth, world Christian relations, and spiritual resources) work under the direction of the executive committee. Four divisions of the National Association provide a Missionary Society, a Building and Loan Fund, a Foundation for Theological Studies, and Congregational Church Development. A unique feature of the organization is found in its Referendum Council, which, upon call of 10 percent of the churches and by a two-thirds vote, may modify any action or proposal of any of the national bodies or officers of the association.

There is no binding ecclesiastical authority and no required subscription to any creed or program. "We are bound together not by uniformity of belief but by the acceptance of a covenant purpose to be 'the people of God.'" The association tends to avoid involvement in controversial social and political questions and action. There is widespread missionary work in the United States and in the Philippines, Mexico, Hong Kong, Formosa, Greece, Italy, Germany, Brazil, Central America, and South India. *The Congregationalist*, a denominational periodical founded in 1849, was revived in 1958 as the journal of the association. Two colleges are supported—Olivet in Michigan and Piedmont in Demorest, Georgia. National offices are maintained in Oak Creek, Wisconsin.

CONGREGATIONAL HOLINESS CHURCH

Founded in 1921 by a group of ministers withdrawing from the Pentecostal Holiness Church in an effort to retain Holiness doctrines and establish a more democratic church polity, this church is Trinitarian, emphasizing the inspiration of the Scriptures, justification, sanctification, divine healing (without objection to medicine), the second coming of Christ, eternal punishment and reward, the merits of the atonement, and the salvation of the entire church.

The Bible is held as the sole rule of conduct; slang, tobacco, membership in oath-bound secret societies, and other forms of worldliness are condemned. Ordinances include baptism, foot washing, and the Lord's Supper. The crowning blessing of religious experience is held to be the baptism of the Holy Ghost and speaking with tongues "as the Spirit [gives] utterance."

Church government is, as the name suggests, congregational. Local churches are grouped in annual associations from which delegates are elected to a general association. Local church officers, elected annually, consist of deacons, trustees, a secretary, and a treasurer. Pastors are called by a majority vote of the congregation; women are licensed to preach but are not ordained. There are 174 churches and 8,347 members in the United States, concentrated in the Southeast. Newer churches and conferences have been established in Mexico, Honduras, Costa Rica, Brazil, Cuba, Spain, and Guatemala.

CONSERVATIVE CONGREGATIONAL CHRISTIAN CONFERENCE

The origins of the CCCC go back to 1935 and the labors of H. B. Sandine, a pastor in Hancock, Minnesota, who was convinced that the denominational establishment of the Congregational Christian Churches had departed from the beliefs, polity, and practices of historic Congregationalism. He carred on a mimeographed educational effort until 1939, when his efforts were consummated in a monthly publication, *The Congregational Beacon,* which later became *The Congregational Christian,* and finally the bi-monthly *Foresee.* A Conservative Congregational Christian Fellowship was organized at Chicago in 1945. The prospect of still another merger (involving Congregational Christian and Evangelical and Reformed churches) precipitated reorganization into the Conservative Congregational Christian Conference in 1948.

Today there are 155 member churches in the conference, with a total of 26,968 members. There are also 20 regional fellowships and associations, some 250 churches, made up of Congregational Christian churches in sympathy with the statement of faith and general polity of the conference; not all of these are directly involved in its official work and actions.

The statement of faith is conservatively evangelical; it includes belief in the infallibility and authority of the Scriptures; the Trinity; the deity, Virgin birth, sinlessness, atoning death, resurrection, ascension, and promised return of Christ; regeneration by the Holy Spirit; the resurrection of both saved and lost; and the spiritual unity of all believers in Christ.

Local churches are completely autonomous; national officers include a president, two vice-presidents, a recording and an executive secretary (missionary-at-large), a treasurer, an editor, and a historian, all elected for three years. A board of directors manages the property and directs the general business of the conference through an executive committee composed of the officers, with the president as chairman. Under the executive committee there are thirteen subordinate committees that guide the various efforts of the conference. Work is largely in the areas of missions, youth, and Christian education, carried on through recognized evangelical home and foreign mission agencies, Bible institutions, colleges, seminaries, and Sunday school publishing houses. An annual meeting is held, usually in August. The CCCC is especially active in the fields of church extension, pastoral placement, and regional activities.

The conference is a member denomination of the National Association of Evangelicals and has recently entered into an international alliance known as the International Evangelical Congregational Union, and similarly minded Congregational groups are at work in Brazil, England, and Australia. Headquarters are in St. Paul, Minnesota.

DIVINE SCIENCE

Three sisters—Alethea Brooks Small, Fannie Brooks James, and Nona Lovell Brooks—of Denver, and Malinda E. Cramer of San Francisco, in the late years of the last century worked out, independently of one another, the principles and practice of Divine Science. They met and joined forces in 1898, incorporating the Divine Science College, and their first church—the First Divine Science Church of Denver—was organized.

The core of its teaching is the principle of the all-inclusive God-mind:

> God [is] the Omnipresence, the Universal Presence, Life, Love, Intelligence and Substance; man, a child of God, is of God, is like God; knowledge of this truth frees man into a larger concept of God and the understanding of man's higher nature; the practice of the Presence of God in daily life results in man's right attitude toward negative thinking; evolution is God's method of accomplishing, and love, conscious unity, is the fulfilling of the law.

The founders had all had the experience of divine healing, and the emphasis upon healing naturally persists. Healing comes through an understanding of the nature of God and the Universal Law and is "the cleansing of the inner man from all that is unlike God." Divine Science does not deny the existence of visible matter but interprets form and substance as manifestations of God.

Divine Science further stands for: (1) the Fatherhood of God as Omnipresent Life, Love, Intelligence, and Wisdom; (2) the "brotherhood" of humankind; (3) the unity of all life; (4) the higher thought in science, philosophy, and religion; (5) the awareness of humanity's relation to God released into expression, in each individual life, of our divine inheritance—health, abundance, peace, and power; (6) the transcendence and immanence of God manifested in all created things.

For many years local churches and colleges of Divine Science were independent of one another. In 1957 some of the ministers and key workers met and organized the Divine Science Federation International. This organization serves its member churches and centers and cooperates with the Divine Science Educational Center, which trains ministers, teachers, and practitioners. Churches, centers, and study groups are found in the major cities of the United States and abroad; headquarters are located in Denver, where all publications are printed and a monthly periodical, *Aspire,* is issued.

EPISCOPAL

It is stated in the preface of the Book of Common Prayer of the Protestant Episcopal Church, since 1967 known as The Episcopal Church, that "this Church is far from intending to depart from the Church of England in any essential point of doctrine, discipline, or worship." Therein lies the hint of its origin: The Episcopal Church constitutes the "self-governing American branch of the Anglican Communion." For a century and a half in this country it bore the name of the Church of England.

Its history runs back to the first missionaries who went to the British Isles from Gaul prior to the Council of Arles in A.D. 314. It is traced down through the days when Henry VIII threw off the supremacy of the pope (Henry, according to Anglican scholars, did not found the Church of England; it was a church that had always been more British than Roman); through the reign of Edward VI, when the Book of Common Prayer and the 42 Articles of Religion were written; through the period of Catholic restoration under Bloody Mary and through her successor Elizabeth, who put the united church and state under the Protestant banner and sent Sir Francis Drake sailing to build an empire.

Drake came ashore in what is now California in 1578. His Church of England chaplain, Francis Fletcher, planted a cross and read a prayer while Drake claimed the new land for the Virgin Queen. Martin Frobisher had reached Labrador in 1576, also with a chaplain. After them came colonists to Virginia under Sir Humphrey Gilbert and Sir Walter Raleigh; Raleigh's chaplain baptized a native named Manteo and a white baby named Virginia Dare before the settlement vanished. With Captain John Smith came Chaplain Robert Hunt, who stretched a sail between two trees for a shelter and read the service from the Book of Common Prayer.

In the South the transplanted Church of England quickly became the established church. It was at heart a tolerant and catholic church; but the control of the crown brought an almost ruthless authority which made the church suspect in the eyes of those colonists who had come here seeking freedom from all such authority. The Virginia House of Burgesses set the salary of the Virginia clergymen at "1,500 pounds of tobacco and 16 barrels of corn." It was a British clergy, supported by public tax and assessment and by contributions from the church in England through the Society for the Propagation of the Gospel. And it was technically under the jurisdiction of the Bishop of London. In that fact lay one of its almost fatal weaknesses; it was necessary for colonial ministers to journey to England for ordination, and few could afford it. This, coupled with the rising tide of the American Revolution, placed the colonial Church of England in an unenviable position.

Yet the church did well. Membership grew rapidly. William and Mary College was established in 1693, and the Church of England became the predominant church in the South. King's Chapel in Boston, the first Episcopal church in New England, was opened in 1689; in 1698 a church was established at Newport, Rhode Island, and another, Trinity Church, in New York City. In 1702 a delegation from the Society for the Propagation of the Gospel arrived from England to survey the colonial church and found about fifty clergymen at work, from the Carolinas to Maine. The visitors sensed the need for American bishops to ordain American clergymen; they also sensed the increasing opposition of American patriots to a British-governed church.

The Revolution almost destroyed the colonial Church of England. Under special oath of allegiance to the king, the clergy either fled to England or Canada or remained as Loyalists in the colonies in the face of overwhelming persecution. That many of them were loyal to the American cause meant little; the Reverend William White was chaplain of the Continental Congress, the Reverend Charles Thurston was a continental colonel, and in the pews of the Episcopal church sat Washington, Jefferson, Patrick Henry, John Jay, Robert Morris, John Marshall, Charles and Light-Horse Harry Lee, and John Randolph. But their presence could not stem the tide. The Anglican house was divided, and it fell. At the war's end there was no episcopacy, no association of the churches, not even the semblance of an establishment. Few thought of any future for this church, which, between Lexington and Yorktown, suffered more than any other in the colonies.

Episcopal Church, The

There was, however, a future—and a great one. In 1782 there appeared a pamphlet entitled *The Case of the Episcopal Churches in the United States Considered,* written by William White. It was a plea for unity and reorganization, and it proposed that the ministry be continued temporarily without the episcopal succession, since the latter "cannot at present be obtained." In 1783 a conference of Episcopal churches met at Annapolis, Maryland, and formally adopted the name Protestant Episcopal Church—Protestant, to distinguish it from the Roman Catholic Church; Episcopal, to distinguish it from the Presbyterian and the Congregational.

Also in 1783 the clergy in Connecticut elected Samuel Seabury as their prospective bishop; he went to England and there waited a year for consecration at the hands of English bishops. When this was denied, he went to Scotland and was consecrated bishop there in 1784. Ultimately Parliament and the Church of England cleared the way, and two other bishops-elect from New York and Pennsylvania were consecrated by the Archbishop of Canterbury in 1787. In 1789 the constitution was adopted in Philadelphia, the Book of Common Prayer was revised for American use, and the Protestant Episcopal Church became an independent, self-governing body.

Complete harmony existed for the next half century. New churches and church institutions were established: Sunday schools; Bible, prayer book, and tract societies; theological seminaries; colleges; boarding schools; guilds for men and women; and a domestic and foreign missionary society. Diocesan organizations replaced state organizations; new bishops moved into the new West. Bishop J. H. Hobart in New York, A. V. Griswold in New England, Richard Channing Moore in Virginia, and Philander Chase in Ohio worked miracles in overcoming Revolutionary prejudices against the church. One of the great Episcopal builders, W. A. Muhlenberg, "organized the first free church of any importance in New York, introduced the male choir, sisterhoods, and the fresh air movement, while his church infirmary suggested to his mind the organization of St. Luke's Hospital [New York], the first church hospital of any Christian communion in the country."

Muhlenberg was a man of wide vision; he inspired a "memorial" calling for a wider catholicity in the Protestant Episcopal church, which resulted in the famous Chicago Lambeth Quadrilateral on Church Unity in 1888 and the movement that produced the further revision of the American Book of Common Prayer in 1892.

With the outbreak of the Civil War, the church was again threatened, but among the major Protestant churches, it alone suffered no division. New England churchmen may have been abolitionists, and a Louisiana bishop, Leonidas Polk, may have been a general under Lee, but Polk prayed for Bishop Charles Pettit McIlvaine of Ohio in public, and the Ohioan prayed for Polk. They were still in one church. A temporary Protestant Episcopal Church in the Confederate States was organized to carry on the work in the South, but the names of the southern bishops were called in the general convention in New York in 1862; and once the war was over, the Episcopal house in 1865 was quickly reunited.

The years following Appomattox were years of new growth. A dispute over churchmanship, rising out of the Oxford Movement in England, resulted in the separation of a group into the Reformed Episcopal Church in 1873, but otherwise Episcopal unity held fast. New theological seminaries were established and old ones were reorganized and strengthened. This period saw the organization of a church congress, the Brotherhood of St. Andrew, and numerous other agencies. The expansion continued into the next century; two world wars failed to halt it. In 1830 the Protestant Episcopal church had 12 bishops, 20 dioceses, 600 clergymen, and 30,000 communicants; in 1930 there were 152 bishops, 105 dioceses, 6,000 clergymen, and 1,250,000 communicants.

The Episcopal form of government closely parallels that of the federal government. It is a federal union, now consisting of 116 dioceses (originally coterminous with the states of the Union), each autonomous in its own sphere, associated originally for the maintenance of a common doctrine, discipline, and worship. To those objectives have been added the unification, development, and prosecution of missionary, educational, and social programs.

Of the dioceses, seventeen are overseas missionary dioceses. Most of the overseas jurisdictions will become either independent or parts of existing Anglican churches in their areas.

Each diocese functions through a bishop (elected locally, with the approval of the whole episcopate and representatives of the clergy and laity of the whole church), who is the spiritual and administrative head. There is a diocesan legislative body (convention, council, or synod) made up of the clergy of the diocese and representatives of the local congregations, meeting annually; a standing committee of clergy and laity who are advisers and assessors to the bishop; and, usually, a program board.

The normal pattern for the local congregation is the parish, which elects its own minister (rector) who is vested with pastoral oversight of the congregation and who, with the wardens and vestry representatives, also administers the temporal affairs and the property of the parish.

Each parish and parochial district (mission or chapel) is represented in the annual diocesan convention by its clergy and elected lay delegates (usually in proportion to the congregation's constituency); each diocese and missionary diocese is represented in the triennial general convention of the church by its bishop or bishops and clerical and lay deputies elected in equal numbers (at present, four of each). The general convention is a bicameral legislature, and the two houses of the convention, bishops and deputies, meet and deliberate separately. Either house may initiate, but the concurrence of both is required to enact legislation.

Between sessions of the general convention, the work of the church is carried on by the presiding bishop (elected for a 12-year term by the House of Bishops with the concurrence of the House of Deputies) and an elective executive council of 40 members—20 elected by the general convention, 18 elected by the provinces (regional groups of dioceses and missionary districts), and 2 ex officio (the presiding bishop and the president of the House of Deputies).

Established in 1919 to unify the work of three previously independent boards, in 1968 the council took the further step of abolishing a more or less rigid departmental structure in favor of a collaborative working relationship among the program areas: national mission, world mission, education, communication, administration, finance, and stewardship.

The Episcopalian accepts two creeds—the Apostles' and the Nicene. The articles of the Church of England, with the exception of the 21st and with modification of the 8th, 35th, and 36th, are accepted as a general statement of doctrine, but adherence to them as a creed is not required. The clergy make the following declaration:

> I do believe the Holy Scriptures of the Old and New Testaments to be the Word of God, and to contain all things necessary to salvation; and I do solemnly engage to conform to the doctrine, discipline, and worship of the Episcopal Church.

The church expects all its members to be loyal to the "doctrine, discipline and worship of the one holy catholic and Apostolic Church" in all the essentials, but permits great liberty in nonessentials. It allows for variation, individuality, independent thinking, and religious liberty. Liberals and conservatives, modernists and fundamentalists, find cordial and common ground for worship in the prayer book, which, second only to the Bible, has probably influenced more people than any other book in the English language.

There are two sacraments, baptism and the Eucharist, recognized as "certain sure witnesses and effectual agencies of God's love and grace." Baptism by pouring or immersion is necessary for either children or adults; baptism by any church in the name of the Trinity is recognized as valid baptism; baptized persons are confirmed as members of the church by the bishop, and those not baptized in infancy or childhood must accept the rite before confirmation. Without stating or defining the holy mystery, The Episcopal Church believes in the real presence of Christ in the elements of the Eucharist. The church also recognizes the sacramental character of confirmation, penance, orders, matrimony, and unction.

Some Episcopal churches are "high" with elaborate ritual and ceremony; others are described as low, with a ritual less involved and with more of an evangelistic emphasis. All members, however, high or low, have a loyalty to their church that is deep and lasting. In more than 300 years this church has known only one minor division; today it stands sixth among all denominations: it has 2,767,440 members in 7,233 churches in the United States.

Stanley I. Stuber has called this the "church of beauty," and it is an apt description. Its prayer book is eloquent in the literature of religious worship, containing the heart of New Testament and Old Testament devotions. Members have built stately cathedrals in this country, among them the Cathedral of St. John the Divine in New York City, the third largest in the world, and the Cathedral of Saints Peter and Paul (national cathedral) in Washington, D.C., sometimes called the American Westminster Abbey. Stained-glass windows, gleaming altars, vested choirs, and a glorious ritual give the worshiper not only beauty but a deep sense of the continuity of the Christian spirit and tradition. Next to the stress on episcopacy, its liturgical worship is a distinguishing feature; varying in degree according to high or low church inclinations, it has its roots in the liturgy of the Church of England and includes the reading, recitation, or intonation by priest, people, and choir of the historic general confession, general thanksgiving, collects, psalms, and prayers.

National church financial support is given to twelve U.S. dioceses, to the Navajoland Episcopal Church (an area mission in the Southwest), and to a coalition of dioceses on the East Coast which share a common ministry to the Appalachian mountain people. Special emphasis is placed upon urban ministries, ministry in college communities, and ministry to black, Hispanic, Native American, and Asian congregations. Overseas missions are located in all American territories and in the Dominican Republic, Haiti, India, Japan, the Near East, Liberia, Mexico, Okinawa, Taiwan, Central America, and the Philippines. The church sponsors 10 accredited seminaries in the United States plus 2 overseas, 9 colleges, a university, about 645 nursery through high schools for boys and girls, 81 homes for the aged, 91 institutions and agencies for child and youth care, 43 hospitals, homes, and convalescent clinics, and work for seamen in 8 dioceses in the United States. The church is unique in Protestantism for its orders of monks and nuns; there are 15 orders for men and 17 for women; both men and women are employed in schools, hospitals, and various forms of missionary work.

Two major developments in The Episcopal Church in the past few years have been subjects of debate: prayer book revision and the ordination of women to the priesthood. The general convention of 1976 gave first approval to a Proposed Book of Common Prayer, the first revision of the American prayer book since 1928 and the first to use contemporary language. Much of the Tudor idiom, however, has been retained. The Holy Eucharist, Morning and Evening Prayer, the Burial of the Dead, and all the Collects for the Church Year appear in both contemporary and traditional language; Archbishop Cranmer's Great Litany has been somewhat revised, but appears in its traditional form only. All other services—such as Baptism, Matrimony, Confirmation, and Ordination—have been revised and/or rewritten in the contemporary idiom. The book is also more comprehensive in such forms as private confession, complete rites for Ash Wednesday and Holy Week, and the addition of three more daily offices between Morning and Evening Prayer. The Eucharistic Lectionary has also been revised to include, for the first time, regular readings from the Old Testament. The Proposed Book was passed by an overwhelming majority at the 1979 convention in Denver and the fully approved version is now in use.

The issue of women's ordination is extremely complex. Actually it goes back to the historical doctrine of the uninterrupted line of succession in the episcopacy from the apostles to the present—the Apostolic Succession—in which men only have been ordained in the threefold ministries of deacon, priest, and bishop. Those in opposition were divided into two opinion groups: those who believed that it was de facto impossible for women to be priests; and those who believed that the general convention—even though it is the supreme legislative authority of The Episcopal Church—had no right to decide this question of women's ordination and that such a decision should have been made only by catholic consensus or in some kind of ecumenical council.

The general convention of 1970 authorized the ordination of women to the deaconate, but "priesting," rejected at that convention and again at the 1973 convention, passed in 1976 by a narrow margin. But even this did not settle the question. In February 1978, three men were consecrated to the episcopate of a newly formed Anglican Church of North America. This body represents scattered groupings of Episcopalians who feel they can no longer remain within The Episcopal Church because of its stand on women in the priesthood, liturgical revision, and divorce and remarriage. It is estimated that about 100 congregations, or parts of congregations, have joined that group, and some 30 to 40 priests have been defrocked by their bishops for having joined. A large number still remain dissatisfied with the ordination of women but seem to have no intention of leaving The Episcopal Church. In fact, most of those who do disapprove have remained. The Archbishop of Canterbury has said that the schismatic group is not to be in communion with the other sister churches of Anglicanism.

The Episcopal Church has an undeserved reputation for exclusiveness and noncooperation with other Protestant bodies; actually it has been most cooperative. The Chicago Lambeth Quadrilateral, already mentioned, was begun by the House of Bishops at the general convention of 1886 and accepted with modifications two years later. It proposed four points for world unity of churches: the Scriptures as the Word of God, the Apostles' and the Nicene creeds as the rule of faith, the two sacraments of baptism and the Lord's Supper, and the episcopate as the central principle of church government. In 1910 the general convention appointed a commission to arrange for a World Conference on Faith and Order; the first conference was held at Geneva in 1920, the second in 1927 at Lausanne, the third at Edinburgh in 1937. The church is active in the National Council of Churches and the World Council of Churches. An unusually effective intercommunion has been established in this country among the Anglican and Old Catholic churches, and abroad with the Church of Finland, Church of Sweden, the Mar Thomas Syrian Church of Malabar, United Church of North India, United Church of Pakistan, Church of South India, and the Philippine Independent Churches—which may be a first step toward mergers among these bodies.

Reformed Episcopal Church

The Reformed Episcopal Church was organized in New York City in 1873 by 8 clergymen and 20 laypeople who formerly had been members of the Protestant Episcopal Church. A long debate over the ritualism and ecclesiasticism of the Protestant Episcopal Church lay behind the separation; the immediate cause of the division lay in the participation of Bishop George David Cummins of Kentucky in a Communion service held in the Fifth Avenue Presbyterian Church in New York City. In the face of criticism and in the conviction that the catholic nature and mission of the Protestant Episcopal Church were being lost, Bishop Cummins withdrew to found the new denomination.

Doctrine and organization are similar to those of the parent church, with several important exceptions. The Reformed Episcopal Church rejects the doctrine that the Lord's Table is an altar on which the body and blood of Christ are offered anew to the Father, that the presence of Christ in the Supper resides in the elements of bread and wine, and that regeneration is inseparably connected with baptism. It also denies that Christian ministers are priests in any sense other than that in which all believers are a "royal priesthood." Clergy ordained in other churches are not reordained on entering the ministry of the Reformed Episcopal Church, and members are admitted on letters of dismissal from other Protestant denominations.

Worship is liturgical; at the morning services on Sunday the use of the prayer book, revised to remove certain objectionable sacerdotal elements, is required. At other services its use is optional, while at any service ex tempore prayer may be used by the minister.

Parish and synodical units prevail in the administration of the church; the triennial general council of the Reformed Episcopal Church is not like the general convention of The Episcopal Church, however, as its bishops do not constitute a separate house.

Foreign missions are maintained in India, France, the Congo, Uganda, Zimbabwe, and Germany. In India and Africa there are 20 primary schools, 2 hospitals, and an orphanage. There are 2 seminaries in the United States, one in Philadelphia, the other recently reopened in Summerville, South Carolina. There are 6,532 members in 64 local churches.

EVANGELICAL CHRISTIAN CHURCHES

These churches trace their origin back to the Arminian preaching and teaching of Horace Bushnell (1802–1876). Bushnell criticized the Calvinistic view that grace is irresistible and election unconditional, insisting that the human race, by free will, cooperates in its own conversion. He is held to have been the spiritual father and head elder of the Evangelical Christian Churches until his death in 1876.

Churches variously known as Evangelical Christian Churches, Christian Churches of North America, Christian Missionary, and Community and Evangelical Christian Churches, were chartered and incorporated as members of the Evangelical Christian Churches in May 1966.

Their doctrines stress the Trinity, the Virgin birth, the plenary inspiration of the Bible, Christ's work of atonement, and his second coming. They recognize the many gifts of the Holy Spirit and that one might experience all the gifts, but they do not condone the charismatic movement. There are 12,711 members in 132 churches located in the United States, Canada, and Haiti.

EVANGELICAL CHURCH OF NORTH AMERICA

When The Methodist Church and the Evangelical United Brethren merged into The United Methodist Church in Dallas, Texas, in 1968, a number of churches in the Brethren body, dissatisfied with the merger, withdrew to form a denomination of their own—the Evangelical Church of North America. In June 1968 the new church was incorporated at Portland, Oregon, and eventually came to include congregations across the country, including those of the former Holiness Methodist Church, and in 1982 union occurred between that body and the Northwest Canada Conference.

The doctrinal position is of the Wesleyan-Arminian persuasion; in organization, there are conference superintendents over each district and annual conference; the general administration of each conference is carried on by the annual conference sessions, the conference Council of Administration, and program agencies such as evangelism, missions, Christian education, and stewardship. A general superintendent is the overseer of the work of the denomination. There is an inclusive membership of 17,170 in 200 churches, with particular strength in the Northwest.

EVANGELICAL CONGREGATIONAL CHURCH

Objecting to the "usurpation of power in violation of the discipline" by bishops, seven annual conferences and from 60,000 to 70,000 members of the Evangelical Association—later known as the Evangelical Church—withdrew from that body in 1894 to organize the United Evangelical

Church. The two churches were reunited in 1922, but again a minority objected and remained aloof from the merger. The East Pennsylvania Conference and several churches in the Central, Pittsburgh, Ohio, Illinois, and West Virginia conferences continued their separate existence under the old name, later changed to Evangelical Congregational Church. Today the boundaries of the Eastern Conference are larger than at the time of the merger; the Midwest churches are joined in a Western Conference.

This church, like its parent Evangelical church, is "Methodist in polity, Arminian in doctrine." There is emphasis upon the inspiration and integrity of the Bible and the "fellowship of all followers of Christ." There are annual and general conferences with equal lay and clerical representation, bishops and district superintendents, and an itinerant ministry. Pastors are appointed yearly by the annual conferences. Local congregations, as the name implies, have more freedom—especially in temporal matters—than congregations in either Evangelical or Methodist churches. The Division of Missions, with two women's auxiliaries, supervises the home and foreign missionary programs. There are 50 missionaries abroad and 36 at home, with 163 nationals at work in various lands.

Large summer assemblies are held in six campsites strategically located in the conferences. Church headquarters, the publishing house, the infirmary, the home for the aging, and the school of theology are located at Myerstown, Pennsylvania. There are 27,203 members and approximately 163 churches.

EVANGELICAL COVENANT CHURCH OF AMERICA

This church traces its roots to the Protestant Reformation, to the biblical instruction of the Lutheran state church of Sweden, and to the great spiritual awakenings of the nineteenth century. These three influences have in large measure shaped its development and should be borne in mind as we seek to understand its distinctive spirit.

The Covenant Church adheres to the affirmations of the Reformation regarding the Holy Scriptures as the Word of God and the only perfect rule for faith, doctrine, and conduct. It has traditionally valued the historic confessions of the Christian church, particularly the Apostles' Creed, while at the same time emphasizing the sovereignty of the Word over all creedal interpretations. It has especially cherished the Pietist restatement of the doctrine of justification by faith as basic to the tasks of evangelism, missionary outreach, Christian nurture, and the advancement of social justice. It treasures the New Testament emphasis upon personal faith in Jesus Christ as Savior and Lord, and the reality of the Church as a fellowship of believers that recognizes but transcends theological differences. Baptism and the Lord's Supper are divinely ordained sacraments. While the denomination has traditionally practiced the baptism of infants, in conformity with the principle of freedom it has given room to divergent views. Its principle of personal freedom, however, is to be distinguished from the individualism that disregards the centrality of the Word of God and the mutual responsibilities and disciplines of the spiritual community.

The local church is administered by a board elected by the membership; it calls its ministers (ordained by the denomination) generally with the aid and guidance of the denominational Pastoral Relations Commission and the conference superintendent. There are nine geographical districts known as regional conferences, each of which elects its own superintendent. The highest constituted authority is vested in an annual meeting composed of ministers and lay people elected as delegates by the constituent churches. An executive board, elected by the annual meeting, implements its decisions.

Mission fields are in Zaire, Taiwan, Ecuador, Colombia, Japan, Mexico, and Thailand. There is a Bible Institute in Canada, Minnehaha Academy in Minneapolis, and North Park College and Theological Seminary in Chicago. The church supports 2 children's homes and a seamen's mission; Swedish Covenant Hospital in Chicago and Emmanuel Medical Center in Turlock, California; and 20 retirement communities and nursing care facilities. There were 82,734 adult members in 577 churches in 1983.

EVANGELICAL FREE CHURCH OF AMERICA

This church began with a group of independent congregations and several churches of the old Swedish Ansgarii Synod and Mission Synod, which met together at Boone, Iowa, in 1884 to form a fellowship of "free" congregations to be known as the Swedish Evangelical Free Mission (later changed to Swedish Evangelical Free Church and still later to Evangelical Free Church of America). In 1950 the Swedish Evangelical Free Church and the Evangelical Free Church Association (formerly the Norwegian and Danish Evangelical Free Church Association) were merged into the present body.

By agreement in the organization of the fellowship in 1884, this was to be a body of self-governing congregations, each free to establish its own doctrine; the several churches elected delegates to an annual conference that was purely advisory in character. A society of ministers and missionaries was organized in 1894 to guide the denomination in doctrine and practice. This is still the guiding principle of the church; the only qualification for membership lies in evidence of conversion and the living of a Christian life. Polity is congregational. A twelve-point doctrinal statement adopted in 1950 is incorporated into the bylaws of most local congregations.

There are approximately 850 churches and a constituency of about 100,000, with 14 districts in the United States and 3 in Canada. There are mission stations in Japan, the Philippines, Hong Kong, Zaire, Singapore/Malaysia, Germany, Venezuela, Belgium, Austria, and Peru, and three schools of higher education—Trinity Evangelical Divinity School and Trinity College in Bannockburn, Illinois, and Trinity Western College in Langley, British Columbia.

The church is a member of the International Federation of Free Evangelical Churches and the National Association of Evangelicals.

FIRE-BAPTIZED HOLINESS CHURCH

A black pentecostal sect, this church was for the first ten years of its existence a part of the white Fire-Baptized Holiness Association of America; the black membership separated in 1908 and in 1922 became the Fire-Baptized Holiness Church.

This church teaches the standard pentecostal and Holiness doctrines of repentance, regeneration, justification, sanctification, pentecostal baptism, speaking with other tongues, divine healing, and the premillennial second coming. It stands opposed to the "so-called Christian Scientists, Spiritualists, Unitarians, Universalists and Mormons." Adventism, immorality, antinomianism, the annihilation of the wicked, the glorification of the body, and "many other modern teachings of the day" are denounced as false, wicked, and unscriptural. Government is by a bishop, two overseers, a general secretary, treasurer, and a board of trustees. Ruling elders, ordained ministers, and pastors are in charge of local churches, and a general convention is held yearly. Today more than 25,000 members are reported in 1,050 churches. The church's bishop resides in Atlanta, and its headquarters are in Greenville, South Carolina.

FOURSQUARE GOSPEL, INTERNATIONAL CHURCH OF THE

Rising out of the evangelistic work of Aimee Semple McPherson, this church is a tribute to the organizing genius and striking methods of its founder. Born in Ontario in 1890, Mrs. McPherson was converted under the preaching of her first husband, Robert Semple, an evangelist. He died in China, and she returned to the United States in 1911 to tour the country in a series of gospel meetings that were spectacular even during the war years. She settled in Los Angeles in 1918, and built the famous Angelus Temple, which was opened January 1, 1923. She also founded the Echo Park Evangelistic Association, the L.I.F.E. Bible College, and the International Church of the Foursquare Gospel religious corporations. The headquarters are still located near Angelus Temple in Los Angeles.

With her great speaking ability and faith in praying for healing of the sick, Mrs. McPherson attracted thousands to her meetings. Her more irreverent critics felt that the meetings were too spectacular, but others appreciated her type of presentation. There was great interest in the sick and the poor; "more than a million and a half" are said to have been fed by the Los Angeles organization in her time. That commissary is still in operation and blesses hundreds annually.

The teaching of the church is set forth in a 21-paragraph Declaration of Faith written by Mrs. McPherson. Strongly fundamental, it is premillennialist, Holiness, and Trinitarian, advocating that the Bible is as "true, immutable, steadfast, unchangeable, as its author, the Lord Jehovah." The Holy Spirit baptism, with the initial evidence of speaking in other tongues, is subsequent to conversion, and there is the power to heal in answer to believing prayer. There are the usual doctrines on the atonement, the second coming of Christ "in clouds of glory," reward for the righteous at the judgment, and eternal punishment for the wicked. Baptism and the Lord's Supper are observed.

Mrs. McPherson was president of the church during her lifetime and was, with a board of directors, its ruling power and voice; her son, Rolf K. McPherson, became president at the time of her death. Today the official business of the church is conducted by a board of directors, the missionary cabinet, and an executive council. The highest seat of authority is the convention body, which alone has the power to make or amend the bylaws of the church. District supervisors are appointed for 9 districts and are ratified by the pastors of the respective districts every 4 years. Each church is governed by a church council and contributes monthly to home and foreign missionary work. Membership is concentrated on the West Coast. There are 526,955 members, 8,923 churches and meeting places in 48 different countries, 20,882 missionaries and national workers, 36 foreign day schools, 75 United States day schools, 55 foreign Bible schools, 2 United States Bible schools, an orphanage in the foreign field, and a net property valuation of $264,059,030.

All members are required to subscribe to the Declaration of Faith. A church flag—red, gold, blue, and purple with a red cross on a Bible background bearing a superimposed 4—is prominently displayed in the churches. A radio station, KFSG, broadcasts from Los Angeles, and a sister station, KHIS, from Bakersfield, California.

FREE CHRISTIAN ZION CHURCH OF CHRIST

Led by E. D. Brown, a local Methodist missionary, a small group of Methodist and Baptist black ministers formed this church in 1905 at Redemption, Arkansas. They objected to the taxing of church membership to provide support for any ecclesiastical organization, feeling that the care and relief of the needy and the poor were the first responsibility of the church. Such relief activities characterize their local churches today.

Doctrine is completely Methodist, and so is government, except for minor titles and details. Chiefs, or superintendents, perform the functions of bishops; a chief pastor is chosen as top administrative officer, making all assignments to pastorates and appointing all church officers. Pastors and deacons head local churches and are responsible for aid to the poor in their congregations. Laymen share in the conduct of the churches and in the annual general assembly. The latest membership report (1956), listed 22,260 members in 742 churches.

FRIENDS (QUAKERS)

With a membership in the United States and Canada of only 123,000, 200,000 around the world, the Friends, better known as Quakers, have had a deep and lasting influence upon Western society. Contributions in both religious and humanitarian spheres have won them universal respect and admiration, and their amazing history and loyalty to their quiet faith offer a challenge and inspiration to all churches.

The Friends' vicissitudes and victories began when George Fox (1624–1691), a British seeker after spiritual truth and peace, failing to find such in the churches of his time, did find them in a new, intimate, personal relationship with Christ. He said, "When all my hopes in [churches and churchmen] were gone . . . then I heard a voice which said, 'There is one, even Christ Jesus, that can speak to thy condition.' " This is the Inner Voice, or Inner Light, of Quakerism, based upon the description of John 1:9—"the true Light, which lighteth every man that cometh into the world"—a voice available to all, having nothing to do with outward forms or ceremonies, rituals, or creeds. To the Quaker, every person is a walking church; every heart is God's altar and shrine.

Quakerism was revolutionary, and it was treated as revolution by the state Church of England. To tell that united state and church that they both were wrong, that their theology and dogma meant nothing, that people need not attend "steeple houses" to find God and that it was equally wrong to pay taxes to support state church clergy—this was rebellion.

Fox and his early followers went even further. They not only refused to go to church but insisted upon freedom of speech, assembly, and worship; they would not take oaths in court; they refused to go to war; they doffed their hats to no one, king or commoner; they made no distinction in sex or social class; they condemned slavery and England's treatment of prisoners and the insane. The very names they adopted—Children of Truth, Children of Light, Friends of Truth, and finally Religious Society of Friends—roused ridicule and fierce opposition. Fox, hauled into court, advised one judge to "tremble at the Word of the Lord" and heard the judge call him "Quaker." But derision was not enough to stop the Friends. So persecution unsheathed its sword.

The Quakers were whipped, jailed, tortured, mutilated, murdered. Fox spent 6 years in jail; others spent decades, dying there. From 1650 until 1689, more than 3,000 suffered for conscience' sake, and 300 to 400 died in prison. Thanks to that persecution the Friends prospered and the society was founded in 1652. When Fox died, there were 50,000 Quakers.

Some were already in America. Ann Austin and Mary Fisher arrived in Massachusetts from Barbados in 1656, were promptly accused of being witches, and deported. Two days later eight more came from England. Laws were passed hastily to keep them out; the whipping post worked overtime and failed. Four were hanged in Boston. But Quakers kept coming—into New England, New York, New Jersey, Maryland, Virginia, and Pennsylvania. Rhode Island and Pennsylvania welcomed them from the start. The long horror in the communities that did not welcome them ended with the passage of the Toleration Act of 1689.

With that law and Fox's death, a new phase began. Persecution waned and died and so did a great deal of revolutionary zeal. The Quakers settled down as businessmen and farmers known for their pacifism and honesty and became quite prosperous.

Yet there were lights in that period of quiet. The meeting organization and community life became well organized. Closely knit family life was emphasized. It was a time of creativeness and mystical inwardness. The period of withdrawal was one in which Quaker philanthropy became widely respected and even admired; their ideas on prison reform began to take effect. Quaker schools increased; as early as 1691 there were 15 Quaker boarding schools in England.

In 1682 William Penn came to Philadelphia. He sat under an elm at Shackamaxon and made a treaty with the Indians—the "only treaty never sworn to and never broken." Treated like human beings, the Indians reacted in kind. If all our cities had been like Philadelphia and all our states like Pennsylvania, our national history might have been vastly different.

But even there the holy experiment had to end. Quakers controlled the Pennsylvania legislature until 1756, when they refused to vote a tax to pay for a war against the Shawnees and Delawares, and consequently stepped down and out of power.

They looked within rather than without and began to enforce discipline upon their membership so strictly that they became in fact a "peculiar people." Members were disowned or dismissed for even minor infractions of the discipline; thousands were cut off for "marrying out of Meeting." Pleasure, music, and art were taboo; sobriety, punctuality, and honesty were demanded in all directions; dress was painfully plain, and speech was biblical. They were "different" and dour; they gained few new converts and lost many old members.

Some few "fighting Quakers" went to battle in the American Revolution, but they were very few; most remained pacifists, working quietly for peace, popular education, temperance, democracy—and against slavery. In 1688 the Friends of Germantown, Pennsylvania, said that slavery violated the Golden Rule and encouraged adultery; they protested that "traffic in the bodies of men" and called it unlawful. Their first attitude of tolerance changed slowly to one of outright opposition; it took nearly a century for the Quakers to rid their own society of slavery, but they did it years in advance of any other religious body in America. Sellers or purchasers of slaves were forbidden membership in the society by the end of the eighteenth century. Persistently across the years, the Quakers dropped their seeds of antislavery agitation into the body politic. First John Woolman, and then the poet Whittier wielded tremendous influence in the fight; and once the Civil War was over, they threw their strength into such organizations as the Freedman's Aid Society. Ever since, they have been active in education and legislative protection for blacks.

Divisions arose within the ranks during those years: The Hicksites separated in 1827, the Wilburites in 1845, and the Primitives (a small group now extinct) in 1861. Of these separations, the one led by Elias Hicks is of primary concern. Hicks was a rural Long Island Quaker whose liberal and rational theological views brought him into conflict with those of more orthodox and evangelical persuasion. The division came in 1827; while it had personal and sociological emphases, the split was basically due to the widespread nineteenth-century conflict between liberalism and rationalism on the one hand and an orthodoxy based on Methodist ideas of evangelism and salvation on the other. Two-thirds of the Philadelphia Yearly Meeting withdrew with the Hicksites (a nickname never officially adopted), and similar divisions followed in the New York, Ohio, Indiana, and Baltimore yearly meetings. A second series of separations, a result of the Wesleyan Methodist influence, were led by Joseph John Gurney and John Wilbur (see Religious Society of Friends [Conservative] below).

The twentieth century thus far has been one of Quaker unity and outreach. A Five Years Meeting (now the Friend's United Meeting) was organized in 1902, merging a large portion of the pastoral yearly meetings. The two Philadelphia meetings, separated since 1827, were united in 1955. In the same year the two New York Yearly Meetings were merged and the three Canada Yearly Meetings came together to form one body. In 1968, two Baltimore Yearly Meetings reunited. Southeastern Meeting, newly founded, affiliated with Friends United Meeting and Friends General Conference in 1972.

In 1917, before the guns of World War I had stopped, Friends from all branches of the society were at work in the American Friends Service Committee in relief and reconstruction efforts abroad. The A.F.S.C. remains today one of the most effective of such agencies in the world. Its volunteers erected demountable houses, staffed hospitals, plowed fields, raised domestic animals, and drove ambulances. Famine relief and child-feeding programs were instituted in Serbia, Poland, Austria, Russia, and Germany; at one time the Friends were feeding more than 1,000,000 German children a day; Greek refugees, Japanese earthquake victims, needy miners' families in Pennsylvania, West Virginia, and Kentucky were helped. Thousands would have perished but for the A.F.S.C.

Quakers drove ambulances and served in the medical corps of both world wars, and some were in combat; probably more young Quakers volunteered for or accepted military service than resisted on grounds of religious principle. They also worked to relieve our displaced Japanese-Americans, and they cooperated with the Brethren and Mennonites in locating our conscientious objectors in work of real importance on farms, in reformatories, hospitals, and mental institutions. They were in Spain soon after the outbreak of the Spanish Civil War and later supplied food for the children in Spain, southern France, Italy, Austria, Holland, North Africa, and Finland. In 1945 alone, they sent 282 tons of clothes, shoes, bedding, and soap to Europe, and still more to China and India. Counting both cash and material gifts, the income of the A.F.S.C. is apt to exceed $7,500,000 annually. At home and abroad, summer camps of young volunteers have inspired incalculable goodwill among nations, and minority groups within nations.

Nor have the Friends been satisfied to work merely in relief. Peace conferences have had a prominent place, ranging from local to international and covering all age groups. Lake Mohonk in New York was founded by a Friend. Scores of youth conferences and camps at home and in foreign fields testify to devotion to the way of Christ; it is little wonder that it is known as a "peace church."

Worship and business in the society are conducted in monthly, quarterly, and yearly meetings. The monthly meeting is the basic unit, made up of one or more meetings in a neighborhood. It convenes each week for worship and once a month for business. It keeps records of membership, births, deaths, and marriages; appoints committees; considers queries on spiritual welfare; and transacts all business of the group. Monthly district meetings join four times a year in a quarterly meeting to stimulate spiritual life and to decide on any business they feel should be brought to the attention of the yearly meeting. The yearly meeting corresponds to a diocese in an episcopal system. There are 27 in the United States and Canada, in touch with Friends all over the world.

They have standing committees on such subjects as publications, education, the social order, missions, peace, charities, and national legislation; they allocate trust fund incomes and generally supervise the work of the society.

Group decisions await the "sense of the meeting." Lacking unity of opinion, the meeting may have a "quiet time" until unity is found, or it may postpone consideration of the matter or refer it to a committee for study. Minority opinion is not outvoted, but convinced. Every man, woman, and child is free to speak in any meeting; delegates are appointed at quarterly and yearly meetings to ensure adequate representation, but they enjoy no unusual position or prerogatives. Women and men hold positions of absolute equality in Quaker polity.

There are, contrary to popular misunderstanding, church officers—elders and ministers—chosen for recognized ability in spiritual leadership, and they too stand on equal footing with the rest of the membership. To the Quaker all members are ministers. A few full-time workers are paid a modest salary, and "recorded" ministers who serve as pastors in meetings that have programmed worship also receive salaries (about 1,000 meetings have no paid pastors).

Quaker worship may be either programmed or unprogrammed, but the two are not always distinct. The former more nearly resembles a simple Protestant service, although there are no rites or outward sacraments. While Friends believe in spiritual communion, partaking of the elements is thought unnecessary. In the unprogrammed meetings there is no choir, collection, singing, or pulpit; the service is devoted to quiet meditation, prayer, and communion. Any vocal contributions are spontaneous. There is no uniform practice; some of the churches greatly prefer to be called meetings.

In business meetings there is often frank inquiry into members' conduct of business, treatment of others, use of narcotics or intoxicants, reading habits, and recreation. No true Quaker gambles, plays the stock market, bets, owns racehorses, or engages in raffles, lotteries, or the liquor business. Some follow conservative religious or theological patterns, and others are liberal; all are guided by the Inner Light.

The Inner Light is highly important in Quaker belief. Grace, power from God to help humans resist evil, is to Quakers universal among all people. They seek not holiness, but perfection—a higher, more spiritual standard of life for both society and the individual—and they believe that the truth is unfolding and continuing. They value the Bible highly but prefer to rely on individual fresh guidance from the Spirit of God which produced the Bible, rather than follow only what has been revealed to others. Some modern groups accept the Bible as the final authority in all religious matters. Rufus Jones says:

> They believe supremely in the nearness of God to the human soul, in direct intercourse and immediate communion, in mystical experience in a firsthand

discovery of God. . . . It means and involves a sensitiveness to the wider spiritual Life above us, around us, and within us, a dedication to duty, a passion for truth, and an appreciation of goodness, an eagerness to let love and the grace of God come freely through one's own life, a reverence for the will of God wherever it is revealed in past or present, and a high faith that Christ is a living presence and a life-giving energy always within reach of the receptive soul.

No Quaker body has ever departed from the Declaration to Charles II in 1661: "We utterly deny all outward wars and strife and fighting with outward weapons, for any end or under any pretense whatever. . . . The spirit of Christ, which leads us into all Truth, will never move us to fight and war against any man with outward weapons, neither for the Kingdom of Christ, not for the kingdoms of this world." However, there is great tolerance toward individual variations in this position. During World War II formal Quaker positions favored applying for conscientious-objector status, either as a noncombatant within the military or in alternate service; in the case of the Vietnam war, corporate positions shifted toward encouraging men to practice draft refusal and go to jail if necessary. In both cases a wide variety of positions was seen as acceptable; the emphasis was on following individual conscience. Quakers who enter military service are no longer disowned from membership, but many leave the society and join a church that does not profess pacifism. Conversely, pacifists brought up in other traditions tend to join the Friends in young adulthood.

Marriage is not necessarily a ceremony to be performed by a minister; in cases where the traditional Quaker marriage is observed, the bride and groom simply stand before a meeting and make mutual vows of love and faithfulness and are thereby married. In certain sections of the country the pastor of the meeting officiates.

The Friends have never been great proselytizers; they depend almost entirely upon birthright membership and membership by "convincement." In many of the bodies, though not in all, every child born of Quaker parents is declared a member of the society. This has resulted in a large number of nominal, or paper, members who contribute little; efforts are being made to correct this custom by establishing a junior, or associate, membership for children. This reliance upon birthright membership has seriously depleted their numbers. There are 30 yearly meetings in America, including one in Canada, one in Cuba, one in Jamaica, and a small group in Mexico. There are also 20 yearly meetings overseas.

If the Friends were ever "exclusive," they no longer are; a world outreach has been evident and growing in recent years. The Friend's United Meeting and the Friends General Conference are members of the World Council of Churches; the Philadelphia Yearly Meeting also belongs to the National Council of Churches. A Friends World Committee for Consultation, organized at Swarthmore, Pennsylvania, following the Second World Conference of Friends in 1937, functions as an agent, or clearinghouse, for the interchange of Quaker aspirations and experiences through regional, national, and international intervisitation, person-to-person consultations, conferences, correspondence, and a variety of publications. The committee has headquarters in Birmingham, England, and offices in Philadelphia, in Plainfield, Indiana, and in Edinburgh, Scotland. The American section has helped some 50 small Friends groups in the United States to attain monthly meeting status. The F.W.C.C. is a nongovernmental organization related to the Economic and Social Council of the United Nations through cooperation with the A.F.S.C.; it helps operate a program at U.N. headquarters to forward world peace and human unity. Something of a world community, or "Franciscan Third Order," has been set up in the organization of the Wider Quaker Fellowship, in which non-Quakers in sympathy with the spirit and program may participate in the work of the Friends without coming into full Quaker membership. This is not so much an organization as "a fellowship of kindred minds—a way of life, a contagion of spirit"; it has 4,200 members, 360 of whom live abroad.

An Evangelical Friends Alliance was formed in 1965 in the interests of evangelical emphasis and denominational unity; it seeks to bring together those interested in an evangelical renewal within Christianity and a renewal of interest in the evangelical emphases of seventeenth-century Quakerism; it includes the Association of Evangelical Friends. Theology here is conservative; local pastors are elected. There are 217 churches and 24,095 members.

A further movement toward unity is found in the Religious Society of Friends (Unaffiliated Meetings), which also stresses elements and teachings of early Friends movements. This group is unique in its wide variety and experimentation in worship and polity; it is not associated with the larger bodies in the society. There are 112 churches with 6,386 members.

Friends General Conference

This is a national organization of yearly meetings (Baltimore, Lake Erie, South Central, Canada, New England, Illinois, Indiana, South Eastern, New York, and Philadelphia). It was established in 1868 as a Sunday school conference and matured in 1900 as a general conference for fellowship across yearly meeting boundaries, as an instrument for deepening the spiritual and social testimonies of the Society of Friends. One of its main features is an annual conference; in 1978 it had 1,500 members, about one-third of whom were children and young people. There are now 26,184 members and 232 meetings in the general conference, a fraction of whom also belong to the Friends United Meeting (described below); this is explained by dual membership in Canada, New York, and New England in the General Conference and the Friends United Meeting.

Friends United Meeting (Five Years Meeting)

With 56,997 members and 538 local meetings in 1981, this is the largest single Quaker body in the United States. The largest yearly meetings in the world are its East Africa, with 40,000 members, and London, with 19,998. Organized in 1902, it brought together in one cooperative relationship 12 yearly meetings at home and three abroad—East Africa, Cuba, and Jamaica—with a somewhat different status. They work together in many departments—such as missionary service and the production of Sunday school materials—and while each is autonomous, they come together for spiritual stimulation, business, and conference every three years.

The ministries of the FUM are carried forward in the interim between triennial sessions by three planning commissions and the general board, which convene semiannually. Affirming the importance of personal religious experience that goes beyond theory or speculation, this group embodies a creative balance of central Quaker accents, evangelism and social concern, mission and service, worship, and ministry. Friends of various persuasions work together within the FUM spectrum. Membership is concentrated in North Carolina, Indiana, Ohio, and Iowa.

Religious Society of Friends (Conservative)

Known also as Wilburites, this group resulted from a second division. Joseph John Gurney, a British evangelical Quaker, came to America in the mid-1800s and began preaching and teaching the final authority of the Bible and acceptance of the doctrines of the atonement, justification, and sanctification. John Wilbur, a Rhode Island conservative, while not denouncing the authority of the Bible and its teachings, felt that Gurney's preaching substituted a creed for the immediate revelation of the Divine Spirit available to human beings. Both men had large followings; the outcome was separation in Kansas, Iowa, Indiana, Ohio, New England, North Carolina, and Canada between 1845 and 1904.

The conservative pattern generally was one "set forth by the Society in the beginning," calling for a silent waiting before God in Quaker meetings, in expectation that the Spirit would instruct and move them to speak or pray without program or ritual. In New England in 1945, and in Canada in 1955, differences were resolved between these conservatives and they were reunited. There are still conservative yearly meetings in Iowa, Ohio, and North Carolina; it cooperates with other Friends groups in various areas of service and in intervisitation. There are 27 monthly meetings and 1,832 members.

GRACE GOSPEL FELLOWSHIP

Dispensational and premillennial, this fellowship had its beginnings in a conference of pastors and missionaries in the First Church of the

Fundamentals in Evanston, Illinois, in 1944, as a pastors' fellowship. A year later its purpose was defined in a constitution: "The purpose of this organization shall be to promote a fellowship among those who believe the truths contained in [our] doctrinal statement and to proclaim the Gospel of the Grace of God in this land, and throughout the world." Its doctrinal statement includes belief in the Bible as infallibly inspired by God, the total depravity of the human race, redemption by God's grace through the blood of Christ by means of faith, eternal security for the saved, the gifts of the Spirit (as enumerated in Eph. 4:7-16), but that the human nature of sin is never eradicated during this life. Its members believe in divine baptism but not in water baptism, and they emphasize the resurrection and the second coming of Christ, and the lasting suffering of the unsaved dead. Any church may vote to become affiliated with Grace Gospel Fellowship, provided it meets the doctrinal standards.

The Fellowship consists of 48 churches and 3,500 members in the United States. Grace Bible College is located in Grand Rapids, Michigan, the headquarters of the fellowship. There are 2 foreign and 1 home missionary organizations—abroad, Fellowship churches are found in Zaire, Puerto Rico, India, Phillipines, Australia, and South America.

INDEPENDENT FUNDAMENTAL CHURCHES OF AMERICA

Organized in 1930 at Cicero, Illinois, by representatives of various independent churches anxious to safeguard fundamentalist doctrine, this body has two types of membership—one for churches and organizations, the other for ministers, missionaries, evangelists, and Christian workers. The organization membership accounts for 692 churches directly affiliated, with 345 other independent churches whose pastors are affiliated. There are 5 Bible camps; 7 Bible institutes; 23 church extension organizations; 2 children's homes; 16 home and 4 foreign mission agencies. More than 1,450 ministers, missionaries, evangelists, and Christian workers are members; total membership is 125,350, with strength in California, Pennsylvania, Michigan, and Illinois.

The president of the body presides over an annual conference in which the members have voting power. An executive committee of 12 serves for 3 years; the constituent churches are completely independent but are required to subscribe to the statement of faith of the organization. A home office is maintained in Westchester, Illinois.

Directly and indirectly, it supports a number of Bible Schools. The official organ is the *Voice*, published bimonthly.

JEHOVAH'S WITNESSES

The people called Jehovah's Witnesses believe that their movement is the true realization of the one faith mentioned by the apostle Paul in

Ephesians 4:5. Their certainty of this, and their zeal in proclaiming it, have made them, at least in point of public interest, an outstanding religious phenomenon in modern America.

They were not known as Jehovah's Witnesses until 1931. Until that time they had been called Millennial Dawnists, International Bible Students, and earlier, Russellites, for the man who brought about their first incorporation in 1884. Pastor Charles Taze Russell, the first president, is acknowledged not as founder (there is no "human" founder) but as general organizer; Joseph F. Rutherford, Russell's successor, claimed that the Witnesses had been on earth as an organization for more than 5,000 years and cited passages (Isa. 43:10-12; Heb. 11; and John 18:37) to prove it.

Russell was deeply influenced by a belief in Christ's second coming; he studied the Bible avidly and attracted huge crowds to hear his lectures. The first formal group organized by Russell was formed in Pittsburgh in 1872; his books, of which 13,000,000 are said to have been circulated, had great influence on the movement. To assist Russell, a board of directors was elected by vote of all members who subscribed $10 or more to the support of the work (a practice discontinued in 1944).

Under Russell's direction the headquarters were moved to Brooklyn in 1909, and another corporation was formed under the laws of the state of New York. In 1956 the name was changed to the Watchtower Bible and Tract Society of New York, Inc. When Russell died in 1916, Rutherford became president. Known widely as Judge Rutherford, he had been a Missouri lawyer who occasionally sat as a circuit court judge. He wrote tirelessly; his books, pamphlets, and tracts supplanted those of Russell, and his neglect of some aspects of Russell's teaching brought dissension.

Administration of the group underwent changes during Rutherford's presidency. The governing body today is in the hands of older and more "spiritually qualified" men who base their judgments upon the authority of the Scriptures; this is not considered a governing hierarchy, but a true imitation of early apostolic Christian organization. Under that system, three corporations eventually came to serve the society: the Watchtower Bible and Tract Society of New York, Inc.; the Watch Tower Bible and Tract Society of Pennsylvania; and the International Bible Students Association of England. Judge Rutherford as president was a moving power in all three.

Under the direction of the leaders at headquarters, local congregations of Witnesses (always called congregations, never churches) are arranged in circuits, with a traveling minister who spends a week with each congregation. Approximately 21 congregations are included in each circuit. Circuits are grouped into districts—38 in the United States. District and circuit organizations are now found in 205 countries and islands around the world.

Meeting in Kingdom halls, and not in churches, the members witness and publish their faith in testimony and in a remarkably comprehensive missionary effort. They do not believe in separation into clergy or laity, since "Christ Jesus did not make such a separation." They never use titles such as *Reverend* or *Rabbi* or *Father*; this, they feel, is not in accordance with the words of Jesus in Matthew 23:6-10. All give generously of their time in proclaiming their faith and teaching in private homes. Called publishers of the Kingdom, they devote time regularly, preaching only from the Bible. Pioneers are required to give at least 90 hours per month; special pioneers and missionaries donate a minimum of 140 hours per month and are sent to isolated areas and foreign lands where new congregations can be formed. All pioneers provide for their own support, but the society gives a small allowance to the special pioneers in view of their special needs. The headquarters staff, including the president of the society, are housed at the Bethel Home in Brooklyn, engage primarily in editorial and printing work, and receive an allowance of $30 a month in addition to room and board. They write, print, and distribute literature in almost astronomical proportions. The official journal, *The Watchtower*, has a circulation of 10,050,000; more than one billion Bibles, books, and leaflets have been distributed since 1920, and these are available in at least 176 languages. More than 2,477,000 Witnesses are active in this work throughout the world.

In the literature (all circulated without by-lines or signatures) is contained the teaching of the society. It rests firmly upon the idea of the theocracy, or rule of God. The world in the beginning, according to the Witnesses, was under the theocratic rule of the Almighty; all then was "happiness, peace, and blessedness." But Satan rebelled and became the ruler of the world, and from that moment on humankind has followed his evil leading. Then came Jesus, "the beginning of the creation by God," as the prophets had predicted, to end Satan's rule; Jesus' rule began in 1914. In 1918 Christ "came to the temple of Jehovah"; and in 1919 when Rutherford reorganized the movement shattered by the war, Jesus, enthroned in the temple, began to illuminate the prophecies and send out his followers to preach.

God, in Witness thinking, will take vengeance upon wicked human beings in our time; he is now showing his great love by "gathering out" multitudes of people of goodwill to whom he will give life in the new world that is to come after the imminent battle of Armageddon. This is to be a universal battle; Christ will lead the army of the righteous, composed of the "host of heaven, the holy angels," and will completely annihilate the army of Satan. The righteous of the earth will watch the battle but will not participate. After the battle a great crowd of people will remain on the earth; these will be believers in God and will be his servants. Those who have proved their integrity under test in the old world will multiply and populate the new earth with righteous people. A resurrection will also take place and will be an additional means of filling the cleansed earth with better inhabitants. After the holocaust, "righteous princes" will rule the earth under Christ, King of the Great Theocracy. One special group—the 144,000 Christians mentioned in Revelations 7 and 14—will become the "bride of Christ" and rule with him in heaven.

Judge Rutherford, who often said that "millions now living will never die" (meaning that Armageddon and the Kingdom were near) died in 1942, leaving guidance of the movement in the hands of Nathan H. Knorr. When Knorr died in 1977, Armageddon had not yet been fought, but the certainty of its imminence persists. Frederick W. Franz is now president.

All these beliefs are based upon the Bible; Witnesses quote elaborately from the Scriptures. All other teachings and interpretations are, to them, suspect and unreliable. They oppose and attack the teachings of the various churches, insisting that they are not denouncing churches or church members, but only doctrines and interpretations of Scripture they consider false. They have been especially active in opposing what they consider the three allies of Satan: false teachings of the churches, tyranny of human governments, and oppressions of business. This "triple alliance" of ecclesiastical, political, and commercial powers has misled and all but destroyed humanity, the Witnesses claim, and must be destroyed at Armageddon before the new world can be born. They refuse, for instance, to salute the flag, bear arms in war, or participate in the affairs of government—not because of any pacifist convictions, but because they consider these to be expressions of Satan's power over humankind. This attitude has brought them into conflict with law enforcement agencies; they have also endured jailings, whippings, assault by mobs, stonings, tar-and-featherings, and the burning of their homes. All this they have accepted in a very submissive spirit; their position is that they will obey the laws of men when those laws are not in conflict with the laws of God; their guide is Acts 5:29.

The ranks of active "publishers" across the world have grown to 2,477,000, of whom approximately 613,000 are in the United States. There are 7,670 congregations in the United States and 44,953 throughout the world. Branch offices are maintained in 95 countries, and work is reported in 216 lands. More than 6,000 people have been trained as foreign missionaries. The Bible School of Gilead was established in 1943 to train missionaries and since 1961 has operated out of the international headquarters in Brooklyn. Kingdom Ministry Schools, designed to provide a brief training course for congregation elders, have been operated in all the major countries of the world since 1959.

JUDAISM

Jews arrived early in the American colonies; some were here before 1650. A small group of Portuguese Jews found safety if not complete understanding in Peter Stuyvesant's New Amsterdam, where they established the first official congregation in North America, Shearith Israel (Remnant of Israel), in 1654. Three years later there was a small group of Jews at Newport, Rhode Island. Jews came to Georgia with Oglethorpe and in 1733 organized a synagogue at Savannah. By 1850 there were 77 Jewish congregations in 21 states, and at the end of the century more than 600 congregations with 1,000,000 Jews. Today 5,728,000 American Jews have a widely varying synagogue membership of approximately 2,750,000 (50 percent).

The historic sense of unity among the Jewish people soon demonstrated itself here as it had abroad. That unity, which has defied centuries of dispersion and persecution, has now welded the followers of Judaism into one of the best organized religious groups in America.

There are two pillars upon which Judaism rests. One is the Old Testament, particularly the Pentateuch, the five books of Moses, known as the Torah. It is the revelation of God, divine in origin and containing the earliest written laws and traditions of the Jewish people. The other pillar is the Talmud, a rabbinical commentary and enlargement of the Torah, an elaborate, discursive compendium containing the written and oral laws of the faith.

In Torah and Talmud are the Jewish foundation principles of justice, purity, hope, thanksgiving, righteousness, love, freedom of will, divine providence and human responsibility, repentance, prayer, and messianic hope. At its heart lies the Hebrew concept of the oneness of God. Every day, the religiously practicing Jew repeats the ancient biblical verse, "Hear, O Israel, the Lord our God is one Lord." All other gods are to be shunned; there is but one Creator of humanity and the world, and he holds the destiny of both in his almighty hands.

Humankind, created by this one God, is inherently good. There is no original sin, no instinctive evil or fundamental impurity; the human being is made in God's image and endowed with an intelligence that enables a person to choose between good and evil. That person has and needs no mediator such as the Christians have in Christ, but approaches God directly. All people—Jews and Gentiles alike—attain immortality as the reward for righteous living.

Judaism looks forward to the perfection of humankind and to the establishment of a divine kingdom of truth and righteousness upon the earth. Orthodox Jews believe the time will come when God will send the Messiah. Conservative and Reconstructionist doctrines teach variations of this idea. Reform Judaism speaks rather of a Messianic age. To work toward the divine kingdom, the Jews have been established by God as a deathless, unique people, "a kingdom of priests and a holy nation," the "servant of the Lord."

Some of their laws provide for the great festivals of the Jewish year: Pesach, or Passover, in late March or early April, a memorial of the Jewish liberation from Egypt; Shabuoth, the Feast of Weeks, or Pentecost, in late May or early June, commemorating the giving of the Ten Commandments to Moses; Sukkoth, or the Feast of Tabernacles, or Booths, in October, marking the years of Jewish wandering in the wilderness; the Feast of Lights, or Hanukkah, in late November or December, celebrating the purification of the temple by the Maccabees after its defilement by Antiochus Epiphanes; the Feast of Lots, or Purim, in February or March, honoring the heroine Esther. Principal minor fasts are also observed: the Fast of Ab, memorializing the fall of Jerusalem and the destruction of the temple; and Yom Kippur, the Day of Atonement. Particularly important to American Jews are Rosh Hashanah, or New Year's Day, and Yom Kippur, closing the Ten Days of Penitence which begin with Rosh Hashanah.

Other laws are kept as reminders of God's covenant with Israel; these include the laws of circumcision and sabbath observance. Still others are held as marks of divine distinction and are kept to preserve the ideal of Israel as a chosen, separate people.

Within the local congregation there is full independence. There are no synods, assemblies, or hierarchies of leaders to control anything whatsoever in the synagogue. Jews are loosely bound by the "rope of sand" of Jewish unity, with wide variation in custom and procedure. They have been influenced deeply by the many peoples and cultures with which they have come in contact and have made adjustments accordingly. Because of differences in historical background over the centuries, some congregations use a German-Polish, or Ashkenazic, version of the Hebrew prayer book; others use a Spanish, or Sephardic, version. Some use English at various points in the service, such as the sermon; but all use Hebrew in the prayers. Traditional Orthodox synagogues have no instrumental music; the congregation worships with covered heads, and the men and women sit separately. In Reform, Conservative, and Reconstructionist houses of worship, sermons are in English and there is no segregation by sex.

At the head of the congregation stands the rabbi, trained in seminary and fully ordained. He is preacher and pastor. He officiates at marriages and grants divorce decrees in accordance with Jewish law after civil divorce has been granted by the state. He conducts funerals and generally supervises burials as Jewish law requires. Congregations usually own their own cemeteries or organize cemetery societies; there are also many private cemetery or burial associations owned and controlled by Jewish benevolent groups. Orthodox rabbis are also charged with the supervision of slaughtering animals for food and with the distribution of kosher meat products in accordance with the dietary laws. Many congregations engage readers or cantors, but it is the rabbi who is the leader and authority on Jewish law and ritual.

There are four divisions in American Judaism: (1) Orthodox Judaism, represented nationally by The Union of Orthodox Jewish Congregations of America, The Rabbinical Council of America, and the Union of Orthodox Rabbis of the United States and Canada; (2) Reform Judaism, affiliated with the Central Conference of American Rabbis and the Union of American Hebrew Congregations—the first national organization of synagogues in the United States, established in 1873; (3) Conservative Judaism, organized in the United Synagogues of America and the Rabbinical Assembly of America; (4) Reconstructionist Judaism, a movement affiliated with Conservative Judaism.

Synagogue membership is difficult to determine; no comprehensive comparison seems available or possible. Research conducted in 1971 disclosed that 11 percent of American Jews identified with Orthodox, 42 percent with Conservative, 33 percent with Reform, and 14 percent either with Reconstructionist or no denomination. The Reconstructionist group, with about 2,500 families, is the smallest. Percentages of increase are usually high; congregations are being formed faster than the various seminaries can ordain rabbis to supply their needs.

The multiplicity of Jewish national organizations is bewildering. The American Jewish Year Book lists the following categories: community relations and political, 26; overseas aid, 12; religious and educational, including colleges, 130; social and mutual benefit, 18; cultural, 37; social welfare, 25; Zionist and pro-Israel, 47; professional associations, 21; women's organizations, 18; youth and student organizations, 24. In more than 225 larger cities and towns, the Jewish population maintains at least one central local organization, perhaps a federation welfare fund or a community council. There are some 200 Jewish periodicals and newspapers in 43 states and the District of Columbia, and two Jewish news syndicates. *American Judaism* is the quarterly Reform organ, the monthly *Jewish Life* speaks for the Orthodox branch, and *Conservative Judaism* is a quarterly for the Conservatives. Of general interest are *Commentary, Midstream, The Reconstructionist, Judaism, Jewish Frontier, Jewish Spectator,* and *National Jewish Post and Opinion.*

Education on all levels is a major Jewish concern. Children are enrolled in Sunday schools, weekday schools, all-day schools, Yiddish schools, and released-time schools. In 1977 there were 357,101 children in all the weekday and Sunday schools, but it was still estimated that not more than 40 percent of available Jewish children were enrolled in Jewish schools.

Jewish institutions of higher learning are largely limited to schools for training rabbis. The most important of these are the Rabbi Isaac Elchanan Theoloical Seminary of Yeshiva University in New York City (Orthodox); the Hebrew Union College in Cincinnati and the Jewish Institute of Religion in New York City (Reform institutions that were merged in 1948 into what is now called H. U. C.—J. I. R.); the Jewish Theological Seminary in New York City (Conservative); and the Reconstructionist Rabbinical College in Philadelphia. The Jewish Theologial Seminary has a branch in Los Angeles, the University of Judaism. Dropsie College ("a postgraduate, nonsectarian institution of Semitic learning") in Philadelphia and the Yivo Institute for Jewish Research in New York City are the only two institutions of higher learning that are independent of Jewish seminaries; Yeshiva University in New York City and Brandeis University in Waltham, Massachusetts, are the only Jewish colleges that award a B.A. degree (Brandeis is actually nonsectarian).

Jewish charity is amazingly efficient. Federations and welfare boards maintain programs costing over $500,000,000 per year; this money is divided among local agencies (health, welfare, education, and recreation), national agencies (civic defense, cultural, religious, and service), and overseas (mainly to help settle refugees in Israel and other countries).

The American Jewish Committee is organized to protect the civil and religious rights of all Jews around the world. It seeks equality in economic, social, and educational opportunities and gives aid and counsel in cases where intolerance or persecution are evident.

Among the Zionist groups, the Zionist Organization of America still remains the largest single body numerically except for Hadassah, the women's Zionist group, the largest and most active in philanthropic and educational programs. In the past decade the most influential representative on behalf of aid to Israel has been the Conference of Presidents of major American Jewish organizations, a coordinating body and a forum of 22 major American Jewish organizations on all questions affecting American-Israeli affairs.

Three trends are noticeable: (1) a relaxation of letter observance of the time-honored Jewish law, one practical expression being found in the Reconstructionist movement, a religious-philosophical development of some influence in both Conservative and Reform Judaism; (2) "emphasis upon youth," in which young Orthodox Jews are organized as Young Israel in the interests of future leadership in the synagogue; (3) a tendency among all groups to consider the inner spiritual strength of Judaism as its only hope for the future. Under this drive, American Jews are moving toward fewer divisions and more cooperation and unity.

Conservative Judaism

Conservative Judaism holds the middle ground between Orthodox and Reform Judaism. It seems to lean closer to the Orthodox, but in some areas it resembles Reform thinking and procedure. Established "for the preservation in America of historical Judaism," it takes from Orthodoxy its belief in the Torah and the observance of the dietary laws of traditional Judaism, the use of the Hebrew language, and the historic custom of men worshiping with heads covered and wearing the *tallis* (prayer shawl) on appropriate occasions.

From Reform comes the tendency to reconcile old beliefs and practices with the cultures in which it finds itself: the use of English as well as Hebrew in the prayer service read from the *siddur* (the prayer book, or service), family pews with men and women sitting together, optional use of instrumental music and mixed choirs, and modern methods of education in the development of schools for children and youths. Generally, to the Conservative, Judaism is not static, but the deepening, growing, widening faith of a people who absorb different influences from other cultures and yet retain their own ethnic and religious aspects.

Orthodox Judaism

Orthodox Judaism has been called Torah-True Judaism; it is the branch that preserves the theology and traditions of Old World Jewry in the New World. It assigns equal authority to the written and oral law and to the ancient Jewish codes embodied in the Torah and the Talmud and their commentaries. The Torah is all-important and basic to all the rest: The

Torah is of God, given to Moses, and there is no way to God except through obedience to the laws of the Torah; Torah is a revelation of the Fatherhood of God and the unity of humankind, and it explains the place of the Jews as the chosen people of God. Everything a Jew needs to know is in the Torah; it governs every moment of life. Moses is believed to have begun an oral tradition that continued down to the time the Torah was first committed to writing. There are, however, two slightly variant emphases: The East European, Hasidic orthodoxy that stems from Hungary resolutely opposes *all* change or innovation in speech, dress, and education; the German and western European is a bit less severe, attempting to preserve the more important elements of traditional Jewish life but accepting modern changes and ideas in those three areas.

Orthodox Jews believe in the political rebirth of their nation, in the return of the Jew to Israel to rebuild the temple on Mount Zion and reestablish the ancient sacrificial ritual. They look forward to the coming of the Messiah, who is to be a descendant of David. The biblical dietary laws are strictly observed, and the traditional holy days and festivals are faithfully kept. The Hebrew language is used in the synagogue prayers, English in the sermons.

Reconstructionism

Within Conservative Judaism there exist Reconstructionist schools of thought which seek to reconstruct Judaism as a natural religion in order to make it relevant to contemporary rational and scientific thought. Originating in 1934 under the leadership of Mordecai M. Kaplan, a member of the faculty of the Jewish Theological Seminary, it is a movement indigenous to America. It defines Judaism as an evolving religious civilization, and attempts to assure physical and spiritual Jewish survival by indicating how a maximum Jewish life can be lived within the setting of a modern democratic state. Though its program is directed specifically to American Jews, its philosophy applies to Jewish life everywhere.

Reform Judaism

Reform Judaism, a liberal Judaism, began in Germany just after the Napoleonic emancipation when "reformers" within Judaism shortened the synagogue services; made use of the vernacular and of organs in those services; and established group, in place of individual confirmation. Some reformers at that time unsuccessfully advocated a complete break with Judaistic traditional forms.

Isaac Mayer Wise, one of Reform's outstanding leaders in the United States, founded the Union of American Congregations (1873), the Hebrew Union College (1975), and the Central Conference of American Rabbis (1889); these important groups sum up the aim of Reform Judaism in their conviction that Judaism should "alter its externals to strengthen its eternals."

Reform holds that there is divine authority only in the written law of the Old Testament; this is its main distinction from Orthodox Judaism. But revelation in Reform is not confined to the Old Testament; it is progressive. Many reform Jews limit themselves to the practice of the ceremonial laws of the Pentateuch, with the exception of those that, like the law of sacrifice, they regard as having no application or purpose in the present day. The sacrifices of the Mosaic era are seen more as reflections of the culture of the time than as eternally commanded observances.

Claiming that the mission of Judaism is the spiritualization of humankind, they see such practices as covering the head at worship, dietary laws, and the wearing of phylacteries as anachronisms that isolate the Jew from the rest of humankind and thus make such spiritualizing impossible. Hence those practices should be abolished. In other words, Orthodox Jews accept the entire body of oral and written law as sanctified by tradition; Reform Jews have simplified the ritual and adapted it to modern needs.

Unlike the Orthodox, they do not believe in the messianic restoration of the Jewish state and the return to Jerusalem; they are abandoning belief in a personal Messiah, but still hold to faith in the coming of a messianic age. They do, however, support return to Israel under the Zionist movement, not so much on spiritual or Talmudic grounds as on the ground that Israel offers a place of refuge for persecuted Jews of the world. They advocate the preservation in the new state of Israel of those Jewish values, customs, and traditions that have inspirational value.

KODESH CHURCH OF IMMANUEL

Formed in 1929 and incorporated in April 1930 by Frank Russell Killingsworth and 120 lay people, some of whom were former members of the African Methodist Episcopal Zion Church, this is an interracial body of approximately 326 members, most of whom are black. The 5 churches of the denomination are located in Pennsylvania, Virginia, and the District of Columbia; a missionary station has recently been established in Liberia, West Africa. Teachings are Wesleyan and Arminian, stressing entire sanctification, or the baptism of the Holy Spirit, and premillennialism. Divine healing is practiced, but not to the exclusion of medicine.

Since the church was founded for the purpose of "conserving and propagating Bible holiness," the use of alcoholic beverages and tobacco is forbidden; pride in dress and behavior, sabbath desecration, secret societies, dissolute dancing, and attendance at inferior and obscene theaters are denounced. Divorce is recognized only on the biblical ground of adultery. Water baptism is by the optional modes of sprinkling, pouring, or immersion.

The churches are under the charge of ministers and the oversight of supervising elders. Ministers are elected and ordained by annual assemblies, to which they report. Elders are elected and consecrated by general assemblies that meet quadrennially to enact all the laws of the church. The work of the entire church, including the support of foreign missionaries, is maintained by free-will offerings and tithes.

LATTER DAY SAINTS (MORMON)

Better known as Mormons, the Latter Day Saints have had one of the most tempestuous histories of any church body in the United States. Attacked by mobs and once invaded by United States Army troops, they built a religious community in what was once a desert and have established themselves as one of the outstanding religious groups of the nation.

Essentially a laypeople's movement in origin, the church is rooted in the visions of Joseph Smith, who organized the movement in 1830 at Fayette, New York. Smith claimed to have experienced a series of heavenly visitations, beginning with the appearance of God and Jesus Christ in 1820, in which he was informed that all existing churches were in error, that the true gospel was yet to be restored, that it would be revealed to him, and that he was to reestablish the true church on earth. He was led by an angel to discover, buried in a hill called Cumorah near Manchester, New York, certain golden plates left there by an ancient prophet and containing the sacred records of the ancient inhabitants of America and the true Word of God. According to the Mormons, America was originally settled by the Jaredites, one of the groups dispersed during the confusion of tongues at the Tower of Babel; the American Indians were direct descendants of the Hebrews who came from Jerusalem in 600 B.C., and Jesus himself visited this country after his resurrection.

Smith translated the hieroglyphics on the golden plates into the *Book of Mormon,* from which the name Mormon comes. Oliver Cowdery acted as his scribe. This *Book of Mormon* is considered by the Saints as equal with, "supporting but not supplanting" the Bible, and equal with the two other writings of Joseph Smith, *Doctrine and Covenants* and *Pearl of Great Price.* These four books contain the foundation teachings of the church. The golden plates were said to have been returned to the angel by Joseph Smith; their authenticity has been challenged by non-Mormon scholars and as ardently defended by the Mormons, who offer the names of eleven other persons beside Smith who saw them. Smith and Cowdery had the "priesthood of Aaron" conferred upon them by a heavenly messenger, John the Baptist, who instructed them to baptize each other. Later, in 1829, a year before the founding of the church with six charter members, three other divine visitants, Peter, James, and John, bestowed upon them the "priesthood of Melchizedek" and gave them the keys of apostleship.

Opposition arose as the church gained strength, and the Mormons left New York in 1831 for Ohio, where headquarters were established at Kirtland. Another large Mormon center developed at Independence, Missouri, where they planned to build the ideal community with a temple at its heart. Friction with other settlers became so acute that the Mormons were expelled from Missouri during 1838 and 1839. They then settled at Nauvoo, Illinois, but violence followed them and reached its peak with the murder of Joseph Smith and Hyrum Smith, his brother, by a mob at Carthage in 1844.

With Smith's death the Quorum of the Twelve Apostles was accepted as the presidency of the church, and Brigham Young as president of the Quorum. A group of the defeated minority, objecting that Young was not the legal successor to Smith, withdrew to form other churches. Some followed James J. Strang to Wisconsin to form the sect known as Strangite; others joined various other splinter groups, but the largest body of "anti-Brighamites" believed that the leadership of the church belonged to direct descendants of Joseph Smith, and in 1847 these people, led by Joseph Smith, Jr., formed the Reorganized Church of Jesus Christ of Latter Day Saints, (a church unaffiliated with the Utah-based church).

Smith later (1860) became president of the group. But Young held his office with the vote of the majority, and he had the courage and the administrative ability to save the church from disruption and further division. He led the Saints when they were driven out of Nauvoo in February 1846 and began their epic march to what is now Utah, arriving in the Salt Lake Valley in July 1847; there they built their famous tabernacle at the heart of what was to become worldwide Mormonism, creating a self-existent community in the desert. In 1850 the Territory of Utah was formed; it became a state in 1896.

Based on *The Book of Mormon* and the Bible, which is accepted "as far as it is translated correctly," the faith of the Mormons is like that found in many conservative Protestant churches, plus the revelations of Joseph Smith. However, certain aspects of Latter Day Saints' theology depart from the traditional orthodoxy of Catholic and Protestant churches. They believe that the three persons comprising the Godhead are the Father, the Son, and the Holy Ghost; that the Father and the Son have bodies of flesh and bones as tangible as a human's, but that the Holy Ghost is a personage of Spirit; that persons will be punished for their own individual sins, not for Adam's transgression. All humankind may be saved through the atonement of Christ and by obedience to the laws and ordinances of the gospel; these laws and ordinances include faith in Christ, repentance, baptism by immersion for the remission of sins, the laying on of hands for the gift of the Holy Ghost, and the observance of the Lord's Supper each Sunday. They believe in the gift of tongues and interpretation of tongues, visions, prophecy, and healing, and that Christ will return to rule the earth from his capitals in Zion and Jerusalem following the restoration of the ten tribes of Israel. In addition, it is believed that the Latter Day

Saints should adhere to the official pronouncements of the living president (prophet) of the church.

Revelation is not to be regarded as being confined to either the Bible or *The Book of Mormon*; it continues today in the living apostles, prophets, pastors, teachers, and evangelists of the modern Mormon church. Baptism is necessary for salvation, and obedience to the priesthood is of first importance. Subjection to civil laws and rules is advocated, together with an insistence upon the right of the individual to worship according to the dictates of conscience.

Two Mormon practices, baptism for the dead and sealing in marriage for eternity, are exclusive with this church. Baptism and salvation for the dead are based upon the conviction that those who died without a chance to hear or accept the gospel cannot possibly be condemned by a just and merciful God. The gospel must be preached to them after death; authority for this is found in I Peter 4:6: "For this cause was the gospel preached also to them that are dead, that they might be judged according to men in the flesh, but live according to God in the spirit." Baptism is considered as essential to the dead as to the living, though the rites will not finally save them; there must be faith and repentance. The ceremony is performed with a living person standing proxy for the dead.

Marriage in Mormonism has two forms: marriage for time and marriage for eternity (or celestial marriage). Mormons who are married by only civil authority still remain in good standing in the church, but marriage for time and eternity in the church's temples is regarded as a prerequisite for the highest opportunity for salvation. In connection with this, it is said that Joseph Smith informed his associates in the 1840s that plural marriage was also sanctioned and commanded by God. Some plural marriages had been contracted secretly for some time before the practice was announced publicly by Brigham Young in 1852.

Following the Civil War, the federal government mounted an increasingly intense campaign against Mormon polygamy. In 1882, the Edmunds Act provided stringent penalties, and in 1887 the church was disincorporated and its properties confiscated. In 1890 the U.S. Supreme Court ruled that it was constitutional to deny all privileges of citizenship to members of the church. Also in 1890, the church president issued a manifesto that officially discontinued the contracting of new plural marriages. Some followers of Joseph Smith, Jr., deny that polygamy was ever sanctioned, but a few in other groups believe that it will never end. These contemporary polygamists are excommunicated from the Mormon church and are known as Fundamentalists.

Organization and government in the church differ in detail among the five Mormon denominations but agree on essentials. They are based upon the two priesthoods: the higher priesthood of Melchizedek, which holds power of presidency and authority over the offices of the church, and whose officers include apostles, patriarchs, high priests, seventies, and elders; and the lesser priesthood of Aaron, which guides the temporal affairs of the church through its bishops, priests, teachers, and deacons.

The presiding council of the church is the First Presidency, made up of three high priests—the president and two counselors. Its authority is final and universal in both spiritual and temporal affairs. The president of the church is "the mouthpiece of God"; through him come the laws of the church by direct revelation.

Next to the presidency stands the Council of the Twelve Apostles, chosen by revelation to supervise, under the direction of the First Presidency, the whole work of the church. The church is divided into stakes (geographical divisions) composed of a number of wards, corresponding to local churches or parishes. High priests, assisted by elders, are in charge of the stakes and wards. Members of the Melchizedek priesthood hold authority under the direction of the presidency to officiate in all ordinances of the gospel. Seventies work under the direction of the First Quorum of the Seventy (a presiding quorum of 70 people); they are organized into quorums of 70 each, with 7 presidents of equal rank presiding over each quorum. Seventies have a responsibility to proselytize. The duties of the apostles and the seventies carry them into all the stakes, wards, and missions throughout the entire church. The duties of the stake presidents, the ward bishops, the patriarchs, high priests, and elders are to supervise the work within the stakes and wards of the church. The Aaronic priesthood is governed by three presiding bishops, who also supervise the work done in the stakes and wards by members of the priesthood. In June of 1978, it was ruled that "all worthy male members of the church may be ordained to the priesthood without regard for race or color."

The church influences every phase of the life of every member; it supplies relief in illness or poverty and assists with education and employment when necessary, but does not educate or employ all members. Such a program has resulted in deep loyalty. Almost 27,000 young Mormons currently serve as full-time missionaries throughout the world without compensation; they give 18 months to the work of spreading the teaching of their church at home and abroad. Only about 60 persons in leadership positions in the church receive a salary. Their missionary experience strengthens them and their church and offers a model of church service.

Church of Christ (Temple Lot)

Claiming status as a remnant of the church founded by Joseph Smith in 1830, this church has 6,000 members in 32 local congregations. After the death of Smith in 1844, and following the western trek of the Mormons, a number of those who remained in the Midwest became convinced that the church leaders were advocating new teachings quite at variance with the original doctrines. By 1852 there were two protesting groups, one known as the New Organization; the other, centered in Crow Creek, Illinois, functioned under the original name, The Church of Christ. This latter group returned to Independence, Missouri, in the "appointed year" of 1867 and began purchasing "temple lots." The revelation concerning the "return" was given in 1864 through the presiding elder at the time, Granville Hedrick.

The temple lots (the subject of controversy and court action between the Church of Christ and the Reorganized Church of Jesus Christ of Latter Day Saints, finally resolved in favor of the Church of Christ) consist of land dedicated in 1831 by Joseph Smith and other Mormon leaders for the building of the Lord's Temple. The belief is that the Lord himself will designate the time of building and that while the people of the church cannot build until the appointed time, they nevertheless have a sacred obligation to "hold and keep this land free; when the time of building comes, it can be accomplished as the Lord sees fit."

The Church of Christ puts its faith in the pattern and thought of the church "as it existed at the time of Christ and His apostles." Hence the highest office in the church is that of apostle, and there are twelve apostles. They are charged with the missionary work and general supervision of the church. Temporal affairs are directly administered by the General Bishopric, under the direction of the general conference and the Council of Apostles; local churches administer their own affairs but must keep their teachings and practice in harmony with those of the denomination. Most of the membership is described as Gentile, with several members among the Maya Indians of Yucatan, Mexico.

The church accepts the King James Version of the Bible and *The Book of Mormon* as its standards. It holds that all latter-day revelation, including that of Joseph Smith, must be tested by these scriptures; it does not accept all that was given through Smith. Because changes were made in the early revelations, this church prefers *The Book of Commandments* to *The Doctrine and Covenants,* which includes these changes. For this reason the doctrines of plural marriage, baptism for the dead, celestial marriage, and plurality of gods are not accepted.

Church of Jesus Christ (Bickertonites)

The founders of this church were at one time members of a Mormon body led by Sidney Rigdon, in Pennsylvania. Rigdon and his followers refused to join the western march under Brigham Young, denouncing Young's teaching of polygamy, the plurality of gods, and baptism for the dead; in 1846 they purchased a farm (later lost at a sheriff's sale) near Greencastle. A small group did not go to Greencastle, but remained at West Elizabeth and, under William Bickerton, who had been one of Rigdon's elders, were formally organized in 1862 as The Church of Jesus Christ. The name "Bickertonite" is employed to distinguish this body from other Mormon groups; members prefer that it be known as "the Bickerton Organization." The current president is Dominic R. Thomas, elected in 1974.

Foot washing is practiced, and members salute one another with the holy kiss. Monogamy "except in case of death" is required, together with obedience to all state and civil laws. They have their own edition of the *Book of Mormon* (in English and Italian) and publish a monthly periodical, *The Gospel News*, along with other denominational material at the headquarters in Monongahela, Pennsylvania, where a general conference meets annually. Missionary work is conducted in Italy, Nigeria, Mexico, and among Native Americans of the United States and Canada. There are 2,500 members in the United States and more than 6,000 worldwide, now including Argentina and Ghana. There are 51 churches in North America.

Church of Jesus Christ of Latter-day Saints, The

The organization and doctrine of the Church of Jesus Christ of Latter-day Saints has been outlined in the preceding section. With headquarters in Salt Lake City, it has an American membership of 3.7 million, and 13,616 congregations in 89 countries and 16 territories, colonies, or possessions—a world membership of more than 5 million. The membership has increased by 65 percent in the last decade. A general conference is held twice a year at Salt Lake City. The church is supported by the tithes of the members, who are expected to give one-tenth of their income.

The missionary effort of this church is constant and vigorous. There are 180 missionary stations throughout the world. The death rate among Mormons is lower than that of any other group of people of the same size anywhere in the world; this is held by some to be the direct result of abstinence from liquor and tobacco. This church maintains storehouses for community food and clothing; members operate vegetable, seed, and wheat farms, orchards, a cotton plantation, dairies, sewing centers, fish canneries, soap processing plants, a vitamin pill factory, and several grain elevators. Most of these products are consumed at home, but thousands of relief packages are sent to Europe under a church-wide relief plan.

Education is of great importance to Latter-day Saints. The church's largest institutions are Brigham Young University, with an enrollment of 26,000, and Ricks College in Idaho, with 6,500. Some 320,500 secondary and post-secondary students are enrolled in seminary and institute classes which provide weekday religious instruction.

Membership is largest in Utah (1,089,000) and contiguous states—Idaho, 257,000, and Arizona, 148,000—but there are 438,000 Saints in California and 123,000 in the state of Washington.

Church of Jesus Christ of Latter Day Saints (Strangite)

This group claims that it is "the one and original" Church of Jesus Christ of Latter Day Saints and that its founder, James J. Strang, is the only legal successor to church leadership with written credentials from Joseph Smith. Strang translated portions of the golden plates; they, together with certain other revelations, are found in *The Book of the Law of the Lord.*

Strang also translated what is called *The Voree Record*—found under an oak tree near Voree, Wisconsin—telling in hieroglyphic-like characters of "an ancient people . . . who no longer exist." He was crowned "king" of this church in 1850 but was murdered in 1856 during a wave of anti-Mormonism in the Great Lakes region.

Organized at Burlington, Wisconsin, in 1844, the church denies the Virgin birth, holds that Adam fell by a law of natural consequences rather than by the breaking of a divine law and that the corruption thus caused can be removed only by the resurrection of Christ. The members deny the Trinity and the plurality of gods, celebrate Saturday as the sabbath day, and believe that baptism is essential for salvation. Due to "lack of prophetic leadership at the present time" they do not practice baptism of the dead.

Chief officer of the church is a high priest in the Melchizedek priesthood, chosen by the general church conference. Membership is given at about 300, in 6 churches, or branches.

Reorganized Church of Jesus Christ of Latter Day Saints

This church claims to be the continuation of the original church organized by Joseph Smith on April 6, 1830. It bases its claim on the rule of lineal succession found in *The Book of Doctrine and Covenants.* Court actions on two occasions—in Ohio in 1880 and in Missouri in 1894—are cited as naming it the legal continuation of the original church. The son of Joseph Smith, it is held, was designated by his father to succeed him.

The Reorganized Church rejected the claims of the Mormons led by Brigham Young because of their abandonment of this rule. Those holding to the "lineal succession" eventually reorganized, the first collective expression of this movement coming at a conference in Beloit, Wisconsin, in 1852. Joseph Smith, Jr., was chosen president in 1860 at Amboy, Illinois. His successors have all been descendants of the founder.

Although the doctrine of polygamy was endorsed by Young's group in 1852, the Reorganized Church held this doctrine to be contrary to the teachings of *The Book of Mormon* and *The Book of Doctrine and Covenants* of the original organization. It also differs on the doctrine of the Godhead, celestial marriage, and baptism of the dead. Basic beliefs include faith in the universality of God the Eternal Father, Jesus Christ as the only begotten Son of the Father, the Holy Spirit, the worth and dignity of others, repentance of sin, baptism by immersion, the efficacy of various sacramental ordinances, the resurrection of the dead, the open canon of Scriptures and the continuity of revelation, the doctrine of stewardship, and the principle of the accountability of all people to God.

The work of the church is supported by tithes and free-will offerings. This is regarded as a divine principle, and the tithe is calculated upon a tenth of each member's annual increase over needs and just wants.

The church has more than 217,000 members, located in 37 countries around the world and on islands in the Caribbean and South Pacific. It has four-year accredited colleges at Lamoni, Iowa (Graceland College), and at Kansas City, Missouri (Park College); a leadership and ministerial school (Temple) is located at Independence, Missouri.

Church doctrines, policies, and matters of legislation must have the approval and action of a delegate conference held biennially at the auditorium in Independence. General adminstration of the church is by a First Presidency of three high priests, a Quorum of Twelve Apostles who represent the presidency in the field, and a pastoral arm under the high priests and elders. The work of the bishops covers church properties, the stewardship of members, and church finances.

LIBERAL CATHOLIC CHURCH

This church originated in Great Britain in the Old Catholic Church movement which began in Holland. Tracing its orders to an apostolic succession that runs back to the Roman Catholic Church under the reign of Pope Urban VIII, and even to the twelve apostles, the Liberal Catholic Church aims at a combination of traditional Catholic forms of worship, but with the utmost freedom of individual conscience and thought. It claims to be neither Roman Catholic nor Protestant, but still *catholic* in the broadest sense of the word. The founding bishops were members of the Theosophical Society. International headquarters are in London; the present presiding bishop resides in Sydney, Australia, and the present Regionary (Bishop) of the United States lives in Ojai, California. Membership stands at just under 3,000.

The Nicene Creed is used in the services generally, but there is no requirement of submission to any creed, Scripture, or tradition; members seek not a common profession of belief, but a corporate worship in a common ritual. While there is no emphasis upon the precepts of the Theosophical Society, theosophia (divine wisdom) is strongly stressed. Paramount in the thinking is a central inspiration from faith in the living Christ, based on the promises of Matthew 18:20 and 28:20. These promises are regarded as "validating all Christian worship," but special channels of Christ's power are found in the seven sacraments of the church: baptism, confirmation, the Holy Eucharist, absolution, holy unction, holy matrimony, and holy orders.

Priests and bishops may or may not marry, and they exact no fee for the administration of the sacraments; many are employed in lay occupations. Divine healing is practiced through "the reviving power of the Holy Spirit, the grace of absolution, the sacred oil for the sick and the sacrament of holy unction," but not to the exclusion of physicians and medicines. Bishops are elected by a general episcopal synod, and a board of trustees meets annually.

LUTHERAN

Lutheran was a nickname fastened upon the followers of Martin Luther by their enemies in the days of the Protestant Reformation; today it stands for something far more comprehensive. "It is clear," said Abdel R. Wentz, "that 'Lutheran' is a very inadequate name to give to a movement that is not limited to a person or an era but is as ecumenical and abiding as Christianity itself." Luther's teachings of justification by faith and of the universal priesthood of believers might be called the cornerstone of Protestantism.

The story of Luther's rebellion against the Roman Catholic Church is well known. His position was, briefly, that the Roman Catholic Church and the papacy has no divine right in things spiritual; that the Scripture, not the priest or the church, has final authority over conscience. "Whatever is not against Scripture is for Scripture, and Scripture is for it," said Luther. People are forgiven and absolved of their sins, he believed, not by good works or by imposition of church rite—and especially not through the purchase of indulgences offered for sale by the Roman Catholic Church—but by their Holy Spirit-empowered action in turning from sin directly to God. Justification is attained through faith, not through ceremony; and faith is not subscription to the dictates of the church, but "the heart's utter trust" in Christ. "The just shall live by faith" was the beginning and the end of Luther's thought. He held that the individual conscience is responsible to God alone; he also held that the Bible is the clear, perfect, inspired, and authoritative Word of God and guide for humankind. God, conscience, and the Book—on these was Lutheranism founded.

In 1529 Luther wrote his Longer and Shorter catechisms. A year later a statement of faith known as the Augsburg Confession was authored by his scholarly associate Philip Melanchthon; 1537 brought the Smalcald Articles of Faith, written by Luther, Melanchthon, and other German Reformers. In 1577 the Formula of Concord was drawn up. These documents in explanation of Luther's ideology and theology form the doctrinal basis of Lutheranism.

The German Reformation resulted not in a united Protestantism, but in a Protestantism with two branches: Evangelical Lutheranism with Luther and Melanchthon as leaders; and the Reformed Church, led by John Calvin, Ulrich Zwingli, and John Knox. Evangelical Lutheranism spread from its birthplace to Poland, Russia, Lithuania, Czechoslovakia, Austria, Hungary, Yugoslavia, France, and Holland; it became in time the state church of Denmark, Norway, Sweden, Finland, Iceland, Estonia, and Latvia. It was mainly from Germany and Scandinavia that Lutheranism came to the United States.

A Lutheran Christmas service was held at Hudson's Bay in 1619; the first European Lutherans to remain permanently in this country arrived at Manhattan Island from Holland in 1623. A congregation worshiped in

New Amsterdam in 1649, but Lutherans did not enjoy full freedom in their worship until the English assumed control of "New York" in 1664. The first independent colony of Lutherans, the colony of New Sweden, was established at Fort Christiana along the Delaware in 1638.

The New York Lutherans were largely German. Exiles from Salzburg also settled in Georgia, where in 1736 they built the first orphanage in America, and Lutherans from Württemberg settled in South Carolina. The great influx, however, went to Pennsylvania, where by the middle of the eighteenth century there were 30,000 Lutherans, of whom four-fifths were German, the remainder Swedish. From Philadelphia they swept into New Jersey, Maryland, Virginia, and North Carolina.

The first churches were small, often without pastors, and because only a minority of the immigrants joined, the churches were poor. The situation was relieved with the coming of Henry Melchoir Muhlenberg from the University of Halle, who brought about the first real merging of American Lutherans. In 1748 he organized pastors and congregations in Pennsylvania, New Jersey, New York, and Maryland into what came to be called the Ministerium of Pennsylvania; it was the first of many Lutheran synods in America. Others followed slowly: New York in 1786, North Carolina in 1803, Maryland in 1820, and Ohio in 1836. Each synod adjusted to its peculiar conditions of language, national background, previous ecclesiastical relationship with Lutheran authorities abroad, and geographic location. The need for even further organization was evident from the ever-increasing emigration of Lutherans from Europe and resulted in the formation of the General Synod in 1820; with that the last real bonds with European Lutheranism began to break, and American Lutheranism was increasingly on its own.

The General Synod was obliged to extend its efforts farther and farther west as German, Swedish, Norwegian, Danish, Icelandic, and Finnish Lutherans came pouring into the new country. The Missouri Synod was formed in 1847. From 1850 until 1860, 1,000,000 Germans arrived, of whom the majority were Lutheran; the German Iowa Synod was organized in 1854; and in the same year, the Norwegian Lutheran Church was established. The Augustana Synod was created in 1860 to care for the Swedish pioneers in the new West. By 1870, Lutherans were the fourth largest Protestant group in the country, with approximately 400,000 members.

The Civil War brought the first serious break in Lutheran ranks with the organization of the United Synod of the South in 1863; three years later a number of other synods led by the Ministerium of Pennsylvania withdrew from the General Synod to form the General Council. To increase the complexity, Lutheran immigrants continued to arrive in larger and larger numbers; from 1870 until 1910, approximately 1,750,000 came from Sweden, Norway, and Denmark; in those years Lutheran church membership leaped from less than 500,000 to nearly 2,250,000. New Lutheran churches, colleges, seminaries, and publications were established from coast to coast.

Since 1910 there has been an almost constant effort toward unification of Lutheran churches and agencies. Three large Norwegian bodies united in 1917 in the Norwegian Lutheran Church of America; some of the Midwest German synods merged in the Joint Synod of Wisconsin in 1918; the synods of Iowa, Ohio, and Buffalo merged in the American Lutheran Church in 1930. The General Synod, the General Council, and the United Synod of the South merged into the United Lutheran Church in 1918, and no less than eight Lutheran churches were included in mergers from 1960 through 1962. In addition to these, the Lutheran Council in the U.S.A. (consisting of the American Lutheran Church, the Lutheran Church in America, the Lutheran Church–Missouri Synod, and the Synod of Evangelical Lutheran Churches) operates through five divisions (Educational Services, Mission and Welfare Services, Public Relations, Service to Military Personnel, and Theological Studies). Perhaps the most cooperative effort in the history of American Lutheranism is found in Lutheran World Action, through which more than $300,000,000 in cash and food (including U.S. government-donated commodities) has been distributed throughout the world.

In spite of their organizational division, there is real unity among Lutherans, a unity based more upon faith than organization. All Lutheran churches represent a single type of Protestant Christianity. Their belief is built upon Luther's principle of justification by faith alone—faith in Jesus Christ; it centers in the gospel for fallen humanity. The Bible is the inspired Word of God and the infallible rule and standard of faith and practice. Lutherans confess their faith through the three general creeds of Christendom, the Apostles', the Nicene, and the Athanasian, which they believe to be in accordance with the Scriptures. They also believe that the unaltered Augsburg Confession is a correct exposition of the faith and doctrine of evangelical Lutheranism. The Apology of the Augsburg Confession, the two catechisms of Luther, the Smalcald Articles, and the Formula of Concord are held to be faithful interpretations of Lutheranism and of the Bible.

The two sacraments, baptism and the Lord's Supper, are not merely signs or memorials, but channels through which God bestows his forgiving and empowering grace upon humankind. The body and blood of Christ are believed to be present "in, with, and under" the bread and wine of the Lord's Supper and are received sacramentally and supernaturally. Consubstantiation, transubstantiation, and impanation are rejected. Infants are baptized, and baptized persons are believed to receive the gift of regeneration from the Holy Ghost.

The congregation is usually administered between its annual meetings by a church council consisting of the pastor and a number of elected lay officers called either elders, deacons, or trustees. There is a growing tendency to call all lay officials deacons. Pastors are elected and called by the voting members of the congregation, but a congregation itself may never depose a pastor from the ministry. As a rule, ministers are ordained at the annual meetings of the synods; almost all are trained in college and seminary.

Congregations are united in synods composed of pastors and lay representatives elected by the congregations and have only such authority as is granted by the synod constitution. In some instances there are territorial districts or conferences instead of synods, operating in the same manner and under the same restrictions; some of these may legislate, while others are for advisory or consultative purposes only.

Synods (conferences, or districts) are united in a general body that may be national, or even international, and is called variously church, synod, or conference. Some of these general bodies are legislative in nature, some consultative; they supervise the work in worship, education, publication, charity, and mission. Congregations have business meetings at least annually; synods, districts, and conferences hold yearly conventions; the general bodies meet annually or biennially.

Worship is liturgical, centering on the altar. "No sect in Western Christendom outside the Church of Rome," said the late Lutheran Archbishop Nathan Söderblom of Sweden, "has accentuated in its doctrine the Real Presence and the mysterious communion of the sacrament as has our Evangelic Lutheran sect, although our faith repudiates any quasi-rational magical explanation of the virtue of the sacrament."

Non-Lutherans are often critical of the divisions among Lutherans, but actually they are not as divided as they may seem. At one time there were 150 Lutheran bodies in this country; consolidation, unification, and federation have now reduced the number to 12. Six of the bodies in the United States account for about 95 percent of all Lutherans in North America. With the old barriers of speech and nationality disappearing, the tendency toward union becomes continually stronger.

The American Lutheran Church is presently in the process of merging with the Lutheran Church in America and the Association of Evangelical Lutheran Churches. It is anticipated that the new Lutheran body will be formed on or about January 1, 1988; it will comprise approximately 5.5 million baptized members and 11,000 congregations.

On the international front, united efforts are noticeable also; groups of lay and ministerial delegates from major Lutheran churches in 22 countries formed a Lutheran World Federation in 1947 for the purpose of relief and rehabilitation on a global scale among Lutherans.

Historically, Lutherans have shown a tendency to remain apart from the rest of Protestantism. In the United States they are identified with churches founded by immigrant groups deeply conscious of their national and linguistic origins—conservative, confessional, nonrevivalistic groups, suspicious of anything that might tend to modify their Old World faith and traditions. These traits seem to be vanishing as the older membership passes and an English-speaking generation takes over. The mother tongues are still used occasionally, but English is predominant. The large Lutheran Church in America is a constituent member of the

National Council of the Churches. Four bodies—the United Lutheran Church, The American Lutheran Church, the Augustana Evangelical Lutheran Church, and the American Evangelical Lutheran Church—participated in the organization of the World Council of Churches; a fifth, the Evangelical Lutheran Church, affiliated with the Council in 1957. Lutheran groups belonging to interdenominational organizations have always insisted upon two principles: the evangelical principle that the churches in the association should be those confessing the deity and saviorhood of Jesus Christ; and the representative principle that the governing and operating units of the organizations should be made up of officially chosen representatives of the churches.

American Lutheran Church, The

At a constituting convention held April 22–24, 1960, in Minneapolis, three major Lutheran churches were formally merged into the body now known as The American Lutheran Church. The three were the American Lutheran Church, of German background, which originated during the formation of the Ohio Synod in 1818; the Evangelical Lutheran Church, of Norwegian heritage, at the time of the merger the third largest Lutheran church in America; and the United Evangelical Lutheran Church, founded in 1896 by Danish immigrants. A fourth body, the Lutheran Free Church, with a Norwegian background, joined those three on February 1, 1963, giving the new American Lutheran Church an inclusive membership of 2,499,373 in 5,239 churches. The Evangelical Church of Canada was founded by this group in 1907. Present baptized membership stands at 2,346,710 in 4,897 congregations. It is expected that in 1988, the American Lutheran, the Lutheran Church in America, and the Association of Evangelical Lutheran Churches will merge into one body, with a combined baptized membership of 5.5 million.

The 1960 merger crossed ethnic lines, and the problems involved were complex in polity and doctrine, but were successfully resolved. In government, the highest constitutional authority is vested in a general convention that meets every 2 years and has approximately 1,000 delegates (500 lay, 500 clergy), elected from the 19 districts into which the church is geographically divided. There are three national officers—a general president, vice-president, and secretary. A church council composed of the general officers and a lay and a clergy representative from each district, together with the district presidents, 2 representatives from the board of trustees, and 2 youths elected by the Luther League to serve in an advisory capacity, meets as the interim body between general conventions and makes recommendations on all matters directed to it by the districts, boards, and standing committees of the church.

Five divisions are maintained as churchwide agencies responsible for mission in behalf of, or directly in service to member congregations. The Division for Life and Mission in the Congregation develops resources for and provides services to the congregations; the Division for Service and Mission in America implements the mission of the church within the

United States; the Division for World Mission and Inter-Church Cooperation is responsible for the mission of the church abroad. These 3 divisions are directed by 22-member boards—19 members elected by the districts, 3 by the church council. The other two divisions, the Division for Theological Education and Ministry, and the Division for College and University Services, are each directed by a board of 9 members elected by the general convention.

There are three service boards established to provide specific services: the Board of Trustees is responsible for the general management of business affairs, financial controls, and property transactions; the Board of Pensions provides for retirement income and major medical/dental coverage for the clergy and eligible laity; the Board of Publication is a nonbudgetary production and distribution unit. Each of these service boards is composed of 9 members elected by the general convention.

There are four administrative offices are maintained as agencies responsible to the general president. The Office of Communication and Mission Support is to interpret the mission of the church and provide support for that mission. The Office of Church in Society is organized to keep the church informed regarding the effects of changes in society. The Office of Support to Ministries supports the various ministries of the church and provides staff services for the Council of Presidents. The Office of the ALC Foundation serves to engender support for the mission of the church through deferred and other special gifts. The offices have standing committees to which they relate. District and national committees on appeals and adjudication exercise judicial authority for the church.

The confession of faith of this church accepts the Bible as divinely inspired, revealed, and inerrant; the three ancient ecumenical creeds (Apostolic, Nicene, and Athanasian); the unaltered Augsburg Confession; Luther's Large and Small catechisms; the Book of Concord of 1580; the Apology; the Smalcald Articles; and the Formula of Concord.

In the field of education there are 4 theological seminaries, 11 senior colleges, a junior college, and an academy. In the area of social services there are 143 homes for the aged, 2 alcohol treatment centers, 8 hospitals, and 34 multiservice agencies. Missionaries are supported in 19 countries overseas and in the United States.

Apostolic Lutheran Church of America

Sometimes called the Church of Laestadius, for Lars Levi Laestadius, a minister of the state church of Sweden, this church originated with Finnish emigrants in and around Calumet, Michigan, in the middle years of the nineteenth century. They worshiped at first in the Lutheran Church of Calumet under a Norwegian minister; however, differences between the two national groups led to the forming, in 1872, of a separate Finnish congregation led by Solomon Korteniemi and called the Solomon Korteniemi Lutheran Society. The church was first incorporated in Michigan in 1879 under the name Finnish Apostolic Lutheran Church of

America; that body was actually a merger of independent Apostolic Lutheran congregations into a national body. Spreading over Michigan, Minnesota, the Dakotas, Massachusetts, Oregon, Washington, and California, the new church was divided into two districts—Eastern and Western—with foreign missions in Nigeria, Liberia, and Guatamala.

A scriptural Christian experience is required for voting membership in spiritual matters; supporting members may vote on temporal matters only. The church accepts the three ecumenical creeds and puts strong emphasis upon the confession of sins, absolution, and regeneration. Confession may be made to another Christian, but if someone has fallen into sins unknown to others, private confession is not sufficient; the person "should confess them publicly before the congregation and receive absolution."

The 64 local congregations of this church are quite free to govern themselves; at the annual church convention where every congregation has a vote, 3 members are elected to a 9-member executive board for 3-year terms; the board elects a president, vice-president, secretary, and treasurer. Three members are also elected to the Eastern and Western mission boards and to the Elder's Home Board. As of 1974, there were 9,384 members.

Church of the Lutheran Brethren of America

This is an independent church body, with churches located throughout the Midwest, on both the East and the West Coast, and in two provinces of Canada. Organized in Milwaukee in 1900, it differs from other Lutheran churches in accepting as members only those who profess a personal experience of salvation, and in stressing nonliturgical worship and lay participation. They have two years of confirmation instruction, but no vow is used at the confirmation service; they instruct children and wait until there is an individual experience and conversion before receiving them as communicant members. Communion is received in the pew; there are no altars in church buildings. Free prayer and personal testimony are stressed.

The church as a body is the supreme administrative unit, with a president, two vice-presidents, secretary, and treasurer. World missions are supervised by a board of nine members, and home missions by a board of nine. With a total membership of 11,160 in 116 congregations, the church conducts foreign missionary work in Africa, Japan, and Taiwan. There are 41 adult missionaries abroad. On an annual budget of $1,273,655 (high among Lutherans in proportion to the membership), the church supports a 3-year high school, a 2-year Bible course, and a 3-year seminary course—all operated by the synod from its headquarters at Fergus Falls, Minnesota.

Church of the Lutheran Confession

This confessional Lutheran church is made up of clergy and lay people who, in 1961, withdrew from several synods of the Synodical Conference of North America as the result of a long debate over conservative and liberal theology. The Church of the Lutheran Confession holds firmly to the scriptural doctrine of verbal inspiration and inerrancy of the Bible; they hold without any reservation whatever to all the historic Confessions of the Lutheran Church and faith. Membership is 8,986 in 74 churches, concentrated in South Dakota, Minnesota, and Wisconsin.

Evangelical Lutheran Synod (Formerly Norwegian Synod)

This synod was formed in 1918 by a minority group that declined to join the other Norwegian groups when they united in the Norwegian Lutheran Church (the former Evangelical Lutheran Church) in 1917. The name was changed as above in 1958.

The jurisdiction of the synod is entirely advisory; all synod resolutions are accepted or rejected by the local congregations. The officers and boards of the synod, however, direct work of common interest insofar as they do not interfere with congregational rights or prerogatives.

For some years the synod used the facilities of the colleges and seminaries of the Missouri and Wisconsin synods, within the framework of the Synodical Conference; in 1963 the Evangelical Lutheran Synod withdrew from the conference because of doctrinal differences with the Missouri Synod. It has maintained Bethany Lutheran College at Mankato, Minnesota, since 1927, and Bethany Lutheran Theological Seminary since 1946. It works overseas in fellowship with the Wisconsin and other smaller synods; there are 12 home mission stations in the United States and foreign mission work in Peru, one preparatory school, and 20,025 members in 110 churches.

Free Lutheran Congregations, The Association of

Established in 1962, this is a conservative and quite independent church in the Lutheran family. Doctrinally, it stresses the inerrancy and supreme authority of the Bible and the conviction that the congregation is actually the final and correct form of the kingdom of God on earth; it admits no authority over itself except that of the Word and Spirit of God. They believe that the spiritual union, fellowship, and cooperation of these believers transcends all synodical, racial, and national boundaries; a widespread evangelistic program calls for personal experience with and devotion to Christ, in addition to a "wholesome Lutheran pietism" in the religious community. They report 16,759 members in 145 churches, principally in Minnesota and North Dakota.

Lutheran Church in America

With over 3,000,000 members, this is the largest Lutheran church in the United States; it represents a consolidation of four Lutheran bodies (the United Lutheran Church in America, the Augustana Evangelical

Lutheran Church, the American Evangelical Lutheran Church, and the Finnish Evangelical Lutheran Church) which came about on June 28, 1962.

The United Lutheran Church was the youngest of the 4 uniting bodies, having been formed in 1918 in the uniting of 45 synods previously found in the General Synod, the General Council, and the United Synod of the South. Some 13 of those synods later withdrew or formed along new lines, but the United Church brought a total of almost 2,500,000 members in 4,600 congregations into the 1962 merger.

The Augustana Evangelical Lutheran Church originated in scattered Swedish families and congregations in Iowa and Illinois in the mid-1800s; the Augustana Synod was formed in 1860, with 5,000 communicants and 49 congregations, of which 36 were Swedish and 13 Norwegian. The name *Augustana* affirmed the group's loyalty to the doctrine of the Augsburg (*Augustana*, in Latin) Confession. Ten years later, the Norwegians withdrew to form a church of their own; at the time of the 1962 merger the Augustana body had more than half a million communicants in 1,200 congregations.

The Finnish Evangelical Lutheran Church (better known as the Suomi Synod) was organized at Calumet, Michigan, in 1890; it was strictly a confessional church, using the three ecumenical creeds and the unaltered Augsburg Confession. Until quite recently the Finnish language was employed in the services of this church, which had 36,000 members and 153 congregations in 1962.

The American Evangelical Lutheran Church was the smallest of the uniting bodies, with 25,000 members in 79 congregations. It was of Danish origin, founded under the direction of ministers sent from Denmark in 1872 and originally named Kirkelig Missionsforening. It was a church deeply concerned with the place and meaning of the Bible in Lutheran theology; yet it had a strong tradition of ecumenical interest and was represented in the National Lutheran Council, the National Council of Churches, and the World Council of Churches.

To combine these four churches into one body necessitated a new confession of faith for the governing documents—one that would preserve the historic creeds and confessions of Lutheranism, yet establish a new broad base of emphasis upon full acceptance of Christ and the Scriptures. That statement of faith is found in Article Two of the constitution of the Lutheran Church in America:

> This church holds that the Gospel is the revelation of God's sovereign will and saving grace in Jesus Christ . . . acknowledges the Holy Scriptures as the norm for the faith and life of the church . . . accepts the Apostles', the Nicene, and the Athanasian creeds as true declarations of the faith of the church . . . accepts the Unaltered Augsburg Confession and Luther's Small Catechism as true witnesses to the Gospel, and acknowledges as one with it in faith and doctrine all churches that likewise accept the teachings of these symbols. . . . [It] accepts the other symbolical books of the evangelical Lutheran church, the Apology of the Augsburg Confession, the Smalcald Articles, Luther's Larger Catechism, and the Formula of

Concord as further valid interpretations of the confession of the church. . . . [It] affirms that the Gospel transmitted by the Holy Scriptures . . . is the true treasure of the church, the substance of its proclamation, and the basis of its unity and continuity.

In administration, the chief officer is a bishop elected for 4 years by a biennial convention; the bishop presides over the convention and over an executive council of 33 members (3 officers, 15 ministers, and 15 lay people) which supervises the work of the following churchwide agencies: Division for Mission in North America, Division for Parish Services, Division for Professional Leadership, Division for World Mission and Ecumenism, Office for Administration and Finance, and Office for Communication. A full-time bishop serves each of the 33 synods which coordinate and direct the work of local congregations. Each minister, whether active or retired, is a member of the annual meetings of the synods, and each congregation is represented by one or more lay delegates.

The LCA is active in missions in 30 foreign countries. Nearly 200 institutions (hospitals, homes for the aged and children, nurseries, etc.) are supported by the church; there are 28 colleges and seminaries.

The Lutheran Church in America is presently in the process of merging with the American Lutheran Church and the Association of Evangelical Lutheran Churches. It is anticipated that the new Lutheran body will be formed on or about January 1, 1988; it will comprise approximately 5.5 million baptized members and 11,000 congregations.

Lutheran Church—Missouri Synod, The

With 2.7 million members and 6,100 churches, this is the second largest Lutheran church in the United States. *Missouri* is included in the name because the denomination was founded in that state by German emigrants in 1847. From the beginning, members have been devoted to the maintenance of confessional Lutheranism, coupled with a strong sense of mission outreach.

Christian education for members of all ages has always been stressed. The synod operates 16 colleges and seminaries in North America, with an enrollment of more than 8,000. Its elementary and secondary system of more than 1,500 schools is the largest of any Protestant denomination in the United States. Mission work is conducted in 30 foreign countries, while more than 100 new North American ministries have been begun each year during the 1980s, toward a goal of 1,000 for the decade.

The synod has long been considered a leader in the field of communications—operating the world's oldest religious radio station, KFUO in Saint Louis; providing the 50-year-old "Lutheran Hour," heard in more than 100 countries; and producing "This Is the Life," after 30 years the longest running dramatic series in the history of television.

A doctrinal controversy in the 1960s concerning the authority and interpretation of Scripture resulted in the departure of about 100,000 members from the church body. Little evidence of that controversy remains in the 1980s. Church observers and historians maintain that it was the first time a major denomination turned back a liberal trend and retained its founding doctrine.

Because of differences in doctrine and practice, the Missouri Synod is not a part of the merger planned by three other Lutheran denominations in America, to take place in the late 1980s. However, it continues to cooperate with those churches in a variety of ministries, particularly in areas of social work such as the resettlement of refugees and world hunger relief.

The church's headquarters are located in the International Center, a new building in suburban Saint Louis. Directors for the church body are set by a triennial convention of pastors and lay people representing the congregations.

Protestant Conference (Lutheran)

A protest against the alleged "high-handed" tactics of church officials, and against the inroads of legalism into the life of the Wisconsin Evangelical Lutheran Synod led to the suspension of 47 pastors and teachers in 1927, and to the formation of this conference. Its purpose, as it has developed in the years since its formation, is to "break down within our Lutheran Church, and wherever else it may flourish, the spirit of self-righteousness and self-sufficiency through a re-emphasis upon the Gospel of forgiveness of sins . . . coupled with the warning of the hardening of hearts and of judgment upon those who reject this message and its implications."

A general conference meets three times a year, and a publication, *Faith-Life*, is issued in LaCrosse, Wisconsin. Membership stands at 1,605 for the 7 churches and several "home" congregations.

Wisconsin Evangelical Lutheran Synod

Organized in 1850 in Milwaukee as the German Evangelical Lutheran Synod of Wisconsin, this church merged with two other synods—Minnesota and Michigan—in 1917 to become the Evangelical Lutheran Joint Synod of Wisconsin and Other States. In 1959 the name was changed to Wisconsin Evangelical Lutheran Synod. This synod subscribes to an orthodox confessional Lutheranism committed without reservation to the inspired, infallible Holy Scriptures. It is opposed to union or cooperation with other church bodies unless there is full agreement in doctrine and practice.

Divided into 12 districts, it maintains its national headquarters in Milwaukee. There is a baptized membership of 413,503 in 1,159 congregations, in all 50 states. Sister mission churches are supported in Zambia, Malawi, Cameroon, Mexico, Puerto Rico, Colombia, Japan, Taiwan, Hong Kong, Indonesia, India, and among Native Americans in Arizona.

For the education of its pastors and Christian day-school teachers, the synod maintains 2 colleges, 3 academies, and a theological seminary. Congregations support 19 Lutheran high schools with an enrollment of 4,414, and 372 Christian day schools with 30,969 students. Associations of congregations operate 7 homes for the aged and a social service agency.

MENNONITE

The first Mennonite congregation of historical record was organized at Zurich, Switzerland, in 1525; it consisted of Swiss Brethren, or *Täufer*, who disagreed with Ulrich Zwingli in his readiness to consent to a union of church and state. They also denied the scriptural validity of infant baptism and hence were labeled Anabaptists, or Re-baptizers. Anabaptist congregations were organized in Holland by Obbe Philips as early as 1534; Obbe baptized Menno Simons (*ca.* 1496–1561) in 1536.

Menno, a converted Roman Catholic priest, organized so many Anabaptist congregations that his name became identified with the movement. Many of his Flemish adherents—Mennonites—crossed the channel at the invitation of Henry VIII. But in England, as well as in Germany, Holland, and Switzerland, they met opposition largely because of their determined distrust of any union of church and state. An impressive martyr role was created; it might have been much greater had it not been for the sudden haven offered in the American colony of William Penn. Thirteen families settled in Germantown near Philadelphia in 1683. Eventually a Mennonite congregation was established there, although many of the members had left the Mennonite fold and united with the Quakers before they left Crefeld, Germany. Mennonite immigrants from Germany and Switzerland spread over Pennsylvania, Ohio, Virginia, Indiana, Illinois, and into the far West and Canada; these were later joined by others from Russia, Prussia, and Poland. Thanks to their historic insistence upon nonresistance, their colonial settlements were comparatively peaceful and prosperous.

The Mennonite belief is based upon a confession of faith signed at Dordrecht, Holland, in 1632. In 18 articles, the following doctrines were laid down: faith in God as creator; humanity's fall and restoration at the coming of Christ; Christ as the Son of God, redeeming humankind on the cross; obedience to Christ's law in the gospel; the necessity of repentance and conversion for salvation; baptism as a public testimony of faith; the Lord's Supper as an expression of common union and fellowship; matrimony only among those "spiritually kindred"; obedience to and respect for civil government except in the use of armed force; exclusion from the church and social ostracism of those who sin willfully; future reward for the faithful and punishment for the wicked.

The Lord's Supper is served twice a year in almost all Mennonite congregations. In most churches baptism is by pouring, and most observe the foot washing ordinance in connection with the Supper, after which they salute one another with the "kiss of peace." The sexes are separated in the last two ceremonies. All Mennonites baptize only on confession of faith, refuse to take oaths before magistrates, oppose secret societies, and strictly follow the teachings of the New Testament. They have a strong intrachurch program of mutual aid and a worldwide relief and eleemosynary service through an all-Mennonite relief organization, the Mennonite Central Committee.

The local congregation is more or less autonomous and authoritative, although in some instances appeals are taken to district or state conferences. The officers of the church are bishops (often called elders), ministers, and deacons (almoners). Many ministers are self-supporting, working in secular employment when not occupied with the work of the church. There are other appointed officers for Sunday school, young people's work, and so forth.

The Amish movement within the ranks of the Mennonites takes its name from Jacob Amman, a Swiss (Bernese) Mennonite bishop of the late seventeenth century who insisted upon strict adherence to the confession of faith, especially in the matter of shunning excommunicated members. This literalism brought about a separation in Switzerland in 1693; about 200 years later the divided bodies, with the exception of three Amish groups, were reunited.

Early Amish immigrants to the United States concentrated in Pennsylvania and moved from there into Ohio, Indiana, Illinois, Nebraska, and other western states; some went into Canada. They have today a common literature. Many of the Amish, distinguished by their severely plain clothing, are found in the Conservative Amish Mennonite Church and the larger Old Order Amish Mennonite Church. They are still the literalists of the movement, clinging tenaciously to the "Pennsylvania Dutch" language and the seventeenth-century culture of their Swiss-German forebears. They oppose automobiles, telephones, and higher education but are recognized as extremely efficient farmers.

Beachy Amish Mennonite Churches

These churches are made up mostly of Amish Mennonites who separated from the more conservative Old Order Amish over a period of years, beginning in 1927 in Somerset County, Pennsylvania. They were led by Bishop Moses M. Beachy, who died in 1946. Today there are 84 congregations and 5,656 members.

They resemble to some degree the Old Order Amish in garb and general attitude, but their discipline is milder and more relaxed. These Mennonites worship in church buildings, have Sunday schools, and are active in supporting missionary work. They sponsor a monthly publication, *Calvary Messenger*, and an annual twelve-week Calvary Bible School.

Church of God in Christ, Mennonite

This church grew out of the preaching and labors of John Holdeman, a member of the Mennonite church in Ohio, who became convinced that his church was apostate and in error in many of its teachings and practices. He preached ardently on the necessity of the new birth, Holy Ghost baptism, more adequate training of children in the fundamentals, disciplining of unfaithful members, avoidance of apostates, and the condemnation of worldly minded churches. He separated, finally, from the Mennonite church and in 1859 began holding meetings with a small group of followers who then formally organized into the Church of God in Christ, Mennonite.

The church holds that the same confession of faith must be believed and practiced by all churches, "from the time of the apostles to the end of the world," and that the Bible, as the inspired, infallible Word of God, must govern all doctrine and teaching. It accepts the Eighteen Articles of Faith drawn up at Dordrecht, Holland, in 1632.

The highest decision-making authority is the General Conference, a convention of ministers, deacons, and delegates that convenes every five years. The church practices the mode form of baptism and teaches nonconformity to the world in dress, bodily adornment, and worldly sports and amusements.

Missions are operated in the United States, Canada, Mexico, Haiti, India, and Nigeria; there are 11,866 members in 95 congregations, from the United States to Brazil. Kansas is the state of heaviest concentration.

Conservative Mennonite Conference

The Conservative Mennonite Conference was first organized in 1910 when church leaders with mutual concerns from Hartville, Ohio; Belleville, Pennsylvania; and Huron County, Michigan, met near Pigeon, Michigan. The organization was known as the Conservative Amish Mennonite Church until the present name was adopted in 1954. The Conference subscribes to the 1963 Mennonite confession of faith, which affirms the full inspiration of the Scriptures, believers' baptism, and nonviolence.

Membership in the United States numbered 7,882 in 1983, with 92 congregations in 20 states. The central church office buildings, which also house the Rosedale Mennonite Missions and Rosedale Bible Institute, are located in Rosedale, Ohio. Churches have been planted in the United States, Central America, Germany, and Turkey, and college-level courses are offered in various Christian studies.

Evangelical Mennonite Brethren Conference

This group, established by Russian Mennonite immigrants in 1896, now has 4,300 members in 35 churches. It concentrates on a strong missionary program, with some 120 missionaries at work overseas. In belief, it adheres to the infallibility of the Scriptures and dispensational interpretation.

Evangelical Mennonite Church

Formerly the Defenseless Mennonite Church, this body was founded about 1865 under the leadership of Henry Egly, to emphasize teachings on regeneration, separation, nonconformity to the world, and nonresistance. Its program today is largely one of missions and church-extension evangelism. There is a children's home in Flanagan, Illinois; 3,857 members are in 24 churches.

General Conference Mennonite Church

A group of Mennonite congregations, eager to improve upon and enlarge foreign missionary efforts, offer better training for prospective leaders, and establish a church periodical, organized at West Point, Iowa, in 1860 to form this church. The desire to unite all Mennonite churches and conferences was, and still is, strong among its members. They accept established Mennonite doctrine, but place strong emphasis upon the autonomy of the local congregation, and in their insistence upon freedom from the traditional Mennonite regulations on attire for men and women, they are marked as "liberal in conduct."

Six district conferences meet annually, and a general conference meets triennially for fellowship and the transaction of official business. Elected commissions—overseas mission, home ministries, education, communication, administration—and a General Board direct the work of the general conference. The conference maintains 2 liberal arts colleges, a Bible college, a junior college, 2 Bible institutes, a theological seminary, several homes for children and the aged, hospitals, and nurses' training schools. There are 37,019 members in 217 churches in the United States, 25,417 members in 122 churches in Canada, and additional churches in Latin America. Mission work is carried on in 15 overseas countries, where the membership totals about 50,000.

Hutterian Brethren

This church was founded by Jacob Hutter, a sixteenth-century Tyrolean Anabaptist who advocated communal ownership of property. He was burned as a heretic in Austria in 1536. Many Hutterites left Russia for Canada and the United States about 1874 and have moved back and forth across that border ever since. Today most are of German ancestry and use the German tongue in their homes and churches. Aside from the idea of common property, they are quite similar to the Old Order Amish; they seek to express their Bible-centered faith in brotherly love and aim at the recovery of the New Testament spirit and fellowship. They feel that this requires nonconformity to the world and, accordingly, practice nonresistance, refuse to participate in local politics, dress differently, make no contribution to community projects, and maintain their own schools, in which the Bible is paramount. Their exclusiveness has made them unwelcome in certain sections of the country, and their status is always somewhat uncertain. There are 3,684 members in 35 colonies in Minnesota, Montana, Washington, and the Dakotas.

Mennonite Brethren Church of North America

Dutch and German in background, this church was organized in 1860 upon the withdrawal of a small group from the Mennonite church in the Ukraine. Pietistic in orientation, it adopted a Baptistic polity, seeking closer attention to prayer and Bible study. Small bodies reached Kansas in 1876 and spread to the Pacific coast and into Canada.

A general conference meets triennially as the chief administrative body, gathering delegates from two areas (Canada and the United States). Each area has a number of districts. The area conferences supervise work in home missions, education, and publications. Foreign missions (a department of the general conference) are found in Africa, Asia, Europe, South America, and Mexico. A radio ministry begun in 1947 broadcasts worldwide in English, German, and Russian. A French-language Bible Institute was established in Quebec in 1976.

The Krimmer Mennonite Brethren merged with this church in 1960, bringing the total membership to 38,000 in 260 churches.

Mennonite Church

This is the largest single group of Mennonites in the United States, with 101,501 members in 1,179 churches; it is the church founded by German immigrants in Germantown, Pennsylvania, in 1683. The Dordrecht Confession was adopted at a conference of the Pennsylvania Mennonite ministers in 1725, and this remained the official statement of faith until the Fundamentals of the Christian Faith, consisting of 18 articles, was adopted in 1921. In 1963 the general conference adopted a revised version, which seeks, without attempting to make the body into a creedal church, to set forth the major doctrines of Scripture as understood in the Anabaptist-Mennonite tradition. The attempt was made to write simply and clearly, and to be more biblical than philosophical or even theological. This 1963 confession of faith stresses faith in Christ, the saved status of children (without any ceremony), the importance of proclaiming God's Word and "making disciples," the baptism of believers, the ethic of absolute love and nonresistance to injustice and maltreatment, the church as a nonhierarchical brotherhood, and the practice of church discipline.

The General Assembly meets every two years; ordained persons, and others present who are not elected delegates from the district or state conferences, may debate but not vote; the elected delegates from the conferences, in cooperation with their respective congregations, set the disciplinary standards for their constituency. Bishops, ministers, and deacons serve as delegates; most districts also have lay delegates.

Churchwide program boards are in charge of mission, congregational ministries, education, publishing, and mutual aid work; all are under the supervision of the church's general board. Home missions stress evangelism; overseas missions are found in Asia, Africa, Europe, and Central and South America. There are 3 colleges, 2 seminaries, and numerous secondary and elementary schools, as well as church-sponsored hospitals, retirement homes, and child welfare services. Membership is strongest in Pennsylvania and the middle western states.

Old Order Amish Church

Continuous with the Amish immigrants of 1720–1740, this church adheres to the older forms of worship and attire, using hooks and eyes instead of buttons, worshiping in private homes, and having no conferences. Members do not believe in missions or benevolent institutions, and they oppose centralized schools; some, however, do contribute to the missions and charities of the Mennonite Church. There are 545 Old Order Amish Church districts listed, and each district averages 110 to 150 members, with approximately half that number baptized.

Old Order (Wisler) Mennonite Church

This church was named for Jacob Wisler, the first Mennonite bishop in Indiana, who led a separation from the Mennonite Church in 1872. Those who separated did so to protest the use of English in the services and the introduction of Sunday schools. Joined in 1886, 1893, and 1901 by groups with similar ideas from Canada, Pennsylvania, and Virginia, the church is still maintained on the basis of those protests.

Each section of the church has its own district conference, and there are home conferences twice each year in each community. All churches take part in relief work, especially to the needy at home and in foreign lands, and some contribute to the work of the Mennonite Church. There are 9,731 members in 38 churches, 19 bishops, and 76 ministers.

Reformed Mennonite Church

Organized under the leadership of John Herr in Lancaster County, Pennsylvania, in 1812, Reformed Mennonites hold closely to New Testament teachings and maintain that there can be but one true church for all believers. They recognize as ordinances baptism, the Lord's Supper, foot washing, marriage, and the kiss of peace; these are "for edification and not a means of salvation." Baptism by pouring or sprinkling is considered an outward testimony of the baptism of the Spirit within the heart, which must precede the reception of water baptism. The Communion service signifies unity with God and with one another and is observed only by members of the church. They carry out strictly the instructions in Matthew 18 regarding laboring in love with an erring brother, greet one another regularly with the kiss of peace, insist upon modest and uniform clothing, and require women to wear head coverings.

They are nonresistant, do not vote or hold any governmental office, and refuse to worship with any who are not united in faith and practice. All converts join the church of their own free will. The bishops, ministers, and deacons are chosen from local congregations and are not paid. They have no Sunday schools, believing it obligatory upon parents to teach their own children.

Unaffiliated Mennonite

A number of small groups hold an unaffiliated status with all other Mennonite bodies. These unaffiliated Mennonite and Amish Mennonite churches claim 5,200 members, enrolled in 87 churches. All the groups hold to the fundamental doctrines of the Christian faith, the necessity of suffering injustice without retaliation, believer's baptism, the New Testament view that Christians must be separate from the evils of an unregenerate society, and moral earnestness. They are widely scattered in the United States, with a few congregations in Canada.

METHODIST

England's famed Oxford University has been called the cradle of lost causes, but at least one cause born there has not been lost—Methodism. Known and ridiculed at Oxford in 1729, today it claims some 13,000,000 adherents in North America and more than 18,000,000 around the world.

The Oxford Methodists, a tiny group of methodically religious students (also dubbed Bible Bigots, Bible Moths, and the Holy Club) who gave stated time to prayer and Bible reading, numbered among their members John and Charles Wesley and George Whitefield. They talked of the necessity of being justified before they could be sanctified and of the need for holiness in human living; they read and discussed William Law's *A Serious Call to a Devout and Holy Life* and *A Treatise on Christian Perfection*. The two Wesleys were sons of a clergyman of the Church of England; with the other members of the Holy Club they stood their ground against jeering students and went out to preach and pray with the poor and desperate commoners of England—prisoners in jail, paupers in hovels, bitter and nearly hopeless "underdogs of a British society that was perilously close to moral and spiritual collapse." Methodism began on a campus and reached for the masses.

The Wesleys arrived in Georgia in 1736. Charles came as secretary to

General Oglethorpe, and John was sent by the Society for the Propagation of the Gospel as a missionary to the Indians. It was an unsuccessful and unhappy two years for John Wesley, with but one bright spot: On shipboard en route to the colonies he met a group of Moravians and was deeply impressed by their piety and humble Christian way of life. Later when he returned to London, he went to the meeting of a religious society in Aldersgate Street, heard the preacher read Luther's preface to the Epistle to the Romans, and felt his heart "strangely warmed" as the meaning of the Reformer's doctrine of justification by faith sank into his soul. It was the evangelistic spark that energized his life and started the flame of the Wesleyan revival in England. From the pious Moravians, via Wesley, came the warmhearted emphases upon conversion and holiness which are still the central themes of Methodism.

Whitefield and the Wesleys were too much afire to be boxed in by the staid Church of England. When its doors were closed to them, they took to the open air, Charles writing the hymns of revival for streets, barns, private homes, and the mining pits of Cornwall, and John preaching repentance, regeneration, justification, holiness, and sanctification. The upper classes laughed, but the lower classes listened to the first words of hope they had heard in many a year. Converts came thick and fast; it became necessary to organize into societies. One was attached to a Moravian congregation in Fetter Lane, London, in 1739 and later moved to its own quarters in an abandoned government building known as the Foundry, where in 1740 it became the first self-sustaining Methodist society in London.

Between 1739 and 1744 the organizational elements of Methodism were instituted; we read of a circuit system and an itinerant ministry, of class meetings and class leaders, of lay preachers and annual conferences. There was phenomenal growth in membership; more than 26,000 Methodists were worshiping in England, Ireland, Scotland, and Wales in 1767. Their impact upon British society was startling; the crudities and barbarisms of the times were alleviated and a "French revolution" averted.

Methodism was primarily a lay movement. Wesley did his best to keep it within the Church of England; an evangelical party grew within that church, but the greater numbers recruited from among the unchurched made a separate organization imperative. In 1739 Wesley drew up a set of general rules, which are still held by modern Methodists, and an ideal delineation of Bible rules and conduct. A Deed of Declaration in 1784 gave legal status to the yearly Methodist conference. But John Wesley was dead in 1791, before Methodism in England became a recognized church, the Wesleyan Methodist Connection.

Meanwhile the movement had invaded Ireland and the American colonies. Wesley had begun to send out leaders; the first in this country were Joseph Pilmoor and Richard Boardman. Philip Embury, an Irish lay leader, encouraged by his cousin Barbara Heck, preached in New York and inspired the organization of the first Methodist society overseas about

1766. By 1769 the New York Methodists had built Wesley Chapel, now known as John Street Methodist Church. Captain Thomas Webb, a veteran of Braddock's ill-fated army, established societies in Philadephia; Robert Strawbridge started a revival in Maryland and built a log-cabin church at Sam's Creek. Devereux Jarratt, a transplanted evangelical Anglican minister, led a revival in Virginia that won thousands. The true center of Methodism in those days lay in the South; of 3,148 Methodists in the colonies in 1775, about 2,000 lived south of Mason and Dixon's Line. Wesley, aware of the rapid spread of the movement in America, sent emissaries to take charge, among them Francis Asbury and Thomas Rankin, the latter as the first full-fledged "superintendent of the entire work of Methodism in America." Rankin presided over the first conference in America, called at Philadelphia in 1773 and attended by ten ministers.

About 1,160 Methodists were represented in the conference of 1773; when the Liberty Bell rang in 1776, there were fewer than 7,000, and they seemed doomed to disappear as quickly as they had gathered. The majority of preachers had come from England; they were incurably British and were so roughly handled by the patriots that by 1779, nearly all had fled either to Canada or home to England. Wesley's pro-British attitude also aroused resentment, and Francis Asbury, working almost singlehandedly, had a difficult time keeping some of the churches alive. But a miracle happened; of all the religious groups in the colonies, the Methodist alone actually seemed to prosper during the Revolution. By the end of the war, the membership had grown to 14,000 and there were nearly 80 preachers. It was, after Yorktown, an American church, free of both England and the Church of England. Wesley accepted the inevitable; he ordained ministers for the colonies and appointed Asbury and Thomas Coke as superintendents.

Coke brought with him from England certain instructions from Wesley, a service book and hymnal, and authority to proceed with the organization. The Christmas Conference, held at Baltimore in December 1784, organized the Methodist Episcopal Church and elected Coke and Asbury as superintendents (later called bishops). The Sunday Service (an abridgment of the Book of Common Prayer) and Articles of Religion were adopted as written by John Wesley, but another article was added: that as good patriots, Methodists should vow allegiance to the United States government. The first general conference of the new church, made up solely of ministers, was held in 1792. It was not until 1872 that the laity was admitted to what had become by that time a quadrennial general conference. Membership soared: From 14,000 in 37 circuits at the close of the Revolution, it had increased to 1,324,000 by the middle of the following century.

Not only did Methodism sweep through the cities; it also developed an amazing strength in small towns and rural areas. There were circuit riders everywhere—ministers on horseback who traveled the expanding frontier—to mountain cabins, prairie churches, schoolhouses, and camp meetings, preaching free grace and individual responsibility and the need for conversion and regeneration. Their itinerant ministry was perfectly adapted to the democratic society of the frontier. The Methodist Book Concern was established in 1789, putting into the saddlebags of the circuit riders a religious literature that followed the march of the American empire south and west. The camp meeting, born among the Presbyterians, though not always carried on by them, was adopted by the Methodists and exploited to the limit. Its revivalistic flavor and method were made to order for the followers of Wesley and Whitefield.

All was not peaceful, however, among the Methodists; divisions came. Objecting, like good democrats, to what they considered abuses of the episcopal system, several bodies broke away: the Republican Methodists, later the Christian Church, withdrew in Virginia; Methodist Protestants seceded in 1830. Between 1813 and 1917, large black groups formed independent churches: the African Methodist Episcopal Church; the Union Church of Africans, now the Union American Methodist Episcopal Church; and the African Methodist Episcopal Zion Church. In 1844 came the most devastating split of all, the bisecting of the Methodist Episcopal Church into the Methodist Episcopal Church, the northern body, and the Methodist Episcopal Church, South.

The cause of this major split was, of course, slavery. Bishop Andrew, a Georgian, owned slaves through inheritance, and his wife also was a slaveholder. It was not possible for them to free their slaves under the laws of Georgia, but the general conference of 1844, held in New York City, requested that the bishop desist from the exercise of his office while he remained a slaveholder. Incensed, the southern delegates rebelled, a provisional plan of separation was formulated, and the southerners went home; they organized their own church in 1845. Basic to the separation was the constitutional question of the power of the general conference, which, the southerners maintained, assumed supreme power in virtually deposing a bishop who had violated no law of the church and against whom no charges had been brought. It was a split that concerned neither doctrine nor polity; purely political and social, it was a wound that was not healed until 1939. In that year the Methodist Episcopal Church, the Methodist Episcopal Church, South, and the Methodist Protestant Church were reunited at Kansas City, Missouri.

The uniting conference of 1939 adopted a new constitution in three sections: an abridgment of the Articles of Religion drawn up by John Wesley and based on the 39 Articles of Religion of the Church of England; the General Rules, covering the conduct of church members and the duties of church officials; and the Articles of Organization and Government, outlining the organization and conduct of conferences and local churches. This constitution cannot be changed by any general conference unless and until every annual conference has acted on the changes proposed.

In matters of faith there has been very little occasion for confusion or difference among Methodists; heresy trials and doctrinal quarrels have been noticeably absent. Historically, they have never built theological fences or walls to keep anyone out; they have stressed the great foundation beliefs of Protestantism and offered common theological ground. Some, but not all the churches repeat the Apostles' Creed in their worship, though the discipline of the church provides for its use in formal worship. The theology is Arminian as interpreted by Wesley in his sermons, his *Notes on the New Testament*, and his Articles of Religion.

The church preaches and teaches the doctrines of the Trinity, the natural sinfulness of humankind, it's fall and the need of conversion and repentance, freedom of the will, justification by faith, sanctification and holiness, future rewards and punishments, the sufficiency of the Scriptures for salvation, the enabling grace of God, and perfection. Two sacraments, baptism and the Lord's Supper, are observed; baptism is administered to both infants and adults, usually by sprinkling. Membership—full, preparatory, or affiliate (the latter arranged for people away from their home church who wish to affiliate where they live)—is based upon confession of faith or by letter of transfer from other evangelical churches; admission of children to membership is usually limited to those 13 years of age or over, though in the South the age may be 2 or 3 years younger. There is wide freedom in the interpretation and practice of all doctrines; liberals and conservatives work in close harmony.

The local churches of Methodism are called charges; their ministers are appointed by the bishop at the annual conference, and each church elects its own Administrative Board, which initiates planning and sets goals and policies on the local level. It is composed of staff people, chairmen of various committees, persons representing various program interests, and members at large. Charge, annual, and general conferences prevail in most Methodist bodies; while Methodist government is popularly called episcopal, it is largely governmental, by this series of conferences. The charge conference meets in the local charge or on the circuit, with the district superintendent presiding. It fixes the salary of the pastor, elects the church officers, and sends delegates to the annual conference. The charge conference may delegate responsibility for many of these duties to the administrative board of the local church. Some areas have a district conference between the charge and the annual conference, but it is not a universal arrangement throughout the church. Annual conferences cover defined geographical areas, ordain and admit ministers to the ministry, vote on constitutional questions, supervise pensions and relief, exchange pastors with other annual conferences through acts of the bishop, and every fourth year elect lay and ministerial delegates to the general conference. The general conference is the lawmaking body of the church, meeting quadrennially; the bishops preside, and the work of the conference is done largely in committees, whose reports when adopted by the general conference become Methodist law.

Worship and liturgy are based upon the English prayer book, with widespread modifications. The language of the prayer book is much in evidence in the sacraments of Methodist churches. In many forms of worship, however, each congregation is free to use or change the accepted pattern as it sees fit.

There are 23 separate Methodist bodies in the United States; The United Methodist Church is numerically the strongest.

African Methodist Episcopal Church

One of the three largest Methodist groups in the United States, this church began with the withdrawal in 1787 of a number of members of St. George's Methodist Episcopal Church in Philadelphia, in protest against racial discrimination. They built Bethel Chapel with the assistance of Bishop William White of the Protestant Episcopal Church. Francis Asbury dedicated the chapel in Philadelphia and ordained one of the members, Richard Allen, as its minister.

The body was formally organized as the African Methodist Episcopal Church in 1816; in the same year, Allen was consecrated as its first bishop, again by Bishop Asbury. From the beginning, it provided social, educational, and journalistic services.

It was a church largely confined, in the years preceding the Civil War, to the northern states; following the war its membership increased rapidly in the South, and today it is found all across the nation. There are 13 bishops, 11 general officers, and 12 connectional officers, in 13 districts. A general conference is held quadrennially. Foreign missions are supported in South Africa, West Africa, India, the Caribbean, and South America. There are 5 colleges, 7 theological schools, and several high schools and elementary schools. The AME Book Concern dates to 1816. The weekly *Christian Recorder* has been published since 1848. Membership stands at 2,210,000 in 6,200 churches.

African Methodist Episcopal Zion Church

This church dates from 1796, when it was organized by a group of black members protesting discrimination in the John Street Church in New York City. Their first church, Zion, was built in 1800; the word was later made part of the denominational name. The first annual conference of the body was held in that church in 1821, with 19 preachers from 6 black Methodist churches in New Haven, Philadelphia, and Newark, presided over by the Reverend William Phoebus of the white Methodist Episcopal Church. James Varick, who had led the John Street dissension, was elected the first bishop. The name African Methodist Episcopal Zion Church was approved in 1848.

This church spread quickly over the northern states; by 1880 there were 15 annual conferences in the South. Livingstone College at Salisbury, North Carolina, the largest educational institution of the church, was established by the general conference in that year. Departments of missions, education, and publications were created in

1892; later came administrative boards to direct work in church extension, evangelism, finance, ministerial relief, and so on. Home missions are supported in Louisiana, Mississippi, and several western states, principally Oklahoma. Foreign missionaries are found in Liberia, Ghana, Nigeria, South America, and the West Indies. There are 5 secondary schools and 2 colleges (Livingstone, and Clinton Junior College in Rock Hill, South Carolina). Membership figures list 1,134,176 in 6,020 churches.

African Union First Colored Methodist Protestant Church, Inc.

Organized in 1866, this body is a union of two black churches, the African Union Church and the First Colored Methodist Protestant Church. Doctrine is in accord with most of Methodism, but there are differences in polity; there are no bishops, and ministers and lay people have equal power in annual and general conferences. There is no foreign missionary program; home missions are maintained by a group of women known as the Grand Body. A general board with a president, secretary, and treasurer directs the denominational effort; the board meets annually, the general conference quadrennially.

Christian Methodist Episcopal Church

This body was established in 1870, in an amicable agreement between white and black members of the Methodist Episcopal Church, South. There were at the time at least 225,000 slave members of the M. E. Church, South, but with the Emancipation Proclamation, all but 80,000 joined the two independent black bodies. When the general conference of the M. E. Church, South, met at New Orleans in 1866, a commission from the black membership asked to separate into a church of its own. The request was granted, and the Colored Methodist Episcopal Church was organized. That name was held until the meeting of its general conference at Memphis in May 1954, when it was changed to Christian Methodist Episcopal Church.

The doctrine is that of the parent church; this denomination adds a local church conference to the quarterly, district, annual, and general conferences usual in Methodism. There are ten episcopal districts, supervised by a presiding bishop. Ten departments oversee the national work, each presided over by a bishop assigned by the College of Bishops as chairperson.

The general secretaries of the various departments are elected every 4 years by the general conference, and the president of the Women's Missionary Council is elected every 4 years by the quadrennial assembly of the Missionary Council. The church issues 2 periodicals and supports 5 colleges, a seminary, a hospital, and several low-rent and senior-citizen housing complexes. There are 800,000 members and 3,000 churches at present.

Congregational Methodist Church

This church was established in Georgia in 1852 by a group withdrawing from the Methodist Episcopal Church, South, in objection to certain features of the episcopacy and the itineracy. Two-thirds of its membership in turn withdrew to join the Congregational Church in 1887 and 1888.

Local pastors are called by the local churches; district conferences grant licenses, ordain ministers, and review local reports. District, annual, and general conferences are all recognized as church courts, ruling on violations of church law, citing offending lay people or ministers, and holding the power of expulsion over unworthy members. There is a home and foreign missionary program among the Navahos in New Mexico and Mexico. A senior college, the denominational headquarters, and a publishing house are located at Florence, Mississippi. There are 25,541 members in 227 churches.

Evangelical Methodist Church

Organized at Memphis in 1946, this church is "fundamental in doctrine, evangelistic in program, and congregational in government." It representes a double protest against what was considered an autocratic and undemocratic government, on the one hand, and a tendency toward modernism, on the other, in The Methodist Church from which the body withdrew.

The church is Arminian in theology and Wesleyan in doctrine. Members seek a return to the original revivalistic thought and program of Wesleyanism; fundamentalist, they oppose the "substituting of social, educational, or other varieties of cultural salvation."

Local churches own and control their own property and select their own pastors. There are 7 districts and 7 district superintendents; Mexico and Bolivia constitute mission conferences. The general conference meets quadrennially; international headquarters are in Wichita, Kansas. There are 138 churches in the Southeast, especially in Virginia and North Carolina, with a membership of more than 10,000.

First Congregational Methodist Church of the U.S.A.

Organized at Forsythe, Georgia, in 1852, this group claims to be the parent body from which the Congregational Methodist Church dissented to form its own organization. Originally under the jurisdiction of the Methodist Episcopal Church, South, some members withdrew from that church in disagreement over the episcopal and itinerant systems. Claiming that the system lacked biblical authority and democratic principles, they set up a church that would be congregational in government. There are local, district, state, and general conferences, and about 7,500 members in 100 churches throughout Alabama, Mississippi, Georgia, Tennessee, Texas, Missouri, Arkansas, and Oklahoma.

Free Methodist Church of North America

This is one of the more conservative among the larger bodies of American Methodism, in both doctrine and standards of Christian practice. Its founders were the Reverend B. T. Roberts and his associates, who objected to "new school" Methodism, which they considered destructive to the Wesleyan standards of the church. They were "read out" of their churches and organized the Free Methodist Church in Pekin, New York, in 1860. The Genesee Conference, of which Roberts had been a member, restored his credentials to his son in 1910, but no reunion of the group with The United Methodist Church has yet been effected. A merger with the Holiness Movement in Canada was approved in 1960.

Doctrinally, the Free Methodists call for a return to primitive Wesleyan teaching; they stress the Virgin birth, the deity of Jesus, and his vicarious atonement and resurrection. No one may be received into membership without undergoing confession and forgiveness of sin, and the experience of entire sanctification is sought in all members. Strict adherence to the general rules of Methodism is demanded, and membership in secret societies is forbidden.

The Free Methodist Church has become a world fellowship consisting of three general conferences—Egypt, Japan, and North America—with a common constitution formally ratified by each general conference in 1964. All legislative actions are reviewed by a constitutional council elected from the general conferences. There are 79,459 members in 1,160 churches in the United States and the United Kingdom, and a world membership of 184,228. Foreign missionary work is conducted in Africa, India, Japan, Taiwan, the Dominican Republic, Hong Kong, the Philippines, Indonesia, Egypt, Brazil, Paraguay, Mexico, and Haiti. There are four senior colleges in the denomination, a Bible college, a cooperative program with other denominations in another senior college, a seminary foundation maintained in cooperation with Asbury Theological Seminary, and Western Evangelical Seminary. Social services include a 177-bed hospital, a home for unwed mothers, 5 retirement and nursing facilities for the elderly, and a children's home.

New Congregational Methodist Church

This church originated in an administrative quarrel in the Georgia Conference of the Methodist Episcopal Church, South, over the consolidation of certain rural properties in the southern section of the state. Protesting, the New Congregational Methodist Church was organized in 1881 on the general plan of the Congregational Methodist Church. There are at present 773 members in 15 churches—7 in northern Florida and 8 in southern Georgia. There are 2 smaller groups in central Georgia and Indiana.

Government is a combination of Methodist and Congregational systems: The episcopacy is rejected—congregations call and elect their own pastors; there are the usual (Methodist) local, district, and general conferences. An unusual feature of this church lies in its practice of foot washing.

People's Methodist Church

Conservative and Holiness, the founders of this church left the Methodist Church in North Carolina at the time of the merger of the three major Methodist churches. There are approximately 25 congregations and 1,000 members, with a Bible school in Greensboro, North Carolina. No information on doctrine or polity is available.

Primitive Methodist Church, U.S.A.

This church was initially organized in England under the influence of Lorenzo Dow, an American camp-meeting revivalist who went to England early in the nineteenth century. He held a series of meetings that resulted in the formation of a number of societies among his converts. The leaders of those societies dropped from the Wesleyan Connection to form the Primitive Methodist Church in 1810. Four missionaries came to America in 1829, settling in New York City and Philadelphia.

The church has a general conference for both administration and legislation, and six districts, or area groups. There is only one salaried official—an executive director. The relationships and assignments of ministers are reviewed annually, and vacancies are filled with student ministers or ordained deacons and elders.

Doctrinally, modified Wesleyan Articles of Religion are accepted. Foreign missionaries are stationed in Guatemala. There are 9,978 members in 87 churches.

Reformed Methodist Union Episcopal Church

This church began in 1885 at Charleston, South Carolina, as a withdrawal from the African Methodist Episcopal Church. The immediate cause of the division was a dispute over the election of ministerial delegates to the general conference. Intended at first as a nonepiscopal church, the body later adopted the complete polity of the Methodist Episcopal Church in its general conferences of 1896 and 1916. Its first bishop was consecrated in 1899 by a bishop of the Reformed Episcopal Church. Class meetings and love feasts are featured in the local congregation; there are 3,800 members in 17 churches.

Reformed Zion Union Apostolic Church

This church was organized at Boydton, Virginia, in 1869 by James R. Howell, a minister of the African Methodist Episcopal Zion Church in New York, as a protest against white discrimination and the ecclesiasticism of other black Methodist churches. Originally known as the Zion

Union Apostolic Church, internal friction completely disrupted the body by 1874, and in 1881–1882 it was reorganized under the present name. There are no basic departures from standard Methodist doctrine or polity, except that only one ordination, that of elder, is required of its ministers. There are 16,000 members in 50 churches.

Southern Methodist Church

Doctrinally, the Southern Methodist Church remains the same as the body from which it came—the Methodist Episcopal Church, South. Its members opposed the merger of that church with the northern Methodist Episcopal Church in 1939, on grounds of "alarming infidelity and apostasy found therein." They regard the Southern Methodist Church not as a separatist body but as a church "brought into existence to perpetuate the faith of John Wesley."

There are no bishops, but there are the usual Methodist annual and general conferences; a president is elected every four years from the elders of the clergy. Lay people and clergy have equal voice and voting privileges in these conferences.

Local churches own and control their own property and buildings, and call their own ministers, who must be approved by their annual conferences. There are 7,500 members in 147 churches, from Virginia to Texas. There is one college, Southern Methodist College, and a publishing house, Foundry Press, located at Orangeburg, South Carolina.

Union American Methodist Episcopal Church

This was one of the first black bodies to establish an independent Methodist church. A group of members left the Asbury Methodist Church in Wilmington, Delaware, in 1805; they worshiped outdoors and in private homes until 1813, when they built their first church and incorporated as the Union Church of Africans. Defections from the membership were responsible for the formation of another body known as the African Union church, which forced the change to the present name.

General, annual, district, and quarterly conferences are held; general conferences are called only to consider proposed changes in name, law, or polity. There are two educational institutions, and the church claims 27,560 members in 256 churches.

United Methodist Church, The

Two mergers of major importance produced The United Methodist Church, the largest Methodist body in this country, with 9,482,000 members in 38,795 local churches. The first was actually a rejoining of three existing Methodist groups: At a uniting conference in Kansas City in 1939, the Methodist Episcopal Church, the Methodist Episcopal Church,

South, and the Methodist Protestant Church were reunited under a new name, The Methodist Church. In 1968 The Methodist Church merged with the Evangelical United Brethren Church to form The United Methodist Church.

The history of the Methodist Episcopal Church and the break between that body and the Methodist Episcopal Church, South, has already been outlined. The Methodist Episcopal Church, South, was organized at Louisville, Kentucky, in 1845 and held its first general conference a year later in Petersburg, Virginia, under the presidency of Bishops James Andrew and Joshua Soule. In 1939 it brought a membership of 2,500,000 to the reunited church. The Methodist Protestant Church was founded at a conference in Baltimore in 1830, in protest against the almost total rule of the clergy in the Methodist Episcopal Church and the exclusion of lay people from its councils. There were about 200,000 members in 1939.

The Evangelical United Brethren Church grew out of a series of mergers in two groups: the United Brethren in Christ and the Evangelical Church. The Evangelical Church, originally the Evangelical Association, began as a result of the labors of Jacob Albright (1759–1808) among the German people of Pennsylvania; preaching first as a Lutheran and then as a Methodist exhorter, Albright was made a bishop at the first annual conference of the Association in 1807. He used the Methodist *Discipline* until 1809, preached Methodist doctrine, and was so effective that for some time his followers were known as the Albrights. A split in 1891 resulted in a separate denomination, the United Evangelical Church; the two groups were reunited in 1922 under the name of the Evangelical Church.

Another group, known as the Church of the United Brethren in Christ, developed in a parallel manner through the preaching of William Otterbein (1726–1813) and Martin Boehm (1725–1812) among the Germans in Pennsylvania, Maryland, and Virginia; they were elected bishops at a conference in September 1800. That conference created the Church of the United Brethren in Christ, which was also strongly Methodistic in polity, doctrine, and practice. Both groups had a *Discipline* modeled on the Methodist, and had too much in common to remain separated. Those two bodies—the Church of the United Brethren in Christ and the Evangelical Church—were merged into the Evangelical United Brethren Church at Johnstown, Pennsylvania, in 1946.

Both the Methodist and the E.U.B. churches, across the years, had been deeply conscious of their common historical and spiritual heritage. Their doctrines were similar; both were episcopal in government; both traced their origins to John Wesley; both had nearly the same *Book of Discipline*. Their preachers often exchanged pulpits and congregations, worked together, and shared the same buildings. The only major difference was that of language—German among the Brethren, English among the Methodists. As new, native-born generations appeared, this barrier meant less and less. Conversations concerning the merging of the churches began as early as 1803 and were consummated when they came together as The United Methodist Church at Dallas, Texas, on April 23, 1968.

There was some dissent at Dallas; 51 congregations and 79 ministers of the Evangelical United Brethren withdrew from the Pacific Northwest Conference to establish the Evangelical Church of North America; 18 of 23 E.U.B. congregations in Montana left to establish the Evangelical Church of North America in Montana; 13 other congregations in the Erie and Ohio Southeast Conferences petitioned to leave, but those petitions were denied. The split mainly concerned theological issues and the question of church ownership. But there were still roughly 750,000 Brethren who accepted the union; their strength gave the new United Methodist Church a membership of nearly 11 million.

In this union no significant changes were made in either doctrine or polity. The Confession of Faith of the Evangelical United Brethren Church, adopted in 1962, was placed beside the Methodist Articles of Religion; Wesleyan standards dominate both statements, and both are used as the congregation of each church elects to use them. The Methodist system of bishops and conferences, already in use in both denominations, is maintained. There are now 73 annual conferences in the United States with a total of 39,395 organized churches and 37,444 ministers. Above the annual conferences are 5 jurisdictional conferences established for geographical convenience in administrative matters. These meet quadrennially, at times determined by the Council of Bishops, to elect new bishops and name the members of the larger boards and commissions. Outside the continental United States, there are central conferences that correspond to the jurisdictional conferences; they meet quadrennially and, when authorized to do so, may elect their own bishops. All bishops are elected for life (except in autonomous overseas conferences, where the term is four years) with retirement set at age 72; there are 59 bishops in the United States and abroad, in charge of the areas of the church—the New York Area, the Denver Area, and so on. Together they constitute the Council of Bishops, which meets at least once a year, and usually twice a year, "for the general oversight and promotion of the temporal and spiritual affairs of the entire church."

The general conference consists of more than 800 delegates, half laity and half clergy, elected on a proportional basis by the annual conferences. A judicial council has been created to determine the constitutionality of any act of the general conference that may be appealed, and to hear and determine any appeal from a bishop's decision on a question of law, in any district or annual, central, or jurisdictional conference. The council is made up of 5 clergy and 4 lay people and has become so important that it is often called the Supreme Court of the church.

The General Conference of 1972 restructured the administrative bodies of the church. The Council of Bishops and a Council on Finance and Administration were made responsible to the general conference, and a new Council on Ministries was set up as a coordinating body between the conference and various other commissions, support services, and program boards. The commissions now include those on archives and history, religion and race, and status and role of women; the support services include a Board of Publication, United Methodist Communications, and a Board of Pensions. The program boards were rearranged to include boards on church and society, discipleship, higher education and ministry, global ministries, and Christian unity and interreligious concerns.

The conference also broadened the basis of doctrine in the church, in the first restatement on doctrine since the eighteenth century. The classic documents of the merging Methodist and Evangelical United Brethren churches were maintained, but the doctrinal door was left open to theological change and revision. Typical of the openness that has always characterized Methodism is the statement in the *Discipline* that the four main sources and guidelines for Christian theology are Scripture, tradition, experience, and reason: "These four are interdependent; none can be defined unambiguously. They allow for, indeed they positively encourage, variety in United Methodist theologizing."

This church has property valued at $12,640,082,011, not including educational plants, hospitals, or homes for the aged. There are 145 institutions devoted to long-term care, 57 to health care, and 58 to child care. There are 81 United Methodist colleges, 8 universities, 13 schools of theology, 14 2-year colleges, 9 secondary schools, an elementary school, and a medical college. The church is at work in 48 countries; 14 bishops administer the work overseas, with a total of 718 missionaries. The United Methodist Publishing House is probably the oldest and largest religious publishing concern in the world; 41 periodicals are sponsored, exclusive of Sunday school materials.

The World Methodist Council, organized in 1881 and designed to draw the whole Wesleyan movement closer together in fellowship and devotion to the Wesleyan heritage, has become increasingly active in recent years. Fourteen ecumenical conferences have been held by the council since 1881; headquarters are established at Lake Junaluska, North Carolina.

METROPOLITAN COMMUNITY CHURCHES, UNIVERSAL FELLOWSHIP OF

Founded in 1968, this Protestant body is best known for its outreach to homosexuals. It professes orthodox Christian theology on such doctrines as Scripture, the Trinity, and the sacraments; that teaching is the basis for its concern to present the good news of God's love to a segment of society often excluded from participation in church life, and sometimes ridiculed—lesbians and gay men.

This awareness prompted the Reverend Troy D. Perry to create a denomination where such people could find genuine acceptance in a context of Christian worship and service. Perry, himself a homosexual, had been discharged from the church he served as pastor and ostracized from his denomination. He called a congregation into being in Los Angeles, and soon churches were organized in other cities. In the summer of 1970, the first General Conference was held.

The church reports a membership of 30,000, with 200 churches in 9 countries. Heterosexuals may and do belong, but a large percentage of the membership is homosexual. The denomination describes its ministry as a shared one: of lay and clergy, women and men, privileged and underprivileged, lesbian, gay, and heterosexual.

The body applied for membership in the National Council of Churches in 1983 and was turned down, but it hopes eventually to become a part of that ecumenical organization, with which it remains in dialogue.

Its membership is active in a variety of ministries, reflecting its primary orientation to such traditions as the social gospel and liberation theology. In particular, it has sought to address the needs of the hungry, the homeless, and the powerless. It supports a freeze on nuclear weapons. It is committed to eradicating sexism in its theology and in society at large. The civil rights of all people are a major concern.

The church faces the controversial nature of its existence by stating that its members accept homosexuality as "a gift from God," just as heterosexuality is "a gift from God." "But our sexuality is not and should not be the focal point of our lives. The MCC emphasizes that everything in our life, including our sexuality, must center on our relationship with God, through faith in Jesus Christ."

MISSIONARY CHURCH

The Missionary Church is made up of two groups that merged in March, 1969: the Missionary Church Association and the United Missionary Church. The new denomination claims 378 congregations and 31,243 members in 12 districts in the United States and Canada.

The Missionary Church Association was founded at Berne, Indiana, in 1889. The United Missionary Church was formed in 1883 in Englewood, Ohio, under the name Mennonite Brethren in Christ; it was renamed in 1947. Both denominations have a Mennonite heritage and came into existence through the Holiness revivals of the late 1800s.

The Missionary Church is conservative and evangelical in theology and practice. Local churches are free to manage their own affairs, but recognize the authority of a general conference made up of ministers, missionaries, and laypeople, which is held biennially. Working under the general conference is a general board made up of the officers of the administrative boards of the church: Christian education, evangelism and church extension, higher education, overseas missions, publications, social concerns. President, vice-president, secretary, and treasurer are elected for a term of four years.

Missions are highly evangelistic; there are 115 missionaries serving in India, Mexico, Haiti, Jamaica, Sierra Leone, Dominican Republic, Ecuador, Brazil, France, and Nigeria. The church is affiliated with two educational institutions in the United States—Bethel College in Mishawaka, Indiana, and Fort Wayne Bible College in Fort Wayne, Indiana; and two in Canada—Emmanuel Bible College in Kitchener, Ontario, and Mountain View Bible College in Didsbury, Alberta.

MORAVIAN

The roots of the Moravian Church run back as far as the ninth century, to the work of Constantine and Methodius among the European Slavs. The Slavic population of Bohemia and Moravia was struggling, at that time, for political and religious freedom. Later the people followed John Hus, who was martyred in 1415, and Jerome of Prague, martyred in 1416. The first association was formed in Bohemia in 1458, and after that time, we find it called *Jednota Bratrska* (The Union of Brethren) and/or *Unitas Fratrum* (Unity of the Brethren).

By the middle of the sixteenth century there were about 60 congregations in Bohemia, between 80 and 90 in Moravia, and, somewhat later, 40 in Poland. The number remained virtually the same (altogether, about 150 congregations) until the outbreak of the Thirty Years' War (1618–1648). Fierce persecution under the Hapsburgs then almost exterminated the members, but they survived. In 1722, two families named Neisser, led by Christian David, fled from Moravia. At the invitation of Nicholas Louis, Count of Zinzendorf, a small band found refuge on his estate in Saxony, where they built the town of Herrnhut. It was the count who called the people Moravians because they came from northern Moravia.

Zinzendorf was made a bishop in 1737. In America (1741–1743) he was active in establishing the church in Pennsylvania, where three towns were founded—Bethlehem, Nazareth, and Lititz—following a failure to plant churches in the colony of Georgia. A church in Hope, New Jersey, and another in Salem, North Carolina, also proved failures. The largest and most successful efforts have been in Pennsylvania, where the current Moravian church *(Unitas Fratrum)* is one of the finest religious establishments in the nation.

Moravian Church *(Unitas Fratrum)*

It is said of the Moravians that "a unified system of doctrine was never developed." That may be an overstatement, but it is certainly true that there is no doctrine peculiar to them; they are broadly evangelical, insisting upon the principle "in essentials unity, in nonessentials liberty, and in all things charity." Their scriptural interpretations agree substantially with the Apostles' Creed, the Westminster and Augsburg confessions, and the Articles of Religion of the Church of England. They hold the Scriptures to be the inspired Word of God and an adequate rule for faith and practice. They have doctrines dealing with the total depravity of humankind, the real Godhead and real humanity of Christ, justification and redemption through the sacrifice of Christ, the work of the Holy Spirit, good works as the fruits of the Spirit, the community of all believers, the second coming of Christ, and the resurrection of the dead to life and judgment. The main doctrinal emphasis may be said to be the love of God manifested in the redemptive life and death of Jesus, the inner testimony of the Spirit, and Christian conduct in everyday affairs.

The sacrament of infant baptism by sprinkling, or occasionally by pouring is practiced. There is a total membership of 56,578 in 157 churches, concentrated in eastern Pennsylvania, North Carolina, and the Kuskokwim River Valley in Alaska. Members are admitted by vote of the congregational board of elders. The Lord's Supper is celebrated at least six times a year, and the custom of the love feast is preserved. A variety of liturgy is used in worship: The church is notable for an especially beautiful outdoor service at Easter.

The Moravian church in the North America is divided into two provinces, northern and southern. The highest administrative body in each is the provincial synod. Composed of ministers and lay people, it meets every three or four years, directs missionary, educational, and publishing work, and elects a provincial elders' conference, or executive board, which functions between synod meetings. Bishops, elected by provincial and general synods, are spiritual, but not administrative leaders in the church.

Missionary work has always been a first concern; with a comparatively small membership, the church conducted the most efficient missionary work of any of the early colonial churches among the Indians. The worldwide Moravian church has 17 provinces in Europe, in North, Central, and South America, and in Africa and the Caribbean. It also sponsors a mission to the Tibetan refugees in northern India and a rehabilitation center for persons with handicaps at Rammallah, near Jerusalem. It maintains 2 colleges, a theological seminary, and a coed Moravian academy.

Unity of the Brethren

Known until 1962 as the Evangelical Unity of the Czech-Moravian Brethren in North America, this body originated among immigrants arriving in Texas in the late nineteenth century. The present name (*Unitas Fratrum*, or *Jednota Bratrska*) is the name used originally in 1457.

A synod meets every 2 years. The church has no colleges or seminaries. In 1964 there were 6,142 members in 32 churches.

MUSLIM

Islam claims more than 3 million adherents in the United States. There is no national organization (there is, indeed, no titular head nor priesthood in all Islam), but there are Islamic Centers in Washington, D.C., Toledo, Detroit, New York, and other large cities. The center in Washington includes a beautiful mosque, library, classrooms for study, and administrative offices; it is open for daily prayer and offers lectures and publications about the philosophy, religion, and art of Islam.

The word *Islam* means "purity, peace, submission to God's will and obedience to his laws." It does not claim to be a new religion formulated by the prophet Mohammed, but rather "the continuation of all former religious principles decreed by God through his revelations to all prophets." The prophets include Jesus Christ (Moslems accept him as prophet but not as divine) and many of the Jewish prophets and leaders of the Old Testament, from Noah to Zephaniah.

The members revere and honor Mohammed but do not worship him; their creed is that "there is no deity worthy of worship except God [Allah], and Mohammed is God's Messenger." This is "the religion of the Book," and the book is the Koran (Quran, to Mohammedans), said to have been dictated to Mohammed (born A.D. 571) by the angel Gabriel. The Koran contains the faith of Islam and describes the manner in which God is to be worshiped; it also outlines legislation concerning civil and criminal laws, laws of war, peace treaties between nations, and laws ruling such matters as marriage, divorce, inheritance, and wills. The Ten Commandments are embodied in the Koran, and it contains the Six Articles of Belief and the Five Pillars of Faith, which are the heart of Islam. The Five Pillars are: (1) recital of the creed; (2) recital of prayer five times daily, facing Mecca (the Cebba at Mecca is held to be the first house built by Abraham, for his son Ishmael, for the worship of God); (3) the giving of tithes for the support of the poor and the expansion of the faith; (4) the observation of Ramadan, the ninth month of the Moslem calendar—fasting during daylight in commemoration of the first revelation of the Koran; (5) a pilgrimage to Mecca, when financially able. The Six Articles of Belief are: (1) God is One, and this is Allah; (2) the Koran is God's truly inspired book; (3) God's angels are heavenly beings created to serve God, and they are opposed to evil spirits; (4) God sent his prophets to earth at stated times for stated purposes; the last of these was Mohammed, and God makes no distinction between his messengers; (5) the Day of Judgment will find good and evil weighed in the balance; (6) the lives and acts of people are foreordained (predestined) by an all-knowing God. Islam, however, still leaves humans "the architect[s] of [their] own destiny, free to make or mar [their] own future through a life of honest endeavor."

Mohammed accomplished his mission, which primarily was to proclaim the unity of God; when he died at 62, the precepts of the Koran became the great unifying force, around which 500,000,000 people eventually were to become followers of Islam (Moslems, or Muslims), with Mecca as their holy city and ardent in their faith in the Islamic trinity of the Koran, Moslem tradition, and the prophet Mohammed. Some divisions and sects have appeared (Shiites, Sunnites, Sufis) with variations in interpretation and practice, but by and large, there is and has been a firm allegiance to the Koran and to traditional Moslem practices.

The true Moslem male prays five times daily, has a service of congregational prayer preceded by a sermon on Friday at noon, eats no pork, drinks no intoxicating liquors, shuns gambling, adultery, and the breaking of one's word. In some countries he practices polygamy and (with less and less insistence) the custom that demands the veiling of Moslem women. He removes his shoes upon entering the mosque and is meticulous in washing feet, hands, head, and arms before prayer. In his moque there are no icons, statues, symbols, pews, chairs, or musical instruments; there is only a constant repetition and echo of the fundamental Koran approach to prayer: "In the name of God, the Beneficent, the Merciful, praise be to God, Lord of the worlds."

Outside the mosque the Moslem is a student. There is a saying that God's first creation was the pen and that the first word God revealed to Mohammed was *read.* To read and to study and to seek knowledge are obligatory in Islam; the ink of the scholar is more valuable than the blood of a martyr.

NEW APOSTOLIC CHURCH OF NORTH AMERICA

The New Apostolic Church of North America is a variant or schism of the Catholic Apostolic Church movement in England. It claims common origin with that church through the appointment of an apostle in the parent body in 1832. Debate arose in 1860 over the appointment of new apostles to fill vacancies left by death. Insisting on twelve apostles at the head of the true church, Bishop Schwarz of Hamburg was excommunicated from the Catholic Apostolic Church in 1862 for proposing the election of new apostles. A priest named Preuss was elected to the office of apostle "through the spirit of prophecy" to lead the dissenting body; Bishop Schwarz served under him until his own elevation to the apostolic office.

Under Preuss and Schwarz the New Apostolic Church spread from Europe to America, where today it is organized into apostles' districts, bishops' districts, and elders' districts. Each church has a rector and one or more assistants (priests, deacons, and so forth) who serve usually without remuneration. All ministers and other "office-bearers" are selected by the apostleship. The American church is a constituent of the international organization supervised by Chief Apostle Hans Urwyler in Zurich, Switzerland.

Just as the true church must be governed on the scriptural pattern by twelve apostles, members of this church believe that only the apostles have received from Christ the commission and power to forgive sin. The New Apostolic Church of North America accepts the Apostles' Creed and stresses the authority and inspiration of the Bible, the apostolic ordinances of the laying on of hands, the necessity of gifts of the Holy Spirit (prophecy, visions, dreams, diverse tongues, songs of praise, wisdom, discrimination of spirits, the power of healing and performing wonders), tithing, and the speedy, personal, premillennial return of Christ. Three means of grace are found in three sacraments: baptism (including children), Holy Communion, and "Holy Sealing" (the dispensing and reception of the Holy Spirit). Work "along broader interior and missionary lines" is conducted in the United States, Canada, Mexico, and Puerto Rico. The United States has 25,900 members in 297 churches and 65 missions; the international organization, about 2 million in 6,000 branches in 88 countries.

OLD CATHOLIC

Old Catholic churches in the United States are outgrowths of the Old Catholic movement of Europe. The European bodies originated in a protest against the doctrine of papal infallibility adopted by the Catholic Vatican Council of 1870; Roman priests in Germany who refused to accept the doctrine were excommunicated and organized the Old Catholic Church under the leadership of Ignatz von Döllinger in 1871. A similar break occurred in Holland and Switzerland where other Old Catholic churches were established.

This revolt did not break completely with Roman Catholicism. It rejected papal infallibility, the doctrine of the immaculate conception, compulsory celibacy of the priesthood, and in some instances the filioque clause of the Nicene Creed, but kept much of the other doctrine, creeds, customs, and liturgy of the Roman Catholic Church. It was also most anxious to preserve the orders and the apostolic succession of its priests and bishops, inasmuch as the apostolic succession was considered vital in a valid Christian ministry. Much confusion has resulted in conflicting claims of succession and validity of orders, especially in American Old Catholic churches. All Old Catholic bodies in this country were at one time or another connected with European bodies, but that is not true today; most American groups have severed their connections with churches abroad. Someone has said that most of the Old Catholics in America are either dissatisfied Anglicans or former Catholics; and there is some truth in that. Several attempts have been made to merge Old Catholic churches with those of the Church of England or the Greek church, and gestures have been made toward membership in the World Council of Churches.

Old Catholic missionaries were in America soon after 1871, establishing scattered congregations. Joseph René Vilatte, a French priest ordained by Old Catholics in Switzerland, attempted to organize these congregations and at once became the storm center of the rising confusion. Vilatte himself vacillated between rival bodies; he studied at a Presbyterian college in Montreal and twice returned to submit to the Roman Catholic Church, dying at last in a French monastery. Vigorously opposed within his own church and by American Protestant Episcopalians, whose ranks he refused to join, he went to Switzerland in 1885 for ordination as an Old Catholic bishop and was finally consecrated as an archbishop by Archbishop Alvarez of Ceylon, who claimed orders through the Syro-Jacobite Church of Malabar. Vilatte then returned to America to found the American Catholic Church.

Separated and competing as they are, the Old Catholics in the United States have a firm common doctrinal basis, similar to that held by the Greek and Latin churches before those bodies separated; among the Old Catholics, it is now more Eastern than Western. They accept the seven ecumenical councils of the church held before the division. Bible reading is encouraged, and national tongues, rather than Latin, are used in all worship. There is a strange blend of orthodoxy and rationalism in both doctrine and ritual.

There are 5 main divisions of Old Catholic churches in the United States, with an approximate total of 500,000 members in 100 churches—the Mariavite Old Catholic Church, the Old Roman Catholic Church (English Rite), the North American Old Roman Catholic Church, Christ Catholic Church of America and Europe (no information available aside from membership, 7,100 in 24 churches), and the American Catholic Church (Syro-Antiochian). The African Orthodox Church, a black group, is listed often as an Old Catholic body but is actually Protestant Episcopalian in origin and connection. The Polish National Catholic Church may be said to have certain Old Catholic origins and doctrines, but it has been listed separately in this book in consideration of its distinctively nationalistic character. The Liberal Catholic Church is also related to the Old Catholic movement.

American Catholic Church (Syro-Antiochian)

Deriving its orders from the Syrian Patriarch of Antioch, this church is better known as the Jacobite Apostolic church. It was organized in the United States in 1915 and is a monophysitic body, as are all Armenian Coptic and Jacobite Syrian churches. *Jacobite* was borrowed from the name of Jacobus Baradeus (d. 578), the Syrian monk who founded the movement. Historically, a bitter quarrel has raged between Jacobites and Orthodox Christians.

This church is Catholic in worship and discipline and has a Catholic liturgy in the administration of the sacraments; otherwise, it is a self-governing American body.

Syrian Jacobites are found in Mesopotamia, Iran, Syria, India, and Kurdistan, where they claim more than 80,000 members. It is from this section of the Middle East that they have migrated to the United States, where they report 750 members in three churches.

Mariavite Old Catholic Church

The Mariavites derive their name from two Latin words, *Mariae* and *vitae*, meaning *life of Mary*, because they desire to imitate closely the life of Mary, the mother of Christ. This ideal originated in late nineteenth-century Poland, a heavily Roman Catholic country. The Mariavite Order was founded in 1893 by Sister Maria Franciska, then the Superior of the Order of the Poor Sisters of St. Clare. Soon thereafter the Mariavite Order of Priests came into being. From the beginning its members endeavored to practice an aesthetical-mystical religious life in accordance with the rule of St. Francis of Assisi. Their goal is to maintain a deep inner life of spirituality through being pastors and servants, not through cloistered or contemplative communities. Requirements are firm and sacrificial with a tendency toward the ascetic.

Ecclesiastical and civil opposition marked the early decades of the Mariavites in Poland, resulting in the formation of a church independent of Rome in 1906; that church is still active in Poland. In 1930 the Mariavite Old Catholic Church was established in the United States. Its work continues under the leadership of priests, brothers and sisters, and a "secular third order," the Mariavite Society.

The church's faith is based on dogmas underscored at the seven ecumenical councils and on the tradition of the universal Church in the early centuries of Christianity. Three creeds are acknowledged—Apostles', Nicene, and Athanasian—as are the traditional seven sacraments. Worship is celebrated in the vernacular in Poland, and in Latin, English, and Polish in the United States. The dogmas of papal infallibility and primacy, the immaculate conception, and the assumption of the Virgin are rejected as being necessary for salvation.

The principal purpose of the Mariavite Church is described as "the propagation of devotion to the Most Blessed Sacrament and the invocation of the Perpetual Help of Mary." The church, in both Poland and the United States, cooperates with all Christian denominations. Each Mariavite observes an hourly adoration of supplication before the "Most Blessed Sacrament" perpetually exposed on all Mariavite altars.

The Mariavite Old Catholic Church numbers 3 bishops, 48 priests, 32 religious sisters, 158 parishes, and 358,560 adherents in North America. It directs missionary work in France and West Germany.

North American Old Roman Catholic Churches

Two Old Catholic groups bear this name, typical of the confusion and debate among Old Catholics. One body, identical in faith, thought, and worship with the Roman Catholic Church but differing in discipline, was "received into union" with the Eastern Orthodox Church by the Archbishop of Beirut in 1911, and again by the Orthodox Patriarch of Alexandria in 1912.

The second church, still in existence as an Old Catholic Church, claims proven succession of Catholic orders; the Knott Missal is used for all Masses, but the Pontificale is used for all Order Rights. It is not under papal control or jurisdiction. Some 61,570 members are reported in 139 churches.

Old Roman Catholic Church (English Rite)

Arnold Harris Matthew, who had been consecrated to the episcopacy by Archbishop Gerard Gul of the Old Catholic Church of Utrect, Holland, in 1911, consecrated Prince de Landes Berghes de la Rache, a Hungarian, in 1912, and sent him to America to consolidate the small, scattered Old Catholic churches in this country. De Landes settled in Waukegan, Illinois, and in October 1916, consecrated William Henry Francis Brothers and Carmel Henry Carfora as bishops. Less than a month later, at the suggestion of Matthew and after a dispute over the question of Minor Orders, de Landes excommunicated Brothers. Carfora then organized and incorporated the North American Old Roman Catholic Church, which remained the official name of the church until 1963, when it was changed to Old Roman Catholic Church (English Rite) following the death of Carfora.

Many immigrants from Poland and Lithuania were brought into the church; in 1973 it had a membership of 65,128 in 186 churches. It is similar to the Roman Catholic Church in worship and discipline, but denies papal infallibility and differs slightly in doctrine. It celebrates the Mass, has seven sacraments, and teaches transubstantiation, "the Veneration and Invocation of the Glorious and Immaculate Mother of God, of the Angels and of the saints." It offers prayers for the dead and advocates celibacy for priests, but permits them to marry. Worship services are in English.

In 1963, the Archbishop Metropolitan for North America, Robert

Alfred Burns, led the church into union with the Old Roman Catholic Church (English Rite) in Great Britain. Upon his death in 1974, Robert William Lane became Archbishop Metropolitan.

OPEN BIBLE STANDARD CHURCHES, INC.

Open Bible Standard Churches, Inc., was originally composed of two revival movements: Bible Standard, Inc., founded in Eugene, Oregon, in 1919; and Open Bible Evangelistic Association, founded in Des Moines, Iowa, in 1932. Similar in doctrine and government, the two groups joined on July 26, 1935, taking the combined name Open Bible Standard Churches, Inc., with headquarters in Des Moines.

The Pacific Coast group, with activities centered in Oregon, spread through Washington, California, and into the Rocky Mountain areas of the West; the Iowa group expanded into Illinois, Missouri, Ohio, Florida, and Pennsylvania. There are now churches in 33 states, concentrated in the central area and far west.

The teachings are "fundamental in doctrine, evangelical in spirit, missionary in vision, and pentecostal in testimony"; they include emphasis on the blood atonement of Christ, divine healing, baptism of the Holy Spirit, personal holiness, the premillennial return of the Lord, and baptism by immersion.

Churches are grouped into 5 geographical divisions, subdivided into 24 districts; district superintendents guide the work under the supervision of divisional superintendents. Individual churches are congregationally governed, locally owned, and affiliated by charter with the national organization. Ten departments function under the leadership of departmental heads, with the advice of a committee, and are represented on the general board of directors. The highest governing body is the general convention, which meets annually and is composed of all licensed and ordained ministers and a lay delegate for each 100 members.

There are 35 missionaries at work in 22 foreign countries, 6 Bible training programs with formal curriculum for the training of national workers, and 3 Bible institutes and colleges with a total enrollment of about 400 students at Des Moines and at Eugene and Dayton, Ohio.

A board of publications is responsible for the preparation of conference literature. The denomination publishes a monthly periodical, *Message of the Open Bible,* and provides lesson materials for Sunday schools through its Christian education department.

The 275 churches—with approximately 40,000 members—hold membership in the Pentecostal Fellowship of North America and the National Association of Evangelicals.

ORTHODOX (EASTERN)

When Constantine moved his capital from Rome to Byzantium in A.D. 330 and began to rule his vast empire from the new Constantinople, the most important split in the history of Christianity was underway. Until that time the church in the West in Rome and the church in the East had formed one body. In the East there were four patriarchs, each traditionally equal with the fifth patriarch, the pope of Rome; all five accepted the Nicene Creed and all were sacramental and apostolic. There were, however, certain basic differences that made for confusion; racially, socially, linguistically, mentally, morally, and philosophically, there were deep gulfs between the two. The East was Greek in blood and speech; the West was Latin. The transference of the capital from West to East meant a shifting of the center of political, social, and intellectual influence. When the Goths swept down upon Rome, that city turned for help—not to Constantinople, but to the Franks; in gratitude for his aid the pope crowned Charles the Great as emperor on Christmas Day in 800, and the Roman Church became coterminous with the Holy Roman Empire.

Conflict deepened between the pope at Rome and the patriarch at Constantinople. In 857 Ignatius, in Constantinople, refused to administer the sacrament to Caesar Bardas on the ground that he was immoral. Tried and imprisoned by the emperor, Ignatius was succeeded by Photius, an intellectual giant for whom the weaker pope was no match. Their increasing friction broke into flame at the Council of St. Sophia, where Photius bitterly condemned the Latin church for adding the word *filioque* to the Nicene Creed. The Eastern church held that the Holy Spirit proceeded directly from the Father; the Western church had adopted the view that the Spirit proceeded from the Father *and* the Son—filioque. Political and ecclesiastical jealousies fanned the flame until, in 1054, the pope excommunicated the patriarch and the patriarch excommunicated the pope, the result being that there were finally two churches, Eastern and Western. The pope remained head of the Western church; at that moment, in the East, there were four patriarchs guiding the destiny of Eastern Orthodoxy. This is important to an understanding of the Eastern Orthodox Church. It is not a monarchy with one all-powerful ruler at the top, but "an oligarchy of patriarchs," based on the body of bishops and responsible to local or general (ecumenical) church councils. No one patriarch is responsible to any other patriarch; yet all are within the jurisdiction of an ecumenical council of all the churches in communion with the patriarch of Constantinople, who holds the title Ecumenical Patriarch.

Today Christendom remains divided into three principal sections: Roman Catholic, Eastern Orthodox (frequently referred to as the Greek church), and Protestant. The Eastern Orthodox Church consists of those churches that accept the decisions and decrees of the first general church councils—2 at Nicea, 3 at Constantinople, 1 at Ephesus, and 1 at Chalcedon—and of such other churches as originated in the missionary activities of these parent churches and have grown to self-government but still maintain communion with them. Certain Eastern bodies refused to accept the christological definition of the Council of Chalcedon (451) and are generally referred to as the Ancient Eastern Churches—Syrian-Antiochian, Malabar Syrians, the Armenians, Copts of Egypt, and Ethiopians.

Claiming to be "the direct heir and true conservator" of the original primitive church, Eastern Orthodoxy has tended historically to divide into independent national and social groups—Syrian, Russian, Serbian, Bulgarian, Romanian, Albanian, Greek, Georgian. These groups have had a bitter struggle for existence, caught between Arab, Tartar, Turkish, and Western armies in endless wars. Generally it may be said that Greek Christianity became the faith of the people of the Middle East and the Slavs in Europe, while Latin Christianity became the religion of Western Europe and the New World.

There are at present the four ancient Eastern Orthodox patriarchates (Constantinople, Alexandria, Antioch, and Jerusalem), with the modern patriarchates of Russia, Serbia, Romania, Bulgaria, and Georgia. In 1970, the former Russian Orthodox Greek Catholic Church in North America was granted autocephaly, with the new name Orthodox Church in America. Mount Sinai, Cyprus, and the National Orthodox churches of Greece, Albania, Finland, Poland, Japan, and Czechoslovakia have autonomous national status.

The Turkish conquest of Constantinople greatly depleted the power of the patriarchate in that city, although it has retained its primacy among the Orthodox—while the First World War and the Russian Revolution of 1917, with the attendant disruption of the Russian Empire, led the Eastern Orthodox churches in Poland, Finland, Estonia, and Latvia to assert their independence. (Lithuania continued loyal to Moscow.) After World War II, Estonia and Latvia were reintegrated into the Russian Orthodox Church. Widely separated, they all still are in essential agreement in doctrine and worship, and together make up what we know as the Holy Eastern Orthodox Church. Nearly all European and Asiatic bodies of the Eastern Orthodox Church have established dioceses in America; some are governed by one or another of the five major patriarchates, while others have declared themselves to be independent and self-governing.

In the United States today, Albanian, Bulgarian, Greek, Romanian, Russian, Serbian, Ukrainian, Carpatho-Russian, and Syrian churches are under the supervision of bishops of their respective nationalities and usually are related to their respective mother churches in tradition and spirit, if not in administration. The patriarch of Moscow and of Alexandria each has jurisdiction over a few parishes in the United States.

Doctrine in Eastern Orthodoxy is based on the Bible, on the holy tradition, and on the decrees of the seven ecumenical councils. The

Nicene Creed is recited in all liturgies and in various other services, the Eastern churches holding that a "creed is an adoring confession of the church engaged in worship"; its faith is expressed more fully in its liturgy than in doctrinal statement. Actually the basis lies in the decisions and statements of the seven councils which defined the ecumenical faith of the early undivided church against the heresies of the period, and in the later statements defining the position of the Orthodox Church of the East with regard to the doctrine and practices of the Roman Catholic and Protestant churches. The Nicene Creed is held in its original form without the "filioque" clause. The dogma of the pope as the sole "vicar of Christ on earth" is rejected, together with the dogma of papal infallibility. Members of Orthodox churches honor the Virgin Mary as *theotokos* but do not dogmatize on the immaculate conception. They also honor the saints and nine orders of angels. They reject the teaching of the surplus merits of the saints and the doctrine of indulgences, but reverence the saints, ikons (consecrated pictures) of revered persons or events, and the cross. The use of carved images is forbidden. Bas-relief is permitted in some Orthodox groups.

There are seven sacraments: baptism, anointing (confirmation or chrismation), Communion, penance, holy orders, marriage, and holy unction. Infants and adults are baptized by threefold immersion. The confirmation sacrament of anointing with chrism, or holy oil, is administered immediately after baptism. Holy unction is administered to the sick, but not always as a last rite. The Holy Eucharist is the chief service on all Sundays and holy days, and all Orthodox churches believe and teach that the consecrated bread and wine are the body and blood of Christ. Purgatory is denied, but the dead are prayed for; and it is believed that the dead pray for those on earth. For justification, both faith and works are considered necessary.

Government is episcopal. There is usually a council of bishops, clergy, and laypeople and a synod of bishops, over which an elected archbishop, metropolitan, or patriarch presides. In the United States each Orthodox jurisdiction is incorporated, with a church assembly of bishops, clergy, and laity. There are three orders in the ministry: deacons (who assist in parish work and in administering the sacraments), priests, and bishops. Deacons and priests may be either secular or monastic; candidates for the deaconate and the priesthood may marry before ordination but are forbidden to marry thereafter. Bishops are chosen from members of the monastic communities; all belong to the same monastic rule of St. Basil the Great and are under lifelong vows of poverty, chastity, and obedience.

Church services are elaborately ritualistic; the liturgy of Holy Communion is a reenactment of the gospel story. Of the worship, Frank Gavin has said:

> In the details of Eastern worship is a rough epitome of the history of Eastern Christendom; the *ikons,* about which a bitter controversy once raged; the service in the vernacular as against Latin; the existence of both a married and a celibate

priesthood; the strong and passionate loyalty to the national allegiance evidenced by the provision of special prayers for the rulers by name—all these mark the characteristics, peculiarities, and contrasts with the customs of the West.

The churches in the United States pray for the President, Congress, the armed forces, and all in places of lawful civil authority.

Membership statistics are confusing and often unreliable, inasmuch as membership is based on baptismal record rather than on communicant status. Infants are confirmed (chrismation) immediately after baptism and are given their first Communion; after the age of seven they must go to confession before taking Communion. Parish membership is frequently determined by the number of males over 21 (often the male head of each family is the voting member in the parish organization). There are probably well over 3 million Orthodox church members in the United States.

It must be kept clear, however, that there are other so-called Orthodox churches in the United States that are not recognized as canonically "Orthodox"—churches that never had or have lost canonical and historical connection with valid, recognized, ancient Orthodoxy. Orthodox churches must be in canonical relationship with the Patriarch of Constantinople and with one another. These irregular Eastern churches might be called autogenic, or self-starting, but they cannot properly be called Orthodox.

Albanian Orthodox Archdiocese in America

The Albanian Orthodox Church in America is the spiritual descendant of the ancient ecclesiastical Western Illyricum (the Holy Illyria) of early Christianity and the early church, and it has suffered a bewildering series of persecutions and changes in the religiopolitical struggles of the Balkan area. Under the peace of Constantine, at the time of the division of the Roman Empire, it was placed under the jurisdiction of the Western church; under the Byzantine (Greek) emperors it was assigned to the Patriarch of Constantinople. Christianized by both Latin and Greek missionaries, Albania, as part of Illyricum, had both Latin- and Greek-rite Christians. There were close ties with Rome and Constantinople until the Moslem Turks became the masters of Albania in 1478–1479, when half its people became Moslems and a small minority remained divided between Latin-rite Christians in the north and Greek-rite Christians, subordinated to Constantinople, in the south. Four centuries of oppression ended in political and religious revolts in the nineteenth and twentieth centuries, and when Albania became independent, its people demanded a church independent of Constantinople.

Meanwhile thousands of Albanians had migrated to America. The Turkish rulers had long refused to allow the maintenance of Albanian-language churches by the church authorities in Constantinople, and accordingly, the Russian Greek Orthodox Catholic Church in America set up Albanian dioceses here under an Albanian archimandrite-administrator, Theophan S. Noli, with a liturgy translated into Albanian in 1908.

With the outbreak of the Russian revolution these ties with the Russian Church were severed, and Noli became the first bishop of a completely independent Albanian-rite church—a "mother church" which, strangely enough, spread its influence back into the motherland of Albania. Noli was consecrated in the Korche Cathedral in Albania as the Archbishop and Metropolitan of Durazzo, and Albanian candidates for the priesthood in America were ordained in Albania. He returned to America to establish a metropolitan throne, with its see in Boston. All Albanian Orthodox in the New World are under this see; it includes 13 organized territorial parishes and some thousands of unorganized, scattered communicants visited by priests on mission circuits. There are 45,250 members in 2 groups: the Albanian Orthodox Archdiocese of America and the Albanian Orthodox Diocese of America. The Archdiocese group is larger, with 40,000 members.

The church has made outstanding contributions, the most notable of which is the production of a liturgical literature in a language that has developed as a composite of ancient Pelasgo-Illyrian dialects, Latin, Greek, and Turkish. Their "Albanian Rite" liturgy actually preceded the liturgy of the Albanian-rite church in Albania. Uniquely, this church has never depended upon the church of its native land. Because of the Iron Curtain, communication between the two churches is no longer possible, but the strong influence of the American church remains.

American Carpatho-Russian Orthodox Greek Catholic Church

The Carpatho-Russian people derive their name from the Carpathian mountain region of eastern Czechoslovakia, where they have resided for centuries. They are akin to the population of Russia because of their geographic location and their common Slavic background and Orthodox religious heritage.

For many years the mother church endured a strife between Orthodoxy and Roman Catholicism; under political pressure in the seventeenth century it became an Uniate church, with Eastern rites and customs, but recognizing the supremacy of the Roman pope.

The desperate struggle to separate from Rome and become completely Eastern was transferred to the United States with the migration of large numbers of the members, especially to the coal-mining and industrial areas of this country. In 1891, Alexis Toth, a Carpatho-Russian Uniate priest, led his Minneapolis parish back to the Orthodox Church, and with several other pastors and parishes was absorbed into the Russian Orthodox Greek Catholic Church in the United States.

In 1938, a new American Carpatho-Russian Orthodox Greek Catholic diocese was established and canonized by Benjamin I, the ecumenical patriarch of Constantinople, with Orestes P. Chornock as its first bishop. In 1977 his auxiliary, John R. Martin, succeeded Chornack as ruling prelate of the diocese.

Under the jurisdiction of the ecumenical patriarchate, the diocese has 65 churches in 10 states and a membership of 56,000. The diocesan headquarters, Christ the Saviour Cathedral, and Christ the Savior Seminary are all located in Johnstown, Pennsylvania. The diocese also has a youth camp, retreat, and conference center in Mercer, Pennsylvania; a monastery in Tuxedo Park, New York; and a retirement facility for the elderly in Philadelphia.

American Holy Orthodox Catholic Eastern Church

Instituted in 1932 and incorporated in 1933, this church is self-governing, "maintaining the Eastern Orthodox faith and rite for all men indiscriminately." Spiritually it "owns no head but the head of the Christian faith, Jesus Christ our Lord," but it considers itself "inseparably joined in faith with the great church of Constantinople and with every other orthodox eastern church of the same profession." The Greek rite is used in all worship services, but it receives into Communion and affiliates with the other churches of Eastern Orthodox belief that desire to retain their national and individual characteristics.

Government is autocephalous: The archbishop does not acknowledge the authority or jurisdiction of any other church or bishop, but he is responsible to the National Council—the supreme legislative, administrative, and judicial authority—made up of bishops, clergy, and laity, which meets every third year. Two lower ecclesiastical bodies, the Holy Synod and the Supreme Ecclesiastical Council, manage the affairs of the church between councils.

The work of the church is religious but also social and educational. It represents an effort, fairly successful, to draw together those of Eastern Orthodox faith into one group, regardless of race, nationality, or language. A provisional synod was set up in 1935 to encourage coordination between the national groups in the various Eastern Orthodox churches, and the Orthodox Catholic Patriarchate of America was fully established in March 1951, in the state of New York. The church and patriarchate have 10 bishops, 25 clergy, 30 churches, and an inclusive membership of approximately 9,000 members.

Antiochian Orthodox Christian Archdiocese of North America

This church is made up of two groups that merged in 1975: the Antiochian Orthodox Christian Archdiocese of New York and All North America (formerly the Syrian Antiochian Orthodox Archdiocese of New York and North America) and the Antiochian Archdiocese of Toledo, Ohio, and Dependencies in North America. It is under the jurisdiction of the Greek Orthodox Patriarch of Antioch and has a membership of 350,000 in 133 churches. These figures reflect a substantial increase in membership, due largely to immigration from the Middle East.

Bulgarian Eastern Orthodox Church

Before the outbreak of the Macedonian revolution in 1903, there was very little Bulgarian immigration to the United States; in 1940 there were only about 60,000 Bulgarian residents here. Coming out of the Bulgarian Orthodox Church, the state church of the country, they brought with them memories of the church's long struggle for independence from the domination of Constantinople. It was in 1872 that the Bulgarian church won its freedom and self-government.

The church was formed in this country in 1909 as the Bulgarian Orthodox Mission and established a bishopric in 1938. It is attached directly to the Holy Synod of Bulgaria, with a membership made up of immigrants from Bulgaria, Macedonia, Thrace, Dobruja, and other parts of the Balkan peninsula. Services are in the Bulgarian and English languages, and doctrine is in accord with that of other Eastern Orthodox churches.

Membership is reported at 86,000 in 13 churches, under the leadership of the Metropolitan Archbishop of North and South America and Australia. There are two American dioceses, located in New York and Akron, Ohio.

Greek Orthodox Archdiocese of North and South America

Greeks arrived in the United States in increasing number between 1890 and 1914, coming from the Greek mainland, the islands of the Aegean Sea, Dodecanese, Cyprus, Constantinople, Smyrna, and other sections of Asia Minor. They asked for and secured the services of Orthodox priests sent to them by the Holy Synod of Greece or by the Ecumenical Patriarchate of Constantinople. Each priest maintained his relation with the synod or patriarchate from which he came; there was at first no central organization.

Following a period of confusion (1908–1922), during which jurisdiction of the American churches was shifted from the Ecumenical Patriarchate of Constantinople to the Holy Synod of Greece and then back again, an act known as the Founding Tome of 1922 established the Greek (Orthodox) Archdiocese of North and South America, consisting of four bishoprics under the supervision of the Archbishop Alexander and the Patriarchate of Constantinople. Alexander's successor, Archbishop Athenagoras, was elected Patriarch of Constantinople in 1948 and was succeeded in turn by Archbishop Michael and Archbishop Iakovos, the present incumbent.

Doctrine, polity, and worship follow the usual Orthodox patterns. There are 1,950,000 members in 535 churches and 11 archdiocesan districts, 18 parochial schools, 9 summer camps, a seminary, 3 homes for teenage boys, and a home for the aged.

Holy Apostolic and Catholic Church of the East (Assyrian)

This is the ancient Church of Persia. Its patriarch originally resided in Chaldea, near the Persian Gulf. It is said that at its peak, throughout most of Asia it had better than 80 million members, but with the exception of that which still exists in India, it was almost completely annihilated in the wars of Ghengis Khan and Tamerlane, and later by the Portuguese and

Turks in 1915; the members scattered through Iraq, Syria, Persia, and Lebanon.

The church claims as its founders Thomas, Thaddeus, Peter, and Bartholomew of the apostles, and Mari and Addai of the seventy. Its theology stresses the two natures of Christ, holding that he was "man and God, two natures and two substances united in one person and one will"; but it insists that Mary should not be granted the name "Mother of God," since she did not give birth "to the divinity, but to the humanity, the temple of divinity," and accordingly is not the mother of God, but the mother of Christ. They believe that it was the man in Christ that died, not the God in Christ.

The American branch of this church came into existence during the wave of immigration in 1911, and nearly all its adherents have arrived during the last half-century. In 1940 the head of the church, then in exile in England, came to the United States; he is Mar Eshai Shimun XXIII, Catholicos Patriarch of the East and Supreme Head of the Assyrian people in the Republic of Iraq. Some 250,000 members are still active in the Middle East, Russia, and India; in the United States there are 30,000 members in 12 churches.

Romanian Orthodox Episcopate of America

This body was organized at a church congress convened in Detroit on April 25, 1929, by clergy and lay representatives of Romanian Orthodox parishes in the United States and Canada. It was under the canonical jurisdiction of the Romanian Orthodox Patriarchate in Bucharest until political conditions forced its separation, and is now under the autocephalous Orthodox Church in America. The bishop is a member of the Holy Synod of the Orthodox Church in America, and the diocese is recognized as an administratively self-governing body.

The episcopate is headed by a bishop elected for life by a special Electoral Congress made up of clerical and lay delegates from the parishes. With the aid of an episcopate council composed of 10 laypeople and five clergy, elected for two years by the church congress, the bishop supervises all matters of administration and also presides at all council meetings, which are held as need arises. The church congress is the chief legislative body, composed of one clerical and two lay representatives from each parish; it meets annually in July.

There are 5 deaneries, or districts, in the United States; some Romanian Orthodox parishes in South America, Western Europe, and Australia are under the jurisdiction of the episcopate. There are 34 churches and 40,000 members in the United States, concentrated in the Great Lakes industrial area.

Russian Orthodox Church

Eastern Orthodoxy came to Russia with the baptism of Grand Prince Vladimir of Kiev in A.D. 988. Government of the church at first was ruled by metropolitans appointed or approved by the Patriarch of Constantinople. About 500 years ago Job became the first patriarch of all Russia. The office of patriarch was abolished, and a Holy Synod was substituted during the reign of Peter the Great; the other Orthodox churches recognized this synod as being patriarchal in effect. From 1721 to 1917 the Holy Synod was made up of three metropolitans and other bishops from various parts of Russia, who sat in rotation at its sessions. A civil officer of the tsar, known as the chief procurator, attended its sessions as the tsar's representative. This pre-1917 church, like every public organization in Russia, was administratively dominated by the tsarist regime.

In 1917 dramatic changes were instituted by the Great Sobor, or church assembly. Administration was changed, the office of chief procurator was abolished, and the church returned to the old patriarchal form of government. As the Great Sobor held its sessions, however, the gunfire of revolution was heard in the streets, and once the followers of Lenin had taken over the state, they immediately applied Marxist-Leninist principles: church was separated from state and school from church, and church activity in large measure was restricted to worship. The patriarch and the synod resisted, but the government found some priests and bishops who were ready to support the new regime. These held a rigged assembly that deposed the patriarch, endorsed communism, and declared itself the governing body of the Russian church. Calling themselves the Renovated, or Living, Church, they changed the ancient disciplinary rules and instituted liturgical reforms. With the support of the Soviet authorities who hoped thus to divide and weaken the church, they held control for several years but were never recognized by the great body of clergy or people. The government considered opposition to the Living Church a civil offense and, on this basis, banished thousands of bishops, clergy, monastics, and lay people to labor camps.

In 1927 the Soviet government prevailed upon Metropolitan Sergius of Nizhni-Novgorod, the deputy *locum tenens* of the then vacant patriarchal see, to submit the policy of the church totally to that of the Soviet regime. This was sine qua non recognition of the church's right to exist as a legal entity. Yet it was not until 1943 that Hitler's success in invading the U.S.S.R. altered his plan for the annihilation of the church, and Stalin engineered the meeting of a small group of bishops to elect Metropolitan Sergius as Patriarch of Moscow and All Russia.

It was this Patriarch Sergius who called on his people to support the government in the defense of their country. This marked a turning point in the Soviet government's policy toward the church; the Living Church was discarded and the patriarch's authority was recognized by the state. Many surviving clergy and bishops who had been banished were permitted to return, and gradually the patriarchal administration became again the sole authority in the Orthodox Church of Russia.

The main missionary efforts of Russian Orthodoxy were historically directed toward the Moslem, Buddhist, animistic populations of Central Asia and Siberia. In the mid-eighteenth century an Orthodox mission was established in China, and in the late nineteenth century one was begun in Japan. Eight Russian Orthodox monks entered Alaska in 1792, established headquarters at Kodiak, and there built the first Eastern Orthodox Church in America; 12,000 people were baptized within two years' time. Orthodox monks and bishops created an alphabet and printed a grammar in the Aleutian language, translated portions of the Bible, and built a cathedral at Sitka.

A chapel was built in the early years of the nineteenth century at a Russian trading post near present-day San Francisco. The episcopal see was transferred to San Francisco in 1872 and moved to New York City in 1905, as waves of immigration brought thousands of Slavs to the eastern states. Immigrants from other countries with Orthodox churches—Serbia, Syria, Greece—were for many years cared for by the Russian hierarchy in America. Many Eastern-rite Catholics from the old Austro-Hungarian empire, traditionally having been in a Uniate church that had grown to impressive numbers, came to this country and found themselves in an embarrassing situation, being placed under the direction of Irish and German Roman Catholic bishops. Torn between conflicting demands and loyalties, many of these Uniate parishes returned to the jurisdiction of the Russian Orthodox Church.

Hard days were ahead, however. The revolution of 1917 cut off the financial support that had come from the mother church, which was now fighting for its life. The Living Church faction in Russia, supported by the communist government, sent an emissary to secure control of Russian Orthodox Greek Catholic Church property in the United States and succeeded, through action in the civil courts, in gaining possession of the cathedral in New York City. An assembly of the Diocese of North America in 1924, attempting to prevent further seizures, declared that, on a temporary basis, it was administratively, legislatively, and jurisdictionally independent of the church in Russia. This autonomy was not recognized by the Patriarchate of Moscow or by the Russian Orthodox Church Outside Russia, headquartered at that time in Yugoslavia. The Russian Orthodox Greek Catholic Church, whose membership in 1951 numbered 55,000 in 81 churches, now is officially titled Orthodox Church in America and has 13 archbishops and bishops and 755,000 members in 352 churches.

The Russian Orthodox Church Outside Russia holds that the Moscow patriarchate has forfeited its right to be considered a true Orthodox church because it has adopted a position of submission to the Soviet regime, not only in regard to politics and external matters, but with respect to its internal policies and affairs.

The metropolitan and synod of this body administer like-minded Russian Orthodox all over the world—largely Russian exiles of the revolution and displaced displaced persons of World War II. When armed resistance to the Soviet revolution finally ceased, many sought refuge abroad. A number of bishops and clergy gathered at Constantinople, later transferred to Sremski Karlovici in Yugoslavia, and there set up a synod to give spiritual leadership to these refugees. During World War II, its administrative headquarters were moved from Belgrade to Munich, a move which proved fortuitous because of the displaced persons' camps set up there in the aftermatch of the war.

Relief programs of the churches brought great numbers to America, and the headquarters of the synod were moved to New York City in 1952. Its complete rejection of the Moscow patriarchate conformed to the attitude of many of these new arrivals and kept them from uniting with the Russian church already established in North America. It maintains bishops and clergy wherever Russian refugees are resettled—in Canada, South America, Australia, Africa, Europe, and the Middle East. With the growth of Orthodox participation in the ecumenical movement, the constituency of the church has been augmented by a significant number of parishes and individuals of other Orthodox jurisdictions because of its steadfast opposition to the ecumenical movement and its theological implications.

The third body is the Patriarchal Parishes of the Russian Orthodox Church in the U.S.A. It accepts the full authority of the Moscow patriarchate and is its representative in America. De facto occupancy of the old Russian cathedral in New York City was established when the former emissary of the Living Church faction submitted to the patriarch's representative. It is governed by a bishop appointed by the patriarch and an assembly elected by the parishes. There are 51,500 members in 51 churches.

Serbian Eastern Orthodox Church in the U.S.A. and Canada

From the seventh century to the thirteenth, the church in Serbia was under the jurisdiction of the Greek Patriarchate of Constantinople and became the independent National Serbian Church in 1219. It made notable contributions to art and architecture and played an important part in the Serbian struggle for independence through the long period of Turkish invasion and domination (1389–1876), during which it suffered unbelievable persecution.

Serbian immigrants to the United States, coming here more for political than economic reasons, began to arrive in large numbers about 1890. They worshiped at first in Russian churches, accepting the ministrations of Russian priests and the supervision of Russian bishops. The Serbian Patriarchate of Yugoslavia approved the organization of the Diocese of the United States and Canada in 1921 and sent its first bishop in 1926. Today there are 77 parishes and 95,000 members. Doctrine and polity are in harmony with other branches of the Orthodox church.

Syrian Orthodox Church of Antioch (Archdiocese of the U.S.A. and Canada)

The word Antioch in the name of this church is important, for its origin is traced back to St. Peter, who is believed to have established the first patriarchate in Antioch. Today the American group is under the jurisdiction of the Syrian Orthodox Patriarch of Antioch and All the East.

Syrians were few in number in the United States until the turn of the last century; their first priest arrived in 1907, their first patriarchal vicar (Archbishop Mar Athanasius Y. Samuel) was appointed in 1949, and the Archdiocese of the Syrian Orthodox Church in the U.S.A. and Canada was organized in 1957.

At the present time there are 15 archdiocesan parishes in 9 states in the United States and 4 in Canada. As of 1980 there were 30,000 members in 10 churches, and an additional (larger) membership is located in the Middle East, India, Europe, and Australia. There is an annual archdiocesan convention.

Ukrainian Orthodox Churches

Eastern Orthodoxy was established as the state religion in Ukraine by a unique procedure. In the tenth century Vladimir the Great, ruler of Kiev, sent investigators abroad to study the doctrines and rituals of Islam and Judaism, as well as those of Christianity. They came back to report that the Eastern Orthodox faith seemed best suited to the needs of their people. Vladimir was immediately baptized Basil in that faith, and by 988 the entire Ukraine population had become Orthodox Christian.

For more than 600 years the Ukrainian church was under the jurisdiction of the Ecumenical Partriarchate of Constantinople. In 1686 it was forcibly placed under the supervision of the Russian Patriarch of Moscow. Rejecting the authority of Moscow after the 1917 revolution, Ukrainians in the United States are still engaged in a bitter dispute among themselves; attempts at union have been made, but to date there are two separate groups. The first, the Ukrainian Orthodox Church of the U.S.A., was formally organized in this country in 1919; Archbishop John Theodorovich arrived in 1924. This group has 107 churches and 87,745 members. The second body, the Ukrainian Orthodox Church of America (Ecumenical Patriarchate), was organized in 1928 and has 12 parishes and 30,000 members. Primary areas of Ukrainian Orthodox strength lie in New England, Chicago, and Pittsburgh and western Pennsylvania.

PENTECOSTAL

Pentecostalism is an inclusive term applied to a large number of revivalistic American sects, assemblies, and churches. Many have either a Methodist or Baptist background, and they are primarily concerned with perfection, Holiness, and the Pentecostal experience.

Their statements of faith are often long, involved, and highly repetitious, but through them run certain common strains and elements. Most believe in the Trinity, original sin, salvation through the atoning blood of Christ, the Virgin birth and deity of Jesus, the divine inspiration and literal infallibility of the Scriptures, manifestations and "blessings" of the working of the Holy Spirit—the fiery Pentecostal baptism of the Spirit, premillennialism, and future rewards and punishments. Two sacraments are found in most sects—baptism, usually by immersion, and the Lord's Supper. Foot washing is frequently observed in connection with the Supper. Many practice divine healing, and speaking in tongues is widespread.

Ultrafundamentalistic, and varying in size from small group meetings to huge mass meetings, pentecostalists are found in every state in the union, with greatest strength in the South, West, and Middle West. The churches bear a great variety of names and do not always include the word *Pentecostal* —for instance, the largest single group, Assemblies of God, with over half a million members, and the Church of God groups. No accurate count of total membership is possible, since many never issue statistical reports of any kind.

Assemblies of God, General Council of

The largest of the Pentecostal bodies, with 1,879,182 members and 10,173 churches, the General Council of the Assemblies of God is actually an aggregation of Pentecostal churches and assemblies accomplished at Hot Springs, Arkansas, in 1914. The founders were former ministers and pastors of evangelical persuasion who wished to unite in the interest of more effective preaching and an enlarged missionary crusade.

Ardently fundamentalist, its theology is Arminian; there is strong belief in the infallibility and inspiration of the Bible, the fall and redemption of the human race, baptism in the Holy Ghost, a life of holiness and separation from the world, divine healing, the second advent of Jesus and his millennial reign, eternal punishment for the wicked and eternal bliss for believers. Two ordinances, baptism and the Lord's Supper, are practiced. Members stand officially opposed to war, but large numbers of their youth accepted noncombatant and even combatant service in World War II. They are especially insistent that baptism in the Holy Spirit is evidenced by speaking in tongues. The Assemblies of God believe that all the gifts of the Spirit should be in operation in the normal New Testament church.

The government of the assemblies is an unusual mixture of presbyterian and congregational systems. Local churches are quite independent in polity and in the conduct of local affairs. District officers have a pastoral ministry to all the churches and are responsible for the promotion of home missions. Work is divided into 57 districts in the United States, including 9 foreign-language districts, each with a district presbytery that examines, licenses, and ordains pastors. The General Council consists of all ordained (not licensed) ministers, and local churches are represented by one lay delegate each. This council elects general officers, sets the doctrinal standards, and provides for church expansion and development.

Missionary work is conducted under the guidance of a central missionary committee; there are 1,220 foreign missionaries at work on a total missionary budget of $48,453,712—unusually high among Protestant churches. A weekly periodical, *The Pentecostal Evangel,* has a circulation of approximately 300,000; a prosperous church press produces books, tracts, and other religious literature. There are 9 Bible colleges; a liberal arts college; a graduate school of theology located in Springfield, Missouri; and 233 Bible institutes abroad. An international weekly radio program, "Revivaltime," is broadcast on 570 stations, and a daily radio program, "Every Day with Jesus," on 42 stations.

Calvary Pentecostal Church, Inc.

This church was founded at Olympia, Washington, in 1931 by a group of ministers who sought a ministerial fellowship, rather than a separate denomination. The body was incorporated in 1932, and a home and foreign missionary society was incorporated in the same year. Home missions today consists mainly of evangelistic work, relief to weak churches, and the establishment of new churches. A general superintendent and executive presbytery board administer the work of the church; the general body meets in convention annually or semiannually. Seminary, college, or Bible school education is considered beneficial, but is not a requirement for ministers of this church, who may be either men or women; those who give evidence of having heard the call of God to preach are qualified by ordination. There are 22 churches and 8,000 members.

Elim Fellowship

Established in 1947, this body is an outgrowth of the missionary-oriented Elim Ministerial Fellowship formed in 1932, and of the work of graduates of the Elim Bible Institute, founded in 1924 in Lima, New York. The organizational pattern is congregational, and doctrine is basically premillennial, holding the usual tenets of belief in an inspired and infallible Bible, the Trinity, sanctification, the baptism of the Holy Spirit, divine healing, and the resurrection of the saved and unsaved for eternal reward or punishment. Some 12,000 members are found in 100 churches, and 125 missionaries are at work in 25 countries in Africa, Asia, Europe, and South America. Headquarters are located on the former campus of Genesee Wesleyan Seminary, purchased in 1951. The assemblies hold membership in the Pentecostal Fellowship of North America and the National Association of Evangelicals.

Emmanuel Holiness Church

The founders of this church had come to a general conference of the Pentecostal Fire-Baptized Holiness Church in 1953 but withdrew from that church in protest against certain positions taken by the conference on doctrine and polity. They now have 1,200 members in 56 churches and tabernacles located in Alabama, Florida, Georgia, North and South Carolina, and Illinois; there is missionary activity in Mexico, Egypt, and France. Their chief administrative body is a general assembly, and their ruling church officer is a general overseer. A periodical, *Emmanuel Messenger*, is published at Franklin Springs, Georgia.

Independent Assemblies of God, International

A Holiness group, this is an incorporated association of Pentecostal ministers. Sometimes called Philadephia, their churches have a Swedish background and work closely with the Swedish Pentecostal movement, with which they conduct an extensive missionary program. It is claimed that their missionary church in Brazil is the largest Protestant church in that country, having "close to half a million followers and really converted people."

The government follows the autonomous pattern of other Pentecostal churches and assemblies. There are 800 churches, 1800 ministers and evangelists, 12 Bible schools, and 200 missionaries in the Philippines.

International Pentecostal Church of Christ

This body was brought into being in 1976 through the consolidation of the International Pentecostal Assemblies and the Pentecostal Church of Christ. Headquarters are located at London, Ohio.

Membership numbers approximately 12,000 in some 80 congregations. The International Pentecostal Assemblies originated in 1907 and were strongest in Atlanta and nearby areas of Georgia. The Pentecostal Church of Christ, founded in 1917 by John Stroup at Flatwoods, Kentucky, was incorporated at Portsmouth, Ohio, in 1927..

The church subscribes to the usual Pentecostal doctrines of the Trinity, regeneration, sanctification, and baptism of the Spirit. It puts strong emphasis on divine healing; the sick are anointed with oil, and prayer is offered for their healing. Foot washing is optional. The group is not opposed to participating in government or in defensive war.

Active mission work is carried on in 13 countries, most notably in Kenya, Brazil, and India. Beulah Heights Bible College, a four-year institution in Atlanta, is supported by this church.

International Pentecostal Holiness Church

This church was organized in 1898 at Anderson, South Carolina, by a number of Holiness associations, and at the time was called the Fire-Baptized Holiness Church. In the same year, in Goldsboro, North Carolina, another group was organized as the Pentecostal Holiness Church. The two bodies united in 1911 at Falcon, North Carolina. A third body, the Tabernacle Pentecostal Church, joined them in 1915. There are 104,011 members in 1,414 churches in the United States, and 157,241 members in foreign mission fields. Principal states of strength are the Carolinas, Virginia, Oklahoma, and Texas.

The theological standards of Methodism prevail, with certain modifications. It accepts the premillennial teaching of the Second Coming and believes that provision was made in the Atonement for healing of the body. Divine healing is practiced but not to the exclusion of medicine. Three distinctive experiences are taught: two works of grace—justification by faith and sanctification; and Spirit baptism, attested by speaking in other tongues. Services are often characterized by "joyous demonstrations."

Polity is also Methodistic. A general executive board of 9 members is elected by a quadrennial conference for a 4-year term and members are limited to 2 consecutive terms in any one office. There is a general superintendent (bishop), 2 assistant general superintendents, a secretary-treasurer, and 5 board members representing geographic areas and the church at large. There are 35 conferences in the United States. Foreign mission stations are located in Hong Kong, India, the Phillipines, Korea, Indonesia, Central and Western Africa, Argentina, Venezuela, Chile, Brazil, Mexico, Cuba, France, Italy, England, and Israel.

Emmanuel College and Oklahoma City Southwestern College are accredited junior colleges, both also offering a four-year ministerial training program, and Holmes Theological Seminary is located at Greenville, South Carolina. There is a children's home at Falcon, North Carolina, a children's convalescent center at Bethany, Oklahoma, and homes for the aged at Falcon and at Carmen, Oklahoma.

Pentecostal Assemblies of the World, Inc.

This was an interracial body at the time of its organization in 1907; some white members withdrew in 1924 to form the Pentecostal Church Inc., which became a constituent body of the United Pentecostal Church in 1945. Origin is traced "directly back to Pentecost, A.D. 33." Doctrine reveals no important departure from that of pentecostalism in general. Secret societies are opposed. Divorce is permitted, but only the grounds of fornication when both man and wife have had the "baptism of the Holy Ghost"; but when the unbeliever in a marriage procures a divorce, the believer may remarry.

Organization is similar to the Methodist: A general assembly meets annually under a presiding bishop; there is a secretary for foreign missions and 123 district elders. An executive board is composed of the 35 bishops, 5 directors, the general secretary, and the general treasurer. An election of officers is held every 3 years by the ministerial members of the national assembly. Local assemblies are under the direction of the bishop. There are 4,500 members in 550 churches.

Pentecostal Church of God

The Pentecostal Church of God, with its international headquarters presently in Joplin, Missouri, was organized in Chicago on December 30, 1919. The name Pentecostal Assemblies of the U.S.A. was used until the general convention on February 22, 1922. At that time the name was changed to Pentecostal Church of God. For a number of years "of America" was a part of the name but this was dropped in 1979.

Evangelical and Pentecostal in doctrine and practice, the church is an active member of both the National Association of Evangelicals and the Pentecostal Fellowship of North America. The doctrines of salvation, divine healing, baptism in the Holy Ghost (with the initial physical evidence of speaking in tongues), and the second coming of Christ are strongly emphasized.

Officers include a general superintendent, general secretary-treasurer, director of world missions, director of Indian missions, director of Christian education, president of Pentecostal ladies auxiliary, district superintendents, district presbyters, and district secretary-treasurers. A general convention meets biennially; most of the 33 districts have annual conventions.

In 1982 there was a total of 1,107 churches with 91,008 members in 42 states, and 1,000 churches and outstations with 80,000 members in 24 other countries. The church owns and operates two Bible colleges—Southern Bible College in Houston, Texas, and Evangelical Christian College in Fresno, California. The School of Bible Theology and Christian Dynamics in San Jacinto, California, is also endorsed by the church. In other countries there are 13 resident Bible schools plus 59 extension training centers, with a student enrollment of 1,600. Messenger Publishing House is located in Joplin, Missouri.

Pentecostal Free-Will Baptist Church, Inc.

As the name suggests, this is a Pentecostal group with a Free-Will Baptist background; it came into existence through the merging of three Free-Will Baptist conferences in North Carolina in 1959. Doctrine is, naturally, a mixture of Baptist and pentecostalist beliefs, including regeneration through faith in the shed blood of Christ, sanctification as a second definite work of grace (subsequent to regeneration), Pentecostal baptism of the Holy Ghost, divine healing, and the premillennial second coming of Christ. Heritage Bible College was established in September, 1972.

Officials include a general superintendent, general secretary, and general treasurer. A general meeting composed of lay and ministerial representatives is held biennially in August.

There are 9,280 members in 127 churches in eastern North Carolina. Mission work is carried on in 7 foreign countries; Bible institutes are operated in Mexico and in the Philippines.

United Pentecostal Church International

The product of a union of two Pentecostal organizations (the Pentecostal Assemblies of Jesus Christ and the Pentecostal Church, Inc.) at St. Louis in 1945, this church stresses the necessity of repentance, water baptism in the name of Christ, and the receiving of the baptism of the Holy Ghost with the initial sign of speaking in tongues. It has 500,000 members in 3,300 churches. The superintendents of geographic districts make up the General Board, the international administrative body.

A foreign missions program supports 4,097 missionaries in 67 foreign countries, with 441,224 members in 5,875 congregations; 37 summer campgrounds are maintained in the United States and Canada. Headquarters and a publishing house that issues the official *Pentecostal Herald* and many other publications are located in St. Louis. The church also sponsors an international radio broadcast on 161 stations, 10 affiliated Bible colleges, and a children's home in Tupelo, Mississippi.

PILLAR OF FIRE

The Pillar of Fire originated in the evangelistic efforts of its founder, Mrs. Alma White. The wife of a Methodist minister in Colorado, Mrs. White often preached from her husband's pulpit. Her fervent exhortations on regeneration and Holiness—and especially her habit of organizing missions and camp meetings on her own authority—brought her into sharp conflict with the bishops and other leaders of Methodism, and she withdrew to become an evangelistic free-lance. She established the Pentecostal Union in 1901; the name was changed to Pillar of Fire in 1917.

Mrs. White's first headquarters were in Denver but later were moved to Zarephath, near Bound Brook, New Jersey. In Denver there are a college, preparatory school, Bible seminary, radio station, and publishing house. Other schools are located in Cincinnati; Zarephath; Los Angeles; Jacksonville, Florida; Pacifica, near San Francisco; Seattle; Liberia, in Africa; and London. Other foreign missions include Nigeria and Spain.

Modernism in theology is condemned by Pillar of Fire; its teaching is based upon primitive Wesleyanism, with doctrines on the inspiration and inerrancy of the Scriptures, repentance, justification, second blessing Holiness, premillennialism, and future judgment. Sacraments include baptism and the Lord's Supper; marriage is a "divine institution."

Mrs. White was the first bishop of Pillar of Fire; on her death, authority passed to her two sons. Bishop White's granddaughter, Arlene White Lawrence, a bishop, is now president and general superintendent. The membership is divided into four classes: probationary, associate, regular, and full, with only regular and full members being allowed to vote on administrative matters. There are deacons and deaconesses, and both men and women are ordained as ministers; there are also consecrated deaconesses, licensed preachers, missionaries, and, as in Methodism, presiding elders (district superintendents) and bishops. Much literature is printed and distributed in the United States, and there are regular broadcasts from WAWZ in Zarephath, KPOF in Denver, and WAKW in Cincinnati. There were approximately 5,000 members and 30 branches in 1983.

PLYMOUTH BRETHREN

The name Plymouth Brethren is a widely used but generally unofficial designation for a loose grouping of churches that have early-nineteenth-century roots in the British Isles. Within these chuches, the common terminology is simply Brethren, or assemblies, or Brethren assemblies. The name Plymouth Brethren will be heard infrequently in casual conversation, but never appears in advertising, on sign boards, or in church bulletins; outsiders combined the two words when the 1,000-member congregation in Plymouth, England, attracted notice with its active evangelism. In Great Britain and the Commonwealth countries, the name Christian Brethren has gradually replaced Plymouth Brethren for governmental purposes, but this changeover is less advanced in the United States.

The matter of names is a sensitive issue among Brethren, reflecting a historical emphasis on the unity of all believers. The movement arose in a highly sectarian age when closed Communion was practiced in most denominations. The early Brethren envisioned a basis for Christian unity—not in the ecumenical merging of denominations, but rather in forsaking denominational structures and names in order to meet simply as Christians, welcoming all who belong to Christ. The designation Plymouth Brethren is inconsistent with this concept because it does not encompass all born-again Christians; the term Brethren by itself is not resented.

The unwillingness to establish a denominational structure makes the autonomy of the local congregation another feature of the movement, coupled with the doctrinal understanding that a *church* is not a building, but rather the gathering of people who meet there. Hence terms like Bible Chapel or Gospel Hall, usually prefixed with the name of the city, community, street, or some biblical term like Grace, Bethel, or Bethany, have been preferred to "Church" when naming a building.

The weekly hour-long "remembrance meeting" is probably the surest way to identify a Brethren assembly. The centrality of the Communion service is characteristic of the movement. The service is unstructured, with all the men of the assembly free to take oral part. This is what is meant by "priesthood of all believers." A preacher may be serving full-time with the local congregation but will not be identified as clergy or given control over the Communion service.

All these features arise from the original emphasis on Christian unity. Under the influence of Anthony Norris Groves, who later became the first Brethren missionary, an initial group of believers meeting in Ireland realized they could break bread scripturally either with or without the presence of the clergy. From that point on Brethren have consistently refused to restrict the administration of baptism and the Lord's Supper to ordained ministers, thus effectively eliminating a clergy/laity distinction and rejecting the traditional concept of ordination.

From the sacraments they moved quickly to the understanding that the Word of God could be ministered by any brother with spiritual gifts. The sharing of preaching responsibilities among men of the congregation has been sometimes a strength, sometimes a weakness of the movement.

Plymouth Brethren are committed to all the fundamentals of orthodox Christianity, including the verbal inspiration of Scripture. They are part of the mainstream of American evangelicalism, strongly emphasizing gospel preaching and the necessity for personal conversion. Except for the weekly breaking of bread and the absence of collections at other meetings, their services are much like those of evangelical Baptist and Bible churches.

Among U. S. evangelicals, Brethren have had an influence out of proportion to their numbers. Their premillennial theology helped shape evangelicalism, especially in the proliferation of independent churches and mission boards. More recently, many have been responding to the Brethren emphasis on plurality of leadership and participatory worship in the local church. Brethren are also characteristically found in leadership positions in interdenominational evangelistic campaigns and in the founding and operation of nondenominational Bible schools, colleges, and seminaries; they have only one multiple-year college-level institution of their own, Emmaus Bible College in Dubuque, Iowa.

As a result of a division in England in 1848, there are two basic types of assemblies, commonly known as *exclusive* and *open*. Led in the beginning by John Nelson Darby, the exclusive assemblies produced most of the movement's well-known Bible teachers (Kelly, Grant, Mackintosh, and so on). They operated on the premise that disciplinary action taken by one assembly was binding on all assemblies. As a result, once started, a division ran to the end of the world, and by the end of the century, exclusive Brethren were divided into seven or eight main groups. Recent mergers have reduced that number somewhat, and an important American group has merged into the open assemblies.

Open assemblies were led by George Muller, well known for his orphanages and life of faith. Their strength has always been in evangelism and foreign missions. Lacking the exclusive disciplinary premise, local disputes spread only as far as there was interest and involvement, and open assemblies have never experienced worldwide division.

Exclusive assemblies were dominant in the nineteenth century, but today there are an estimated 850 open assemblies in the United States, while there are only 250 exclusive groups. The number of people has been estimated at 80,000 and 20,000, respectively. Precise figures are difficult to obtain since the assemblies do not maintain membership rolls, emphasizing instead "fellowship at the Lord's table."

Letters of Interest Associates publishes a monthly magazine, address lists of North American open assemblies, and those of full-time Christian workers serving those assemblies in the United States, Canada, and the Bahamas. Christian Missions in Many Lands, Inc., publishes a missionary magazine and an address list of missionaries serving overseas. In keeping with Brethren concepts of ministers' and missionaries' direct responsibility to the Lord, neither organization assigns workers to specific tasks or locations, or assumes responsibility for their financial support. In these respects, there are no mission boards in the conventional sense.

Plymouth Brethren are strongest in the New York and Chicago metropolitan areas and in the states of Pennsylvania, North Carolina, Florida, Michigan, Iowa, and California. Apart from the Los Angeles and San Francisco metropolitan areas, there are only scattered assemblies in the western half of the country.

POLISH NATIONAL CATHOLIC CHURCH OF AMERICA

A strictly American church born on American soil, this body was formally organized at Scranton, Pennsylvania, on March 14, 1897, after a long period of conflict between the Roman Catholic Church and many of the Poles who had immigrated to the United States around the turn of the century. Roman Catholic in background, they objected that in the United States they had no bishops and few priests who were Polish, that they could not teach in Polish in their parish schools, and that under the ruling of the Roman Catholic Council of Baltimore in 1884, they had no right to establish parishes of their own. All this, they felt, gave the Roman hierarchy and priesthood an unwarranted religious, political, financial, and social power over the parishioners and permitted "an unlawful encroachment upon their right to private ownership and paved the way for the political and social exploitation of the Polish people." (Some scholars feel that the cause of dissension has roots farther back, in the demand during the Reformation era for a Polish National Church.) Resentment smoldered gradually into open revolt in Chicago, Detroit, Cleveland, Buffalo, and Scranton and gradually resulted in the founding of an independent Polish body with approximately 20,000 members, mainly in the eastern states. This was the only break of any considerable size from the Roman Catholic Church in the United States; but some groups among Slovaks, Lithuanians, Ruthenians, and Hungarians also have broken away. Several Slovak and Lithuanian parishes have merged with the Polish National Catholic Church.

A constitution for the new church was adopted by the Scranton parish in 1897, claiming the right for the Polish to control all churches built and maintained by them, and to administer such property through a committee chosen by the parish. The first synod was held in 1904, with 146 clerical and lay delegates representing parishes in Pennsylvania, Maryland, Massachusetts, and New Jersey. Francis Hodur, the organizer and dominant figure in the group, was chosen bishop-elect; he was consecrated in 1907 at Utrecht, Holland, by three bishops of the Old Catholic Church. Following the synod, Polish gradually replaced Latin as the liturgical language.

The doctrine of this church is founded in the Holy Scripture, holy traditions, and four ecumenical synods of the undivided church; however, the three councils that followed are not rejected. The Apostles' and Nicene creeds are accepted. Doctrine is expanded in a confession of faith that includes belief in the Trinity; the Holy Spirit as the ruler of the world and the source of grace; the necessity for spiritual unity of all Christians; Christ's one Body, the Church apostolic and universal, as teacher, steward of grace, and a light unto salvation; the equal right of all to life, happiness, and growth in perfection; equal responsibility toward God of all people and nations; immortality and the future justice and judgment of God. The doctrine of eternal damnation and punishment is supplanted in the church's Eleven Great Principles by an expressed hope and surety of universal salvation as taught in the church by Gregory of Nyssa and Clement of Alexandria. The seventh of their Eleven Great Principles reads:

> We cannot conceive that God created man out of sheer caprice, nor selfishness . . . nor for the purpose of delivering him to devils for them to abuse and treat him cruelly by physical and spiritual torment and torture . . . but He created man that he should live his own life according to his creator's image.

Faith is necessary to salvation but must be manifest in good works. Sin is:

> a misunderstanding of the being and purpose of God on the part of the individual, the nation, and even all humanity. Left to himself . . . sinful man . . . deteriorates, wastes away; and surely would perish if not for the help of the Father Creator who does not desire the death of a sinner but rather that he be converted and live.

Seven sacraments are observed, with baptism and confirmation as one sacrament—confirmation is regarded as a completion of baptism. The seventh sacrament is hearing the Word of God proclaimed by the church. Two forms of confession are in general use—a private confession for children and youths and a general confession for adults only.

A general synod is the highest legislative authority in the government of the church. It meets every four years, except for such special sessions as may be considered necessary, and is composed of active bishops, clergy, and lay delegates from every parish. The administration and destiny of this church, according to its constitution, rests with the Prime Bishop. A Supreme Council meets annually or on call and is composed of all active bishops and 6 clerical and 14 lay delegates approved by the general synod. In like manner the authority of the diocese is vested in a diocesan bishop and a diocesan synod which meets every four years. Each parish is governed by an elected board of trustees. There are 272,082 members in 162 parishes in the United States and Canada, divided into 5 dioceses: Buffalo, Pittsburgh, Canadian, Eastern, and Western. Polish and English are used in worship and in the educational programs of parish schools, taught largely by pastors. The clergy may marry, but only with the knowledge and permission of the bishops.

The Polish National Union, a fraternal and insurance organization established by Bishop Hodur in 1908, is set up on parish lines as an adjunct to parish life. It consists of 12 districts, divided into 224 branches, and has approximately 32,000 members, not all of whom are required to be members of the church.There is a theological seminary in Scranton, Pennsylvania, and a home for the aged at Spojnia Farm, Waymart, Pennsylvania.

Missionary work was begun in Poland in 1919, and by 1939 there were more than 50 parishes and a theological seminary in Krakow. Missionary bishop Padewski was arrested by the communists and died in prison the same year; since that time the church in Poland has become autocephalous, but the two churches remain in theological and ideological harmony.

In 1912 the Lithuanian National Catholic Church was established under the jurisdiction of the Polish National Catholic Church. This church also does missionary work among the Poles in Brazil. As the only member of the Old Catholic Union of Utrecht, it has in recent years strengthened its ties with European Old Catholics.

PRESBYTERIAN

Presbyterianism has two firm and deep roots: One leads back to the Greek *presbuteros* (elder) and has to do with the system of church government of ancient and apostolic times; the other leads back to John Calvin and the Protestant Reformation; it pertains to the form of government used by all people calling themselves Presbyterian and holding the faith of the Reformed churches.

Calvin (1509–1564) was a Frenchman trained in the law. Turning to theology, his keen legalistic mind and his lust for freedom from the rigid, confining forms of Roman Catholicism drove him as a fugitive to Geneva, where he quickly grasped the reins of leadership in the Reformed sector. Resolute and often harsh with his opponents, he established himself and his theological system at the heart of a "city of God" in the Swiss capital, making it, according to Macaulay, the "cleanest and most wholesome city in Europe."

Calvin's whole thought revolved around the concept of sovereignty: "The sovereignty of God in his universe, the sovereignty of Christ in salvation, the sovereignty of the Scriptures in faith and conduct, the sovereignty of the individual conscience in the interpretation of the Will and Word of God."

His system has been summarized in five main points. Greatly simplified, these are human impotence, unconditional predestination, limited atonement, irresistible grace, and final perseverance. God, according to Calvin, is the sovereign and eternal ruler of the world; humans are completely dominated by and dependent upon God.

> The doctrine of God's eternal decree is held in harmony with the doctrine of his love to all mankind, his gift of his Son to be the propitiation for the sins of the whole world, and his readiness to bestow his saving grace on all who seek it; that concerning those who perish, the doctrine of God's eternal decree is held in harmony with the doctrine that God desires not the death of any sinner, but has provided in Christ a salvation sufficient for all, adapted to all, and freely offered in the gospel to all; that men are fully responsible for their treatment of God's gracious offer; that his decree hinders no man from accepting that offer; and that no man is condemned except on the ground of his sin. All dying in infancy are excluded in the election of grace, and are regenerated and saved by Christ through the Spirit, who works when and where and how he pleases.
>
> (The Constitution of the United Presbyterian Church)

Out of Calvinism came miracles of reform; few have made as many contributions as John Calvin in so many fields at once—education, building of an intelligent ministry, liberation of the oppressed and persecuted, and establishment of democratic forms of government in both church and state. In his thought lay the germ that in time destroyed the divine right of kings. He gave a new dignity to the people and brought representative government to their parliaments and church councils. He struck the final blow at feudalism and offered a spiritual and moral tone for dawning capitalism.

Strictly speaking, John Calvin did not found Presbyterianism; he laid the foundations upon which it was constructed in Switzerland, Holland, France, England, Scotland, and Ireland. He inspired the French, from whose ranks came the Huguenots; by 1560 there were 2,000 churches of Presbyterian complexion in France. He influenced the people of Holland who established the Dutch Reformed Church. He gave courage to British Presbyterians in their bitter struggle against the Roman Catholic queen, "Bloody Mary" Tudor. From Calvin came the Scottish Covenanters and John Knox, who cried, "Great God, give me Scotland, or I die!"

A delegation of Scots sat in the Westminster Assembly of Divines (1643–1648) with 121 English ministers, 10 peers, and 20 members of the House of Commons. They resolved to have "no bishop, and no king." That assembly, a milestone in Presbyterian history, meeting in 1,163 sessions at the call of Parliament to resolve the struggle over the compulsory use of the Anglican Book of Common Prayer, produced a Larger and a Shorter Catechism, a directory for the public worship of God, a form of government, and the Westminster Confession of Faith. That document, built upon the Old and New Testaments, became the doctrinal standard of Scottish, British, and American Presbyterianism.

Dominant in the Westminster Assembly, the Presbyterians soon also dominated the British government. Oliver Cromwell completed the ousting of the monarch and established a commonwealth; the commonwealth subsequently crashed, the monarchy returned, the fires of persecution flamed again, and British Presbyterians fled to America with the Puritans. An attempt to establish episcopacy in Scotland after 1662 sent many Presbyterians out of Scotland into Ireland, where economic difficulties and religious inequalities drove them on to America. These British and Scotch-Irish became the founders of Presbyterianism in America. From 1710 until mid-century, between 3,000 to 6,000 Scotch-Irish arrived annually in America, settling at first in New England and the middle colonies, then spreading out more widely than any other ethnic group.

But there were Presbyterian congregations in the colonies long before the immigration of 1710–1750. One was worshiping in Virginia in 1611; others were underway in Massachusetts and Connecticut in 1630. Long Island and New York had congregations by 1640 and 1643, respectively. Francis Makemie, an Irish minister, ranged the coast from Boston to the Carolinas, planting churches. Six groups were united into the first presbytery in Philadelphia in 1706 and by 1716 had become a synod made up of four presbyteries; it held its first meeting in 1717.

Associate Reformed Presbyterian Church

This is a continuing synod of the former Associate Reformed Presbyterian church; it is a body of Covenanter and Seceder origins and traditions. (*Covenant* here refers to the Reformed branch of the church. The Associate Presbyterian Church of North America, in distinction, is of *Seceder* origin; the Associate Reformed Church is a result of the union of the two groups.) Feeling that the distances that separated it from its fellow members in the North were too great, the synod of the Carolinas withdrew in 1822 from the Associate Reformed Church to form the Associate Reformed Synod of the South. Following the creation of the United Presbyterian Church in 1848 (which this group never joined), it dropped the phrase "of the South," thereby becoming the Associate Reformed Presbyterian Church. It became a general synod in 1935.

The standards of the Westminster Confession are followed. For some years the only music in this church was the singing of the psalms; this was modified in 1946 to permit the use of hymns. Foreign mission fields are located in Pakistan and Mexico. *The Associate Reformed Presbyterian* is published monthly at Greenville, South Carolina; Erskine College and Erskine Theological Seminary are located at Due West, South Carolina;

three retirement centers are supported.There is an assembly ground, "Bonclarken," at Flat Rock, North Carolina. Total membership is 35,000 in 167 churches, most located in the Carolinas.

Bible Presbyterian Church

On June 11, 1936, during the fundamentalist-modernist controversy, a group of about 300 people, led by J. Gresham Machen of Princeton Theological Seminary, met in Philadelphia to form a new church that would be true to the Bible. The name chosen was The Presbyterian Church of America, and Dr. Machen was unanimously elected the first moderator.

A year later it became apparent that the new church was actually composed of two groups with views so divergent as to make continued unity impossible. Therefore in 1939 one group formed the Bible Presbyterian Church; the other took the name Orthodox Presbyterian Church.

In 1941, the Bible Presbyterians joined with other like-minded churches to found the American Council of Christian Churches, in opposition to the Federal Council of Churches; in 1948 the International Council of Christian Churches was formed to provide a worldwide body of association. Membership in 1983 included 399 denominations from 93 nations.

Bible is included in the name of this church to emphasize its Bible-based position. It is thoroughly fundamentalist, subscribing to the Westminster Standards (the Confession of Faith, the Shorter and Larger Catechisms), and is strongly Reformed. It opposes all forms of the social gospel and liberation theology and refuses to cooperate with those who compromise such doctrines as the inerrancy and infallibility of the Bible, the Virgin birth and deity of Christ, his blood atonement and bodily resurrection, and his literal coming again. It continues to oppose the policies of the National and World Council of Churches because of what is seen as their "departure from historic Christianity."

The properties of the local church are guaranteed to the church itself. Local congregations may call their pastors "without interference" from presbyteries or synods. Any church may withdraw at any time "for reasons sufficient to themselves." The work of the church is carried on through independent agencies rather than denominational boards. Among its approved agencies are Faith Theological Seminary, Shelton College, and The Independent Board for Presbyterian Foreign Missions. Presbyteries and synods are meetings for edification and fellowship rather than administration. There are about 10,000 members in the United States and Canada. Some 47 missionaries now serve in 11 foreign mission fields.

Cumberland Presbyterian Church

An outgrowth of the great revival of 1800, the Cumberland Presbytery was organized on February 4, 1810, in Dickson County, Tennessee, by three Presbyterian ministers, Finis Ewing, Samuel King, and Samuel McAdow. Contributing factors to the organization were a rejection of the doctrine of double predestination in the Westminster Confession of Faith and an insistence that the rigid standards of the Presbyterian church for the education of the clergy be relaxed in the light of extraordinary circumstances existing on the American frontier. The General Assembly was organized in 1829.

A union with the Presbyterian Church, U.S.A. in 1906 was only partially successful. A considerable segment, to whom the terms of union were unsatisfactory, perpetuated the Cumberland Presbyterian Church as a separate denomination.

This church reports 84,059 members in 841 congregations, located for the most part in 11 southern states with some congregations in Indiana, Illinois, Michigan, Iowa, Kansas, New Mexico, Arizona, and California.

The church sponsors missionaries in Colombia, Japan, Hong Kong, and Liberia, West Africa. It supports Bethel College in McKenzie, Tennessee, and Memphis Theological Seminary. There is a children's home at Denton, Texas. Denominational headquarters, Frontier Press, and a resource center are located in Memphis.

Orthodox Presbyterian Church

This church was organized June 11, 1936, in protest against what were believed to be modernistic tendencies in the Presbyterian Church in the U.S.A. Led by J. Gresham Machen, the dissenters had formed a foreign missionary society which they were ordered to disband. Refusing, they were suspended from the Presbyterian Church in the U.S.A. and organized the Presbyterian Church of America; an injunction brought against the use of that name by the parent body resulted in the change in 1938 to the name Orthodox Presbyterian Church.

The Westminster Confession and the Westminster Larger and Shorter Catechism are accepted as subordinate doctrinal standards or creedal statements. Strong emphasis is laid upon the infallibility and inerrancy of the Bible (the books of the Bible were written by men "so guided by Him that their original manuscripts were without error in fact or doctrine"); original sin; the Virgin birth, deity, and substitutionary atonement of Christ; his resurrection and ascension; his role as judge at the end of the world and the consummation of the Kingdom; the sovereignty of God; and salvation through the sacrifice and power of Christ for those "whom the Father purposes to save." Salvation is "not because of good works, [but] in order to do good works."

The Presbyterian system of government is followed; a general assembly meets annually. The church constitution contains the creedal statement of the group, a form of government, book of discipline, and directory for the worship of God. The church has published the *Trinity Hymnal*, probably the only hymnal designed as a worship supplement to the Westminster Confession of Faith. Committees appointed by the general assembly conduct work in home and foreign mission, Christian education, and general benevolence. The church supports a seminary in Philadelphia. With 17,500 members in 165 congregations, it is a constituent member of the Reformed Ecumenical Synod, an international association of churches holding the Reformed faith, and of the North American Presbyterian and Reformed Council. Membership is concentrated in eastern Pennsylvania, New Jersey, and southern California.

Presbyterian Church (U.S.A.)

Following formal separation that began during the Civil War and lasted for 122 years, the two largest American Presbyterian churches were reunited on June 10, 1983, in a historic Communion service celebrated by some 15,000 persons in the Georgia World Congress Center in Atlanta, and by many more on a nationwide television link. The creation of the new Presbyterian Church (U.S.A.) came during the simultaneous general assemblies of the former denominations, the United Presbyterian Church in the U.S.A. (the "northern"church, hereafter called UPCUSA) and the Presbyterian Church in the United States (the "southern" church, hereafter called PCUS). The Reverend J. Randolph Taylor, pastor of Myers Park Presbyterian Church in Charlotte, North Carolina, was elected the new group's first moderator.

While the ceremonies in Atlanta made reunion official, the full combining of functions from the UPCUSA offices in New York and the PCUS offices in Atlanta is expected to take several years. A General Assembly Council was created to oversee this work, and it began meeting at once to tackle the problems of merging budgets, creating a single ministerial candidacy system, and deciding locations of the new denomination's administrative offices, among many other questions. The timetable for these processes, while subject to the will of the Council, is anticipated to be finished in a decade.

The origins of the new church go back to the first American presbytery, founded in Philadelphia in 1706. Since then, the two churches' histories have flowed in sometimes separate but always parallel streams until the reunification in 1983.

American Presbyterians met in a general synod in 1729 and adopted the Westminster Confession of Faith and the Larger and Shorter catechisms, "as being, in all essential and necessary articles, good forms of sound words, and systems of Christian doctrine." The same synod denied civil magistrates any power over the church and banned the persecution of anyone for religious faith.

Free in the new land and fired with their Scotch-Irish and Covenanter backgrounds, the Presbyterians quickly began to procure trained ministers; creeds and colleges have been Presbyterian hallmarks from the earliest days. William Tennent, Sr., organized a "log college" in a cabin at Neshaminy, Pennsylvania, with three of his four sons as his first pupils. This family school grew into the most important Presyterian institution of higher learning in the colonies. From it came the College of New Jersey (later Princeton University) and a stream of revivalistic Presbyterian preachers who played leading roles in the Great Awakening of the early eighteenth century. Prominent among them were William Tennent, Jr., and his brother Gilbert, who met and came to like British revivalist George Whitefield. They followed him in preaching an emotional "new birth" revivalism that conflicted with the old creedal Calvinism. The camp meeting revival grew out of the Great Awakening enthusiasm; it was born as a Presbyterian institution and continued by Methodists when the Presbyterians dropped it.

Presbyterian objection to emotional revivalism went deep and split the church. Preachers on the "old side" opposed revivalism, while those of the"new side" endorsed it, claiming that less attention should be paid to college training of ministers and more to recruiting regenerated common men. The two sides quarreled until they reunited in 1757. The next year, in the first united synod, there were 98 ministers in the colonial Presbyterian Church, 200 congregations, and 10,000 members. One of the ablest of the new-side preachers was John Witherspoon, president of Princeton, a member of the Continental Congress, and the only clergyman to sign the Declaration of Independence.

Witherspoon may have been instrumental in having the general synod call upon the Presbyterian Churches to "uphold and promote" the resolutions of the Continental Congress. The Scotch-Irish accepted the Revolution with relish; their persecution in England and Northern Ireland had made them into solid anti-British dissenters. Their old cry, "No bishop and no king," was heard back in England—statesman Horace Walpole supposedly remarked that "Cousin America" had run off with a Presbyterian parson.

The Presbyterians moved swiftly to strengthen their church after the colonial victory at Yorktown, meeting as a synod in Philadelphia in 1788 while the new nation's constitution was being drafted in the same city. The national administrative body of American Presbyterianism was known as The Presbytery from 1706 to 1716, as The Synod from 1717 to 1788, and as The General Assembly from 1789 to the present.

From 1790 to 1837, membership in the Presbyterian Church in the U.S.A. (as it was now called) increased from 18,000 to 220,557. This growth was due to the revivalism sweeping the country and to the plan of union with the Congregationalists. Under that plan, Presbyterian and Congregational preachers and lay people who were moving into the new western territory worked and built together. Preachers of the two groups preached in each other's pulpits, and members held the right of representation in both Congregational association and Presbyterian presbytery. The plan worked well on the whole, absorbing the fruits of the national revivals and giving real impetus to missionary work at home and abroad.

Then came disagreements between Old School and New School factions within the church over matters of discipline and the expenditure of missionary money. The General Assembly of 1837 expelled four New

School presbyteries, which promptly met in their own convention at Auburn, New York. The Presbyterian Church in the U.S.A. (PCUSA) remained split between the New School advocates who wanted to continue working with the Congregationalists, and those of the Old School, who were suspicious of the "novelties of New England [Congregational] theology."

Those years promised to be an era of Presbyterian expansion. Marcus Whitman drove the first team and wagon over the south pass of the Rockies into the great Northwest. After him came hosts of Presbyterians and lay people, building churches, schools, colleges, and seminaries. Between 1812 and 1836, Presbyterians built their great theological seminaries: Princeton, Allegheny, Auburn, Columbia, Lane, McCormick, Union in Virginia, and Union in New York City. They set up missionary and educational societies.

But the era of unity suddenly became an era of schism. Back in 1810, even before the Old School-New School division, the Cumberland presbytery had broken away in a dispute over the educational qualifications of ministers and formed the Cumberland Presbyterian Church. Antislavery sentiment was increasing. In 1846 the Old School assembly regarded slavery in the southern states as no bar to Christian communion, but the New School took action that year and condemned the practice strongly. By 1857, several southern synods of the new school had withdrawn to form the United Synod of the Presbyterian Church. The greater break came in 1861, following the outbreak of the Civil War, when 47 southern presbyteries of the Old School formed the General Assembly of the Presbyterian Church in the Confederate States of America. In 1865, following the war, the United Synod and the Confederate churches merged to form the Presbyterian Church in the United States; the Synod of Kentucky joined in 1869 and the Synod of Missouri, in 1874. But the separation of northern from southern continued until the reunion of 1983.

The Southern Church

The Presbyterian Church in the United States (PCUS), being initially Old School in doctrine, remained separate from the northern bodies long after the end of Civil War hostilities; indeed, the regional churches were, at least officially, not on speaking terms until well into the twentieth century. But the southern Presbyterians continued to develop their own style of faith and practice.

Presbyterians in the South had long made special contributions to the nation. Presbyteries in Virginia and North Carolina were calling for American independence well before the Boston riots and the Liberty Bell, and Mecklenburg Presbytery in North Carolina was the first ecclesiastical body in the colonies to approve the Declaration of Independence. Presbyterian civic leaders brought law and order to many parts of the South before colonial officials could assume such duties, and Presbyterian ministers taught school prior to the establishment of public school systems. Presbyterians were prominent during both the French and Indian War and the Revolution, and with Baptists, they laid the political, spiritual, moral, and intellectual foundations for the famous Jeffersonian "Act for Establishing Religious Freedom" in Virginia, which preceded similar statements in the Constitution and elsewhere.

The PCUS organization developed parallel to that of the northern churches. Offices for the various functions, located in several Southern cities, were gradually centralized in Atlanta under the General Assembly Mission Board. Mission work was always active on a worldwide scale, being a special source of pride for southern Presbyterians. In 1982, just prior to reunion, there were 814,931 members of the PCUS in 2,704 churches, with 61 presbyteries (17 already functioning as "union" bodies with UPCUSA presbyteries) and 7 synods. There were 6,077 ordained ministers on the rolls. The PCUS supported seminaries: Austin, Columbia, Louisville and Union in Richmond, as well as the Presbyterian School of Christian Education, a unique institution. There were several secondary schools and mission schools, as well as colleges, children's homes, and homes for the aged.

The Northern Church

The Old School and New School bodies, which had held separate assemblies since 1837, were united in 1870 on the basis of the Westminster Confession. Most of the Cumberland churches joined them in 1907; the Welsh Calvinistic Methodists, in 1920.

In the decades from 1920 to 1950, the emphases of theology and unity were evident. The former was seen in a liberal-conservative struggle; the latter in the proposed merger with the Protestant Episcopal Church, which did not take place, and the accomplished merger of the Presbyterian Church in the U.S.A. and the United Presbyterian Church of North America (UPCNA) in 1958.

The UPCNA had been formed exactly a century earlier by a merger of the Associate Presbyterian Church and the Associate Reformed Presbyterian Church. The doctrines, traditions, and institutions of those bodies were preserved in the new church's Presbyterian-style government of local sessions, presbyteries, synods, and a general assembly.

The UPCNA doctrine rested on the Westminster Confession, with a few modifications, one of which amended its chapter on the power of civil magistrates. A 1925 confessional statement of 44 articles contained the substance of Westminster, but restricted divorce to marital infidelity, denied infant damnation, extended the sacraments to all who professed faith in Christ and led Christian lives, and withdrew the old protest against secret societies. It also abandoned the exclusive use of the Psalms, maintained belief in the verbal inspiration of the Scriptures, affirmed the sufficiency and fullness of the provisions of God for the needs of Christ, emphasized the renewing and sanctifying power of the Holy Spirit, and held salvation to be free to all sinners.

There were no insurmountable doctrinal differences when the UPCNA and the Presbyterian Church in the U.S.A. merged in 1958 to become the United Presbyterian Church in the United States of America (UPCUSA);

there were only the usual disagreements between theological conservatives and liberals. On the whole, all found agreement in the Westminster Confession, the accepted doctrinal statement of American Presbyterians since 1729.

But the Westminster Confession was 300 years old, and many had come to believe that a new statement was needed to proclaim the gospel in twentieth-century language. After eight years of work, a special committee presented a draft to the General Assembly in 1967, which ratified this first major new doctrinal statement in 300 years.

The UPCUSA now had a Book of Confessions with nine creeds: the Nicene Creed of A.D. 325, the Apostles' Creed of the second century, the Scots Confession of 1560, the Heidelberg Confession of 1563, the Second Helvetic Confession of 1566, the Westminster Confession of 1647, the Shorter Catechism of 1647, the 1934 Theological Declaration of Barmen, and the Confession of 1967. These were grouped togther to trace the development of the great Christian affirmations, especially in the Reformed tradition, to make clear the common beliefs of most of the world's Christians, and to offer common ground for unity among Reformed churches.

The brief 4,200-word Confession of 1967 avoids the confusing terminology of the Westminster Confession and stresses the concepts of love, sin, eternal life, and especially the work of reconciliation in God, Christ, and the church. It is Christ-centered and generally repeats the Westminster tenets in modern speech. Some opposition persisted, on the ground that the new document waters down the Westminster, but most United Presbyterians accepted the document as reflecting the mind of true Presbyterianism and offering a wide theological base on which all Presbyterians can stand together.

The UPCUSA eventually reorganized its offices into three agencies based in New York City. The Program Agency sends missionaries, supports education and human ministries, and aids in church development and disaster relief, among other functions. The Vocation Agency develops new ministries and helps prepare people for the ministry. The Support Agency works in communication, research, and finance. Coordinating all three was the General Assembly Mission Council, until its termination at the time of the reunion in 1983.

In 1982, on the eve of reunion, the UPCUSA had 2,351,119 members nationwide and 15,178 ordained ministers. Its 8,975 churches were grouped into 151 presbyteries and 15 synods; 17 of the presbyteries were joint "union" bodies with similar units in the PCUS.

The New Church

The new Presbyterian Church (U.S.A.) created in 1983 has a total of 3,166,050 members and 21,255 ministers nationwide. There are 11,679 churches, organized into 195 presbyteries and 20 synods (the former "union" presbytery pairs are now counted as one, and two pairs of synods in overlapping areas have already consolidated). Since the boundaries of synods and presbyteries in the southern states now overlap, the number will doubtless be reduced further over the next few years as these regional bodies move to consolidate their functions. The former UPCUSA had churches nationwide, which explains the existence of its synods and presbyteries in the southern states alongside those of the former PCUS.

Always interested in education, the new church now has an expanded network of schools. There are 71 Presbyterian-related colleges, 11 seminaries, and 7 secondary schools in the United States.

The church operates two book-publishing companies, The Westminster Press in Philadelphia and John Knox Press in Atlanta. The church's official periodical is the monthly *Presbyterian Survey*, published in Atlanta.

Under the Presbyterian system of government, each congregation has its local session, made up of the elders, with the pastor as moderator. The session governs the local church, receiving and disciplining members as well as acting for the church's welfare. Presbyteries made up of congregations in a local district examine, ordain, and install ministers and review reports from sessions, as well as hearing their complaints. The synods, occupying larger boundaries, review the presbytery records, organize new presbyteries, and act in helping to administer denominational matters. The highest judiciary body is the general assembly, made up of lay and clerical delegates who meet yearly, having been elected by their presbyteries on a proportional plan of representation. The general assembly settles all matters of discipline and doctrine referred to it by the lower bodies, establishes new synods, appoints agencies and commissions, and reviews all appeals. Its decisions are final, except that it cannot, of itself, amend the church's constitution. The officers of the general assembly are the stated clerk (the chief executive officer of the church), who is elected for five years and may be reelected, and the moderator, who is chosen each year to preside over the meetings and who often speaks for the church during the year.

While Presbyterians are found throughout the United States, there are several areas of concentration. About 40 percent of the 3.16 million members live in the area of the former PCUS, the South. The most populous synod is the Synod of the Trinity (Pennsylvania and West Virginia), where about 8 percent of PCUSA members live. The PCUSA is largely an urban church with membership greatest in the larger cities. There are concentrations in Ohio, Pennsylvania, New York, Virginia, North Carolina, Florida, and Texas.

Presbyterian Church in America, The

Organized at a constitutional assembly in December 1973, this church was known first as the Continuing Presbyterian Church, then as the National Presbyterian Church, and finally as The Presbyterian Church in America (PCA). It represents a separation from the Presbyterian Church in the United States (southern). The dissenting group stood in opposition to what they considered a long-developing liberalism in that church, a liberalism that did not emphasize the historic Presbyterian positions on the inerrancy and infallibility of Scripture. Also involved were questions of the position of the church on marriage and divorce, the admission of women to church offices, the affiliation of the parent body with the National Council of Churches and World Council of Churches, and the movement toward merger with the more liberal United Presbyterian Church in the U.S.A. (northern).

Basic in the debates that led to the separation was the question of firm subscription to the Westminster Confession of Faith and the Larger and Shorter Catechisms of the Westminster Assembly, with their distinctive doctrines. The dissenting body "readopted" the confession and the catechism; they hold firmly to a conservative Calvinism in doctrine and theology.

The PCA maintains the historic Presbyterian polity and the rule of the church by elders; there is the usual session, presbytery, and general assembly, but it puts a new emphasis on the parity of the teaching ministers, elders, and the ruling elders; these are viewed as of equal authority in all the church courts. The work of the church is carried on by three major committees—Mission to the World, Mission to the United States, and Christian Education and Publications. At the present time it has no central headquarters but has administrative offices in Columbus, Georgia; Jackson, Mississippi; Decatur, Georgia; and Montgomery, Alabama. The stated clerk is located in Clinton, Mississippi.

Statistics reveal 136,582 members in 698 churches.

Reformed Presbyterian Church, Evangelical Synod

This body was formed in 1965 when the Reformed Presbyterian Church, founded in 1774 in Dolphin County, Pennsylvania, merged with the Evangelical Presbyterian Church, which had split from the Orthodox Presbyterian Church in 1937.

It is biblical in theology and subscribes to the Westminster Confession and catechisms. It operates Covenant Theological Seminary in St. Louis and Covenant College at Lookout Mountain, Georgia. Its National Missions Board assists in establishing new local churches in the United States and Canada, and a Board of Home Ministries and Christian Training is active in educational work. It has 10 chaplains on active duty with the armed forces. There are 19,669 members in 154 churches and 21 missions. The church is currently exploring possibilities of merger with the Presbyterian Church in America and/or the Orthodox Presbyterian Church.

Reformed Presbyterian Church of North America

A body of direct Covenanter lineage, this church's first minister came to the colonies from the Reformed Presbytery of Scotland in 1752. Most of the early membership joined the union with the Associate Presbytery in 1782, but a small group remained outside the union and reorganized at Philadelphia under the name Reformed Presbytery in 1798. A synod was constituted at Philadelphia in 1809, only to split in 1833 into Old Light and New Light groups, in a dispute over citizenship and the right of its members to vote or participate generally in public affairs; the general synod of the Reformed Presbyterian Church (New Light) imposed no such restriction. This restriction was finally removed in 1964; members are free to participate in civil government and to vote on issues and for candidates who are committed to Christian principles of civil government. The Reformed Church merged with the Associate Presbyterian Church of North America in 1969.

Special emphasis is given to the inerrancy of Scripture, the sovereignty of God, and the Lordship of Christ over every area of human life. The government is thoroughly Presbyterian, except that there is no general assembly. Members use only the psalms in their worship services, and no instrumental music is permitted. Members cannot join secret societies.

Home missionaries are opening new work in seven states under a Board of Home Missions and Church Extension; foreign missionaries are stationed in Japan and Taiwan. Geneva College is located at Beaver Falls, Pennsylvania, a theological seminary at Pittsburgh, and there is one home for the aged. The denomination is a member of the National Association of Evangelicals and of the North American Presbyterian and Reformed Council. There are 5,236 members in 70 congregations and 6 mission stations. Strength in the United States lies in western Pennsylvania and eastern Kansas.

Second Cumberland Presbyterian Church in the United States

This church, formerly the Colored Cumberland Presbyterian Church, was built on the 20,000 black membership of the pre-Civil War Cumberland Presbyterian Church, with the full approval of the general assembly of that church, held in 1869. The first three presbyteries were established in Tennessee, where the first synod, the Tennessee Synod, was organized in 1871. In doctrine this church follows the Westminster Confession, with four reservations: (1) there are no eternal reprobates; (2) Christ died for all humankind, not for the elect alone; (3) there is no infant damnation; and (4) the Spirit of God operates in the world coextensively with Christ's atonement, in such manner "as to leave all men inexcusable."

In 1984, there were 15 presbyteries and 4 synods, with 18,000 communicants in 143 congregations. The Alabama Synod comprises nearly one-fourth of the constituency. The church's ministers are trained at the college and seminary of the Cumberland Presbyterian Church, in McKenzie, Tennessee, and Memphis, respectively.

REFORMED

When the Belgic Confession was written in 1561 as the creedal cornerstone of the Reformed churches in Belgium and Holland, the

"Churches in the Netherlands which sit under the Cross" gave thanks to their God in the preface of that document: "The blood of our brethren . . . crieth out." There was real cause for crying out, but the Reformation was spreading from Switzerland in the midst of the Netherlands' long struggle against Catholic Spain. The Dutch Reformed Church was cradled in cruelty.

Those Reformation-founded churches called Reformed, as distinguished from those called Lutheran, originated in Switzerland under Zwingli, Calvin, and Melanchthon: They were Reformed in Switzerland, Holland, and Germany; Presbyterian in England and Scotland; Huguenot in France; and still others in Bohemia and Hungary used national names. As they moved overseas to the American colonies, they formed into four groups: two from Holland became the Reformed Church in America and the Christian Reformed Church; one from the German Palatinate became the Reformed Church in the United States, later known as the Evangelical and Reformed Church and now merged with the Congregational Christian churches in the United Church of Christ; the fourth, coming from Hungary, became the Free Magyar Reformed Church in America. All were and still are Calvinistic and conservative, basing their doctrine generally upon the Heidelberg Catechism, the Belgic Confession, and the Canons of the Synod of Dort. They use a modified Presbyterian form of government.

Christian Reformed Church

With a membership of 299,685 in 828 churches, this Reformed group originated in Michigan in 1847 and was affiliated with the Reformed Church in America from 1850 until 1857, when it found itself in disagreement with the parent church on matters of doctrine and discipline. A conference held in 1857 at Holland, Michigan, effected the separation of the True Holland Reformed Church, which, after a series of changes in name, became the present Christian Reformed Church. Emigration from Holland brought several other groups into the new organization, rapidly increasing its membership.

The Christian Reformed Church today is largely English-speaking, although the Dutch, Spanish, French, Navajo, Zuni, Korean, Chinese, and Vietnamese languages are used in some of the churches. Doctrine shows no important differences from accepted Reformed standards; the three historic formulas of unity are accepted: the Belgic Confession, the Canons of Dort, and the Heidelberg Catechism. Organization bears the usual Reformed characteristics, including 40 classis that meet every 4 months (in some cases every 6 months), but with no intermediate or particular synods between the classes; a general synod made up of 2 ministers and 2 elders from each classis meets annually.

There are 238 home mission personnel in Canada and the United States who maintain ministries among Navajos, Zunis, Blacks, Chinese, Spanish-Americans, Koreans, Cambodians, Vietnamese, and Laotians, and on many university campuses; 185 foreign missionaries are stationed in Japan, South America, northern Nigeria, Cuba, Taiwan, Mexico, Guam, Puerto Rico, the Philippines, Australia, Honduras, Sierra Leone, New Guinea, the Dominican Republic, Costa Rica, Hong Kong, the Ivory Coast, and Liberia. The Christian Reformed World Relief Committee carries on a worldwide relief program.

The "Back to God Hour" radio program, broadcast from a chain of stations in the United States and superpower stations abroad, reaches Canada, Europe, Africa, and Asia as well as North and South America; a television ministry also broadcasts in the United States and Canada. There are five colleges—Calvin College and Seminary in Grand Rapids, Michigan; Dordt College in Sioux Center, Iowa; Trinity Christian College in Palos Heights, Illinois; Redeemer Reformed College, Hamilton, Ontario; and The King's College, Edmonton, Alberta. A publishing house in Grand Rapids provides literature for the Christian Reformed Church and its agencies, as well as educational material for many other churches. Closely associated with the church are unique Christian school societies made up of parents who serve and support a national educational program.

Hungarian Reformed Church in America

The Hungarian Reformed Church in America is successor to a work begun in the United States by the Reformed Church of Hungary in 1904. Work among Hungarian Reformed people had actually begun in 1891 under the auspices of other interested Calvinistic groups, but that sponsored by the parent body in Hungary soon became the most vital and popular, and by 1912 there were two classes affiliated with the church in Hungary. With the break-up of the Austro-Hungarian Empire and the impoverishment of Hungary, the Reformed Church in that country transferred jurisdiction of its churches in the United States to the Reformed Church in the United States, in an agreement reached at Tiffin, Ohio, in 1921. Three of the original congregations, and four more recently organized, refused to accept the agreement and united to form the Free Magyar Reformed Church in America at Duquesne, Pennsylvania, in 1924. The present name was adopted in 1958.

The church's polity is a combination of Synod-Presbyterian elements developed in Hungary in the eighteenth century. It is made up of three classes—New York, Eastern, and Western—that form a diocese headed by an elected bishop and a lay curator. Doctrinal standards are those of the Heidelberg Catechism and the Second Helvetic Confession. Synodical meetings are held annually, and a "constitutional" meeting is held every three years. There are 31 congregations with 10,500 baptized members, in Connecticut, New York, New Jersey, Arizona, the District of Columbia, Pennsylvania, Ohio, Michigan, Florida, and California, and two congregations in Ontario, Canada. The church is a constituent member of the World Alliance of Reformed Churches, the National Council of Churches, and the World Council of Churches.

Netherlands Reformed Congregations

This is the smallest of all the Reformed groups in the United States; it has 22 churches, with 7,319 communicants and 4,195 baptized members. Its short history began when it seceded from the state church in Holland. Dutch emigrants formed the first two churches in South Holland, Illinois (1865), and in Grand Rapids, Michigan (1870), basing their belief on the Belgic Confession, the Heidelberg Catechism, and the Canons of Dort. There are 9 additional churches in Canada, with a total of 8 Sunday schools and 7 clergy; a synod meets every 2 years.

Protestant Reformed Churches in America

Three consistories of the Classis Grand Rapids East and Grand Rapids West of the Christian Reformed Church, and their pastors, were deposed from that church as the result of a disagreement over the doctrine of common grace (Arminianism). The debate began in 1923; the dissenters formally organized as Protestant Reformed Churches of America in 1926. They stand for particular grace, for the elect alone, and hold to the three Reformed confessions—the Heidelberg Catechism; the Belgic, or Netherlands, Confession; and the Canons of Dordrecht—as the basis of their belief in the infallible Word of God. In government they are Presbyterian, subscribing to the 87 Articles of the Church Order of Dordrecht. A general synod meets annually in June.

A small theological seminary is maintained at Grand Rapids. The Reformed Free Publishing Association publishes a bimonthly periodical, *The Standard Bearer*; a monthly publication, *Beacon Lights*, is issued by the young people's federation. There are 4,700 members in 21 churches, located in Michigan, Illinois, Iowa, Wisconsin, Minnesota, Colorado, California, Washington, North and South Dakota, Texas, New Jersey, and Canada.

Several home mission fields and two foreign fields—Jamaica and Singapore—are supported.

Reformed Church in America

This church had an unorganized membership along the upper reaches of the Hudson River in the neighborhood of Fort Orange (Albany), New York, in 1614. There were no regularly established congregations or churches, but members were numerous enough to require the services of Reformed ministers, two of whom came from Holland in 1623 as "comforters of the sick." By 1628 the Dutch in New Amsterdam had a pastor of their own, Jonas Michaelius, and an organized Collegiate Church, to become the oldest church in the middle colonies and the oldest church in America with an uninterrupted ministry.

When the English took possession of New Amsterdam in 1664, Dutch churches were thriving in Albany, Kingston, Brooklyn, Manhattan, and at Bergen in New Jersey. When the immigration from Holland ceased, there were perhaps 8,000 Dutch churchpeople in the country, holding their services in Dutch and served by either native clergy or pastors sent from Holland. It was difficult and expensive to send native-born ministerial candidates to Holland for education and ordination; the question rent the Reformed Church and was finally resolved by the building of a college and seminary at New Brunswick (Queen's College, later Rutgers). It was the first theological seminary built in this country, and was fathered by the famous Theodore Frelinghuysen, who also took a leading part in the revival called the Great Awakening.

A sharp controversy over the authority of the classis of Amsterdam resulted in the complete independence of the Dutch churches in America; a general body and five particular bodies were created, a constitution was drawn up in 1792, and the general synod was organized in 1794. The names Dutch Reformed Church in North America and Reformed Dutch Church in the United States of America were both in use in 1792; in 1819 the church was incorporated as the Reformed Protestant Dutch Church, and in 1867 it became the Reformed Church in America.

The American Revolution had little effect upon the church except to offer the Dutch people a chance to even matters with the English. Once the war was over, Scots, English, and Germans began joining the church, creating a problem in the use of the Dutch tongue which took years to resolve. A second emigration from the Netherlands began in the middle of the nineteenth century, bringing whole congregations with their pastors. One group led by Albertus van Raalte settled in western Michigan and established a community called Holland, known today for Hope College, Western Theological Seminary, and an annual tulip festival. Van Raalte and his group became part of the Reformed Church in America in 1850. Another colony led by Dominie Scholte settled in Pella, Iowa, in 1847–1848, and in 1856, except for a small dissenting group, it merged with the Reformed Church in America.

Domestic missions began in 1786; actually, missionary work among Native Americans had begun much earlier. Needy and destitute churches in New York, Pennsylvania, and Kentucky were assisted by the domestic missionaries of the classis of Albany for many years, and in 1806 the general synod assumed administration of all missionary agencies, in cooperation with the American Board of Commissioners for Foreign Mission. In 1832 the Board of Foreign Missions was created, but it continued to work through the American Board until 1857, after which it has operated independently. Insisting from the start upon seven years of college and seminary training for its ministers, in 1828 the church established the Education Society of the Reformed Church in America, later the Board of Education of the General Synod.

The explicit statements and principles of the Belgic Confession, the Heidelberg Catechism, and the Synod of Dort are still the doctrinal standard of the Reformed Church in America. The mild and gentle spirit of the confession, with its emphasis upon salvation through Christ, is a central theme; the primacy of God's power in human life is at the heart of the preaching of the church, as it is at the heart of the Canons of Dort; and the Heidelberg Catechism, based on the Apostles' Creed, is employed in many catechetical classes. The divine authority of the Scriptures is important: "The final authority in the Reformed faith is the Holy Scripture, the living Word of God, spoken to every man through the Holy Spirit of God."

Worship is semi-liturgical, but it is an optional liturgy; only the forms for baptism and the Lord's Supper, the two recognized sacraments of the church, are obligatory. It is a corporate, or congregational, way of worship, blending form and freedom and distinguishing this church from other Protestant communions. A new edition of the Liturgy and Psalter was published in 1968.

Government of the church stands midway between the episcopal and presbyterian forms; it might be called "modified presbyterian." The governing body in the local church is the consistory, made up of elders, deacons, and the pastor, who is always president. Elders are charged with the guidance of the spiritual life of the church and deacons are in charge of benevolences; but they generally meet and act as one body. A number of churches in a limited area are grouped into a classis, which has immediate supervision of the churches and the ministry and is composed of all the ministers of the area and an elder from each consistory. Classes are grouped into six particular synods, made up of an equal number of ministers and elders from each classis. These meet annually to supervise the planning and programming of the churches within the area. The higher court of the church is the general synod, representing the entire church. It meets once a year and is composed of delegations of ministers and elders from each classis; the size of the delegation depends upon the size of the classis.

In 1968 this church underwent a process of restructure. The former boards and agencies have been unified in a general program council, resulting in fewer board members. Each of the 45 classes in the United States has a representative on the council. The program staff is assisted by three "service offices"—administration and finance, promotion, communications and development, and human resources.

Foreign missionaries are appointed to work in 19 countries abroad. Through minority councils at home, the denomination relates to Chinese, Japanese-Americans, Blacks and Native Americans. Scholarships and student aid are provided in 3 colleges and 2 seminaries. Membership in 1982 stood at 353,184 in 943 churches, with greatest strength in New York, New Jersey, Michigan, Iowa, and California.

Reformed Church in the United States

This body originally was made up of Swiss and German emigrants who arrived in this country in the 1700s. It formerly operated under the auspices of the Dutch Reformed Synod of South and North Holland, but separated from the synod in 1793. Since 1869 it has been known as the Reformed Church in the United States. Most of its churches merged into the Evangelical and Reformed Church in 1934 and, in 1957, with the

Congregational and Christian churches to become the United Church of Christ. One group, the Eureka Classis in South Dakota, refused to become a part of the united church and continues as the Reformed Church in the United States. The doctrines are those set forth in the Heidelberg Catechism; there are 30 churches, with an inclusive membership of 3,710 baptized and communicant members and 31 active ministers.

ROMAN CATHOLIC CHURCH

For the first 1,500 years of Christendom until the time of the Protestant Reformation, the Western world was almost solidly Roman Catholic. The eleventh-century separation divided the faith between Roman Catholic and Eastern Orthodox sectors. The Reformation divided continental Europe and the British Isles among Roman Catholic, Lutheran, Anglican, and Reformed churches, with the prospect of still further division as denominationalism increased.

The Roman Catholic Church dates its beginning from the moment of Christ's selection of the apostle Peter as guardian of the keys of heaven and earth and as chief of the apostles, and it claims the Fisherman as its first pope. It gained temporal authority and power when it arose as the only body strong enough to rule after the fall of Rome in A.D. 410. A house of terror, ravaged first by Goths, Vandals, and Franks and then by Saxons, Danes, Alemanni, Lombards, and Burgundians, Europe found its only steadying hand in the church. Without the church, anarchy would have been king from Britain to the Bosphorus.

The first mention of the term *Catholic* (universal) was made by Ignatius about A.D. 110–115, but the first real demonstrations of its authority came as it won the barbarians to its banners while it kept the flame of faith burning in its churches and the candle of wisdom alive in its monastic schools. Augustine deeply influenced its theological and philosophical structure and he gave papacy its finest justification and defense. He left it strong enough to bestow crowns or to deny them to Europe's kings.

The church beat back the threats of its enemies at home and afar; it converted the barbarian, defeated the Saracen, and employed the Inquisition against the heretic boring from within. It brought the hopeful interval known as the Peace of God; it also supported chivalry and feudalism, fought the Crusades, built schools, and created a noble art and literature. For long centuries the Benedictine monasteries guarded and preserved learning and culture in Europe; this order of monks was founded in 529 in Italy by St. Benedict; since its founding, more than 4 million men have practiced the Benedictine rule of life. Centuries later in 1209, St. Francis of Assisi established the Franciscan order, and at about the same time, St. Dominic began his Order of Friars Preachers (Dominicans).

Inevitably there arose temptations of power and prosperity. Then came the Reformation. Roman Catholic scholars readily admit that there were corrupt individuals within the church and that reform was necessary. Indeed, reform was underway before the Reformation broke; Martin Luther himself was a Catholic reformer within the church. Erasmus and Savonarola wrote and preached against the corruption and worldliness of certain Roman Catholic leaders and laypeople, but they stayed within the church. That all these reformers had a case against members of the Roman church is not denied by Roman Catholics; they do, however, maintain that while priests and bishops and even popes may err, the one true church cannot err, and Luther was wrong in rebelling against it. But rebel he did, and the Roman church suffered its most fateful division.

There were, too, other reasons for the revolt. There was the growth of nationalism and secularism, the ambitions of political princes and rulers with great personal ambitions who wanted no interference from the church. And there was the Renaissance, with its revival of Greek and Roman pagan influences and emphases. All those forces worked together to produce the Reformation. The Counter Reformation was effective in halting the spread of the new Protestantism in Europe and won back some areas to the Roman Catholic Church; one of its chief instruments was the Society of Jesus (Jesuits), an educational and missionary order founded by Ignatius of Loyola in 1534.

But long before Luther's times, Roman Catholics had reached America. The first diocese on this side of the Atlantic was established in Greenland in 1125; there were bishops in residence there until 1377. Priests of Spain came with Columbus in 1492; missionaries came with Coronado and the other early Spanish explorers. Most perished, but one of them started the first permanent parish in America at St. Augustine, Florida, in 1565.

French explorers, voyageurs, and colonizers—Cartier, Joliet, Marquette, and others—were generally Roman Catholics accompanied by missionary groups. Among them were the Recollects, Jesuits, Sulpicians, Capuchins, and the secular clergy. New France became a vicariate apostolic in 1658 with Bishop Laval at its head. The See of Quebec (1675) had spiritual jurisdiction over the vast province of France in North America, reaching down the valley of the Mississippi to Louisiana.

In 1634 Roman Catholics founded Maryland; later they were restricted by law in Maryland and in most other colonies, and the restrictions were not removed until after the Revolution. In the face of these restrictions and in view of the fact that most of the colonial immigrants were Protestants, the Roman Catholic Church grew slowly. In 1696 there were only 7 Catholic families in New York, and 80 years later they were still traveling to Philadelphia to receive the sacraments. In 1763 there were fewer than 25,000 Catholics out of a population of 2,200,000; they were under the jurisdiction of the vicar apostolic of London.

Among the signatures on the Articles of Confederation, the Declaration of Independence, and the Constitution are found those of Thomas Fitzsimmons, Daniel Carroll, and Charles Carroll of Carrollton, all of whom were Catholics. The Revolution brought them religious as well as political freedom; religious equality became the law with the adoption of the Constitution in 1787.

There was no immediate hierarchal superior in the United States when the war ended, and the vicar apostolic in London refused to exercise jurisdiction over the "rebels." After long investigation and delay and an appeal to Rome, John Carroll was named Superior, or prefect apostolic, of the church in the 13 original states. At that time there were 15,800 Catholics in Maryland, 700 in Pennsylvania, 200 in Virginia, and 1,500 in New York, unorganized and with no priests. At the turn of the century there were 80 churches and about 150,000 Roman Catholics; by 1890 there were 6,231,417—a growth due primarily to the flood tide of emigration from the Catholic countries of Europe. Today the 51 million members of the Roman Catholic Church make up about 22 percent of the population of the United States.

Baltimore became the first American diocese in 1789 and an archdiocese in 1808; other dioceses and archdioceses were formed as the church expanded. Three plenary, or national, councils were held at Baltimore in 1852, 1866, and 1884. Archbishop John McCloskey of New York became the first American cardinal in 1875, and Archbishop James Gibbons of Baltimore was elevated to the same rank in 1877.

The Civil War and two world wars failed to disturb the work of the church or interrupt its growth; indeed, World War I produced one of the ablest hierarchal Roman Catholic agencies in the country—the National War Council, now known as the United States Catholic Conference. There were 18,608,003 Catholics in the United States in 1926; in 1982 the Roman Catholic Church (long the largest church in the United States) reported 51,207,579 members in approximately 18,250 churches.

The faith and doctrine of Catholicism are founded upon "that deposit of faith given to it by Christ and through his apostles, sustained by the Bible and by tradition." Thus they accept the Apostles' Creed, the Nicene-Constantinople Creed, the Athanasian Creed, and the Creed of Pius IV, also called the Creedal Statement of the Council of Trent.

Roman Catholics, like the Eastern Orthodox, believe in seven sacraments. Baptism, necessary for membership in the church, is administered to infants and adults by pouring or immersion, and all baptized persons are considered members of the church. Confirmation by the laying on of hands and anointing with the holy chrism in the form of a cross follows baptism; the ordinary minister of this sacrament is the bishop, but priests may also confirm. The laity usually receive the Eucharist (Lord's Supper) in the form of bread alone; the body and blood of Christ are considered actually present in the eucharistic elements. The sacrament of penance is one through which postbaptismal sins are forgiven. The anointing of the sick is for the seriously ill, injured, or aged. The sacrament of holy orders is one of ordination for deacons, priests, and bishops. Marriage is a sacrament that "cannot be dissolved by any human power"; this rules out divorce with remarriage. Members are required to attend Mass on Sundays and obligatory holy days, to fast and abstain on certain appointed days, to confess at least once a year, to receive the Holy Eucharist during the Easter season, to contribute to support of pastors, and to observe strictly the marriage regulations of the church.

The government of the Roman Catholic Church is hierarchical and authoritarian, but laypeople are frequently consulted. (The trend is toward more and more lay participation, since Vatican Council II.) At the head of the structure stands the pope, who is also Bishop of Rome, "Vicar of Christ on earth and the Visible Head of the Church." His authority is supreme in all matters of faith and discipline. Next is the College of Cardinals. Although lay people were once chosen to be cardinals, the office has been limited to priests since 1918; the last lay cardinal died in 1876. Many of the cardinals live in Rome, acting as advisors to the pope and as heads or members of the various congregations or commissions supervising the administration of the church. When a pope dies, the cardinals elect the successor; they hold authority in the interim. The Roman Curia is the official body of papal administrative offices through which the pope governs the church; it is composed of congregations, tribunals, and curial offices.

In the United States there are 9 active cardinals, 39 archbishops (8 also are cardinals), 309 bishops, and more than 58,000 priests. The archbishop is in charge of the archdiocese and has precedence in that province. There are 33 archdioceses and 142 dioceses. Bishops are the ruling authority in the dioceses, but appeals from their decisions may be taken to the apostolic delegate at Washington and even to Rome. The parish pastor, responsible to the bishop, is appointed by the bishop or archbishop and holds authority to celebrate Mass and administer the sacraments with the help of such other priests as the parish may need. Bishops are appointed from Rome, usually upon suggestions from the hierarchy in the United States.

The clergy of the church includes deacons, priests, and bishops. There are 11,645 candidates for orders studying in diocesan and religious-order seminaries. The usual seminary course covers a period of 8 years of study after high school—4 years of philosophy and 4 years of theology. Those in religious orders also spend 1 or 2 years in a novitiate.

Since the restoration of the Permanent Deaconate in 1967, more than 5,400 men have completed the training course and been ordained deacons. Most of these men are married and over 35. They are empowered to preach, baptize, distribute Holy Communion, and officiate at weddings. Most deacons support themselves in secular jobs and exercise their ministry on weekends and evenings.

In 1982 there were 35,813 diocesan or secular priests in the United States and 22,572 priests who belong to religious orders and congregations. Add to these the 7,880 lay brothers and 121,370 sisters engaged in the work, and their importance in the overall task of the church becomes clear. The official *Catholic Directory* lists a total of 101 religious orders of priests and brothers, 32 religious orders for brothers only, and over 400 orders of women. They differ widely in their work. Some are "contemplative" orders, remaining in their monasteries or cloistered convents. Those in active or mixed religious orders engage in teaching, care of the sick, missionary work, writing, or social work. Those in brotherhoods or sisterhoods are required to take vows of poverty, chastity, and obedience but are not ordained; they engage primarily in educational, philanthropic, and charitable work. (Technically the only "orders" for ordained men are the Dominicans, Carmelites, Benedictines, Augustinians, and Jesuits, but usually any religious community of men or women is called a religious order.)

Besides religious orders and congregations, Catholics may join secular institutions whose members also observe poverty, chastity, and obedience but do not wear any distinctive garb or live together in a community; before receiving approval as secular institutes engaged in apostolic work, these groups may operate as approved "pious unions." Worldwide membership in these institutes and unions exceeds 15,000. Some members are also ordained priests.

Three ecclesiastical councils form an important part of the Catholic system; they are known as general, or ecumenical; plenary, or national; and provincial councils. A general council is called by the pope or with his consent; it is composed of all Catholic bishops of the world, and its actions on matters of doctrine and discipline must be approved by the pope. Plenary councils are made up of the bishops resident in a given country; their acts, too, must be submitted to the Holy See before promulgation. The diocesan and provincial councils make further promulgation and application of the decrees passed by the other councils and approved by the pope. Pope John XXIII summoned the bishops of the church to the twenty-first ecumenical council, the Second Vatican Council. Following Pope John's death, Pope Paul VI reconvened the council, which stimulated liturgical reform, Catholic participation in the ecumenical movement, updated many church practices, and inaugurated the idea of collegiality among the bishops. In 1968 Paul VI reaffirmed the official church position against any form of birth control except total or partial abstinence from sex relations in marriage; many theologians, priests, and laypeople protested this, voicing opposition to the encyclical *Humanae Vitae;* the hierarchies of such countries as France, Canada, Belgium, Holland, Switzerland, Austria, and West Germany interpreted the papal position in the light of the freedom of the individual conscience.

The central act of worship is the Mass; its two principal parts are the Liturgy of the Word and the Eucharistic Liturgy. The chief parts of the Liturgy of the Word are readings from the Old and New Testaments; the homily, or sermon; the Nicene Creed; and the Prayer of the Faithful. The eucharistic liturgy includes the offering of the bread and wine, the consecration, the Lord's Prayer, and the Communion. From the third century to 1963 the Western church prescribed Latin as the liturgical language; now the entire Mass is recited in the vernacular by both priest and people. Besides the Mass, Catholics may participate in popular devotions such as the benedictions, rosary, stations of the cross, novenas, and Bible vigils.

With the most centralized government in Christendom, the Holy See at Rome has representatives in many countries of the world. Roman Catholic churches have been established in 217 countries with a total membership of over 633,000,000. The majority of Italians, Spanish, Irish, Austrians, Poles, Latin Americans, Belgians, Hungarians, Southern Germans, Portugese, French, and Filipinos are baptized Roman Catholics. The Society for the Propagation of the Faith is the overall representative missionary body. In 110 foreign countries there are 7,699 missionaries sent out from the United States.

Education has been a primary concern of American Catholics since the establishment of a classical school at St. Augustine, Florida, in 1606. As of 1982 there were 7,761 elementary parochial and private schools in this country with 2,265,764 students and 1,470 Catholic high schools with 833,900 students. More than 533,086 students attend 237 Catholic colleges and universities, including Notre Dame, Fordham, Georgetown, Boston College, St. Louis, Marquette, Catholic, Loyola, and Villanova. There are 173,230 full-time teachers in Catholic schools, of whom 5,101 are priests, 2,889 are brothers, 36,066 are sisters, and 129,014 are lay teachers. An estimated total of 1,400,000 Catholics attend non-Catholic colleges and universities.

Almost every diocese publishes a weekly newspaper; more than 400 Catholic newspapers and magazines are published in the United States and Canada. Some of the largest and most influential are *The National Catholic Reporter*, *Commonweal*, *America*, *Columbia*, *U.S. Catholic*, *St. Anthony Messenger*, *Catholic Digest*, *Catholic World*, and *Ligourian*. Periodicals reflecting a more conservative position include *The Wanderer*, *Twin Circle*, and *The National Catholic Register*.

Roman Catholic charity and welfare work is conducted by many different organizations, religious and otherwise. The National Conference on Catholic Charities helps to coordinate work on state and national levels; work is also conducted by several religious orders of men and women who devote full time to the relief of the poor in homes or in institutions; there are also bureaus of charities in many of the dioceses. The Society of St. Vincent de Paul is perhaps the largest and most effective charity organization; numerous others—Little Sisters of the Poor, Sisters of Charity, Daughters of Charity of the Society of St. Vincent de Paul, Sisters of Mercy, the Third Order of Franciscans—are active among the poor in Catholic hospitals, orphanages, and homes for the aged. There are 710 general and special hospitals treating over 36,000,000 patients annually; 1 out of every 3 beds in the nation's private hospitals has been provided by the Catholic hospital system. There are 560 homes for the aged and 190 orphanages.

The members of the hierarchy are also members of the United States

Catholic Conference, which operates as a clearinghouse for information; this is not a council or a legislative body, so the resolutions of its meetings do not have the force of law. It facilitates discussion of all policies affecting the interests and activities of the church and unifies, coordinates, and organizes work in social welfare, education, and other activities. Every bishop in the United States and its territories and possessions has a voice in this conference.

A new phenomenon of the church will have important effect in the shaping of future structures: lay parish councils, created to aid the priests in the management of the parish, have consultative powers; new diocesan senates, composed of priests, assist the bishop in the setting of policies in the diocese.

While most Roman Catholics belong to the Latin Rite, there are at least 20 groups of churches and an estimated 10 to 12 million other Catholics belonging to the Eastern Rites. These Catholics hold identical doctrinal beliefs and recognize the authority of the pope, but differ in language, liturgy, customs, church laws, and tradition. Generally they follow one of five historic rites: Byzantine, Alexandrian, Antiochian, Armenian, or Chaldean. Across the world the main Eastern Rite bodies are the Catholic Copts, Ethiopian Catholics, Syrians, Chaldeans, Catholic Armenians, Malabar Catholics, Byzantine Catholics, and Maronites.

Some 586,000 Eastern Rite Catholics, mostly Ukrainians and Ruthenians, live in the United States. Smaller groups include the Maronites, Melkites, Romanians, Russians, and Armenians. All these rites are jurisdictionally related to one or another of the Eastern Patriarchs.

The Roman Catholic Church today finds itself in an era of change, tension, and some dissension. Pope John XXIII and Vatican II brought about new programs and approaches in the fields of ecumenism, religious liberty, the liturgy, biblical studies, and social action. Priests now face their people as they say Mass; Masses once said only in Latin are now said in the modern vernacular of the people. Many Catholics may now choose to practice confession by sitting down and discussing their sins and spiritual problems face-to-face with the priest, and many may choose one of several forms of penance. Before Vatican II, Catholics were forbidden to attend meetings of the World Council of Churches; now Catholic observers attend council sessions as observers, and Catholic bishops have entered into theological dialogue with several of the larger Protestant denominations. A Catholic Pentecostal Movement stressing the charismatic gifts of speaking in tongues, healing, interpretation, and prophecy now claims 300,000 Catholics meeting in charismatic prayer groups across the country. Dissension is found in the questioning of celibacy, birth control, abortion, the authority of bishops, and the anti-sex positions of many of the Fathers of the early church.

Vatican II opened the way for many of these changes and reforms; it now remains to be seen what Pope John Paul II will do with or about them. It is a crucial day for this great, historic church.

SALVATION ARMY

William Booth, an ordained minister in the Methodist New Connexion in England, regretfully left the pulpit of that church in 1861 to become a free-lance evangelistic preacher. This step led him, in 1865, to the slum areas in London's East End and to a dedication of his life to the poverty-stricken unchurched masses in that area. His first plan was to make his work supplementary to that of the churches, but this proved impractical because many converts did not want to go where they were sent; often when they did go, they were not accepted, and Booth soon found that he needed his converts to help handle the great crowds that came to his meetings. He began his work in Mile End Waste under the name Christian Mission; in 1878 the name was changed to The Salvation Army.

Being a Methodist, Booth first organized his movement along lines of Methodist polity, with annual conferences at which reports were made and programs planned. With the changing of the name, the whole organization became dominated by the new title. Articles of War (declaration of faith) were drawn up, and soon the mission stations became corps, members became soldiers, evangelists became officers, and converts were listed as seekers. Booth was designated as "general," and gradually he set up his organization on a military pattern that provided a direct line of authority and a practical system of training personnel for effective action. The leader reasoned that it was "just as valid to build an army of crusaders to save souls as it has been to send armies to recover a sepulchre."

The work spread quickly over England, Scotland, and Wales and, in 1880, was officially established in the United States by a pioneer group under the direction of George Scott Railton. Once committed to a policy of expansion, Booth lost no time in sending pioneering parties in different directions, reaching Australia and France in 1881; Switzerland, Sweden, India, and Canada in 1882; New Zealand and South Africa in 1883; and Germany in 1886. Today The Salvation Army works in 85 lands with approximately 25,000 officers; preaches the gospel in some 112 languages, at 15,450 evangelical centers; and operates more than 3,038 social institutions, hospitals, schools, and agencies. There is a general membership of about 2,000,000.

Administratively, the Army is under the command of "the General," with top leaders in charge in 85 countries and colonies. The Army conducts its religious and social programs in all 50 states, preaching the gospel and effecting the spiritual, moral, and physical reclamation of persons coming under its influence through 11,158 centers of operation, including 7,246 service extension units. These are administered by more than 5,000 officers assisted by about 25,000 employees. The unit of the Army is the corps, of which there may be several in a city. Each corps is commanded by an officer ranging in rank from lieutenant to brigadier, who is responsible to divisional headquarters. Each of the 38 divisions in the United States consists of a number of corps, and the work of each division is under the direct supervision of a divisional commander. The divisions are grouped into four territories—Eastern, Central, Southern, and Western—with headquarters in New York City, Chicago, Atlanta, and Rancho Palos Verdes, California. Territorial commanders are in charge of the work in each territory, and the four territorial headquarters are composed of departments to facilitate all phases of Army work. National headquarters in Verona, New Jersey, is the coordinating office for the entire country, and the national commander is the chief administrative officer, official spokesman, and president of all Salvation Army corporations in the United States. Property and revenues are in the custody of a board of trustees, or directors, and citizens' advisory boards assist in interpreting the work of the Army to the general public.

Within the structure of the Army, converts who desire to become soldiers (members) are required to sign the Articles of War, after which, as members, they give volunteer service. The function of officers , who are commissioned to full-time Salvation Army service, is similar to that of ministers of other churches.

Basic training for each officer is a two-year in-residence course at one of the Army's four schools for officers' training located in Suffern, New York; Chicago; Atlanta; and Rancho Palos Verdes. The chief source of officer candidates is the Salvation Army corps. A soldier who has served actively for at least six months may make application for officership and, if accepted, may enter the School for Officers' Training where the curriculum, in addition to formal study, includes practical field experience in corps and social service institutions as well as orientation in all possible areas of Salvation Army service. The officer graduates from the school as a lieutenant and, following additional studies, is eligible to attain the ranks of captain, major, lieutenant colonel, colonel, and commissioner.

The motivating force of the Salvation Army is the religious faith of its officers and soldiers, and the fundamental doctrines of the organization are stated in the eleven cardinal affirmations of its Foundation Deed of 1878. These statements document the Army's recognition of the Bible as the only rule of Christian faith and practice; of God as the creator and Father of all humankind; the Trinity of Father, Son, and Holy Ghost; Jesus Christ as Son of God and "Son of man"; sin as the great destroyer of soul and society; salvation as God's remedy for human sin and the ultimate and eternal hope made available through Christ; sanctification as the individual's present and maturing experience of a life set apart for the holy purposes of the kingdom of God; and an eternal destiny that may triumph over sin and death. While the Army has a dual function of church and social agency, its first purpose is the salvation of people "by the power of the Holy Spirit combined with the influence of human ingenuity and love." To The Salvation Army, its social services are merely a means of putting the socially disinherited—the needy in both the physical and spiritual realm—into a condition to be physically and spiritually uplifted. In meeting the needs of the "whole person," the Army has established a widespread social welfare program.

The work of the Army in the United States includes 115 adult rehabilitation centers, aiding almost 72,000 annually. In 28 homes and hospitals, more than 4,500 unwed mothers are cared for. A total of 52,860 were admitted last year to the Army's 7 general hospitals and related institutions; 143,568 persons were given outpatient care; 53 camps provided camping facilities for more than 47,000 children, mothers, and senior citizens. The Army maintained more than 274 boys' and girls' clubs; 1,115 corps community centers with more than 700,000 members; a Red Shield club for servicemen with a total attendance of 44,795; 239 canteens serving more than 650,000 persons in emergencies; family service bureaus serving 812,912 families; hotels and lodges for men and women, settlements, missing persons' bureaus, day-care centers, alcoholic care, correctional service bureaus for prisoners and their families, community centers for all ages, and other allied services. These services are given without respect to race, color, creed, or condition; the whole work is financed largely through voluntary subscriptions, federal funds, and annual maintenance appeals from each service.

SCHWENKFELDER CHURCH

Caspar Schwenckfeld von Ossig (1498–1561), a Silesian nobleman baptized and raised in the Roman Catholic Church, experienced a spiritual awakening in 1519. Disappointed in his hope to help reform the Roman Catholic Church from within, he played a leading role in the Reformation, advocating wider reading of the Bible by laypeople, urging the need of power, guidance, and leading of the Holy Spirit, and preaching that the sacramental consuming of the Lord's Supper is a mystical partaking of Christ as food for the soul—that the food is really bread. This interpretation of the Lord's Supper, together with his insistence upon complete separation of church and state, led him into disagreement with Luther and Lutheranism.

He founded a number of spiritual brotherhoods whose members in time came to be known as Schwenkfelders. The body has disappeared in Europe but persists in the United States, in a church of 2,700 members in 5 local congregations. A large body arrived in this country in 1734; the first formal society of Schwenkfelders was organized in 1782. The 5 churches today are all located within a radius of 50 miles of Philadelphia.

All theology, the members hold, should be constructed from the Bible, but the Scriptures are considered dead without the indwelling Word. Christ's divinity was progressive, his human nature becoming more and more divine without "losing its identity"; faith, regeneration, and subsequent spiritual growth change human nature; but justification by faith must not obscure the positive regeneration imparted by Christ.

The theology is thus Christocentric. In polity it is congregational, each church being incorporated, self-sustaining, and conducting its affairs through its district or local conference. A general conference composed of all the local churches meets twice a year to develop the larger program of education and missions. The general conference sponsored the founding of the Perkiomen School for boys at Pennsburg, Pennsylvania, in 1892; and a majority of the board of trustees are still members of Schwenkfelder churches. A home for the elderly is located at Lansdale, Pennsylvania.

SOCIAL BRETHREN

This is a body organized in Illinois in 1867 by a small group of persons from various denominations, who held quite orthodox doctrines but disagreed with those denominations in certain matters of interpretation of Scripture, discipline, and decorum. In 1983 it reported 3 associations, each meeting annually, a general assembly meeting biennially, 26 churches in Illinois, Michigan, and Indiana, and 1,165 members. Recently a church was organized in the Philippines.

The confession of faith emphasizes the following points: The infinite power, wisdom, and goodness of God, in whom are united three persons of one substance, power, and eternity—the Father, Son, and Holy Ghost; the authority and consistency of the Scriptures, comprising the Old and New Testaments, as containing all things necessary to salvation, "so that whatsoever is not read therein nor may be proved thereby is not required of any man that it should be believed as an article of faith or thought to be requisite or necessary to salvation"; regeneration and sanctification through Christ; and eternal salvation of the redeemed and eternal punishment for apostasy.

The ordinances of baptism and the Lord's Supper are for true believers only; baptism may be by sprinkling, pouring, or immersion. Lay members of the church have the right of suffrage and free speech, but ministers are called to preach the gospel, not political speeches. Polity is a fusion of Baptist and Methodist structures and customs. The work of the Social Brethren, aside from efforts in mutual aid and assistance, is largely evangelistic.

SPIRITUALIST

This movement is known popularly for its mediums, séances, clairvoyance, and so on. Ouija boards, table tipping, spirit rappings and conversations have attracted thousands anxious to communicate with their departed ones. But Spiritualism has genuine religious bases and connotations as well as psychic experiments. The movement has become a church. The National Spiritual Alliance (NSA) offers a Declaration of Principles:

1. We believe in Infinite Intelligence.
2. We believe that the phenomena of Nature, both physical and spiritual, are the expression of Infinite Intelligence.
3. We affirm that a correct understanding of such expression, and living in accordance therewith, constitute true religion.
4. We affirm that the existence and personal identity of the individual continue after the change called death.
5. We affirm that communication with the so-called dead is a fact scientifically proven by the phenomena of Spiritualism.
6. We believe that the highest morality is contained in the Golden Rule. . . .
7. We affirm the moral responsibility of the individual and that he makes his own happiness or unhappiness as he obeys or disobeys Nature's physical and spiritual laws.
8. We affirm that the doorway to reformation is never closed against any human soul, here or hereafter.
9. We affirm that the practice of Prophecy, as authorized by the Holy Bible, is a divine and God-given gift, reestablished and proven through mediumship by the phenomena of Spiritualism.

The teaching of God as love is central in Spiritualism; the Lord's Prayer is used in both public worship and private séance. Christ is recognized as a medium; the annunciation was a message from the spirit world, the transfiguration was an opportunity for the materialization of the spirits of Moses and Elias, and the Resurrection was evidence that all people live on in the spirit world. The soul is often called the astral body; at death the material body dissolves, and the soul as the body of the spirit progresses through a series of spheres to a higher and higher existence. There are two lower spheres in which those of lower character or sinful record are purified and made ready for the higher existences. Most of the departed are to be found in the third sphere, called the summer land; above this are the philosopher's sphere, the advanced contemplative and intellectual sphere, the love sphere, and the Christ sphere. All reach the higher spheres eventually; Spiritualists do not believe in heaven or hell, or that any are ever lost.

Services and séances are held in private homes, rented halls, or churches. Most Spiritualist churches have regular services with prayer, singing, music, selections from the *Spiritualist Manual*, a sermon or lecture, and spirit messages from the departed. The churches and ministers are supported by freewill offerings; mediums and ministers also gain support from classes and séances in which fees are charged. The attendance at church services is invariably small; one authority estimates the average congregation at 20 to 25. But membership cannot be estimated on the basis of church attendance; for every enrolled member there are at least 15 who are not enrolled but are interested in the movement and in attending services. More than 180,000 have been reported as members, but this is not comprehensive or inclusive of all using the services of the church.

Administration and government differ slightly in the various groups, but most have district or state associations and an annual general convention. All have mediums, and most have ministers in charge of the congregations. Requirements for licensing and ordination also differ, but a determined effort is being made to raise the standards of education and character in the larger groups.

International General Assembly of Spiritualists

Organized at Buffalo, New York, in 1936, this is a cooperative body that is endeavoring to establish cohesion and unity in the Spiritualist movement. In 1956 it had an inclusive membership of 164,072 in 209 churches. It was originally organized as an auxiliary of the General Assembly of Spiritualists in New York to care for churches outside that state. Its present purpose is to charter new Spiritualist churches; headquarters are located at Norfolk, Virginia.

National Spiritual Alliance of the U.S.A.

This body was founded in 1913 by G. Tabor Thompson and has its headquarters at Lake Pleasant, Massachusetts, where it was incorporated. Holding general Spiritualist doctrines, the alliance stresses paranormal and impersonal manifestations and intercommunication with the spirit world. Salvation is held to be through the development of personal character; "one reaps as he sows, yet . . . all things are working together for good and evolution obtains perpetually in all persons."

The local churches of the alliance elect their own officers and choose their own ministers; a three-day convention is held annually with delegates from all the churches electing national officers—president, secretary, and treasurer. An official board of directors directs the missionary work of ministers and certified mediums; college training is not required, but a minister must have passed a course of study arranged by the alliance. Mediums may baptize, but only ministers may officiate at the ceremonies of ordination and marriage. The work of the alliance is mainly in benevolent, literary, educational, music, and scientific activities. There are 3,230 members and 34 churches, located in Central Massachusetts and Connecticut.

National Spiritualist Association of Churches

This association is influential far beyond its immediate membership, furnishing literature for the whole movement and advocating higher qualifications in mediums and ministers. It has a seminary, the Morris Pratt Institute, for the training of its ministers; a great deal of its work is done by correspondence. A national director of education directs a training course for members, licentiates, lecturers, mediums, and ordained ministers. The NSA holds an annual legislative convention that elects officers triennially. This is the orthodox body of American Spiritualism, having been organized in Chicago in 1893. Its membership totals 5,168 in 164 churches.

Progressive Spiritual Church

This church was founded in Chicago in 1907 by G. Cordingley and has its own confession of faith. It was organized "to lift spiritualism above mere psychic research, to establish it upon a sound, religious basis, and to secure its recognition among other Christian denominations." The confession of faith states the members' belief in the communion of spirits, in the restoration of humans to everlasting life, in God as an absolute divine Spirit, and in angels who, as departed spirits, communicate with the living by means of mediums. Jesus Christ is recognized as a medium controlled by the spirits of Elias and Moses, and John the Baptist. "The fingers of the hand of a medium under control can write and deliver divine messages and vision. . . . A divine understanding of dreams can be had. . . . The stars divine the pathway of life of every character." The Bible is acknowledged as the inspired Word of God, a guide to the spirit life as well as to the phases and phenomena of Spiritualism: prophecies and spiritual palmistry, automatic writing, materialization, trumpet speaking, healing by magnetized articles, and so forth. Heaven and hell are believed to be conditions, not locations.

Four sacraments—baptism, marriage, spiritual communion, and funerals—are observed. Ministers, who may be of either sex, must pass a course of instruction in the church seminary. Church officers include a supreme pastor, secretary, treasurer, and board of trustees. Local churches elect their own officers but are subject to the constitution and bylaws of the mother church. The work of the church is largely benevolent, social, literary, scientific, and psychical. There are 11,347 members in 21 churches.

SWEDENBORGIAN (The New Jerusalem)

Commonly called Swedenborgian, the Churches of the New Jerusalem are based upon the teachings of Emmanuel Swedenborg and exist in three main bodies: the General Convention of the New Jerusalem in the U.S.A (the older U.S. body); the General Church of the New Jerusalem, which broke from the older group in 1890; and the General Conference in England.

Swedenborg, born in Stockholm in 1688, was a scientist distinguished in the fields of mathematics, geology, cosmology, and anatomy before he turned seriously to theology. Items in his theology dealing with the nature of the one God, heaven and hell, human freedom, the Bible, marriage, and so on, are held to have been revealed by God through things heard and seen by Swedenborg in the spirit world; he was "uniquely permitted to have communication with the other world." His writings disclaim spiritism but claim almost daily visions of heaven and hell, which he describes in full detail. He wrote also of frequent conversations with spirits, through whom he learned that a new Christian church was to be born and that his written works would be the basis of its teachings. He died in London in 1772 and was buried a Lutheran, but his teachings were definitely different.

Certain that he was divinely commissioned to teach the doctrines of this "New Church," Swedenborg taught that "God is man," meaning that the origin of all that is truly human is in one God. The Divine Humanity is, however, Christ's glorified and risen Humanity, in which the human is manifested and which is God. These doctrines are accepted and preached by his followers, who consider him to have been a divinely illuminated seer and revelator. Against the background of his concept of "correspondence" of the natural world with the spirit world, he expounded an additional sense of the Scriptures considered to be consistent with science and reason. Swedenborg himself never preached or founded a church, but his followers felt that the need for a separate denomination was implicit in the New Revelation. They stand on the conviction that a new epoch is opening in the spiritual life of the human race.

The New Church as an organization started in London in 1783 when Robert Hindmarsh, a printer, gathered a few friends to discuss the writings of Swedenborg; they formed a general conference of their societies in 1815. The first Swedenborgian Society in America was organized at Baltimore in 1792; in 1817 the General Convention of the New Jerusalem in the U.S.A. was established.

The doctrines of the General Convention of the New Jerusalem are set forth in its liturgy:

1. That there is one God, in whom there is a Divine Trinity; and that He is the Lord Jesus Christ.
2. That saving faith is to believe in Him.
3. Every man is born to evils of every kind, and unless through repentance he removes them in part, he remains in them, and he who remains in them cannot be saved.
4. That good actions are to be done, because they are of God and from God.
5. That these are to be done by a man as from himself; but that it ought to be believed that they are done from the Lord with him and by him.

The societies are grouped into a general convention that meets annually; there are also state regulations. Each society is self-regulating. There are ministers and general pastors (in charge of state associations). Services are liturgical but with a wide latitude, based upon the book of worship issued by the general convention. The convention now has 1,820 members active in 31 societies; a theological school is located at Newton, Massachusetts; the Swedenborg Foundation in New York City distributes his writings.

The General Church of the New Jerusalem accepts the full divine authority of the writings, acknowledging them as being not really *his*, but rather "from the Lord alone." There is no fixed constitution in this church; polity is based upon "essential unanimity" in free council and assembly. There are ministers, pastors, and bishops, the latter being chosen by a general assembly that meets every 3 or 4 years; 3,297 members are reported in 21 organized circles and 15 organized groups. Eight of these societies have parochial elementary schools with an enrollment of 627; there is a theological school, a college, and a secondary school. Headquarters are at Bryn Athyn, Pennsylvania, where a cathedral has been built.

THEOSOPHY

Theosophy holds that there is a universal perennial philosophy underlying all religions, and thus it draws from both Eastern and Western philosophical and religious teaching. Its founder was Helena Petrovna Blavatsky, who was born in Russia in 1831 and traveled over the world in search of "a knowledge of the laws which govern the universe." She arrived in the United States in 1872 and, with Henry Steel Olcott and William Q. Judge, founded the Theosophical Society of New York in 1875. Her purpose and aim was "to form a nucleus of the Universal Brotherhood of Humanity, without distinction of race, creed, sex, cast, or color; to encourage the study of comparative religion, philosophy and science; and to investigate the unexplained laws of Nature and the powers latent in man."

Mrs. Blavatsky brought out the teachings of the great thinkers of various religions, science, and philosophies, both ancient and of her time. Proceeding from the premise that God is immanent in the hidden forces of nature and that people can attain perfection through their own powers, she described God as impersonal. God is the Absolute Principle of pantheistic Hinduism, the Tao of Taoism, the Godhead of Christianity. Each person is a part of God and has a divine potential within; therefore all are related. She held that all religions stem from a hierarchy that includes Jesus, Buddha, and other master thinkers who have experienced a series of rebirths, or reincarnations, to ultimately attain divinity. Reincarnation is a central theme in Theosophy; it is the method through which men and women rid themselves of all impurities and unfold their inner potentials through varied experiences.

When Mrs. Blavatsky died in 1891, Annie Besant took over leadership of the movement, and established headquarters in Adyar, India. Conflicts developed during this period between Mrs. Besant and the leaders of other Theosophical groups in Europe and the United States; in 1895 William Q. Judge, one of the three founders and president of the American society, established the independent Theosophical Society in America; those loyal to Mrs. Besant worked in the Theosophical Society of New York. Other splits developed in the years following, and the fragmentation is still evident, but the basic teachings of Mrs. Blavatsky still hold in all groups.

No accurate report of membership seems possible among these groups, but it is estimated that there are upward of 40,000 Theosophists worldwide, perhaps 5,000 in the United States. The Theosophical Society was the first to bring out the philosophy behind occultism. Its influence, thanks to the current interest in oriental philosophy and religion, is felt in many other occult groups unconnected with any Theosophical Society.

TRIUMPH THE CHURCH AND KINGDOM OF GOD IN CHRIST

Founded in Georgia in 1902 by E. D. Smith, this church teaches the cleansing from sin in all "justified" believers through the shed blood of Christ; entire sanctification as an instantaneous, definite work of second grace obtained through the faith of the consecrated believer; the second coming of Christ; and baptism by fire as a scriptural experience also obtainable by faith. General Overseers are the chief officers of the body; they meet quadrennially in what is called the International Religious Congress; otherwise the work of the church is carried on by state, county, and local officers. There are 54,307 members and 475 churches.

UNITARIAN UNIVERSALIST ASSOCIATION

In May 1961, the Unitarian and Universalist churches in the United State and Canada were consolidated as the Unitarian Universalist Association of Congregations in North America, one of the most influential liberal churches in this country. The two former bodies have separate and interesting origins and history.

It has often been claimed by Unitarians that their thought reaches back into the early Christian centuries before the concept of Trinitarianism developed. Unitarianism as we know it today, however, began with the Protestant Reformation, among Anti-Trinitarians and Socinians. The movement spread from independent thinkers and Anabaptists in Switzerland, Hungary, Transylvania, Holland, Poland, and Italy to England, where it found champions in such leaders as Newton, Locke, and Milton. No attempt was made to organize the movement in England until late in the eighteenth century.

American Unitarianism, however, developed independently from New England Congregationalism. Members of the liberal wing of the Congregational Church in eastern Massachusetts, asked only to join a covenant in that church and never to subscribe to a creed, were branded as Unitarian while still within the Congregational membership. The first organized church to turn to Unitarianism as a body, however, was not a Congregational church but the Episcopal King's Chapel in Boston in 1785.

In the second half of the eighteenth century many older and larger Congregational churches moving toward Unitarianism were known as Liberal Christian churches or groups; the name Unitarian was finally accepted in 1819.

The split within Congregationalism came into the open in 1805 with the appointment of Henry Ware as professor of theology at Harvard; it was confirmed when William Ellery Channing of Boston preached his famous Baltimore sermon in 1819, outlining the Unitarian view. In that sermon, the liberals had their platform. A missionary and publication society known as the American Unitarian Association was formed in 1825, and with it began activity that looked forward to the formation of a separate denomination. A national conference was established in 1865.

Channing defined the true church in these words:

> By his Church our Savior does not mean a party bearing the name of a human leader, distinguished by a form or an opinion, and on the ground of this distinction, denying the name and character of Christians to all but themselves. . . . These are the church—men made better, made holy, virtuous by his religion—men who, hoping in his promises, keep his commands.

From this, Unitarians proceeded to formulate their views. They have no creed; the constitution of the general conference stated that "these churches accept the religion of Jesus, holding in accordance with his teaching that practical religion is summed up in the love to God and love to man." Cardinal points in their doctrinal attitudes are those of the oneness of God (as opposed to Trinitarianism), the strict humanity of Jesus, the perfectibility of human character, the natural character of the Bible, and the ultimate salvation of all souls. They deny the doctrine of total depravity and believe in the perfectible nature of humankind; Trinitarianism is rejected as unscriptural, and they reject the deity of Christ but say that they believe in his divinity as all persons are divine as the children of God. Salvation is by character; character is not an end, but a means, and salvation lies in being saved from sin here, not from punishment hereafter. Hell and eternal punishment are held to be inconsistent with the concept of a loving and all-powerful God; to admit that God would permit eternal punishment would be to admit that God was powerless to save. Heaven is a state, not a place. Unitarians do not accept the doctrine of the infallibility of the Bible; they believe the Bible is not a book, but a library of books, all of which cannot be accepted as of equal value and importance. These ideas have been prominent in Unitarianism, but within this ideological framework the widest possible freedom is encouraged in personal interpretation and belief; even students and teachers in Unitarian theological schools are not required to subscribe to any dogmatic teaching or doctrinal tests. Emphasis upon individual freedom of belief, democratic principles, hospitality to the methods of science in seeking truth, and less concern with traditional doctrinal matters characterize the Unitarian movement.

In accordance with its charter, the American Unitarian Association (1825-1961) considered itself to be devoted to certain moral, religious, educational, and charitable purposes, which, to the non-Unitarian may be as enlightening as an analysis of their religious or doctrinal statements:

(1) Diffuse the knowledge and promote the interests of religion that Jesus taught as love to God and love to man;
(2) Strengthen the churches and fellowships that unite in the association for more and better work for the kingdom of God;
(3) Organize new churches and fellowships for the extension of Unitarianism in our own countries and in other lands; and
(4) Encourage sympathy and cooperation among religious liberals at home and abroad.

Organization has always been liberally congregational; independent local churches were grouped in local, county, district, state, and regional conferences and were united in an international association for purposes of fellowship, counsel, and promotion of mutual interests.

At the time of merger, there were 4 denominational seminaries, 2 preparatory schools, 386 churches, and approximately 115,000 members. Foreign work is conducted through the International Association for Liberal Christianity and Religious Freedom with headquarters at Utrecht, Holland; the International Association has correspondents in 22 countries.

The Universalists draw their inspiration and find evidence of their thinking and philosophy in many cultural streams; much that is basic in Universalism is discovered throughout the world's several religions. Universalism is not exclusively a Christian denomination, having roots in both pre-Christian and contemporary world faiths; yet within the Christian frame of reference, Universalists claim roots in the early Christian Gnostics, Clement of Alexandria and Theodore of Mopsuestia, the Anabaptists of Reformation times, and the seventeenth- and eighteenth-century German mystical universalists. American Universalism has its direct origin in the work of George DeBenneville, a lay theologian; John Murray, the British anti-Calvinist; and Hosea Ballou, an original universalist thinker.

DeBenneville, the English-educated son of French Huguenot *émigrés*, studied medicine in Germany, and in 1741 came under the influence of the early Brethren, the Friends of God, and the German pietists in Pennsylvania. He preached his gospel of universal salvation as he practiced medicine among the settlers and Native Americans.

In 1759 James Relly of England wrote *Union*, in which he opposed the Calvinistic doctrine of the election of the few. Relly's conviction of universal salvation deeply influenced John Murray, a Wesleyan evangelist who came to New Jersey in 1770; Murray found groups of universalist-minded people scattered along the Atlantic coast, and became minister to one such group in Gloucester, Massachusetts. The Independent Christian Church of Gloucester became the first organized Universalist church in America in 1779. One of its charter members was Gloucester Dalton, a black. Murray served briefly as a Revolutionary War chaplain in the armies of Washington and Greene.

The Universalists met at Philadelphia in 1790 to draft their first declaration of faith and plan of government. Government was established as strictly congregational; doctrinally, they proclaimed their belief in the Scriptures as containing a revelation of the perfections and will of God and the rule of faith and practice, faith in God, faith in Christ as a mediator who had redeemed all people by his blood, in the Holy Ghost, and in the obligation of the moral law as the rule of life. War was condemned; statements approving settlement of disputes out of court, abolition of slavery and education of blacks, testimony by affirmation rather than by oath, and free public education were approved. This Philadelphia declaration was adopted by a group of New England Universalists in 1793; at about the same time Hosea Ballou, a schoolteacher and itinerant preacher in Vermont, was ordained to the Universalist ministry.

Ballou broke radically with Murray's thought; in 1805 he published *Treatise on Atonement*, giving Universalists their first consistent philosophy. Ballou rejected the theories of total depravity, endless punishment in hell, the Trinity, and the miracles. Humankind, said Ballou, was potentially good and capable of perfectibility; God, being a God of infinite love, recognized humanity's heavenly nature and extraction and loved the human race as his own offspring. The meaning of the Atonement was found not in bloody sacrifice to appease divine wrath, but in the heroic sacrifice of Jesus, who was not God but a Son of the eternal and universal God, revealing the love of God and anxious to win all persons to that love. It was an avowedly Unitarian-Universalist statement of theology that deeply influenced American Universalism. Ballou made another lasting contribution with his insistence that the base of Christian community lay not in creeds but in mutual good faith and goodwill; from this principle came two consistent aspects of modern Universalism—a broad liberalism in theology and a universal concern for people.

It must be made clear that Universalists have never had an *official* statement of faith or covenant. From time to time they have set down their basic principles—not as tests of membership nor to be used in any official way, but only to examine their emphases at a given moment in history. Accordingly, in four successive statements, they have grown progressively more liberal and inclusive: The Philadelphia statement of 1790 had obvious Trinitarian overtones and spoke in prevailing orthodox terms on the Scriptures, God, the Mediator, and the Holy Ghost; but the Winchester Profession of 1803 humanized Jesus and thus directly opposed Trinitarianism and reemphasized salvation for the whole family of humankind; it also saw the Bible as one revelation of the character of God. A statement of Universalist principles in Boston in 1899 liberalized their doctrine still further, and in 1935 in Washington, D.C., they adopted the latest statement:

> The bond of fellowship in this Convention shall be a common purpose to do the will of God as Jesus revealed it and to cooperate in establishing the kingdom for which He lived and died.
>
> To that end we avow our faith in God as Eternal and All-Conquering Love, in the spiritual leadership of Jesus, in the supreme worth of every human personality, in the authority of truth known or to be known, and in the power of men of good will and sacrificial spirit to overcome all evil and progressively establish the kingdom of God. Neither this nor any other statement shall be imposed as a creedal test, provided that the faith thus indicated be professed.

In 1942 the charter of the Universalist Church of America was changed to read: "To promote harmony among adherents of all religious faiths, whether Christian or otherwise." This was the last of a long series of steps calculated to meet the challenges of intellectual and social developments and to safeguard the Universalist conviction that no doctrinal statements should be employed as creedal tests. Consequently Universalism has become a harmonious body of theists, naturalists, humanists, mystics, Christians, and non-Christians who find great significance and meaning in a universal approach to life.

A keen sense of ethical responsibility has accompanied this sense of the importance of freedom. Universalists were active very early in movements of reform for prisons and working women; they opposed slavery from their earliest days, stood for separation of church and state, and maintained a continuing interest in the fields of science, labor management, civil rights, and human concern. In modern times, they have placed medical workers in West Berlin and southern German refugee centers; international student work-camp teams are serving underprivileged children and refugee youths in Europe. American Universalists feed children in Japan; develop community centers in India; provide child care for black children in Virginia and a social center at an interracial public housing development in Chicago; and work in various state mental hospitals. They have founded several colleges and universities—Tufts, St. Lawrence, Lombard (now linked to the University of Chicago), Goddard, California Institute of Technology, Akron, Dean Junior College, and Westbrook Junior College. Through membership in the International Association for Religious Freedom, they contribute to the support of liberal religious groups in 22 countries abroad, and they maintain a close affiliation with Universalist groups in Holland, Japan, Korea, and the Philippines. At the time of the formation of the Unitarian Universalist Association, there were 68,949 members in 334 churches.

In the new association, neither Unitarians nor Universalists seem to have lost anything of their original ideology, theology, or purpose. Except for matters of organization and government, the churches involved will continue as they have across the years; no minister, member, or congregation "shall be required to subscribe to any particular interpretation of religion, or to any particular religious belief or creed." The aims and purposes of the Association were set forth in 1974 in a revised statement:

The Association, dedicated to the principles of a free faith, shall:

(a) Support the free and disciplined search for truth as the foundation of religious fellowship;

(b) Cherish and spread the universal truths taught by the great prophets and teachers of humanity in every age and tradition, immemorially summarized in the Judeo-Christian heritage as love to God and love to humankind;

(c) Affirm, defend and promote the supreme worth of every human personality, and the use of the democratic method in human relationships;

(d) Implement the vision of one world by striving for a world community founded on ideals of brotherhood, justice, and peace;

(e) Serve the needs of member societies;

(f) Organize new churches and fellowships and otherwise extend and strengthen liberal religion;

(g) Encourage cooperation among people of good will in every land.

Under the constitution a general assembly is the overall policy-making body for carrying out the purposes and objectives of the association. Ministers and laity are represented in this assembly. The general assembly meets annually, or in such special sessions as may be called by the board of trustees. The elected officers of the association—a moderator, president, 2 vice-moderators, secretary, and treasurer, all elected for 4-year terms—together with 24 other elected members, constitute a board of trustees which appoints the executive and administrative officers and generally carries out the policies and directives. Members of this board have the usual powers of corporate directors as provided by law. The trustees meet four times a year, between regular meetings of the general assembly. A series of committees is appointed to facilitate and coordinate the association's work. Under the general assembly there are a nominating committee, program and business committees, and a commission on appraisal; under the board of trustees, an executive committee, a ministerial fellowship committee, finance committee, and investment committee.

Among its most notable and successful achievements are its publishing house, Beacon Press, which produces and circulates more than one million books every year to students, teachers, libraries, counselors, bookstores, Unitarian Universalists, and the world at large; a newspaper,

The UU World, sent out 12 times a year to more than 100,000 Unitarian Universalist families; a Unitarian Universalist Service Committee which provides leadership and materials in the field of social change; and a religious education curriculum that ranks as one of the best in the United States.

Continental headquarters are in Boston; 23 district offices have been established on regional or geographic bases; there were 175,233 adherents in 1,005 congregations in 1983.

In recent years the Association has been heavily involved in numerous causes and concerns: the issue of black power; the rise of feminist consciousness; scholarship in church history and process theology; inner-city ministries; and the development of lay religious life.

UNITED CHURCH OF CHRIST

Four churches of historic importance constitute the United Church of Christ: the Congregational Church, the Christian Church, the Evangelical Synod, and the Reformed Church. The first two merged to become the Congregational Christian Churches in 1931; they were joined in 1957 by the by-then merged Evangelical and Reformed churches. The union was completed when the constitution was adopted at Philadelphia in July 1961. So important is the background of these denominations, each of which has a long life of its own, that attention is given to them following a description of the present-day body itself.

On July 8, 1959, at Oberlin, Ohio, representatives of the Congregational Christian Churches and the Evangelical and Reformed Church adopted a statement of faith for the United Church of Christ, into which they were merging.

We believe in God, the Eternal Spirit, Father of our Lord Jesus Christ and our Father, and to his deeds we testify:

He calls the worlds into being, creates man in his own image and sets before him the ways of life and death.

He seeks in holy love to save all people from aimlessness and sin.

He judges men and nations by his righteous will declared through prophets and apostles.

In Jesus Christ, the man of Nazareth, our crucified and risen Lord, he has come to us and shared our common lot, conquering sin and death and reconciling the world to himself.

He bestows upon us his Holy Spirit, creating and renewing the Church of Jesus Christ, binding in covenant faithful people of all ages, tongues, and races.

He calls us into his Church to accept the cost and joy of discipleship, to be his servants in the service of men, to proclaim the gospel to all the world and resist the powers of evil, to share in Christ's baptism and eat at his table, to join him in his passion and victory.

He promises to all who trust him forgiveness of sins and fullness of grace, courage in the struggle for justice and peace, his presence in trial and rejoicing, and eternal life in his kingdom which has no end.

Blessing and honor, glory and power be unto him. Amen.

This is "a testimony rather than a test of faith"; it is not intended to set forth doctrinal positions (the doctrines and theological positions of the four churches now within the United Church of Christ remain as they were before the union was accomplished), or to stand as a substitute for the historic creeds, confessions, and covenants of the churches involved. It is not binding, in any creedal or theological sense, upon any local church in the denomination; no congregation is required to subscribe to the statement. But it does stand as a tribute to the faith, charity, and understanding of the merging groups.

Equally impressive is the understanding and cooperation evident in the governmental provisions of the constitution. The United Church of Christ represents a union of congregationalism and presbyterianism—"It establishes congregationalism as the rule for the local congregation and presbyterianism as the basis for organization of the connectional life of the churches" (Harold E. Fey). The constitution is explicit: "The autonomy of the local church is inherent and modifiable only by its own action. Nothing . . . shall destroy or limit the right of each local church to continue to operate *in the way customary to it*." But above the local church, protected as it is, are associations, conferences, and the general synod. Local churches in a geographic area are grouped into associations. The association is concerned with the welfare of the churches within its area: It assists needy churches; receives new churches in the United Church of Christ; licences, ordains, and installs ministers; adopts its own constitution, bylaws, and rules of procedure; and is made up of the ordained ministers and elected lay delegates of the area. The association meets annually and is related to the general synod through its conference.

Associations are grouped into conferences, again by geographic areas. The voting members of the conference are ordained ministers of the associations in the conference and lay delegates elected from the local churches. The conference acts on requests, counsel, and references from the local churches, associations, general synod, and other bodies. It meets annually, and its main function is to coordinate the work and witness of the local churches and associations, render counsel and advisory service, and establish conference offices, centers, institutions, and other agencies.

The general synod is the top representative body of the church; it meets biennially and is composed of 675 to 725 delegates chosen by the conferences, and ex officio delegates (the elected officers of the church, members of the executive council, the moderator, and assistant moderators). The conference delegates are clergy, laymen, and laywomen, in equal numbers; there are also associate delegates, with voice but with no vote. The general synod has no power to "invade" local churches, associations, or conferences; it nominates and elects the officers of the church (a president, secretary, director of finance, and treasurer) for 4-year terms, and a moderator and 2 assistant moderators who preside over the session of the general synod and hold office for one year only. (The duties are quite similar to those of a moderator among the Presbyterians.)

The major boards, commissions, councils, offices, and "other instrumentalities" of the church are established by the general synod; these include the Board for World Ministries (foreign missions in Europe, Southern Asia, and Latin America), made up of 225 ministers and laypeople; the Board for Homeland Ministries (home missions), also with 225 ministers and laypeople; the Council for Health and Welfare Services, administered by the heads of 65 church institutions in those fields; the Office for Church in Society, the Office for Church Life and Leadership, the Commission for Racial Justice, and the Stewardship Council, which is responsible for program development, information, promotion, and social audiovisual resources. Pension and relief activities are administered by a nonprofit corporation responsible to and reporting annually to the general synod. Two committees (nominating and credentials) are also appointed by the general synod, which also is authorized to appoint other necessary committees.

An executive council of 43 voting members and 9 ex officio members (ministers and laypeople) is elected by the general synod to act for the synod in the interims between synod meetings. It determines the salaries of the officers of the church, has responsibility for the church's publications,prepares the agenda for all meetings of the general synod, and appoints committees not otherwise provided; it also submits to the general synod "any recommendation it may deem useful" for the work of the church.

As of 1959, there were 1,419,171 members and 5,500 churches in the Congregational Christian churches; there were approximately 810,000 members in 2,740 churches in the Evangelical and Reformed Church. While some local churches in both groups declined to enter the merger, there are today 1,726,244 members and 6,443 churches in the United Church of Christ.

The national church holds membership in the National and World councils of churches and the World Alliance of Reformed Churches.

The United Church of Christ has its oldest and deepest roots in the congregational tradition of Protestantism. That movement of early modern England and colonial America enjoyed clear identity and primary prominence until Independence. It lost membership to the Unitarian exodus and relative standing among the denominations as frontier conditions began to give shape to Americanized religious patterns. The Evangelical and Reformed tradition brought to the stream of the United Church of Christ varieties of German confessional Protestantism and a sizable membership with a progressive outlook. The Christian Church—this particular body known by that name—contributed an indigenously American, even a frontier and southern form to the stream.

Long ecumenical despite American Congregationalism's early career as an established church, the United Church of Christ remains a leader in cooperative Christianity, especially through its ministries in education and social action and service. The words of John Robinson as he bade the Pilgrims godspeed in 1619 endure as a keynote to this denomination's life: "God hath yet more truth and light to break forth from His Holy Word."

Congregational Church

Congregationalism has been an issue in Christianity from the beginning; it began, as Gaius Glenn Atkins suggests, "without a name and with no sense of its destiny." Even before the Reformation broke over Europe, there were little dissenting groups of churchpeople in England "seeking a better way" than that of the established church (Anglican, or Church of England). As the Reformation developed, dissent took corporate form in the Puritan movement, of which Congregationalism was the most radical wing.

Until a few years ago it was generally believed that Congregationalism rose from separatism, a movement that began in the days of Queen Elizabeth and held that the Church of England was unchristian; that to attempt to reform it from within was hopeless; and that the only course for a true Christian was to separate from it completely. Recent historians, however, have proved that though Robert Browne and other separatist leaders developed sundry ideas that were identical with those of early Congregationalism, the two groups were wholly distinct: the former being perfectionists, refusing to cooperate with other branches of the church; the latter being as cooperative as possible without giving up its principles.

John Robinson, one of its most influential early leaders, first entered church history as a separatist; in 1609 he fled persecution in England and settled at Leiden in the Netherlands with the exiled congregation from Scrooby in Nottinghamshire. There he met William Ames, Congregationalism's first great theologian, and Henry Jacob, its first great pamphleteer and organizer. These men were also fugitives from the ecclesiastical courts of Britain. Robinson was converted by them from rigid separatism to the position of congregationalism.

For twelve years Robinson and his congregation enjoyed peace and freedom under the Dutch; but haunted by the conviction that their children would not grow up as English people, a large part of the company sailed for America in 1620 aboard the historic *Mayflower*. In a hostile new world with the wilderness before them and the sea at their backs, they helped lay the foundations of the American commonwealth; the democratic ideals of their Plymouth colony, worked out slowly and painfully, were the cornerstone of the structure which gave us our free state, free schools, and free social and political life.

Other Congregational churches were established at Barnstable, Salem, and elsewhere along the Massachusetts coast. Between 1630 and 1640, 20,000 Puritans came to Massachusetts Bay. It was inevitable that the "Bay People" who came direct from England and the "Plymouth People" from the Netherlands should join forces to establish an all-powerful theocratic government over both settlements.

Church and commonwealth were this theocracy's two instruments. It was a stern—and at times an intolerant—regime. Suffrage was limited to church members; Anne Hutchinson and Roger Williams were banished;

Baptists were hauled into court; and four Quakers were hanged on Boston Common. It was a dark but comparatively short period, ending with the Act of Toleration in 1689.

In 1636 Thomas Hooker led a company of 100 to what is now Hartford, Connecticut; the freeman's constitution drawn up by Hooker and his associates became the model of the American Constitution. Dissenting from the rigidity of current church worship, Congregationalists such as Jonathan Edwards of Northampton played leading roles in the Great Awakening which broke in 1734; that revival was marked not only by the eloquence of George Whitefield but by the vigorous writings and preaching of Edwards, whose books are now regarded as American classics.

Emerging stronger than ever from the Revolution, in the preparation for which it played a great heroic part, for the next century Congregationalism was concerned with five significant developments: higher education, missions, the Unitarian separation, the formation of a national council, and the production of a uniform statement of belief. In the field of education this church had already made tremendous contributions: it had founded Harvard in 1636; Yale (1707) was a Congregational project for the education of its clergy; Dartmouth (1769) developed from Eleazer Wheelock's School for Indians. These, with Williams, Amherst, Bowdoin, and Middlebury, were among the first colleges in New England. By 1953 there were 48 colleges and 10 theological seminaries in the United States with Congregational Christian origin or connection.

Interest in missions among American Congregationalists began the day the Pilgrims landed at Plymouth. The Mayhews, David Brainerd, and John Eliot were soon at work among Native Americans. Eliot spent seven years mastering their tongue, put the Bible in their language, and published a catechism in 1653, the first book to be printed in their language. By 1674 there were 4,000 "praying Indians" in New England, with 24 native preachers. When the wagon trains went West after the Revolution, the families of Congregational ministers and missionaries were prominent. Manasseh Cutler, a preacher from Hamilton, Massachusetts, was instrumental in framing the famous Northwest Territory Ordinance of 1787; other ministers led in the founding of Marietta, Ohio, the first permanent settlement in the Northwest Territory.

The American Board of Commissioners for Foreign Missions was organized in 1810 and was concerned at first with both home and foreign missionary work. On it served not only Congregationalists, but representatives of Presbyterian, Dutch Reformed, and Associate Reformed churches. This was the first foreign missionary society in the country, and it was interdenominational. The first people ordained were the young men who had participated in the famous "haystack" meeting at Williams College. Missionaries were sent to more than 30 foreign countries and American territories, not the least of which was Hawaii, where within 25 years, Congregational missionaries taught a whole nation of people to read and write, laid the foundations of a constitutional democratic government, and made of the beautiful islands a sociological laboratory filled with many races. The Congregational achievement in Hawaii is one of the greatest in the whole history of Protestant missions.

The rise of denominationalism worked against the interdenominational complexion of the American Board, and by mid-century all the non-Congregationalists had withdrawn to go their separate ways. The American Board was no longer interdenominational.

Moving westward, Congregationalists from New England came into contact with Presbyterians coming from the middle and southern states. To avoid competition and duplication of effort, a plan was developed under which ministers and members from both churches were exchanged and accepted on equal basis. Adopted in 1801, the plan eventually worked to the advantage of Presbyterians; it was discontinued in 1852, leaving the Presbyterians stronger in the West and the Congregationalists with a virtual church monopoly in New England. But the plan did much to inspire new Congregational missionary work. In 1826 the American Home Missionary Society was founded; it was active in the South before the Civil War and especially effective there toward the end of that conflict, with its "contraband" schools for blacks, one of which became Hampton Institute.

Meanwhile differences of opinion between theological liberals and conservatives were developing within the church. Strict Calvinists and Trinitarians were opposed by Unitarians, and a famous sermon by William Ellery Channing at Baltimore in 1819 made a division inevitable. The American Unitarian Association was established in 1825. Almost all the older Congregational churches in eastern Massachusetts went Unitarian; only one Congregational church was left in Boston. Debate and legal action over property and funds were not concluded until about 1840.

In spite of the Unitarian defection, Congregationalism continued to grow. It assumed such proportions that a national supervisory body became necessary. A national council held at Boston in 1865 was so effective that a regular system of councils was established. Following conferences between the associations into which the churches had grouped themselves, the first of the national councils was called at Oberlin, Ohio, in 1871. Known as the General Council of the Congregational Christian Churches, it met biennially and acted as an overall advisory body for the entire fellowship.

The council of 1913 at Kansas City adopted a declaration on faith, polity, and wider fellowship which has been accepted by many churches as a statement of faith. While it did not in any way modify the independence of local churches, it did give a new spiritual unity to the church:

Faith—We believe in God the Father, infinite in wisdom, goodness, and love; and in Jesus Christ, His Son, our Lord and Savior, who for us and our salvation lived and died and rose again and liveth evermore; and in the Holy Spirit, who taketh of the things of Christ and revealeth them to us, renewing, comforting, and inspiring the souls of men. We are united in striving to know the will of God, as taught in the Holy Scriptures, and in our purpose to walk in the ways of the Lord, made known or to be made known to us. We hold it to be the mission of the Church of Christ to proclaim the Gospel to all mankind, exalting the worship of the true God, and laboring for the progress of knowledge, the promotion of justice, and reign of peace, and the realization of human brotherhood. Depending, as did our fathers, upon the continued guidance of the Holy Spirit to lead us into all truth, we work and pray for the transformation of the world into the kingdom of God; and we look with faith for the triumph of righteousness and the life everlasting.

Polity—We believe in the freedom and responsibility of the individual soul and the right of private judgment. We hold to the autonomy of the local church and its independence of all ecclesiastical control. We cherish the fellowship of the churches united in district, state, and national bodies, for counsel and cooperation in matters of common concern.

The Wider Fellowship—While affirming the liberty of our churches, and the validity of our ministry, we hold to the unity and catholicity of the Church of Christ, and will unite with all its branches in hearty cooperation; and will earnestly seek, so far as in us lies, that the prayer of our Lord for His disciples may be answered that they all may be one.

The "wider fellowship" is taken seriously; unity and cooperation across denominational lines have been outstanding characteristics of Congregationalism all through its history. Christian Endeavor, the largest young people's organization in all Protestantism, was founded by a Congregationalist, Francis E. Clark, in 1881; by 1885 it had become an interdenominational organization known all over the world as the United Society of Christian Endeavor. In 1924 the Evangelical Protestant Church of North America was received into the National Council of Congregational Churches as the Evangelical Protestant Conference of Congregational Churches; the comparative closeness of the two mergers with the Christian Church and the Evangelical and Reformed Church again witnesses to the widening fellowship and vision of Congregationalists. Into the most recent merger they brought 47 church-related (not church-*controlled*) colleges, 11 theological seminaries, foreign mission stations in Africa, Mexico, Japan, the Philippines, India, Ceylon, Greece, Lebanon, Syria, Turkey, Korea, and Micronesia, and home missionaries in every state in the Union and Puerto Rico.

Christian Church

The Christian Church, like the Congregational, was born in protest against ecclesiasticism and the denial of individual freedom in churches. There were actually three revolts that resulted in the establishment of the Christian Church in New England and in the South.

The first was in 1792, when James O'Kelly, a Methodist minister in Virginia, withdrew from that church in protest against the development of the superintendency into an episcopacy, especially insofar as it gave the bishops absolute power in appointing ministers to their charges. O'Kelly and his followers organized under the name Republican Methodists; this was later changed to "Christian," with the new church insisting that the Bible be taken as the only rule and discipline, and that Christian character be made the only requirement of church membership.

Abner Jones, convinced that "sectarian names and human creeds should be abandoned," left the Vermont Baptists in 1801 to organize the First Christian Church at Lyndon, Vermont. This was done not as much in objection to Baptist organization or doctrine as from a desire to secure a wider freedom in religious thought and fellowship. Like O'Kelly, Jones insisted that piety and character were to be the sole test of Christian fellowship.

In the Great Awakening that swept Tennessee and Kentucky in 1801, there was a great deal of preaching that either ignored the old emphasis on the doctrines of the various denominations involved or was in direct contradiction to them. Barton W. Stone, accused of anti-Presbyterian preaching, led a number of Presbyterians out of the Synod of Kentucky to organize a Springfield presbytery. This presbytery was discontinued as its members gradually came to accept the ideology of James O'Kelly and Abner Jones, and adopted the name Christians. Stone, an ardent revivalist, was deeply influenced by the preaching of Alexander Campbell and led many of his followers and churches into the fold of the Disciples of Christ. But the large majority of his Christian churches remained with the original Christian body.

The groups under O'Kelly, Jones, and Stone engaged in a long series of conferences which resulted in their union on 6 basic Christian principles:

1. Christ, the only head of the Church.
2. The Bible, sufficient rule of faith and practice.
3. Christian character, the measure of membership.
4. A right, individual interpretation of the Scripture, as a way of life.
5. "Christian," the name taken as worthy of the followers of Christ.
6. Unity, Christians working together to save the world.

No council or other body in the Christian church has ever drawn up any other creed or statement. Its creed is the Bible. Its interpretation of Bible teaching might be called evangelical, but no sincere follower of Christ is barred from membership because of difference in theological belief. Open Communion is practiced; baptism is considered a duty but is not required; immersion is used generally, but any mode may be employed.

The union of the Congregational and Christian churches has been thoroughly democratic, leaving both free to continue their own forms of worship and each with its own polity and doctrine. Adhering strictly to the congregational idea, each local church is at liberty to call itself either Congregational or Christian, and the same choice is found in the self-governing district and state associations into which the churches are organized.

Evangelical and Reformed Church

The Evangelical and Reformed Church was the product of a union established at Cleveland, Ohio, on June 26, 1934, by two bodies of Swiss and German background with basic agreements in doctrine, polity, and culture—the Evangelical Synod of North America and the Reformed Church in the United States.

The Evangelical Synod, the younger of the bodies, originated when six ministers of Lutheran and Reformed churches in the Evangelical United Church of Prussia met at Gravois Settlement near St. Louis in 1840 to form the Evangelical Union of the West. Two had been sent to America by the Rhenish Missionary Society and two by the Missionary Society of Basel; the others were independent, one coming from Bremen and the other from Strasbourg.

The Evangelical Union of the West was a cooperative ministerial association until 1849, when the first permanent organization was established. As the movement spread east and northwest among German-speaking Lutheran and Reformed peoples, headquarters were established at St. Louis, and a new name, German Evangelical Synod of North America, was adopted. A series of amalgamations with four other bodies of similar belief and polity—the German Evangelical Church Association of Ohio, the German United Evangelical Synod of the East, the Evangelical Synod of the Northwest, and the United Evangelical Synod of the East—resulted in the formation of the Evangelical Synod of North America, giving it a membership of 281,598 at the time of the merger with the Reformed Church in the United States.

The Reformed Church in the United States had its origin in Switzerland and Germany, particularly in the flood tide of German immigration to Pennsylvania in the eighteenth century. More than half the Germans in Pennsylvania in 1730 were Reformed; the congregations were widely separated along the frontier and, lacking ministers, they often employed schoolteachers to lead the services. Three pastors, Johann Philip Boehm, George Michael Weiss, and Johann Bartholomaeus Rieger, were deeply influenced by Michael Schlatter, who had been sent to America by the (Dutch Reformed) Synod of South and North Holland; with him they organized in 1747 a coetus (synod) in Philadelphia, directly responsible to and in part financially supported by the synod in Holland. It declared its independence in 1793, taking the name German Reformed Church; in that year it reported 178 congregations and 15,000 communicants. The word German was dropped in 1869, and thereafter the denomination was called the Reformed Church in the United States.

Reformed church missionaries went across the Alleghenies into Ohio and south into North Carolina. An overall synod of the church divided the country into eight districts or classes, in 1819, and an independent Ohio classis was formed in 1824. Franklin College (now Franklin and Marshall) was founded at Lancaster, Pennsylvania, with the support of Benjamin Franklin; a theological seminary was opened at Carlisle and later moved to Lancaster; an academy that later became Marshall College was established in 1836. The Synod of Ohio established a theological school and Heidelberg University at Tiffin, Ohio, in 1850. The mother synod in the East and the Ohio synod were united in the general synod in 1836, which functioned until the merger with the Evangelical Synod of North America in 1934.

Difficulties arose in the early years of the last century: the older Germans preferred the use of German; the second-generation members demanded English. Inevitably in a church of such mixed membership, there was conflict between conservatives and liberals. Some churches withdrew and formed a separate synod but returned in 1837 when wiser heads prevailed and compromises were made. New district synods of both German-speaking and English-speaking congregations were created, and two Hungarian classes from the Old Hungarian Reformed Church were added in 1924.

By 1934 the boards of the church were directing widespread home missions and foreign missionary work in Japan, China, and Mesopotamia. There were 12 institutions of higher learning, three theological seminaries, and three orphanages. There were 348,189 members in the Reformed Church at the time of the 1934 merger, largely concentrated in Pennsylvania and Ohio.

Few difficulties were encountered in reconciling the doctrines of the two bodies when the union was finally accomplished. Both churches were German Calvinistic; the Reformed church had been based historically on the Heidelberg Catechism, the Evangelical Synod on the Heidelberg Cathechism, the Augsburg Confession, and Luther's Catechism. These three standards of faith were woven into one in the new constitution of the Evangelical and Reformed Church:

> The Holy Scriptures of the Old and New Testaments are recognized as the Word of God and the ultimate rule of Christian faith and practice.
>
> The doctrinal standards of the Evangelical and Reformed Church are the Heidelberg Catechism, Luther's Catechism, and the Augsburg Confession. They are accepted as an authoritative interpretation of the essential truth taught in the Holy Scriptures.
>
> Wherever these doctrinal standards differ, ministers, members, and congregations, in accordance with the liberty of conscience inherent in the Gospel, are allowed to adhere to the interpretation of one of these confessions. However, in each case the final norm is the Word of God.

Two sacraments—baptism, usually administered to infants, and the Lord's Supper—are accepted; confirmation—generally before the thirteenth or fourteenth year—ordination, consecration, marriage, and burial are considered rites. Although hymns and forms of worship are provided for general use, a wide freedom of worship is encouraged.

Church polity, when this church joined the Congregational Christians in 1957, was modified presbyterian; each local church was governed by a consistory or church council elected from its own membership. Local churches formed 34 synods, each made up of a pastor and lay delegate from each charge. The synod met twice a year and had jurisdiction over all ministers and congregations; examined, licensed, and ordained all pastors; and elected its own officers—a procedure quite different from that of the Congregational Christian churches. It led many to wonder whether a union between two such different forms of government could possibly work, and this hesitancy is a root cause of the refusal of a few churches to cooperate in the merger.

The Evangelical and Reformed Church was a thriving church when the details of union were being worked out. In 1959 there were 810,000 members in 2,740 churches, 8 colleges, 3 theological schools, and 2 academies; foreign missionaries in India, Japan, Hong Kong, Iraq, Africa, and Honduras; and a widespread home missionary work among the people of the Ozarks, Native Americans, Volga Germans, Hungarians, and Japanese.

UNITED HOLY CHURCH OF AMERICA, INC.

A pentecostal church organized at Method, North Carolina, in a meeting held by Isaac Cheshier in 1886, this body was successively called the Holy Church of North Carolina, the Holy Church of North Carolina and Virginia, and finally (1918) the United Holy Church of America, Inc. Its purpose is to establish and maintain holy convocations, assemblies, conventions, conferences, public worship, missionary and school work, orphanages, manual and trade training, and religious resorts, both permanent and temporary.

Articles of faith contain statements of belief in the Trinity, the record of God's revelation of himself in the Bible, redemption through Christ, justification with instantaneous sanctification, the baptism of the Holy Spirit, divine healing, and the ultimate reign of Christ over the earth. Baptism by immersion, the Lord's Supper, and foot washing are observed as ordinances.

The chief officer is the president; the board of bishops supervises the general work of the church. There were 28,980 members in 470 churches in 1960.

UNITY SCHOOL OF CHRISTIANITY

In 1860, Charles Fillmore, bankrupt and a cripple, and his wife Myrtle, seriously ill with tuberculosis, discovered an affirmative prayer approach. The treatment, or system, is offered today in the Unity School of

Christianity as a curative in many areas beyond physical healing. Unity is not a church or a denomination, but a nonsectarian religious educational institution devoted to demonstrating that the teaching of Jesus Christ is a practical, seven-day-a-week way of life. "The true church is a state of consciousness in man."

The Fillmores held that "whatever man wants he can have by voicing his desire in the right way into the Universal Mind," an emphasis found originally in Christian Science. Both studied Christian Science, though neither was ever a part of the movement. They also studied New Thought, Quakerism, Theosophy, Rosicrucianism, Spiritism, and Hinduism; out of their studies came an ideology both old and original, built on ancient truth and concepts but moving in a new direction.

Unity teaches that all thought goes back to God, who is "Principle, Law, Being, Mind, Spirit, All Good, omnipotent, omniscient, unchangeable, Creator, Father, Cause and Source of all that is." In the attribute of Mind is found the "meeting ground of man and God." Unity has a Trinity: "The Father is Principle, the Son is that Principle revealed in a creative plan. The Holy Spirit is the executive power of both Father and Son carrying out the creative plan." Jesus Christ is "Spiritual man . . . the direct offspring of Divine Mind, God's idea of perfect man." Humans are children of God, filled with the Christ consciousness. It is through Christ, or the Christ consciousness, that the human gains eternal *life* and *salvation*, both terms having meanings different from those in orthodox Christianity. *Salvation* may be said to mean the attainment of that true spiritual body which replaces the physical body when a human being becomes like Christ. This transformation takes place not in any hereafter, but "here in this earth" through a series of reincarnations and regenerations. A person suffers no final death but changes into increasingly better states until finally becoming like Christ. All people will have this experience.

Unity has been described as "a religious philosophy with an 'open end,' seeking to find God's truth in all of life, wherever it may be." It has no strict creed or dogma; it finds good in all religions, and we should keep our minds open to receive that goodness. Each person must achieve it alone. Others may help, but ultimately it must be a relationship between God and the individual. Knowing and loving God is the key to peace and success: "To them that love God all things work together for good."

Unlike Christian Science, Unity recognizes the reality of matter, the world, sin, and sickness. Sin and sickness are real but may be overcome: health is natural; sickness is unnatural. Anything that injures the body is to be avoided—emotions, for instance, such as strife, anger, hatred, or self-interest. But all this is strictly personal, a matter of individual decision; Unity lays down no laws concerning health but concentrates on spiritual goals, knowing that healthful living habits will follow. Some Unity students are vegetarians in the interests of health; many are not. Unity is personal; there are no social or health programs as such, no hospitals or relief agencies.

Solutions are suggested for every human want and illness. The follower is told to repeat certain affirmations which develop the all-powerful mind and bring from the Divine Mind whatever the follower needs. The Bible is used constantly in Unity but is not considered the sole or final authority in faith and practice; people must be in direct, personal communion with God, not dependent upon such secondary sources as the Scriptures.

The Association of Unity Churches (AUC), an independent but related organization of ministers and licensed teachers, is not a department of Unity School. It handles ordination and placement of ministers. The AUC is self-supporting and has conventions.

Unity School has not in the past approved or disapproved of ministers or been involved in placement. It has, however, begun directing the educational process and thus will have some voice in ordination.

Unity does not have annual conferences, nor is there a statement of faith. Its real work is done through what is called Silent Unity. A large staff of workers in Unity Village, near Kansas City, is available for consultation day and night, answering telephone calls, telegrams, and letters—an average of 15,000 calls a week and 2.5 million letters annually. It is a service of counsel, prayer, and affirmation, offering help on every conceivable problem. Each case or call is assigned to one member of the staff, who suggests the proper affirmations. The whole staff joins in group prayer and meditation several times a day. All calls and requests are answered. There is no charge for this service, but love offerings are accepted. Unity answers 750,000 such calls yearly, most of them coming from members of various Christian churches. Correspondents are never asked to leave the churches to which they belong.

Some 200,000,000 books, booklets, tracts, and magazines are published and undoubtedly used by many who never contact headquarters at all and never in any sense become members of the school. About 15 new cassettes are produced annually, and more than 1,000 radio and television stations broadcast 250 Unity programs a week.

UNIVERSAL CHRISTIAN SPIRITUAL FAITH AND CHURCHES FOR ALL NATIONS, THE

This body was founded as the National David Spiritual Temple of Christ Church Union (Inc.), U.S.A. in 1932 by David William Short, a former minister of the Missionary Baptist Church. Dr. Short wished to "proclaim the Orthodox Christian spiritual faith"; he was convinced that no one has the right or spiritual power "to make laws, rules, or doctrines for the real church founded by Jesus Christ" and that the denominational churches were founded in error and in disregard of the apostolic example. He held wisdom, knowledge, faith, healing, miracles, prophecy, discerning of spirits, and diverse kinds of tongues to be spiritual gifts of the Holy Ghost and parts of the church of Christ. He believed that all races should and must be accepted in the true church.

The members of this church consider themselves the true and universal church of Christ, not just another denomination. They rely entirely upon the Holy Ghost for inspiration and direction; their church constitution, they claim, is found in I Corinthians 12:1-31 and Ephesians 4:11. Their organization is made up of pastors, prophets, prophetesses, bishops, archbishops, elders, overseers, divine healers, deacons, and missionaries. Archbishop Short is the chief governing officer; there is a national executive board that holds a national annual assembly.

Home missionary work is conducted in hospitals, and a nursing home is maintained. A monthly newspaper, *The Christian Spiritual Voice,* is published at Kansas City, Missouri. Archbishop Short is also founder, president, and mentor of the St. David Orthodox Christian Spiritual Seminary, dedicated in 1949 at Des Moines; in 1952 he was elected archbishop and chief apostle of the new Universal Christian Spiritual Faith and Churches for All Nations, which represented a merger of the National David Spiritual Temple, the St. Paul's Spiritual Church Convocation, and King David's Spiritual Temple of Truth Association. The organization has a membership of 40,816 in 60 churches, prayer bands, and missions.

VEDANTA SOCIETY

The members of the Vedanta Society base their faith and philosophy upon the writings of the Vedas, the scriptures of the Indo-Aryans. This Indian philosophy, explaining the nature and end of all wisdom, harmonizes the findings of modern science, offers a scientific and philosophical basis for religion—rational, nondogmatic, and liberal—and stresses the oneness of all religions as taught in the Upanishads and the Bhagavad Gita. It was first expounded in this country by Swami Vivekananda at the World's Parliament of Religions held in Chicago in 1893; he founded the Vedanta Society of New York in 1894.

There are 13 Vedanta centers, 3 monasteries, and 2 convents in the United States; all belong to and are under the management of the Ramakrishna Math and Mission founded by Swami Vivekananda, with headquarters in Belur Math, near Calcutta. Each center is an independent self-supporting unit with its own board of trustees, made up mostly of American citizens. The swamis are ordained monks and visit as guest teachers. There are public lectures and classes that seek not to convert, but to enlighten. There are 1,600 members.

VOLUNTEERS OF AMERICA

The Volunteers of America (VOA) is a religious social-welfare organization founded and incorporated in New York in 1896 by the late Ballington and Maud Booth. More than 36,000 members were reported in 1978, but this figure hardly tells the whole story of services rendered to hundreds of thousands of people in the principal cities of the United States.

Religious services are offered in missions, Volunteer churches, Sunday schools, companionship leagues, prisons, and on the streets; the organization has its own rituals for baptism, the Lord's Supper, and marriage. Doctrine is evangelical, with strong emphasis on the saving grace of God, the Trinity, the atonement of Christ, regeneration through the Holy Spirit, the necessity of repentance and conversion, immortality, and future rewards and punishments.

Organization of the Volunteers is based on a semimilitary structure. All officers bear military titles and wear uniforms. The chief governing body, the Grand Field Council, is composed of officers bearing the rank of lieutenant major or above. A board of ten members, the National Executive Board, functions when the Grand Field Council is not in session. There are nine directors, who are the responsible financial officers and act as trustees and custodians of all property. Military regulations do not apply in the selection of these officers; they are chosen by democratic election. The commander in chief is elected for 5 years and is also president of the corporate body. There are 4 administrative regions—Eastern, Western, Midwestern, and Southern. National office and staff are located in New York City.

The social welfare programs include departments of family welfare, salvage, health camps, hospices for working girls, maternity homes, nursing homes, homes for mothers and children, adoptive placements, clubs and homes for the aged, rehabilitation workshops, family counseling centers, transient men's homes, and boys' and girls' clubs. There is an excellent prison department which assists discharged and paroled prisoners, men and women in prison, and their families; more than 100,000 prisoners are enrolled in the Volunteer Prison League—a self-help group, organized by inmates in various correctional institutions with VOA consultation and guidance. Recent program developments include 40 prerelease centers or half-way house facilities. There are also 28 housing projects for low and moderate income families and senior citizens, providing more than 7,500 units and serving nearly 30,000 families and individuals.

During 1972 nearly 6,000,000 people received material assistance through various departments, exclusive of religious service. There were 9,000,000 meals and 2,000,000 lodgings furnished; in addition, more than 6,500 children were cared for in such child service centers as day care centers, foster day care, group homes, summer camps, and so on. Nearly

100,000 elderly persons participated in the Sunset Club program. More than 16,000 interviews were held in prisons; 160,000 prisoners attended Volunteer religious services; and 2,000 prisoners were paroled in their custody. Nearly 60,000 men were given job opportunities in the Men's Rehabilitation Centers, and 30,000 unemployed men were aided in securing work in business and industry. Over 30,000,000 articles such as furniture, household appliances, and clothing were distributed free or at a nominal cost to low income families and individuals. The annual budget of the Volunteers is in excess of $45 million.

WESLEYAN CHURCH, THE

Until 1968 this body was called the Wesleyan Methodist Church of America. At the time of its founding in 1843, it represented a protest against slavery and the Methodist episcopacy, predating by one year the historic division of the Methodist Episcopal Church and the Methodist Episcopal Church, South. With the slavery issue settled by the Civil War, other differences—entire sanctification and the issue of the liquor traffic—seemed important enough to continue its separate existence.

In June 1968 the Wesleyan Methodist Church merged with the Pilgrim Holiness Church to become The Wesleyan Church. The Pilgrim Holiness Church, founded in 1897, was close in doctrine and polity to the Church of the Nazarene and thus close to Methodism and in agreement with Wesleyan doctrines; there was no shift or change in doctrinal emphases when the two churches joined. The time-honored teaching of entire sanctification is still central. Candidates for church membership are required to disavow the use, sale, or manufacture of tobacco and alcoholic beverages and to refrain from membership in secret societies.

Present membership totals 111,111 in 1,711 churches in the United States and Canada, with areas of greatest strength in Indiana, Michigan, Ohio, and North Carolina. An enlarging evangelistic and missionary activity is directed from world headquarters in Marion, Indiana. In 1983, 46 districts had missionaries at work in many countries of Asia, Africa, the Caribbean, and Latin America. There are now 3 liberal arts colleges, 2 Bible colleges, and a seminary foundation.

WORLDWIDE CHURCH OF GOD

Founded in 1931 by Herbert W. Armstrong, a businessman, this independent body of conservative Protestants claims historic kinship with ancient and medieval dissenters from the Catholic Church. In this country it is a descendant of several Adventist and Sabbatarian movements. Since 1934 it has been a quite singular body, adhering strictly to its own course.

The Worldwide Church of God is best known for its monthly magazine, *Plain Truth*, and its radio and television program, "Garner Ted Armstrong Presents." Rivalry for leadership between the founder, the elder Armstrong, and Garner Ted, his son, has brought the body to public attention.

Its "Fundamentals of Belief" do not teach the doctrine of the Trinity, regarded as pagan, but do affirm faith in one God, in Jesus of Nazareth as "the Christ, the divine Son of the living God," and in the Holy Spirit as "the Spirit of God and of Christ Jesus." It stresses the reality of Satan as a personality. Concerning human nature, the inspiration of the Scriptures, Christ's resurrection, and baptism, the church holds to rather traditional positions, and it takes a strong stand against bearing arms and the taking of human life.

Its affinity for the subject of Israel and some of the teachings of classical Judaism are striking: The Lord's Supper is stressed as a continuation of Passover; the Sabbath (Friday sunset to Saturday sunset) is observed as the day of worship; seven annual holy days are observed, and certain "unclean" foods must be avoided. Some divine promises pertain only to Israel; other prophecies, however, pertain to the white English-speaking peoples of America and Britain. A strong dispensationalist strain is present, with an eager expectation of Christ's return to establish the kingdom of God on earth.

Each local congregation is called The Church of God; collectively, the Churches of God. A worldwide ministry is carried out from the headquarters in Pasadena, California. Baptized adult membership is about 67,000, most in the United States.

MAKING SENSE OF BEWILDERMENT

Understanding the Current Scene in American Religion

In the mid-1980s two conditions stand out as most prominent in the religious life of the American people. One is the large and growing evangelical family within Christianity, which has achieved distribution into all parts of the country and all social classes. The other is the ongoing, growing, and powerful movement called secularism, a way of understanding and living that is indifferent to religion—in fact, not even concerned enough to pay it any attention, much less oppose it.

Thus one "conservative" and one "liberal" force are the most visible at work in American society today. Their prominence and visibility are far from misleading. They *are* significant features in contemporary American life. But of course much more is going on; it is important to look at some of that also.

Familiarity with the huge number of religious bodies surveyed in this *Handbook* sheds some light on the current scene. It reveals that religious patterns are highly diverse. It also implies that we continue to be a religiously pluralistic nation—that is, we agree to value respect for the rights of others to practice their religious faith differently, even if we may regard some particular practices as strange or perhaps regrettable. Only in the United States of America are there so many religious bodies, and only here is such diversity tolerated and even accepted.

Yet it is fascinating to note how little change has been taking place as far as denominational groupings are concerned. Few new denominations have come into being in the past 50 or more years— that is, apart from new Eastern faiths or Orient-related movements. And only a small number have disappeared, all small and showing membership decline over the past several decades. American religion is indeed active, growing, and changing—a dynamic entity in American life. But this action is not a result of the formation of new bodies and the demise of old ones.

Instead, the dynamics of contemporary American religion resides in the growth and vitalization of existing denominations—in particular, more conservative Protestant Christian ones. Latter Day Saints (Mormon) and Southern Baptist Convention growth are remarkable, statistically speaking, since those organizations were already very large. The Pentecostal bodies show sizable increases, most phenomenally the black Church of God in Christ, which reports a membership of over 3,700,000 and has recently opened All Saints University in Memphis. Similarly, Assemblies of God shows a dramatic increase, as do Seventh-Day Adventists and the Baptist Bible Fellowship, a very conservative independent body representing more than one million members (the most famous of whom is Jerry Falwell).

Conservative movements like these once occupied marginal positions in American society. During and since the late 1970s they have striven for and achieved access to prominence in the society at large. Drawing upon huge resources provided by generous members, they have entered the television field, syndicating programs or even operating networks of their own. In some cases they have become active politically. The Moral Majority, Inc., is only the best known of several New Christian Right ventures into the public realm for the sake of electing their chosen candidates to office and supporting legislation in line with their moral and philosophical convictions. For the groups within the conservative range correctly described as fundamentalist, this is revolutionary behavior indeed, since they traditionally have prided themselves on withdrawal from the society, refusing to compromise with a culture perverse in its inclinations.

Less visible, but perhaps more effectual and certainly more appreciated by the public at large, are other conservative Protestant denominations—those that are evangelical but not fundamentalist. Some of the groups properly so described are the Evangelical Covenant Church and the Evangelical Free Church, the Conservative Baptist Association of America, the Christian Reformed Church, and the Presbyterian Church in America. In addition to whole denominations, there are thousands of Methodists, Mennonites, and American Baptists, among others, who identify with this kind of authority and manifest a high-intensity personal faith. Christians such as these are politically active, often on the "liberal" side with reference to issues like foreign policy and capital punishment but without forming quasi-Christian parties to accomplish their ends. Also, they sponsor colleges and seminaries well within the main stream of American education, though grounded in particularist philosophies and practices.

Thus the most evident new developments are occurring among conservatives within the evangelical Protestant camp. At the same time millions of Americans continue to find meaning in and give dedication to the more traditional bodies. These probably are times of transition and reorientation for such bodies as the United Church of Christ, the Presbyterian Church (U.S.A.), The United Methodist Church, and the Lutheran Church in America. But their membership figures have stabilized after several years of gradual decrease, their influence remains very strong, and they are still "home" for a great many people. One of several reasons for their recovery may well be the infusion of fresh strength by evangelical cadres within their own ranks—that is, some members who hold more firmly to traditional authority and others who manifest spiritual gifts (charisma). In addition, these churches have begun to generate a revitalized program of Christian education for children and adults alike. Their commitments to social ministries, long prominent and vital, persist.

How are these specific new directions related to the two features mentioned at the beginning as standing out in present-day American religious life? Relative to the surge of evangelical strength, evangelical groups themselves are growing in numbers and capacity for making impact and, in a variety of ways, are insinuating their concerns into the public life of all the American people. That surge is also making its presence felt, somewhat indirectly, within the mainline denominations as well. As far as the second feature is concerned, secularism is more attractive to mainline communities than to evangelicals (although it is hardly absent from the latter). But as it becomes easier to admit that one really is secular in life practice, and as the mainline churches tighten up their identities somewhat, we may suppose that their members' conscious and open affirmation of Christian identity will deepen and mature.

Of abiding importance is interaction and dialogue between people with a Christian world-view and secularists, sometimes described as practicing the absence of God. Curiously, these days evangelicals, extremist evangelicals (fundamentalists), and mainline denominations are all interacting with the secular world and, in the first and last cases, carrying on dialogue with people in it. Thus one of the primary items on the old "liberal" agenda has now appeared on the lists of other kinds of Christians as well.

This emerging trend toward a more particularized Protestant population—soon we will look at Roman Catholicism—is arresting a drift that gained a full head of steam after two developments early in this century: (1) the passing of the last major wave of immigration during the 1920s; and (2) the bursting of modernity upon more isolated areas and more traditionalist denominations between the 1880s and the 1920s.

In the first case, the arrival of immigrant peoples in a nation with few familiar landmarks made the church of the old country very attractive to a great many, some of whom had merely taken the church's presence for granted back in Poland, Sicily, Ireland, or Greece. During that period, many new American religious organizations took form or enlarged greatly: the various national Orthodox bodies (Greek, Russian, Albanian, et al.), the Old Catholic churches (from Germany, Poland, Switzerland, et al.), the Roman Catholic Church, and several Lutheran national churches together with Pietist groups that had broken away from them. New or existing bodies thus were formed or their membership swelled, and immigrants affiliated with them meaningfully.

In the second case, indigenously American sects appeared on the scene, as the Holiness and Pentecostal movements erupted and expanded. Decrying accommodation to modernity (referred to as *modernism*), they took a firm grip on the Bible as infallible authority. In many cases they found in the Bible doctrines rarely practiced, such as "entire sanctification," "Baptism of the Spirit," and "speaking in tongues." In appropriating these, they sought to restore authenticity and power to strayed Methodist, Baptist, and Presbyterian traditions. From unimpressive beginnings in southern Appalachia, a number of new denominations appeared. Out of the Tennessee animation came, earlier and later, the Church of God (Cleveland, Tennessee), the (Original) Church of God, the Church of God of Prophecy, and the Church of God (headquarters in Huntsville, Alabama). From northwest South Carolina and nearby parts of Georgia arose the Pentecostal Holiness Chuch and the Fire-Baptized Holiness Church. Blacks participated in this Holiness revival as well, whence came the Church of God in Christ. In Arkansas and Missouri, too, the Spirit moved, bringing to life the Assemblies of God. In Los Angeles, the Azusa Street Mission effervescence of 1906 bore fruit in many vineyards. The Midwest witnessed the emergence of the Church of God (Anderson, Indiana) which was "holiness" without being "pentecostal."

The first congeries served the growing human needs of immigrant peoples alienated from the culture they had chosen—and rather soon became an accepted part of. The second group reflected "becoming somebody" in the Lord's eyes, and in one another's. Thousands of Americans from the lower classes, typically divorced from advancing through mainstream culture, saw new visions and strove to create pure communities of the faithful.

It is likely that both the abounding secularism and the resurging evangelicalism of the past quarter-century trace some roots to those early-century developments. The process of secularization has been enhanced by the lessening, or at least the shifting appeal to ethnic groups of ethnic churches. Sociologically less necessary to people now quite at home in American culture, the various ethnic denominations either hold those people for other reasons, or have lost them, since that factor which was once so vital has faded in importance.

The Pentecostal and Holiness movements forfeited some gains, as those groups often shunned "the world" in favor of retaining purity. Their hostility toward public culture and their sect-minded withdrawal in time lost them some members, especially potential recruits. It also set the stage for evangelicalism's bursting upon the public scene in the 1970s and 1980s. Somewhat earlier, the more moderate sector in the American evangelical community began to develop a socal ethic and assume for itself public responsibility. Within the past decade the more fundamentalist branches have surfaced as the New Right, as much up to their steeples in politics as the more liberal denominations have been for a long time—with radically different positions, needless to say. After a long season of isolation from the society, they have lately "gone public."

The ethnic churches, through the reform and revitalization of their traditions, have recently taken a role in the more conservative of the two major developments. In some cases they have participated in the "charismatic" movement, in that prayer, Spirit experience, and more demonstrative forms of faith have been introduced. In others they have tightened their traditions, insisting on the defined authority of both priestly office and liturgical texts. Several of the new "denominations" that have appeared were formed so that the catholic tradition could be conserved.

Both of those developments during the years before and after 1900 have run their courses by the mid-1980s. This does not mean, however, that these movements have lost their vitality and place. Conservators of tradition and Spirit-filled Christians are abundant in this decade. But the current scene is operating on a new cycle. Nevertheless, as we have been seeing, there is continuity as well as discontinuity between the earlier and newer cycles.

One of the major aspects of what is occurring in this decade is the infusion of unfamiliar styles of Christian practice and expression into existing denominations—a quite different thing from the formation of new bodies. Some Lutherans, Episcopalians, and Roman Catholics are becoming charismatic. Such people are not disposed to join Pentecostal or Holiness bodies; any such denomination shifting is a rarity. They remain happily Lutheran or Episcopalian or Catholic while embracing new forms of spirituality that are more often "Spirit-filled" than "pentecostal." That is to say, their faith is now more demonstrative, enthusiastic, and expressive, but it stops short of extranatural phenomena such as speaking in tongues.

Summarizing, we may say that the paucity of newly organized religious bodies in our time is both a fact and a fact that could mislead. There are not dozens of new denominations. At the same time, many of the impulses that gave rise to new groups in earlier periods, especially before and after 1900, continue to make impact. We see them in those same bodies that originated in those earlier times and that are now, in several cases, quite large denominations. But now they are also present in traditionally low-intensity, nondemonstrative mainline Christian communions. The high-intensity dimension of spirituality persists as a significant force in American Christianity. We are indeed in a different cycle but the animation is much the same.

Depiction of groups, concerns, and trends by such terms as *conservative, liberal, evangelical, mainline, conservators of tradition, high-intensity*, and so on suggests the desirability of examining what those terms mean and where those qualities fit in the current religious scene.

What is liberal? What is conservative? These are questions that defy easy answers. The ascription of "liberal" to another group than one's own tells something about that group, of course, but also about the one who thinks of the other in that way. It can indicate areas of disagreement between two groups where labeling or classifying seems appropriate. Beyond that, it points to concerns they place high on their list of values and priorities, especially the basic items that simply must not be compromised.

A number of concrete examples come to mind. Those who view personal morality with supreme earnestness, who make personal purity or piety a paramount concern, are apt to accuse people who drink alcoholic beverages of being "liberals." Yet some of the most "conservative" Christians, from a doctrinal perspective—for instance, Missouri Synod Lutherans—think nothing of having a glass of beer or wine. Christians of the latter persuasion—"liberals" by one set of standards and "conservatives" by another—may well view some pietists ("conservatives") as quite "liberal" on the issue of doctrinal firmness; for example, Mennonites and many Methodists are faulted for being more concerned with faithful life-style than with fastidious doctrine.

Or take the case of Roman Catholics alongside Presbyterians when the issue (as focused on here) is conservation of the Christian tradition as contrasted with reaching back over or under the tradition to New Testament events, practices, and messages themselves in their stark integrity. Which is "conservative" in this case? Both communions live and die by being "conservative," yet how greatly they differ on what that means! Presbyterians so disposed might well characterize Roman Catholicism as "liberal" in the sense that it has tampered with the authoritative Word of God by adding the "traditions of men." Roman Catholics, by contrast, might well respond with the judgment that Presbyterianism has ignored the continuing presence and witness of God through the church over the centuries. And on and on the story might go. Who is liberal and who is conservative are questions answerable by reference to several, not just one or two basic categories of Christianity—personal morality, authority, and doctrinal propriety being prominent among them. (There are other basic categories as well—for example, social responsibility and church organization.)

Perhaps a more fruitful solution to the liberal/conservative classification is the construction of a spectrum with families of Christians placed upon it. The extremes are Right and Left, with Right referring to traditionalist, Left to immediatist. Examples will clarify this. Roman Catholicism belongs at the Right end of the spectrum since it gives a place of authority to the tradition of the church, its experiences, teachings, and practices, and to its saintly members from the time of Christ and the apostles to the present. It thus has access to a number of instruments which mediate the presence and power of God: the church, priests, liturgy, the sacraments, departed saints, visual and tactile signs and symbols, and so on. It is not the case that one cannot "pray directly to God" (as more Left Christians may put it), but it is true that such traditionalist Christianity places in the hands of its members a large number of instruments on earth and in heaven that bring God and people together.

On the Left, a radically different understanding prevails—an immediatist view. For radical Protestants (many of whom are fundamentalists), the God who spoke definitively once in Christ and through Scripture continues to speak to people and through events. And God speaks directly, immediately, without any "instruments" apart from the message of the Bible as directed by the Holy Spirit. Christians of this kind turn only to the Bible, not to the tradition of Christianity between the time of the giving of the normative revelation contained in the Bible and the present. They do not acknowledge any valid intermediaries, largely because there is no need for any. It follows that emphasis falls on the individual and his or her own daily experience, conversion, and spiritual sensitivity and discipline; it also falls on the congregation and on the preacher's interpretation and effectiveness.

Moving from Right to Left on this spectrum, then, is moving from tradition to immediacy; from church as authoritative institution to free-form congregations and each individual; from prescribed worship to informal gatherings; from orientation toward objective means and instruments to the hold of texts on a person's life and individual spiritual experience; from organized corporateness to spontaneous expression of the individual and the assemblage.

The examples given for the extremes of the spectrum, Roman Catholicism on the Right and radical Protestantism on the Left, must be set alongside the many stations that line the spectrum between the two. Those denominations, taken together, are often referred to as mainline Protestant. They include most prominently (though there are others), the Episcopal, Lutheran, Presbyterian, Methodist, Congregational, and Disciples of Christ families of Protestantism.

It has been said that Roman Catholicism and the Baptist-like position are the extremes within Christianity and that all the others differ about as much as Tweedle-dum and Tweedle-dee. That playful assessment does make a certain amount of sense. Yet the differences are there and need delineation.

By major categories we may divide the spectrum into (1) Liturgical, (2) Word and Sacrament, (3) Experiential, and (4) Sectarian. (Several smaller categories will be touched on later.) In the process of treating discrete denominations, some overlapping occurs since different groups share perspectives with others, one shading into another. This is even true of one of our "extreme" examples, Roman Catholicism, as we shall see.

The Liturgical cluster of Christians regards worship as the central act of life. Roman Catholics, Orthodox (members of the Eastern churches), and Episcopalians are very much at home in the church, the place of worship. While their prescribed forms of worship (liturgies) differ somewhat in the three instances, they all do use set forms. And these forms are derived from the Christian tradition—that is, from prayers, creeds, lectionaries, special ceremonies, and the like developed by Christians long ago. For instance, a particular prayer or creed may have begun in simple form in the third century, have evolved gradually, and come to its present formulation through elaboration and revision over the next millennium, more or less. Thus these Liturgical bodies are heirs to and participants in the catholic (universal) tradition. Worship is their stock-in-trade—the forms are prescribed and those forms are hundreds of years old.

In addition, this way of approaching Christianity regards the Eucharist or Holy Communion as the central element in worship. Without exception the bread and wine are taken as bearers of mystery—that is to say, they are more than or different from what their mere physical attributes suggest. (Roman Catholicism goes farthest in claiming that the bread *is* the body of Christ and the wine *is* his blood.) This teaching is correlated with the conviction that the service at the altar is some kind of representation of Christ's sacrificial death on Calvary. In turn, this claim is correlated with the role of the ordained officiant at the service (often called the Mass). It is logical that the priest can perform some rites that no lay person is authorized to conduct (although that does not make the priest superior or "a better Christian" in any way).

Thus Liturgical Christianity places the act of worship at the center of faith, identifies with the Christian tradition that has developed from the time of Christ and his apostles to the present, and accords to the ordained officer specific and exclusive roles. As for what is believed, the biblical message shapes and defines its teachings, with attention also given to how that message has been interpreted and applied over the centuries. Yet heavier stress is placed on the adaptation of that message to worship forms and expression than to formal and required doctrinal positions (especially in the Episcopal and Orthodox churches).

The Word and Sacrament families of Christianity are next left on the spectrum, still somewhat traditionalist ("conservative" in that sense) yet also Protestant. Lutherans and Presbyterians are the major denominations here. Concerning their traditionalism, they honor the experience and fruits of the Church over the centuries, but do not accord them any normative status. They too grant to public corporate worship a role of great importance. In the Lutheran case, a prescribed liturgical form is followed, one that has much in common with the Episcopal, Orthodox, and Catholic (the traditional Christian) forms. Also, Holy Communion not only is given a high place but the dimension of mystery in the two elements and their meaning is upheld. Among Presbyterians, worship is rather formal, done in "decency and order," but no set forms are employed. Communion is viewed as very important but is treated as "enacted words" rather than as a mystery located in the elements. In both cases the role of the minister is highly appreciated—for example, education is essential and a cultivated intelligence is prized. Basically, however, the minister is a preacher, a proclaimer of the Word (the message of the Bible) and as such is an interpreter of a message intended for all. The minister is not viewed as the officiant of a celebration associated with the act of Christ's sacrificial death. Clearly, then, these are more "democratic" types of church life, although they are not strictly congregational.

Looming somewhat larger in Lutheran and Presbyterian life is its "very Protestant" character, which insists that the Bible is the sole authority for faith and action. The question is not What does the tradition deliver from the Christian past to the present? but rather, What does the Bible say? It is not surprising then that preaching and preacher are so vital to these denominations, nor that training and learning are important. Moreover, theology—correct thinking and teaching about Christian doctrine—rank high on the list of priorities. Lutherans and Presbyterians are supposed to know Christian doctrine, proclaim it, and live by it. A theologian is highly respected in this family of Protestantism. At the same time, each Christian is urged to be a serious interpreter and an earnest practitioner of the normative biblical message.

Just as Liturgical Christianity overlapped with Word and Sacrament, so we find the latter overlapping with the next family to the left on our spectrum, Experiential, the Protestantism that expresses personal experience. The most prominent denominations are Methodist, Congregational, and Baptist. All share the Lutheran and Presbyterian exaltation of the Bible as the only authority for faith; all are vigorously Protestant. These groups pay less (sometimes no) attention to tradition than to the religious experience of the individual and the will of "the people" in local congregations. In stopping at these stations on the spectrum we have moved from priest to minister to preacher—from worship (whether before an altar or from a pulpit) to the response of the individual member or the congregation.

As stated, the Bible is central, basic, and indispensable. Its message is essential and its authority is binding. And its message takes form less in worship and doctrine than in personal expressiveness. One is in touch directly with the Lord—spoken as "the Lord" more often than the less intimate term "God"—no intermediaries are necessary or permitted. Here is direct access to heaven for a sense of relationship with "my own Lord" or, if not always quite that, an awareness of direct participation in the reality. The Bible is proclaimed with the result that the Lord is present in me, to me, to us. In the Baptist case, this often amounts to internal assurance of personal salvation. In the Congregational setting today, it usually means a call to direct involvement in caring Christian service. For Methodists, the response may include personal salvation, ethical involvement, and a keen devotional sense.

Clearly there are distinctions to be drawn within the Experiential family in regard to emphasis, basic direction, degree of openness to change, and church government. But all uphold the centrality of the Bible, all teach the direct participation of each person in the Christian life, and all repudiate formal means of access to God.

The fourth and most radical family is the Sectarian. While many groups populate this family, each typically having little or nothing to do with the others, they share devout commitment to perfect revelation, whether in the Bible or through overpowering experience of the Holy Spirit, or both. The key is "revelation" and the fact that it is "perfect." Such Christians hold to the infallible and inerrant Word of God; they are fundamentalistic about the Bible. Many also believe in the baptism of the Spirit, or speaking in tongues. In other words, Spirit experience is as precise and definable, its reality and authenticity as certifiable as a mathematical formula—or as the inspired Word of God. For this family the distance between heaven and earth has been shortened considerably. Or, to change the metaphor, the pipeline that connects God to each Christian is straight, clean, and altogether reliable. Other Christians may trust; these Christians know with certainty, precisely.

Sectarian in respect to their refusal to compromise or even to flirt with anything manufactured or "of this world," these groups repudiate critical textual study of the Bible; the Book is to be taken at face value, "for what it says," not tampered with by people (scholars or anyone else) to conform to what they think it says or want it to say. Thus science is either kept in its own compartment or used to bolster biblical truth. By definition, religious truth cannot *share* truthfulness with any other agency of truth, nor can any secular or naturalistic truth possess any religious credibility.

In other words, a sharp distinction is drawn between God's truth—revealed in the Bible—and all other truth. Science may be respected for what it can say about physical nature. But science must be seen either as supporting Bible teaching or as a rival and false system of truth. Similarly, philosophy—the conviction is firm, indeed absolute, that nothing Christian can reside within philosophy or science, in and of themselves. They are either co-opted to prove Christianity's (the Bible's) case or they are viewed as the enemy. God and the world are, in this sense, in contention. A Sectarian attitude is at the heart of the outlook of people in this family—examples appear within the Pentecostal bodies, the Holiness bodies, independent Baptist and scholastic Presbyterian congregations, the Churches of Christ, and others correctly called fundamentalist.

Consistent with this view of perfect truth and unimpeachable experience is the contention that most, if not all other denominations or interpretations of Christianity, are in error. Some cooperative activities do take place within this family, some respect does bind one group to another. The momentum, however, is in the direction of preoccupation with one's own group's vision of the truth. Thus a number of Christians and Christian bodies hold themselves aloof from others who go by the Christian name but whose credentials are held suspect.

Throughout, the observer can see a tendency toward taking sides, toward seeing everything as black or white. These Christians claim purity and integrity and judge that other groups have forsaken the plain truth of the self-evidently authoritative biblical text. Some groups within the Sectarian family are totally withdrawn. Others only oppose divine revelation toward anything of human origin. A more moderate camp is merely preoccupied with the position, the mission, and the fellowship of its own church home and simply does not often engage other Sectarians (or any other people or ideologies).

The spectrum we have been looking at is already quite wide. Great differences separate Roman Catholics from fundamentalists, even Lutherans from Baptists. (It is also true that a great deal is held in common by *all* these Christian bodies: All are followers of Christ; know about him through the Bible; have access to the Holy Spirit; come together with others to worship, study, and serve; and much more.) A number of discernible groupings do show up along that broad span, each made up of several bodies which are, themselves, distinctive. But there are more "denominations" than the spectrum can accommodate: Latter Day Saints (Mormons), Friends (Quakers), Unitarians, Unity, Christian Science,

Jehovah's Witnesses, and still others. Mormons add other history and texts to those of orthodox Christianity. In a very different way, Christian Science strikes a similar note by honoring a correlative text. Quaker teaching posits the Inner Light within every person, an internal spiritual center which has an objective authority as sturdy as the Bible's. And so on. The point is that the complexity and diversity are so vast that no attempt at classifying America's denominations can be altogether successful.

The faith of Afro-American people—black religion—also does not quite fit a scheme which, after all, grows out of European Christianity as that heritage has been modified by American conditions. Black religion is an Afro-American adaptation of a Euro-American adaptation of the European tradition. Thus it goes largely by familiar names— Baptist, Methodist, Pentecostal, for example—but those names are applied to somewhat distinctive forms of Christianity. The black denominations are not misrepresented by being placed on our spectrum, but some important explanations are called for in the interest of accuracy, owing to the unique cultural experience of black Americans.

America's Jews make up a significant aspect of the national religious scene. *Denomination* is not the term Jews would naturally use to refer to Judaism, the religion of the Jewish people, but in this setting it is intelligible. (A number of other bodies, including many Christian ones, also do not prefer that term.) What is essential to a clear understanding is that non-Jews—Christians especially—recognize that Judaism is a unique faith. It must be understood on its own terms. No knowledge is gained by treating it as a variation on Christianity. For example, it is not correctly or helpfully viewed as a religion of the Christian Bible with the New Testament taken away and Jesus not regarded as the Messiah. The spectrum used here to aid in reducing the perplexity of American religious patterns simply does not apply to Judaism. Incidentally, Judaism has it own "denominations" which could be deployed along a spectrum. There the issues and criteria would be peculiar to that distinctive faith.

Comparable descriptions apply to the Eastern, East-oriented, and Orient-derived "denominations." The same is true of Islam and the several Spiritualist groups. Having outlooks and histories that differ so sharply from the Euro-American Christian tradition, they must be seen in their uniqueness.

It is the nature of a reference book to call primary attention to diversity, not to unity or similarity. That is dramatically true for a handbook of denominations in the United States. The prevalence of some unity and much similarity, however, lies behind the construction of the spectrum. And there is some momentum toward unity in American religion, at least toward the overcoming of differences in the hope that cooperation and a common oneness can be achieved. That momentum is present, indeed strong, within the mainline Protestant families—Lutheran, Presbyterian, Methodist, Disciples of Christ, and the United Church of Christ. One finds it also among American ("northern") Baptists and many black Methodists and Baptists. The recent history of several of these bodies reveals a willingness to merge. Northern and Southern Presbyterians became one in 1983. Three Lutheran bodies plan to merge in 1988. The United Church of Christ is a result of the major mergers of 1931 and 1958. The United Methodist Church reflects action of this kind from 1968. The Disciples of Christ tradition, theologically intended to be ecumenical, lives a cooperative existence and engages in merger talks.

Unity, then, is a commitment of the mainline Protestant churches as reflected in actual organizational cooperation. But the same spirit pervades the regular, informal operation of many within this grouping. It views the "fracturing of the Body of Christ" as sinful. It also regards *all* interpretation and institutional practice as partial and imperfect, including that of each mainline denomination; therefore no body of Christians has a corner on the truth. Practically, one incentive for cooperation (and especially for merger consideration) has been the decline in membership in recent years.

Earlier, we glanced at the family of Christians called evangelical and noted that they are spread through many denominations. Evangelicalism, as a way of understanding Christianity, is not identifiable with a list of specific denominations. The same is true of the liberal family of Christians. Somewhat less identifiable than evangelicalism, liberalism does dominate a few denominations such as the Unitarian-Universalist and the United Church of Christ, but it is more commonly an outlook, a spirit, and a set of values. The liberal spirit is embodied as openness to change, as flexibility and tolerance, and as the refusal to absolutize anything in history—not biblical texts, not church offices or officers, and not any program, whether of church or society. A number of nonliberals respect this outlook and, in some ways, reflect it themselves. However, they part company when the liberal spirit becomes "liberal theology," inasmuch as it then is not authority-minded. More dedicated to the journey toward the truth and to putting the message into ethical practice than in defining or defending authoritative claims, thoroughgoing liberals flirt with heterodoxy and sometimes have actually departed from historic doctrine.

A bewildering variety, a perplexing diversity, a mystery, a puzzle, an enigma. Many such exclamations fit the American religious scene—and have for a long time. The trained eye can see, however, that some of the many can be grouped together in families or by shared outlook. It is hoped that some training of the eye is achieved by the devices of analysis suggested here. Whether that has occurred or not, we may be certain that the occasion for confusion continues. Every pertinent factor in American religious history makes a contribution to religious diversity: the First Amendment's provision for religious liberty; the early inheritance of several religious bodies; American society's penchant for giving birth to new groups; the impact of immigrants bringing ethnic churches; the influence of the East; the singular experience of Afro-Americans; the presence of 5.8 million Jews.

Since so much diversity is here and will continue to be, why not try to make sense of it? This essay is offered as a beginning.

HEADQUARTERS OF DENOMINATIONS

Adventist:

Advent Christian Church: 14601 Albemarle Rd., Charlotte, NC 28212

Church of God General Conference: Box 100, Oregon, IL 61061

Primitive Advent Christian Church: Sec., Hugh W. Good, Elkview, WV 25071

Seventh-day Adventist: 6840 Eastern Avenue, Washington, DC 20012

African Orthodox Church: 122 West 129th St., New York, NY 10027

Amana Church Society: Pres., Charles L. Selzer, Homestead, IA 52236

American Ethical Union: 2 West 64th St., New York, NY 10023

American Evangelical Christian Churches: Box 331, Pineland, FL 33945

American Rescue Workers: 2827 Frankford Ave., Philadelphia, PA 19134

Anglican Episcopal Church of North America: the Rev. G. O. Wiebe, 730 Blossom Way, Hayward, CA 94541

Anglican Orthodox Church: Bishop James Parker Dees, P.O. Box 128, Statesville, NC 28677

Apostolic Christian Church (Nazarean): P.O. Box 151, Tremont, IL 61568

Apostolic Christian Church of America: Dale R. Eisenmann, 6913 Wilmette Ave., Darien, IL 60559

Apostolic Faith: 6615 S.E. 52nd Ave., Portland, OR 97212

Apostolic Overcoming Holy Church of God: 514 10th Ave., Birmingham, AL 35204

Armenian Church: St. Varton Cathedral, 630 Second Ave., New York, NY 10016

Baha'i: 536 Sheridan Road, Wilmette IL 60091

Baptist:

American Baptist Association: 4605 N. State Line Ave., P.O. Box 901, Texarkana, TX 75501

American Baptist Churches in the U.S.A.: Valley Forge, PA 19481

Baptist Bible Fellowship, International: P.O. Box 191, Springfield, MO 65801

Baptist General Conference: 2002 S. Arlington Heights Rd., Arlington Heights, IL 60005

Baptist Missionary Association of America: Sec., the Rev. Ralph Cottrell, P.O. Box 2866, Texarkana, AR 75501

Bethel Ministerial Association: Box 5353, Evansville, IN 47715

Central Baptist Association: Larry Browder, Route 1, Timbertree Road, Kingsport, TN 37660

Conservative Baptist Association of America: P.O. Box 66, Wheaton, IL 60187

Duck River (and Kindred) Associations of Baptists: Clerk, Marvin Davenport, Auburntown, TN 37061

Free Will Baptist: 1134 Murfreesboro Rd., Nashville, TN 37202

General Association of Regular Baptist Churches: 1300 N. Meacham Rd., Schaumburg, IL 60185

General Baptist: Poplar Bluff, MO 63901

General Conference of the Evangelical Baptist Church, Inc.: Kevetter Bldg., 2400 E. Ash St., Goldsboro, NC 27530

Landmark Baptist: Dr. I. K. Cross, P.O. Box 848, Bellflower, CA 90706

National Baptist Convention of America: Sec., the Rev. Billy H. Wilson, 2620 S. Marsallis Ave., Dallas, TX 77020

National Baptist Convention U.S.A., Inc.: Sec., the Rev. T. J. Jemison, 915 Spain St., Baton Rouge, LA 70872
National Baptist Evangelical Life and Soul Saving Assembly of the U.S.A.: 441 Monroe Ave., Detroit, MI 48226
National Primitive Baptist Convention of the U.S.A: P.O. Box 2355, Tallahassee, FL 32301
North American Baptist Conference: 1 S. 210 Summit Ave., Oakbrook Terrace, IL 60181
Primitive Baptist: Elder W. H. Cayce, S. Second St., Thornton, AR 71766
Progressive National Baptist Convention, Inc.: 601 50th St. NE, Washington, DC 20019
Reformed Baptist: J. Zens, P.O. Box 548, St. Croix Falls, WI 54024
Separate Baptists in Christ: Floyd Wilson, 59 Greenspring St., Indianapolis, IN 46224
Seventh Day Baptist General Conference: P.O. Box 167, Janesville, WI 53547
Southern Baptist Convention: 460 James Robertson Pkwy, Nashville, TN 37209
United Free Will Baptist Church: Kinston College, 1000 University St., Kinston, NC 18501

Berean Fundamental Church: North Platte, NE 69101
Bible Protestant Church: 84 Clementon Rd., Gibbsboro, NJ 08206
Bible Way Church, Worldwide: 1130 New Jersey Ave. NW, Washington, DC 20001
Brethren
Dunkers:
Brethren Church: 524 College Ave., Ashland, OH 44805
Church of the Brethren: 1451 Dundee Ave., Elgin, IL 60120
Fellowship of Grace Brethren Churches: 1108 Chestnut Ave., Winona Lake, IN 46590
Old German Baptist Brethren: Elder Clement Skiles, Route 1, Box 140, Bringhurst, IN 46913
River Brethren:
Brethren in Christ Church: P.O. Box 245, Upland, CA 91786
Old Order (Yorker) Brethren: Laban T. Brechbill, 945 E. King St., Lancaster, PA 19101
United Zion Church: Sec., the Rev. J. Paul Martin, Box 212 D, Route 1, Annville, PA 17003
United Brethren:
Church of the United Brethren in Christ: 302 Lake St., P.O. Box 650, Huntington, IN 46750
United Christian Church: Elder Henry C. Heagy, R.D. 4, Lebanon, PA 17012

Buddhist Churches of America: 1710 Octavia St., San Francisco, CA 94109
Christadelphian: H. P. Zilmer, 1002 Webster Lane, Des Plaines, IL 60016
Christian and Missionary Alliance: 350 N. Highland Ave., Nyack, NY 10960
Christian Catholic Church: Dowie Memorial Dr., Zion, IL 60099
Christian Church (Disciples of Christ): 222 S. Downey Ave., Indianapolis, IN 46219
Christian Church of North America: Box 141-A, R.D. 1, Transfer, PA 16154

Christian Churches and Churches of Christ: 3533 Epley Rd., Cincinnati, OH 45231

Christian Congregation: Supt., Ora Wilbert Eads, 804 W. Hemlock St., La Follette, TN 37766

Christian Union: 106 W. Broadway, Excelsior Springs, MO 64024

Christ's Sanctified Holy Church: South Cutting Ave. & East Spencer St., Jennings, LA 70546

Church of Christ (Holiness) U.S.A.: 329 E. Monument St., Jackson, MS 39202

Church of Christ, Scientist: Christian Science Center, Boston, MA 02115

Church of God:

Church of God (Anderson, Ind.): Box 2420, Anderson, IN 46018

Church of God (Apostolic): St. Peter's Church of God (Apostolic), 11th and Hickory St., Winston Salem, NC 27101

Church of God (Original): P.O. Box 3086, Chattanooga, TN 37404

Church of God (Cleveland, Tenn.): Keith St. at 25th NW, Cleveland, TN 37311

Church of God (Seventh Day, Denver, Colorado): P.O. Box 2370, Denver, CO 80201

Church of God (Seventh Day, Salem, W. Va.): 79 Water St., Salem, WV 26426

Church of God (New Testament Judaism): P.O. Box 1207, Jerusalem Acres, Cleveland, TN 37311

Church of God (Tomlinson): 2504 Arrow Wood Dr., Huntsville, AL 35803

Church of God and Saints of Christ: Belleville, Portsmouth, VA 23704

Church of God by Faith: 3220 Haines St., Jacksonville, FL 32206

Church of God in Christ: P.O. Box 320, Memphis, TN 38101

Church of God in Christ (International): 170 Adelphi St., Brooklyn, NY 11025

Church of God of Prophecy: Bible Place, Cleveland, TN 37311

Church of Illumination: Beverly Hall, Quakertown, PA 18951

Church of Jesus Christ: P.O. Box 1414, Cleveland, TN 37311

Church of Our Lord Jesus Christ of the Apostolic Faith, Inc.: 2081 Adam Clayton Powell Blvd., New York, NY 10027

Church of the Nazarene: 6401 The Paseo, Kansas City, MO 64131

Churches of Christ: Ed., J. Roy Vaughan, *Gospel Advocate*, 1006 Elm Hill Rd., Nashville, TN 37210

Churches of Christ in Christian Union: 459 E. Ohio St., Box 30, Circleville, OH 43113

Churches of God, General Conference: P.O. Box 926, Findlay, OH 45840

Churches of God, Holiness: 170 Ashby St., NW, Atlanta, GA 30314

Churches of the Living God:

Church of the Living God (Christian Workers for Fellowship): Bishop F. C. Scott, 801 NE 17 St., Oklahoma City, OK 73105

House of God, Which Is the Church of the Living God: Bishop A. H. White, 6107 Cobbs Creek Pkwy., Philadelphia, PA 19143

Community Churches, National Council of: 900 Ridge Rd., Suite LL 1, Homewood, IL 60430

Congregational Bible Holiness Church, International: P.O. Box 2776, New Bern, NC 28561

Congregational Christian Churches (National Association): P.O. Box 1620, Oak Creek, WI 53154

Congregational Holiness Church: 3888 Fayetteville Highway, Griffin, GA 30223
Conservative Congregational Christian Conference: 7582 Currell Blvd., Suite 108, St. Paul, MN 55125
Divine Science: 1819 E. 14th Ave., Denver CO 80218
Episcopal
  Episcopal Church, The: 815 Second Avenue, New York, NY 10017
  Reformed Episcopal Church: Mrs. Bonnie C. Abboud, 4225 Chestnut St., Philadelphia, PA 19104
Evangelical Church of North America: Supt., Dr. V. A. Ballantyne, 8719 John Dr., Indianapolis, IN 46234
Evangelical Congregational Church: 100 W. Park Ave., Myerstown, PA 17067
Evangelical Covenant Church of America: 5101 N. Francisco Ave., Chicago, IL 60625
Evangelical Free Baptist Church, Inc.: P.O. Box 529, Addison, IL 60101
Evangelical Free Church of America: 1515 E. 66th St., Minneapolis, MN 55423
Fire-Baptized Holiness Church: Bishop William Edward Fuller, Jr., 2889 Chaucer Dr., Atlanta, GA 30311
Foursquare Gospel, International Church of the: 1100 Glendale Blvd., Los Angeles, CA 90026
Free Christian Zion Church of Christ: 1315 Hutchinson St., Nashville, AR 71852
Friends (Quaker):
  Friends General Conference: 1520-B Race St., Philadelphia, PA 19102
  Friends United Meeting: Gen Sec., Lorton G. Heusel, 101 Quaker Hill Dr., Richmond, IN 47374
  Religious Society of Friends (Conservative): George C. Parker, North Carolina Yearly Meeting, Route 1, Box 10, Woodland, NC 27897
Grace Gospel Fellowship: 1011 Aldon St. SW, Grand Rapids, MI 49509
Independent Fundamental Churches of America: 1860 Mannheim Rd., Westchester, IL 60153
Jehovah's Witnesses: 25 Columbia Heights, Brooklyn, NY 11201
Judaism: American Jewish Committee, 165 East 56th St., New York, NY 10022
Kodesh Church of Immanuel: 1509 S St., NW, Washington, DC 20009
Latter Day Saints:
  Church of Christ (Temple Lot): Temple Lot, Independence, MO 64000
  Church of Jesus Christ (Bickertonites): Sixth and Lincoln, Monongahela, PA 15063
  Church of Jesus Christ of Latter Day Saints (Strangite): Elder Vernon D. Swift, P.O. Box 522, Artesia, NM 88210
  Church of Jesus Christ of Latter-day Saints: 150 E. North Temple St., Salt Lake City, UT 84150
  Reorganized Church of Jesus Christ of Latter Day Saints: Saints Auditorium, Independence, MO 64051
Liberal Catholic Church: Krotona 62, Ojai, CA 93023

Lutheran:

American Lutheran Church: 422 S. 5th Street, Minneapolis, MN 55415

Apostolic Lutheran Church of America: Sec., James Johnson, Route 2, Box 729, L'Anse, MI 49946

Church of the Lutheran Brethren of America: Fergus Falls, MN 56537

Church of the Lutheran Confession: 460 75th Ave. NE, Minneapolis, MN 55432

Evangelical Lutheran Synod: the Rev. Alf Merseth, 106 13th St., Northwood, IA 50459

Free Lutheran Congregations, Association of: 3110 E. Medicine Lake Blvd., Minneapolis, MN 55441

Lutheran Church in America: 231 Madison Ave., New York, NY 10016

Protestant Conference (Lutheran): Sec., the Rev. Gerald Hinz, Shiocton, WI 54170

Wisconsin Evangelical Lutheran Synod: 3512 W. North Ave., Milwaukee, WI 53208

Mennonite:

Beachy Amish Mennonite Churches: Ervin N. Hershberger, R.D. 1, Meyersdale, PA 15552

Church of God in Christ, Mennonite: 420 Wedel St., Moundridge, KS 67107

Conservative Mennonite Conference: Rosedale Mennonite Missions, Irwin, OH 43029

Evangelical Mennonite Brethren Conference: 5800 S. 14th Street, Omaha, NE 68107

Evangelical Mennonite Church.: 1420 Kerrway Court, Fort Wayne, IN 46805

General Conference Mennonite Church: 722 Main St., Newton, KS 67114

Hutterian Brethren: Joseph J. Waldner, P.O. Box 628, Havre, MT 59501

Mennonite Brethren Church of North America: Dr. Frank C. Peters, Winnipeg, Man., Canada

Mennonite Church: 528 E. Madison Street, Lombard, IL 60148

Old Order Amish Church: ℅ Raber's Book Store, Baltic, OH 43804

Old Order (Wisler) Mennonite Church: Henry W. Riehl, 3702 State Route 14A, Columbiana, OH 44408

Reformed Mennonite Church: Bishop Earl Basinger, 1036 Lincoln Heights Ave., Ephrata, PA 17522

Unaffiliated Mennonite: Dr. J. C. Wenger, Goshen Biblical Seminary, 3003 Benham Ave., Elkhart, IN 46517

Methodist:

African Methodist Episcopal Church: Sec., the Rev. Richard A. Chappelle, 3526 Dodier, St. Louis, MO 63107

African Methodist Episcopal Zion Church: Sec., Herman L. Anderson, P.O. Box 1401, Charlotte, NC 28232

Christian Methodist Episcopal Church: 564 E. Frank Ave., Memphis, TN 38006

Congregational Methodist Church: Sec., the Rev. A. F. O'Connor, P.O. Box 555, Florence, MS 39073

Evangelical Methodist Church: 3000 W. Kellogg Dr., Wichita, KS 67213

Free Methodist Church of North America: 901 College Ave., Winona Lake, IN 46590

Primitive Methodist Church, U.S.A.: The Rev. Jerry Brown, 4 Longmeadow Dr., R.D. 2, Staatsburg, NY 12590

Reformed Methodist Union Episcopal Church: the Rev. Eugene Davis, Jr., 1219 Carnegie Ave., Charleston, SC 29407

Reformed Zion Union Apostolic Church: Deacon James C. Feggins, 416 South Hill Ave., South Hill, VA 23907

Southern Methodist Church: Pres., the Rev. J. B. Gamble, P.O. Box 132, Orangeburg, SC 29115

Union American Methodist Episcopal Church: the Rev. David M. Harmon, 774 Pine Street, Camden, NJ 08123

United Methodist Church, The: 475 Riverside Drive, New York, NY 10027

Metropolitan Community Churches: 5300 Santa Monica Blvd., Suite 304, Los Angeles, CA 90029

Missionary Church: 3901 S. Wayne Ave., Fort Wayne, IN 46807

Moravian:

Moravian Church (*Unitas Fratrum*): 69 West Church St., P.O. Box 1245, Bethlehem, PA 18018

Unity of the Brethren: Pres., the Rev. John Baletka, 3829 Sandstone, San Angelo, TX 76904

Muslim: The Islamic Center of Washington, 2551 Massachusetts Ave., NW, Washington, DC 20008

New Apostolic Church of North America: 3753 N. Troy St., Chicago, IL 60618

Old Catholic:

American Catholic Church (Syro-Antiochian): St. Peter's Cathedral, 1811 NW 4th Court, Miami, FL 33136

Mariavite Old Catholic Church: 2803 10th St., Wyandotte, MI 48192

North American Old Roman Catholic Church: 236 Wyona St., Brooklyn, NY 11207

Old Roman Catholic Church (English Rite): St. Mary Magdalene Church, 2820 N. Lincoln Ave., Chicago, IL 60657

Open Bible Standard Churches, Inc.: 2020 Bell Ave., Des Moines, IA 50315

Orthodox (Eastern):

Albanian Orthodox Archdiocese in America: 529 E. Broadway, Boston, MA, 02127

American Carpatho-Russian Orthodox Greek Catholic Church: 312 Garfield St., Johnstown, PA 15906

American Holy Orthodox Catholic Eastern Church: His Holiness Patriarch Clement, 247 E. 126th St., New York, NY 10035

Antiochian Orthodox Christian Archdiocese of North America: 358 Mountain Rd., Englewood, NJ 07631

Bulgarian Eastern Orthodox Church: 550-A W. 50 St., New York, NY 10025

Greek Orthodox Archdiocese of North and South America: 8-10 E. 79th Street, New York, NY 10021

Holy Apostolic and Catholic Church of the East (Assyrian): 554 Arball Dr., San Francisco, CA 94132

Romanian Orthodox Episcopate of America: 2522 Grey Tower Rd., Jackson, MI 49201

Russian Orthodox Church in the U.S.A.: St. Nicholas Patriarchal Cathedral, 15 E. 97th St., New York, NY 10029

Russian Orthodox Church Outside Russia: 75 E. 93rd St., New York, NY 10028

Serbian Eastern Orthodox Church in the U.S.A. and Canada: St. Sava Monastery, P.O. Box 519, Libertyville, IL 60048

Syrian Orthodox Church of Antioch: 292 Hamilton Pl., Hackensak, NJ 07601

Ukrainian Orthodox Churches: South Bond Brook, NJ 08880

Pentecostal:

Assemblies of God, General Council of: 1445 Boonville Avenue, Springfield, MO 65802

Elim Fellowship: Carlton Spencer, Elim Fellowship, Lima, NY 14485

Emmanuel Holiness Church: Sec., J. Robert Hicks, Route 3, Box 157, Anderson, SC 29621

Independent Assemblies of God, International: 3840 Fifth Ave., San Diego, CA 92103

International Pentecostal Church of Christ: Box 439, London, OH 43140

International Pentecostal Holiness Church: P.O. Box 12609, Oklahoma City, OK 73157

Pentecostal Assemblies of the World, Inc.: 3040 N. Illinois St., Indianapolis, IN 46208

Pentecostal Church of God: 221 Main St., Joplin, MO 64801

Pentecostal Free-will Baptist Church, Inc.: P.O. Box 1568, Dunn, NC 28334

United Pentecostal Church International: 8855 Dunn Rd., Hazelwood, MO 63042

Pillar of Fire: Zarephath, NJ 08890

Plymouth Brethren: P.O. Box 294, 218 W. Willow, Wheaton, IL 60187

Polish National Catholic Church of America: 529 E. Locust St., Scranton, PA 18505

Presbyterian:

Associate Reformed Presbyterian Church: One Cleveland St., Greenville, SC 29601

Bible Presbyterian Church: Haddon Ave. and Cuthbert Blvd., Collingswood, NJ 08108

Cumberland Presbyterian Church: 1978 Union Ave., Memphis, TN 38104

Orthodox Presbyterian Church: 7401 Old York Rd., Philadelphia, PA 19126

Presbyterian Church (U.S.A.): 341 Ponce de Leon Ave., NE, Atlanta, GA 30365

Presbyterian Church in America: P.O. Box 256, Clinton, MS 39056

Reformed Presbyterian Church, Evangelical Synod: Clerk, Dr. Paul R. Gilchrist, 107 Hardy Rd., Lookout Mountain, TN 37350

Reformed Presbyterian Church of North America: Clerk, Louis D. Hutmire, 7418 Penn Ave., Pittsburgh, PA 15208

Second Cumberland Presbyterian Church in the United States: 226 Church St., Huntsville, AL 35801

Reformed:

Christian Reformed Church: Stated Clerk, William P. Brink, 2850 Kalamazoo Ave. S., Grand Rapids, MI 49508

Hungarian Reformed Church in America: Bishop Dezso Abraham, 18700 Midway Ave., Allen Park, MI 48101

Netherlands Reformed Congregations: Pres. of Synod, the Rev. W. C. Lamain, 2115 Romence Dr. NE, Grand Rapids, MI 49503

Protestant Reformed Churches in America: 16515 S. Park Ave., South Holland, IL 60473

Reformed Church in America: 475 Riverside Dr., New York, NY 10027

Reformed Church in the United States: Clerk, the Rev. Steven E. Work, Route 3, Box 16, Garner, IA 50438

Roman Catholic Church: U.S. Catholic Conference, 1312 Massachusetts Ave. NW, Washington, DC 20005

Salvation Army: 799 Bloomfield Ave., Verona, NJ 07044

Schwenkfelder Church: Pennsburg, PA 18073

Social Brethren: the Rev. John Bailey, R.R. 1, Box 122, Simpson, IL 62985

Spiritualist:

International General Assembly of Spiritualists: 1809 E. Bayview Blvd., Norfolk, VA 23503

National Spiritual Alliance of the U.S.A.: the Rev. Albert Armstrong, Edgewood Apartments, Maple House, Apt. 21, Rt. 8, Keene, NH 03431

National Spiritualist Association of Churches: Sec., the Rev. Alice M. Hull, P.O. Box 128, Cassadaga, FL 37206

Swedenborgian Church, General Convention of: Pretty Prairie, KS 67570

Theosophy: Theosophical Publishing House, 306 W. Geneva Rd., Wheaton, IL 60189

Triumph the Church and Kingdom of God in Christ (International): 213 Farrington Ave., Atlanta, GA 30318

Unitarian Universalist Association: 25 Beacon St., Boston, MA 02108

United Church of Christ: 105 Madison Ave., New York, NY 10016

United Holy Church of America, Inc.: 159 W. Coulter St., Philadelphia, PA 19144

Unity School of Christianity: Unity Village, MO 64065

Vedanta Society: 34 W. 71st St., New York, NY 10023

Volunteers of America: 340 W. 85th St., New York, NY 10024

Wesleyan Church, The: Gen. Sec. the Rev. D. Wayne Brown, P.O. Box 2000, Marion, IN 46952

Worldwide Church of God: Ambassador College, Pasadena, CA 91123

GLOSSARY OF TERMS

Absolution: The remission of guilt by a priest, following confession.
Adoration: An act of homage to God.
Advent: The coming of God in Christ, or the Incarnation. May refer to the Second Coming.
Affusion: The pouring or sprinkling of water in baptism.
Allah: In Islam, the name of the Supreme Being, or all-powerful God.
Anathema: Anything cursed or despised.
Anchorite: A monk or zealous one who lives in isolation.
Antichrist: The one against Christ, to be destroyed at Christ's second coming.
Annunciation: The announcement by the angel Gabriel to the Virgin Mary that she was to be the mother of Christ.
Anointing: The act of consecrating, by the application of oil, candidates for baptism or the sick (as in the Anointing of the Sick).
Antinomianism: The doctrine that the gospel does away with prescribed moral laws so that the Christian is not bound by them.
Apocalyptic: Literally, pertaining to the revelation of the end time.
Apocrypha: A group of writings regarded by many Protestants as noncanonical or not authoritative, but worthy of study for their religious and historical value.
Apostolic: Of or pertaining to the apostles, the 12 men Jesus sent forth with authority.
Apostolic Succession: The doctrine of an unbroken line of succession in the episcopacy, from the apostles to the present time, maintained in Eastern, Roman, and Anglican churches.
Arminian: The spiritual heirs of Arminius (1560–1609), a Dutch Protestant theologian, in support of the freedom of the will. Arminius denied the later Calvinist doctrine of unconditional limited atonement and irresistible grace.
Athanasian: The belief of Athanasius (293–373), a defender of the orthodox view of the divinity of Christ. He opposed and won over Arius at the Council of Nicaea; Arius held that Christ was created by, but was essentially different from the Father.
Atonement: The reconciliation of the sinner with God through the sufferings of Jesus Christ.
Autocephalous: Ecclesiastically self-controlling, or having jurisdiction as an independent head. *Autocephali* was a term applied in early Christian times to bishops who recognized no ecclesiastical superior.
Autonomous: Self-governing, or independent, as in a local congregation.
Ban, The: A sentence that amounts to excommunication or outlawry by the church, upon those guilty of an act or speech forbidden by the church.
Baptism: The ceremonial application of water to a person by either sprinkling, immersion, or affusion as a sign of the washing away of sin, rebirth or new life, and of admission into the church as commanded by Christ in Matthew 28:19. Spirit baptism in some denominations is a baptism by the Holy Spirit, not with water.
Born Again: The experience of a second birth in the Spirit.

Byzantine: Related to the city of Byzantium (Constantinople), a historic center of Eastern Orthodoxy.

Calvinists: Those holding the faith of John Calvin (1509–1564), typically in Presbyterian and Reformed churches.

Canon: The books admitted to the Bible as authoritative—39 in the Old Testament, 27 in the New.

Catechism: The form or guide used in instruction of candidates for church membership, preceding baptism. A book containing items for such instruction.

Catholicos: The title given to the chief bishop of a church, usually in the East.

Celibacy: The state of being unmarried, a requirement for Roman Catholic priests and the members of some orders.

Cenobite: Person in a religious order who lives in a separate cell, but shares a common life with other such persons.

Chalice: A cup used at Communion services.

Charisma: Spiritual giftedness (in Greek, *grace*) enabling one to manifest an unusual ability for the benefit of others.

Chastity: The state of refraining from sexual relations in order to consecrate one's sexuality to spiritual ends.

Chrism: An ungent, usually olive oil or balm, used in Orthodox, Anglican, and Roman Catholic churches for anointing at baptism, confirmation, ordination, or consecration services, and sometimes for the sick. *Chrismation* is the act of anointing.

Christocentric: With Christ as the center.

Christology: A systematic teaching about Christ.

Collect: A brief prayer, highly stylized. In Roman and Anglican liturgies, a prayer read before the Gospel and Epistle.

Communicant: A church member who participates in the Lord's Supper.

Communion: The Lord's Supper. "Open" Communion is open to all Christians; "closed" Communion is closed to all except those of a particular faith or belief. The word is also used occasionally as a synonym for denomination.

Communion of Saints: The spiritual union in the Christian community, including the dead.

Confession: A statement of the religious beliefs of a religious body, or an admission of sin.

Confirmation: The initiatory rite by which persons are inducted into the church. In some churches, a sacrament.

Congregational: The church polity that makes the authority of the local congregation supreme within its own area.

Consecrate: To set apart as sacred certain persons, animals, places, objects, or times.

Consubstantiation: The theory that, following the words of institution in the Lord's Supper, the substantial body and blood of Christ join sacramentally with the bread and wine (which remains unchanged), the union remaining only until the purpose of the consecration is fulfilled. Applied sometimes to Lutheran doctrine, but not accepted by Lutherans.

Contrition: Sorrow for sin.

Conversion: Religiously, a radical spiritual and moral change, commonly attending a change of belief, and involving profoundly altered spirit and conduct—"a change of heart."

Covenant: Sacred relationship between God and an individual or a people. The Latin term *testament* is a translation of the Greek work for *covenant*—hence "Old Testament" and "New Testament."

Creed: A statement of belief including the fundamentals considered essential to salvation; a creed differs from a confession in that it may be held by Christians and recited in public worship.

Deacon: The principal lay officer in some denominations, especially Baptist. Its origin is often identified with the appointment of the Seven in Acts 6:1-6.

Decalogue: The Ten Commandments.

Deism: A form of Christianity in which God's existence or will is in universal natural law rather than through revelation.

Diocese: The territory of a church under the jurisdiction of a bishop.

Dispensationalism: The concept that God deals with the world in different time periods, or "dispensations," usually 7 in number.

Doctrine: That which is taught as the belief of a church.

Dogma: Belief generally regarded as necessary for salvation.

Ecclesiastical: Pertaining to the church.

Ecumenical or Ocumenical: General, universal, representing the whole Christian church.

Ecumenical Councils, The: The 7 early church councils of Nicaea (I) in 325, Constantinople (I) in 381, Ephesus in 431, Chalcedon in 451, Constantinople (II) in 553, Constantinople (III) in 680, and Nicaea (II) in 787.

Election: God's choice of an individual or a people for salvation.

Encyclical: A letter sent to local churches, usually a communication from the pope but more recently used in a broader sense, to report the actions or findings of church conferences.

Episcopal: Having to do with bishops, or governed by bishops.

Eschatology: Study of the last things, involving the final coming and triumph of Christ and God's rule, and sometimes the resurrection.

Esoteric: Restricted to an inner circle, from the custom in the Greek Mystery religions, and explaining advanced doctrines only to the fully initiated.

Eucharist: Holy Communion, or the Lord's Supper.

Evangelical: Loyal to the gospel of Christ; used in history to distinguish those kinds of Christianity that stress evangelism and conversion.

Excommunication: Exclusion from the religious fellowship of the church, either permanent or temporary.

Extreme Unction: *See* **Anointing.**

Fall, The: Estrangement from God through sin, as symbolized by the disobedience of Adam and Eve.

Fasting: Going without food, or certain foods, for a specified period.

Feast Day: A day in the church calendar set aside for celebration—for feasting, not fasting—such as Christmas or Easter.

Foot Washing: The practice of washing the feet, observed regularly by some Protestant bodies, and on special occasions by many Catholic Christians.

Fornication: Sexual intercourse outside marriage.

Free Will: The power to choose between good and evil, without compulsion or necessity.

Fundamentalism: The belief in certain fundamentals of Christian teaching, notably the inerrancy of the Bible, as distinguished from modernism, which interprets the Bible in accordance with more modern scholarship and scientific knowledge.

General Confession: A public, congregational confession of sin; among Roman Catholics, a confession in which the individual sums up past sins; among Protestants, a part of worship recited in unison by pastor and congregation, modeled on historic Roman Catholic and Anglican forms.

Genuflection: The act of bending one knee—in worship, upon entering the sanctuary, or when approaching the altar, as a gesture of reverence or adoration—a custom dating from the early church, usually found in Roman Catholic and some Episcopal churches.

Glossolalia: Speaking in tongues, as a manifestation of baptism with the Holy Spirit. The religious phenomenon described in the account of Pentecost in Acts 2.

Grace: God's favor or unmerited love; a gift received from God.

Heterodox: Not orthodox; contrary to accepted teachings.

Hierarchy: The body or organization empowered to administer sacred things.

Holiness: Negatively, removal from what is sinful; positively, consecration to God.

Holy Orders: The power granted the ecclesiastical leaders of the church, especially among Catholic bodies, to perform the acts proper to the ministry.

Immaculate Conception, The: The dogma that the Virgin Mary was conceived in her mother's womb, preserved from all stain of original sin.

Immanence: The presence of God in the world, as opposed to transcendence.

Immersion: Baptism by submerging the candidate in water.

Immortality: Life exempt from death.

Incarnation: God's becoming a human being in the historical person of Jesus Christ.

Indulgence: In the Roman Catholic Church, a remission "of the temporal punishment due to sins, the guilt of which has already been remitted." Granted only when penance is shown.

Inerrant: The quality of being truthful or without fault; applied to the text of the Bible by some Christians.

Infallibility: Immunity from error, as applied to the pope or to Scripture.

Inspiration, Verbal: Signifying the supernatural influence upon the writers of the Scriptures by which authority was given their work.

Judgment, Judgment Day: The act of judging by God on the last "judgment day," when rewards and punishments will be declared.

Justification: Gaining righteousness from a belief in Jesus Christ, rather than by one's own merit.

Kiss of Peace, or Holy Kiss: A religious greeting or ceremony, usually during the Eucharist.

Laity: Often taken to mean those members of the church who are not clergy; in actuality, the whole body of Christian people.

Laying on of Hands: A rite of consecration or blessing.

Litany: Form of prayer, made up of a series of petitions and offered by the leader, with congregational responses.

Liturgy, Liturgical: Literally, the "work of the people"; therefore, the public worship of the people of God. More narrowly, a prescribed form of worship as used in Roman Catholic, Orthodox, Anglican, and Lutheran services.
Logos: Christ as the Word of God, a teaching highlighted in John's Gospel.
Love Feast: A common meal of Christians, often culminating in the Eucharist, and sometimes called agape.
Mass, The: The central worship service of the Roman Catholic Church, celebrating the Holy Eucharist.
Medium: A person through whom messages from the spiritual world are sent, as in Spiritualism.
Metropolitan: In an Eastern church, a bishop who has provincial as well as diocesan powers.
Modernist: *See* **Fundamentalist.**
Monophysitism: The doctrine that Christ's human nature is absorbed in his divine nature.
Monotheism: Belief in one, and only one God, as opposed to polytheism or pantheism.
Mysticism: Knowledge of God by immediate experience; a direct and intimate consciousness of divine reality.
Nestorian: A follower of Nestorius, a fifth-century Syrian patriarch of Constantinople condemned for teaching that Christ was two persons, divine and human. Still found in Iran, Iraq, and South India.
Nicene: Pertaining to Nicaea, when the Nicene Creed was adopted at the famous council of 325, temporarily settling the controversy concerning the persons of the Trinity; properly called the Niceno-Constantinopolitan Creed.
Nonconformist: One who does not accept, or dissents from, the Church of England.
Ordinance: A religious rite or ceremony used in preference to sacrament in nonliturgical churches.
Orthodoxy: Belief in a doctrine or practice considered correct or sound.
Pacifism: Dedication to peace, usually on religious grounds.
Passover: The Jewish festival commemorating the time when the angel of death "passed over" Israelite homes but required the death of Egyptian firstborn.
Patriarch: In the Old Testament, the chief of a tribe of Israel; in Christianity, a bishop in a principal center in the East, such as Alexandria and Antioch.
Peace Churches: Churches historically holding a pacifist position, such as Friends and Mennonites.
Penance: Actions indicative of conversion or contrition, sometimes including fasting or abstinence.
Pentecostalism: The experience of baptism with the Holy Spirit, often accompanied by speaking in tongues and other charismatic gifts.
Perfection: The complete love of God with one's whole being, a doctrine taught by John Wesley.
Pietism: Specifically, a German Lutheran movement of the seventeenth and eighteenth centuries, in the interest of spiritual renewal. Generally, a term used to designate those movements in Christianity that emphasize zeal for missions and the personal, spiritual, and practical, rather than the institutional, formal, and intellectual aspects of faith.

Plenary: Full, complete; a plenary council is attended by all its qualified members.
Polity: The particular form or system of government used by a denomination.
Predestinarian: A believer in predestination—that each person's eternal destiny is fixed by divine decree.
Premillennialism: Belief that the personal visible return of Christ will precede his reign for a thousand years on earth. ***Post*millennarians** believe that the return will come at the end of the millennium.
Presbytery: A church court or assembly having the ecclesiastical or spiritual rule and oversight of a district; the district itself.
Reconciliation: The process of being brought back into fellowship with God.
Redemption: God's deliverance from sin and death through the sacrificial atonement of Christ.
Regeneration: A new birth, re-creation, a radical renewal of life, or conversion.
Religious: Those Roman Catholics who are members of a religious community.
Remission of Sin: Pardon or forgiveness for sin.
Repentance: Conversion to God from a sinful life.
Reprobation: The divine decree concerning those who do not attain salvation.
Revelation: God's self-disclosure, as in historical events or in Scripture.
Ritual: A form or office of worship.
Sabbatarian: One who believes that the seventh day should be observed as the Lord's day, or regards Sunday as a day of abstinence from work and amusement.
Sacerdotal: A religious system in which the priestly order has special or sacred powers.
Sacrament: A "visible sign of an invisible grace, instituted by Christ." In the Roman Catholic Church there are seven sacraments—the Eucharist, baptism, confirmation, penance, holy matrimony, holy orders, and the anointing of the sick; in Protestantism, the first two (and sometimes penance).
Sacramentals: Certain practices or objects, such as the sign of the cross or the use of holy water or candles, symbolizing spiritual reality.
Salvation: Deliverance from sin and death by God's act.
Sanctification: The work of the Holy Spirit beyond justification, toward holiness of life.
Second Coming: The second advent of Jesus.
See: The jurisdiction of a bishop.
Speaking in Tongues: *See* **Glossolalia**.
Synod: An ecclesiastical council either of regular standing or appointed as needed; in Presbyterian churches, a body between the presbyteries and the general assembly.
Total Depravity: The condition created by the Fall, every human faculty having an innate evil taint.
Tongues, Gift of: An ecstatic utterance induced by religious excitement.
Transcendence: The absolute exaltation of God above the universe and its limitations.
Transfiguration: Change in form or appearance, such as the transfiguration of Jesus (Mark 9:2-10).
Transmutation: The change from one nature, substance, or form to another.

Transubstantiation: The doctrine that there is present in the Eucharist, after consecration of the elements, the substance of Christ's body and blood.
Trinitarian: A believer in the Trinity—that there is a union of Father, Son, and Holy Ghost in one divine nature.
Triune: Having the quality of three-in-oneness; a reference to the Trinitarian God.
Unction: Anointing with oil, as in the case of sickness or imminent death. (Extreme unction, a sacrament, is now designated as "the anointing of the sick.")
Uniate: Persons or churches acknowledging the supremacy of the pope but maintaining their own liturgies or rites.
Unitarian: The theology that insists upon the unity of God, denying the doctrine of the Trinity.
Universalism: Universal salvation.
Unleavened Bread: Bread made without yeast, necessary for Jewish Passover, and often used in Christian eucharistic services.
Venerable: Anglican title for archdeacon; Catholic title for one who has reached a particular point in the process of beatification; title of honor for one of unusual sanctity, as the Venerable Bede.
Venial Sin: In Roman Catholic doctrine, a slight offense that does not require the sacrament of penance; a sin that is not mortal (meriting eternal death).
Venite: "Oh come," Latin version of Psalm 95, used frequently in the service of Morning Prayer.
Versicle: Literally, "little verse," a short statement followed by a congregational or choral response.
Vestment: Article of clothing worn by religious official.
Vicar: Incumbent of a parish; member of the clergy who serves as the deputy or substitute for another.
Vocation: The calling to serve God in one's work and life; for some, entailing ordination.
Vulgate: Latin version of the Bible, translated by Jerome (d. 420).
Warden: Head of an ecclesiastical institution, or official, entrusted with the temporal affairs or the protection of property in a parish.
Western Church: Term for Christianity in Europe or America, or for Roman Catholicism as opposed to Eastern Orthodoxy.
Whitsunday: "White Sunday," or Pentecost, Christian festival on the seventh Sunday after Easter.
Yahweh: The divine name in the Hebrew Scriptures.
Zionism: The modern movement that sought the colonizing of the Jews in Palestine. Historically, the return of the Jews to their homeland. The forming of the state of Israel in 1948 was in part a result of the Zionist movement.

BIBLIOGRAPHY

General

Ahlstrom, Sydney E. *A Religious History of the American People*. New Haven: Yale University Press, 1972.

Albanese, Catherine L. *America: Religions and Religion*. Belmont, Calif.: Wadsworth Publishing Co., 1981.

Backman, Milton V., Jr. *Christian Churches of America: Origins and Beliefs*. New York: Scribner's, 1983.

Banks, William L. *The Black Church in the U.S.* Chicago: Moody Press, 1972.

Bednarowski, Mary Farrell. *American Religion: A Cultural Perspective*. Englewood Cliffs, N.J.: Prentice-Hall, 1984.

Brauer, J. C. *Protestantism in America*. Philadelphia: Westminster Press, 1953.

Carroll, Jackson W., et. al. *Religion in America: 1950 to the Present*. New York: Harper & Row, 1979.

Clark, Elmer T. *The Small Sects in America*. Nashville: Abingdon Press, 1949.

Cobb, John B. *Varieties of Protestantism*. Philadelphia: Westminster Press, 1960.

Dillenberger, John, and Welch, Claude. *Protestant Christianity*. New York: Scribner's, 1954.

Gaustad, Edwin Scott. *A Documentary History of Religion in America*. 2 vols. Grand Rapids: Eerdmans Publishing Co., 1982–1983.

———. *Historical Atlas of Religion in America*. Rev. Ed. New York: Harper & Row, 1976.

Handy, Robert T. *A Christian America: Protestant Hopes and Historical Realities*. 2d Ed. New York: Oxford University Press, 1984.

———. *A History of Churches in the United States and Canada*. New York: Oxford University Press, 1976.

Herberg, Will. *Protestant-Catholic-Jew*. Reprinted Ed. Chicago: University of Chicago Press, 1984.

Hudson, W. S. *American Protestantism*. Chicago: University of Chicago Press, 1961.

———. *The Great Tradition of American Churches*. New York: Peter Smith, 1963.

———. *Religion in America*. 3d.Ed. New York: Scribner's, 1981.

Jacquet, Constant H., Jr., ed. *Yearbook of American and Canadian Churches*. Nashville: Abingdon Press, (annual).

James, Janet W., ed. *Women in American Religion*. Philadelphia: University of Pennsylvania Press, 1980.

Johnson, D. W., and Cornell, G. W. *Punctured Preconceptions: What North American Christians Think About the Church*. New York: Friendship Press, 1972.

Kennedy, Roger G. *American Churches*. New York: Crossroad, 1982.

Latourette, Kenneth S. *Christianity in a Revolutionary Age: The 20th Century Outside Europe*. New York: Harper & Row, 1962.

Lincoln, C. Eric, ed. *The Black Experience in Religion*. Garden City, N.Y.: Doubleday, 1974.

Marty, Martin E., *A Nation of Behavers*. Chicago: University of Chicago Press, 1976.

———. *The Public Church: Mainline-Evangelical-Catholic*. New York: Crossroad, 1981.

———. *The Righteous Empire: The Protestant Experience in America*. New York: Dial Press, 1970.

Mayer, F. E. *The Religious Bodies of America*. 4th Ed. St. Louis: Concordia Publishing House, 1961.

Mead, Sidney E. *The Lively Experiment: The Shaping of Christianity in America*. New York: Harper & Row, 1963.

———. *The Nation with the Soul of a Church*. New York: Harper & Row, 1975.

Melton, J. Gordon. *The Enclyclopedia of American Religions*. 2 vols. Wilmington, N.C.: McGrath Publishing Co., 1978.

Niebuhr, H. Richard. *The Kingdom of God in America*. New York: Harper & Brothers, 1937.

Noll, Mark A., et. al., eds. *Eerdmans Handbook to Christianity in America*. Grand Rapids: Eerdmans Publishing Co., 1983.

Piepkorn, Arthur C. *Profiles in Belief: The Religious Bodies of the United States and Canada*. 4 vols. New York: Harper & Row, 1977–1979.

Raboteau, Albert J. *Slave Religion: The "Invisible Institution" in the Antebellum South*. New York: Oxford University Press, 1978.

Rosten, Leo. *A Guide to the Religions of America*. St. Louis: Bethany Press, 1963.

Scherer, Lester B. *A Short History of Religion in America*. Reynoldsburg, Ohio: Advocate Press, 1980.

Smith, H. Shelton; Handy, Robert T.; and Loetscher, Lefferts A. *American Christianity: An Historical Interpretation with Representative Documents*. 2 vols. New York: Scribner's, 1960–1963.

Smith, James W., and Jamison, A. Leland. *Religion in American Life*. 4 vols. Princeton, N.J.: Princeton University Press, 1961.

Stuber, Stanley I. *How We Got Our Denominations*. New York: Association Press, 1948.

Sweet, W. W. *Religion in the Development of American Culture*. New York: Scribner's, 1952.

———. *The Story of Religion in Ameria*. 2d Ed. Rev. New York: Harper & Row, 1950.

Walker, Williston. *History of the Christian Church*. 3rd Ed. New York: Scribner's, 1970.

Whalen, William J. *Separated Brethren*. Milwaukee: Our Sunday Visitor Press, 1979.

Williams, J. Paul. *What Americans Believe and How They Worship*. Rev. Ed. New York: Harper & Row, 1962.

Denominational

Adventist

Froom, Le Roy E. *The Prophetic Faith of Our Fathers*. 4 vols. Washington, D.C.: Review & Herald Publishing Assn., 1946-1954.

Hasel, Gerard F. *Old Testament Theology: Basic Issues in the Current Debate*. Grand Rapids: Eerdmans Publishing Co., 1972.

Herndon, Booton. *The Seventh Day: The Story of the Seventh-day Adventists*. New York: McGraw-Hill, 1960.

Johnsen, Carsten. *Man: The Invisible*. Oslo: Universitetsforlaget, 1971.

Martin, Walter R. *The Truth About Seventh-day Adventism*. Grand Rapids: Zondervan, 1960.

Seventh-Day Adventist Enclyclopedia. Ed. Dan F. Neufeld. Rev. Ed. Washington, D.C.: Review & Herald Publishing Assn., 1976.

Seventh-day Adventists Answer Questions on Doctrines. Washington, D.C.: Review & Herald Publishing Assn., 1957.

Spalding, Arthur W. *Origin and History of Seventh-day Adventists*. 4 vols. Washington, D.C.: Review & Herald Publishing Assn., 1961.

White, Ellen G. *The Desire of Ages*. Mountain View, Calif.: Pacific Press Publishing Assn., 1940.

———. *The Great Controversy Between Christ and Satan*. Mountain View, Calif.: Pacific Press Publishing Assn., 1927.

Baptist

Baker, Robert A. *The Southern Baptist Convention and Its People, 1607–1972*. Nashville: Broadman Press, 1974.

Cox, Norman W. *Encyclopedia of Southern Baptists*. Nashville: Broadman Press, 1958–1982.

Gaustad, Edwin S., ed. *The Bible, Church Order, and the Churches*. New York: Arno Press, 1980.

Lumpkin, William L. *Baptist Confessions of Faith*. Valley Forge, Penna.: Judson Press, 1969.

Maring, Norman H., and Hudson, Winthrop, S. *A Baptist Manual of Polity and Practice*. Valley Forge, Penna.: Judson Press, 1963.

McLoughlin, William G. *New England Dissent, 1620–1833: Baptists and the Separation of Church and State*. Cambridge: Harvard University Press, 1971.

Olson, Adolf. *A Centenary History*. Chicago: Baptist Conference Press, 1952. (Baptist General Conference of America).

Pelt, Owen C., and Smith, Ralph Lee. *The Story of the National Baptists*. New York: Vantage Press, 1960.

Wood, James E., Jr., ed. *Baptists and the American Experience*. Valley Forge, Penna.: Judson Press, 1976.

Woolley, D. C., ed. *Baptist Advance: Achievements of the Baptists of North America for a Century and a Half*. Nashville: Broadman Press, 1964.

Woyke, Frank. *Heritage and Ministry of the North Amerian Baptist Conference*. Oakbrook Terrace, Ill.: North American Baptist Conference, 1979.

Black Churches

Booth, William D. *The Progressive Story: New Baptist Roots*. St. Paul: Braun Press, 1981.

Bragg, George Freeman. *History of the Afro-American Group of the Episcopal Church*. Baltimore: Church Advocate Press, 1922, 1968.

Cobbins, editor-in-chief. *History of the Church of Christ (Holiness), U.S.A., 1895–1965*. New York: Vantage Press, 1966.

Erskine, Noel Leo. *Black People and the Reformed Church in America. Lansing, Ill.: Reformed Church Press, 1978.*

Frazier, E. Franklin. *The Negro Church in America*. Bound with: Lincoln, C. Eric. *The Black Church Since Frazier*. New York: Schocken Books, 1973.

Gillard, John T. *The Catholic Church and the American Negro*. Baltimore: St. Joseph's Society Press, 1929; New York: Johnson Reprint Corporation, 1968.

Jackson, Joseph H. *A Story of Christian Activism: A History of the National Baptist Convention, U.S.A., Inc.* Nashville: Townsend Press, 1980.

Lakey, Othal Hawthorne. *The Rise of "Colored Methodism": A Study of the Background and the Beginnings of the Christian Methodist Episcopal Church*. Dallas: Crescendo Book Publications, 1972.

Morrison-Reed, Mark D. *Black Pioneers in a White Denomination*. Boston: Skinner House, 1980. (A history of Blacks in the Unitarian Universalist Association.)

Murray, Andrew E. *Presbyterians and the Negro: A History*. Philadelphia: Presbyterian Historical Society, 1966.

Patterson, J. O.; Ross, German O.; and Atkins, Julia Mason. *History and Formative Years of the Church of God in Christ with Excerpts from the Life and Works of Its Founder—Bishop C. H. Mason*. Memphis: Church of God in Christ Publishing House, 1969.

Richardson, Harry V. *Dark Salvation: The Story of Methodism as It Developed Among Blacks in America*. Garden City, N.Y.: Doubleday, 1976.

Simpson, George Eaton. *Black Religions in the New World*. New York: Columbia University Press, 1978.

Singleton, George. *The Romance of African Methodism: A Study of the African Methodist Church*. New York: Exposition Press, 1952.

Stanley, A. Knighton. *The Children Is Crying: Congregationalism Among Black People*. New York: Pilgrim Press, 1979.

Walls, William Jacob. *The African Methodist Episcopal Zion Church: The Reality of the Black Church*. Charlotte, N.C.: A.M.E. Zion Publishing House, 1974.

Wilmore, Gayraud S. *Black Religion and Black Radicalism: An Interpretation of the Religious History of Afro-American People*. 2d Ed. Maryknoll, N.Y.: Orbis Books, 1983.

Woodson, Carter G. *The History of the Negro Church*. 2d Ed. Washington, D. C.: Associated Publishers, 1921.

Brethren

Bittenger, Emmert F. *Heritage and Promise*. Elgin, Ill.: Brethren Press, 1970.

Durnbaugh, Donald F. *The Brethren in Colonial America*. Elgin, Ill.: Brethren Press, 1967.

———. ed. *The Brethren Encyclopedia.* 3 vols. Philadelphia/Oak Brook, Ill.: Brethren Enclyclopedia, 1983–1984.

Sappington, Roger E. *Brethren and Social Policy 1908–1958.* Elgin, Ill.: Brethren Press, 1961.

———. *The Brethren in the New Nation.* Elgin, Ill.: Brethren Press, 1976.

Christian Science

A Century of Christian Science Healing. Boston: Christian Science Publishing Society, 1966.

Beasley, Norman. *The Cross and the Crown: The History of Christian Science.* New York: Duell, Sloan & Pearce, 1952.

Canham, Erwin D. *Commitment to Freedom: The Story of the Christian Science Monitor.* Boston: Houghton Mifflin, 1958.

DeWitt, John. *The Christian Science Way of Life.* Boston: Christian Science Publishing Society, 1971.

Eddy, Mary Baker. *Science and Health with Key to the Scriptures.* Boston: Christian Science Board of Directors. Many editions.

Gottschalk, Stephen. *The Emergence of Christian Science in American Religious Life.* Berkeley: University of California Press, 1973.

Leishman, Thomas. *Why I Am a Christian Scientist.* Camden, N.J.: Thomas Nelson, 1958.

Peel, Robert. *Mary Baker Eddy: The Years of Discovery.* New York: Holt, Rinehart & Winston, 1977.

———. *Mary Baker Eddy: The Years of Trial.* New York: Holt, Rinehart & Winston, 1971.

———. *Christian Science: Its Encounter with American Culture.* New York: Holt, Rinehart & Winston, 1958.

Church of God

Brown, C. E. *When the Trumpet Sounded.* Anderson, Ind.: Warner Press, 1951. (History of the Church of God of Anderson, Ind.)

Conn, Charles W. *Like a Mighty Army Moves the Church of God, 1886–1955.* Cleveland, Tenn.: Church of God Publishing House, 1955.

Diary of Ambrose Jessup Tomlinson. Homer A. Tomlinson, ed. 3 vols. Queens Village, N.Y.: The Church of God, World Headquarters, 1949–1955.

Frodsham, S. H. *With Signs Following.* Springfield, Mo.: Gospel Publishing House, 1941.

Riggs, R. M. *The Spirit Himself.* Springfield, Mo.: Gospel Publishing House, 1949.

Stone, James. *The Church of God of Prophecy: History and Polity.* Cleveland, Tenn.: White Wing Publishing House, 1977.

Tomlinson, Homer A. *The Shout of a King.* Queens Village, N.Y.: The Church of God, World Headquarters, 1968.

Church of the Nazarene

Purkiser, W. T., ed. *Exploring Our Christian Faith.* Kansas City, Mo.: Beacon Hill Press, 1966.

Redford, M. E. *The Rise of the Church of the Nazarene*. Kansas City: Nazarene Publishing House, 1951.

Smith, Timothy L. *Called to Holiness: The Story of the Nazarenes, The Formative Years*. Kansas City, Mo.: Nazarene Publishing House, 1962.

Taylor, Richard S. *Life in the Spirit*. Kansas City, Mo.: Beacon Hill Press, 1966.

Churches of Christ

Harrell, David E., Jr. *Quest for a Christian America: The Disciples of Christ and American Society to 1866*. Nashville: The Disciples of Christ Historical Society, 1966.

———. *The Social Sources of Division in the Disciples of Christ, 1865–1900*. Atlanta/Athens: Publishing Systems, 1973.

West, Earl Irvin. *The Search for the Ancient Order*. 3 vols. Indianapolis: Religious Book Service, 1950, 1964, 1979.

Woodson, William. *Standing for Their Faith: A History of Churches of Christ in Tennessee, 1900–1950*. Henderson, Tenn.: J & W Publications, 1979.

Disciples of Christ

Beazley, George G., Jr. *The Christian Church (Disciples of Christ): An Interpretative Examination in the Cultural Context*. St. Louis: Bethany Press, 1973.

Campbell, Alexander. *Creative Freedom in Action*. 1832.

Crain, James Andrew. *The Development of Social Ideas Among the Disciples of Christ*. St. Louis: Bethany Press, 1969.

Garrison, W. E., and DeGroot, A. T. *Disciples of Christ: A History*. St. Louis: Bethany Press, 1958.

Garrison, Winifred E. *Heritage and Destiny*. St. Louis: Bethany Press, 1963.

Harrell, David Edwin, Jr. *Quest for a Christian America: The Disciples of Christ and American Society to 1866*. Nashville: The Disciples of Christ Historical Society, 1966.

Humbert, Royal, ed. *A Compend of Alexander Campbell's Theology*. St. Louis: Bethany Press, 1961.

Lair, Loren E. *The Christian Churches and Their Work*. St. Louis: Bethany Press, 1963.

McAllister, Lester G., and Tucker, William E. *Journey in Faith*. St. Louis: Bethany Press, 1975.

Panel of Scholars. *The Renewal of Church*. St. Louis: Bethany Press, 1963.

Teegarden, Kenneth L. *We Call Ourselves Disciples*. St. Louis: Bethany Press, 1976.

Whitley, Oliver R. *The Trumpet Call of Reformation*. St. Louis: Bethany Press, 1963.

Episcopal

Addison, J. T. *The Episcopal Church in the United States: 1789–1831*. New York: Scribner's, 1951.

Albright, Raymond W. *History of the Protestant Episcopal Church*. New York: Macmillan, 1964.

Chorley, E. C. *Men and Movements in the American Episcopal Church*. New York: Scribner's, 1946.

Damrosch, Frank, Jr. *The Faith of the Episcopal Church*. New York: Morehouse-Gorham, 1946.

DeMille, George E. *The Episcopal Church Since 1900*. New York: Morehouse-Barlow, 1955.

Krumm, John McGill. *Why I Am an Episcopalian*. Boston: Beacon Press, 1957.

Manross, W. W. *A History of the American Episcopal Church*. New York: Morehouse-Gorham, 1950.

McConnell, S. D. *History of the American Episcopal Church*. Milwaukee: Morehouse Publishing Co., 1916.

Pittenger, W. Norman. *The Episcopal Way of Life*. Englewood Cliffs, N.J.: Prentice-Hall, 1957.

Simcox, Carroll E. *Approach to the Episcopal Church*. New York: Morehouse-Barlow, 1961.

Friends (Quakers)

Bacon, M. *Quiet Rebels*. New York: Basic Books, 1969.

Bolding, K. E. *Evolutionary Potential of Quakerism*. Pamphlet. Wallingford, Penna.: Pendle Hill Publications, 1964.

Brinton, Howard H. *Quaker Education: In Theory and Practice*. Wallingford, Penna.: Pendle Hill Publications, 1958.

———. *Friends for 300 Years*. Wallingford, Penna.: Pendle Hill Publications, 1965.

Comfort, W. W. *The Quaker Way: Just Among Friends*. Philadelphia: American Friends Service Committee, 1968.

Cooper, C. W., ed. *Break the New Ground: Seven Essays by Contemporary Quakers*. Philadelphia: Friends World Committee, 1969.

Hall, Francis. *Friends in the Americas*. Philadelphia: Friends World Committee, 1976.

———. *Quaker Worship in North America*. Richmond, Ind.: Friends United Press, 1979.

Jonas, G. *On Doing Good*. New York: Scribner's, 1971.

Loukes, H. *Quaker Contribution*. New York: Macmillan, 1965.

Russell, Elbert. *The History of Quakerism*. New York: Macmillan, 1943; Richmond, Ind.: Friends United Press, 1980.

Sheeran, Michael. *Friendly Persuasion*. Philadelphia: Friends World Committee, 1984.

West, J. *Quaker Reader*. New York: Viking Press, 1969.

Jehovah's Witnesses

Cole, Marley. *Jehovah's Witnesses: The New World Society*. New York: Vantage Press, 1955.

Jehovah's Witnesses in the Divine Purpose. New York: Watch Tower Bible & Tract Society, 1959.

Let God Be True. New York: Watch Tower Bible & Tract Society, 1946.
New World Translation of the Holy Scriptures. New York: Watch Tower Bible & Tract Society, 1961.
The Truth That Leads to Eternal Life. New York: Watch Tower Bible & Tract Society, 1968.
True Peace and Security—From What Source? New York: Watch Tower Bible & Tract Society, 1973.

Judaism

Agus, Jacob Bernard. *Guideposts in Modern Judaism*. New York: Bloch Publishing Co., 1954.
Bamberger, B. J. *The Story of Judaism*. New York: Union of American Hebrew Congregations, 1957.
Donin, Rabbi Hayim Halevy. *To Be a Jew*. New York: Basic Books, 1973.
Eban, Abba. *My People*. New York: Random House, 1984.
Elazar, Daniel. *Community and Polity*. Philadelphia: Jewish Publication Society, 1976.
Encyclopedia Judaica. 16 vols. Jerusalem: Encyclopedia Judaica, 1972.
Finkelstein, Louis. *The Jews: Their History, Culture and Religion*. 2 vols. 3d Ed. New York: Harper & Row, 1949; Shocken Books, 1970.
Gay, Ruth. *Jews in America: A Short History*. New York: Basic Books, 1965.
Gaer, Joseph. *Our Jewish Heritage*. New York: Holt, Rinehart & Winston, 1957.
Glazer, Nathan. *American Judaism*. Chicago: University of Chicago Press, 1957.
Gross, David C. *1001 Questions and Answers About Judaism*. New York: Doubleday, 1978.
Hertzberg, A. *Judaism*. New York: George Braziller, 1961.
Isaacson, Rabbi Benjamin, and Wigoder, Deborah. *The International Jewish Encyclopedia*. Englewood Cliffs, N.J.: Prentice-Hall, 1973.
Jacobs, Louis. *Jewish Thought Today*. New York: Behrman House, 1970.
Karp, Abraham J. *The Jewish Way of Life*. Englewood Cliffs, N.J.: Prentice-Hall, 1962.
Liebman, Charles S. *The Ambivalent American Jew*. Philadelphia: Jewish Publication Society, 1973.
Neusner, Jacob. *The Way of Torah*. Belmont, Calif.: Wadsworth Publishing Co., 1979.
Rosenthal, Gilbert. *The Many Faces of Judaism: Orthodox, Conservative, Reconstructionist, and Reform*. Ed. S. Roesel. New York: Behrman House, 1978.
Roth, Leon. *Judaism: A Portrait*. New York: Viking Press, 1961.
Sklare, Marshall. *America's Jews*. New York: Random House, 1971.
Steinberg, Milton. *Basic Judaism*. New York: Harcourt, 1947.
Wallach, Michael, ed. *Jewish Year Book*. New York: Hartmore, (annual).
Waxman, Chaim. *America's Jews in Transition*. Philadelphia: Temple University Press, 1983.
Wouk, Herman. *This Is My God*. Garden City, N.Y.: Doubleday, 1959.

BIBLIOGRAPHY

Latter Day Saints (Mormons)

Allen, James B., and Leonard, Glen M. *The Story of the Latter-day Saints*. Salt Lake City: Deseret Book Co., 1976.

Anderson, Nels. *Desert Saints: The Mormon Frontier in Utah*. Chicago: University of Chicago Press, 1966.

Arrington, L. J. *Great Basin Kingdom: An Economic History of the Latter-day Saints*. Cambridge: Harvard University Press, 1958.

Arrington, L. J., and Bitton, Davis. *The Morman Experience: A History of the Latter-day Saints*. New York: Alfred A. Knopf, 1979.

Backman, Milton V., Jr. *Eyewitness Accounts of the Restoration*. Orem, Utah: Grandin Press, 1983.

England, Eugene. *Brother Brigham*. Salt Lake City: Bookcraft, 1980.

Hill, Donna. *Joseph Smith: The First Mormon*. Garden City, N.Y.: Doubleday, 1977.

Hill, M. S., and Allen, J. B., eds. *Mormonism and American Culture*. New York: Harper & Row, 1972.

O'Dea, Thomas F. *The Mormons*. Chicago: University of Chicago Press, 1957.

Richards, Legrand. *Marvelous Work and a Wonder*. Salt Lake City: Desert Book Co., 1972.

Smith, Joseph. *The Book of Mormon*. Salt Lake City: Deseret Book Co., 1972.

———. *The Doctrine and Covenants*. Salt Lake City: Deseret Book Co., 1971.

———. *The Pearl of Great Price*. Salt Lake City: Deseret Book Co., 1971.

———. *History of the Church of Jesus Christ of Latter-day Saints*. Ed. B. H. Roberts. 7 vols. Salt Lake City: The Church of Jesus Christ of Latter-day Saints, 1932–1951.

Smith, Joseph Fielding, comp. *Teachings of the Prophet Joseph Smith*. Salt Lake City: Deseret Book Co., 1961.

Talmage, James E. *Articles of Faith*. Salt Lake City: Deseret Book Co., 1971.

Lutheran

Allbeck, Willard D. *Studies in the Lutheran Confessions*. Philadelphia: Fortress Press, 1968.

Arden, G. Everett. *Augustana Heritage*. Rock Island: Augustana Press, 1963.

Bainton, Roland. *Here I Stand*. Nashville: Abingdon Press, 1950.

Bergendoff, Conrad. *The Church of the Lutheran Reformation*. St. Louis: Concordia Publishing House, 1967.

Bodensieck, Julius, ed. *The Encyclopedia of the Lutheran Church*. Philadelphia: Fortress Press, 1965.

Dillenberger, John, ed. *Martin Luther: Selections from His Writings*. Garden City, N.Y.: Doubleday, 1961.

Ebeling, Gerhard. *Luther: An Introduction to His Thought*. Philadelphia: Fortress Press, 1970.

Kerr, H. T., ed. *A Compend of Luther's Theology*. Philadelphia: Westminster Press, 1943, 1966.

Lowe, Ralph W. *The Lutheran Way of Life*. Englewood Cliffs, N.J.: Prentice-Hall, 1966.

Nelson, E. Clifford. *Lutheranism in North America: 1914–1970*. Minneapolis: Augsburg Publishing House, 1972.

Neve, H. T., and Anderson, B. A., eds. *The Maturing of American Lutheranism*. Minneapolis: Augsburg Publishing House, 1968.

Neve, J. L. *Introduction to the Symbolical Books of the Lutheran Church*. Columbus: Lutheran Book Concern, 1926.

Scherer, James A. *Mission and Unity in Lutheranism*. Philadelphia: Fortress Press, 1969.

Schlink, Edmund. *Theology of the Lutheran Confessions*. Philadelphia: Muhlenberg Press, 1961.

Schmidt, John. *The Lutheran Confessions: Their Value and Meaning*. Philadelphia: Muhlenberg Press, 1956.

Swihart, Altman K. *Luther and the Lutheran Church, 1483–1960*. New York: Philosophical Library, 1960.

Tappert, Theodore G., ed. *The Book of Concord: The Confessions of the Evangelical Lutheran Church*. Philadelphia: Muhlenberg Press, 1959.

———. *Lutheran Confessional Theology in America 1840–1880*. Library of Protestant Thought. New York: Oxford University Press, 1972.

Watson, Philip S. *Let God Be God!* Philadelphia: Muhlenberg Press, 1948.

Wentz, Abdel Ross. *A Basic History of Lutheranism in America*. Philadelphia: Fortress Press, 1964.

———. *The Lutheran Church in American History*. Philadelphia: United Lutheran Publication House, 1933.

Wentz, Frederick K. *Lutherans in Concert*. Philadelphia: Fortress Press, 1969.

Wolf, R. C. *Documents of Lutheran Unity in America*. Philadelphia: Fortress Press, 1966.

Methodist

Armstrong, James. *United Methodist Primer*. Nashville: Tidings, 1972.

Asbury, Francis. *Journals and Letters*. Elmer T. Clark, ed. Nashville: Abingdon Press, 1958.

Book of Discipline of The United Methodist Church. Nashville: The United Methodist Church, 1984.

Bucke, Emory S., ed. *History of American Methodism*. Nashville: Abingdon Press, 1964.

Carter, Henry. *The Methodist Heritage*. Nashville: Abingdon Press, 1952.

Colaw, Emerson. *Beliefs of a United Methodist Christian*. Nashville: Tidings, 1972.

Harmon, Nolan B. *Understanding the Methodist Church*. Nashville: Abingdon Press, 1977.

Heitzenrater, Richard P. *The Elusive Mr. Wesley*. 2 vols. Nashville: Abingdon Press, 1984.

Kennedy, Gerald H. *The Methodist Way of Life*. Englewood Cliffs, N.J.: Prentice-Hall, 1958.

Kirkpatrick, Dow, ed. *The Doctrine of the Church*. Oxford Institute on Methodist Theological Studies, 1962; Nashville: Abingdon Press, 1964.

Moore, John M. *The Long Road to Methodist Union*. Nashville: Abingdon Press, 1943.

Norwood, Frederick A. *The Story of American Methodism*. Nashville: Abingdon Press, 1975.

Stokes, Mack B. *Major United Methodist Beliefs*. Nashville: Abingdon Press, 1972.

Sweet, W. W. *Methodism in American History*. Nashville: Abingdon Press, 1954.

Tuell, Jack Marvin. *The Organization of The United Methodist Church*. Nashville: Abingdon Press, 1977, 1985.

Wesley, John. *John Wesley's Theology: A Collection from His Works*. Burtner, Robert W., and Chiles, Robert E., eds. Nashville: Abingdon Press, 1954, 1982.

Wesley, John. *The Works of John Wesley*. Frank Baker, editor-in-chief. 4 vols. Nashville: Abingdon Press, 1984–1986.

Williams, Colin W. *John Wesley's Theology Today*. Nashville: Abingdon Press, 1960.

Moravian

Fries, Adelaide. *Records of the Moravians in North Carolina*. 10 vols. Raleigh: State Department of Archives, 1968.

Gollin, Gillian Lindt. *Moravians in Two Worlds*. New York: Columbia University Press, 1967.

Hamilton, J. T., and Hamilton, K.G. *History of the Moravian Church: The Renewed Unitas Fratrum from 1722–1957*. Bethlehem, Penna.: Interprovincial Board of Christian Education, 1967.

Lewis, Arthur J. *Zinzendorf, The Ecumenical Pioneer: A Study of the Moravian Contribution to Christian Mission and Unity*. London: SCM Press, 1962.

Weinlick, John R. *Count Zinzendorf*. Nashville: Abingdon Press, 1956.

———. *The Moravian Church Through the Ages*. Bethlehem, Penna.: Interprovisional Board of Christian Education, 1966.

Old Catholic

Anson, Peter. *Bishops at Large*. London: Faber & Faber, 1964.

Moss, C. B. *The Old Catholic Movement*. New York: Morehouse-Barlow: 1964.

Pruter, Fr. Karl. *A History of the Old Catholic Church*. Scottsdale, Ariz.: St. Willibrord's Press, 1973.

Orthodox

Benz, Ernst. *The Eastern Orthodox Church: Its Thought and Life*. Trans. Winston, Richard, and Winston, Clara. Chicago: Aldine Publishing Co., 1963.

Bespuda, Anastasia. *Guide to Orthodox America*. Tuckahoe, N.Y.: Saint Vladimir's Press, 1965.

Bogolepov, Alexander A. *Toward an American Orthodox Church: The Establishment of an Autocephalous Orthodox Church*. New York: Morehouse-Barlow, 1963.

Bratsiotis, Panagiotis. *The Greek Catholic Church*. Notre Dame/London: University of Notre Dame Press, 1967.

Bulgakov, Sergius. *The Orthodox Church*. Milwaukee: Morehouse Publishing Co., 1935.

Constantelos, Demetrios J. *The Greek Orthodox Church.* New York: The Seabury Press, 1967.
Emhardt, Chauncy, et al. *The Eastern Church in the Western World.* Milwaukee: Morehouse Publishing Co., 1828.
LeGuillou, M. J. *The Spirit of Eastern Orthodoxy.* New York: Hawthorne Books, 1962.
Meyendorff, John. *The Orthodox Church: Its Past and Its Role in the World Today.* Tuckahoe, N.Y.: St. Vladimir's Press, 1981.
Salutos, Theodore. *The Greeks in America.* Cambridge, Mass.: Harvard University Press, 1964.
Schmemann, Alexander. *The Historical Road of Eastern Orthodoxy.* New York: Holt, Rinehart & Winston, 1963.
Ware, Timothy. *The Orthodox Church.* Baltimore: Penguin Books, 1964.
Zernov, Nicholas. *Eastern Christendom: A Study of the Origin and Development of the Eastern Orthodox Church.* New York: G. P. Putnam's Sons, 1961.

Pentecostal

Anderson, Robert Mapes. *Vision of the Disinherited.* New York: Oxford University Press, 1979.
Bennett, Dennis J. *Nine O'clock in the Morning.* Plainfield, N.J.: Logos International, 1970.
Bloch-Hoell, Nils Egede. *The Pentecostal Movement: Its Origin, Development, and Distinctive Character.* New York: Humanities Press, 1964.
Clark, E. T. *The Small Sects in America.* Nashville: Abingdon Press, 1949.
Conn, Charles. *Like a Mighty Army.* Cleveland, Tenn.: Pathway Press, 1955.
Cunningham, Robert C. *Filled with the Spirit.* Springfield, Mo.: Gospel Publishing House, 1972.
Durasoff, Steve. *Bright Wind of the Spirit.* Englewood Cliffs, N.J.: Prentice-Hall, 1972.
Frodsham, S. H. *With Signs Following.* Springfield, Mo.: Gospel Publishing House, 1946.
Gaver, Jessyca Russell. *Pentecostalism.* New York: Universal Publishing & Distribution Corp., 1971.
Gee, Donald. *Concerning Spiritual Gifts.* Springfield, Mo.: Gospel Publishing House, 1972.
Harper, Michael. *As at the Beginning: The Twentieth Century Pentecostal Revival.* Plainfield, N.J.: Logos International, 1971.
Harris, Ralph W. *Spoken by the Spirit.* Springfield, Mo.: Gospel Publishing House, 1973.
Hollenweger, Walter. *The Pentecostals: The Charismatic Movement in the Churches.* Minneapolis: Augsburg Publishing House, 1972.
Menzies, William W. *Anointed to Serve: The Story of the Assemblies of God.* Springfield Mo.: Gospel Publishing House, 1971.
Moon, Elmer Louis. *The Pentecostal Church.* New York: Carlton Press, 1966. (A history of the Pentecostal Church of God in America, Inc.)
Nichol, John Thomas. *The Pentecostals.* Plainfield, N.J.: Logos International, 1971.
Riggs, R. M. *The Spirit Himself.* Springfield, Mo.: Gospel Publishing House, 1949.

Sherrill, John. *They Speak with Other Tongues.* Old Tappan, N.J.: Fleming H. Revell, 1964.

Synan, Vinson. *The Holiness-Pentecostal Movement in the United States.* Grand Rapids: Eerdmans Publishing Co., 1972.

———. *The Old-Time Power.* Franklin Springs, Ga.: Advocate Press, 1973.

Presbyterian

Armstrong, Maurice W.; Loetscher, Lefferts A.; and Anderson, Charles A. *The Presbyterian Enterprise.* Presbyterian Historical Society Publications. Philadelphia: Westminster Press, 1956.

Briggs, C. A. *American Presbyterianism.* New York: Scribner's, 1885.

Calvin, John. *Institutes of the Christian Religion.* Philadelphia: Westminster Press, 1960.

Davies, A. Mervin. *The Presbyterian Heritage.* Richmond: John Knox Press, 1965.

Drury, C. M. *Presbyterian Panorama.* Philadelphia: Westminster Press, 1952.

Jamison, Wallace N. *The United Presbyterian Story,* 1858–1958. Pittsburgh: Geneva Press, 1958.

Lingle, Walter W., and Kuykendall, John W. *Presbyterians: Their History and Beliefs.* Richmond: John Knox Press, 1978.

Loetscher, Lefferts A. *A Brief History of the Presbyterians.* Philadelphia: Westminster Press, 1978.

———. *The Broadening Church.* Philadelphia: University of Pennsylvania Press, 1954.

Mackay, John A. *The Presbyterian Way of Life.* Englewood Cliffs, N.J.: Prentice-Hall, 1960.

Melton, Julius. *Presbyterian Worship in America.* Richmond: John Knox Press, 1967.

Miller, Park Hays. *Why I Am a Presbyterian.* New York: Thomas Nelson, 1956.

Reed, R. C. *History of the Presbyterian Churches of the World.* Philadelphia: Westminster Press, 1905.

Slosser, Gaius J., ed. *They Seek a Country: The American Presbyterians.* New York: Macmillan, 1955.

Thompson, Ernest Trice. *Presbyterians in the South.* 3 vols. Richmond: John Knox Press, 1963–1973.

Thompson, R. E. *A History of the Presbyterian Churches in the United States.* American Church History Series. New York: Scribner's, 1895.

Trinterud, Leonard J. *The Forming of an American Tradition.* Philadelphia: Westminster Press, 1949.

Reformed

American Calvinistic Conference. *The Word of God and the Reformed Faith.* Grand Rapids: Baker Book House, 1942.

Berts, H. *The Christian Reformed Church in North America.* Grand Rapids: Eastern Avenue Book Store, 1932.

Boettner, Loraine. *Studies in Theology.* Grand Rapids: Eerdmans Publishing Co., 1941.

Brown, W. D. *History of the Reformed Church in America*. New York: Board of Publication of the Reformed Church in America, 1928.

Brouwer, Arie R. *Reformed Church Roots*. New York: Reformed Church Press, 1977.

Corwin, E. T., et al. *A History of the Reformed Church, Dutch, the Reformed Church, German, and the Moravian Church in the United States*. American Church History Series. New York: Scribner's, 1895.

Hageman, Howard. *Lily Among the Thorns*. New York: Half Moon Press, 1953.

———. *Our Reformed Church*. 11th ed. Lansing: RCA Distribution Center, 1976.

Hoekema, H. *The Protestant Reformed Churches in America*. Grand Rapids: Eerdman's Publishing Co., 1936.

Roman Catholic Church

Abbott, Walter M., S.J., ed. *Documents of Vatican II*. New York: American Press, 1966.

Bokenkotter, Thomas W. *A Concise History of the Catholic Church*. Garden City, N.Y.: Doubleday, 1979.

Catholic Almanac. Huntington, Ind.: Our Sunday Visitor Press, (annual).

Ellis, John Tracy. *American Catholicism*. 2d Ed. Chicago: University of Chicago Press, 1969.

Greeley, Andrew. *The American Catholic*. New York: Basic Books, 1977.

Hardon, John A., S. J. *Modern Catholic Dictionary*. Garden City, N.Y.: Doubleday, 1980.

Hennessey, James, S.J. *American Catholics*. New York: Oxford University Press, 1981.

Holmes, J. Derek, and Bickers, Bernard W. *A Short History of the Catholic Church*. New York: Paulist Press, 1984.

Kung, Hans. *The Church*. New York: Sheed & Ward, 1967.

McBrien, Richard P. *Catholicism*. Minneapolis: Winston Press, 1980.

McKenzie, John L. *The Roman Catholic Church*. Garden City, N.Y.: Image Books, 1971.

New Catholic Encyclopedia. New York: McGraw-Hill Book Co., 1967.

Official Catholic Directory. New York: P. J. Kenedy & Sons, (annual).

Spiritualist

Bach, Marcus. *They Have Found a Faith*. Indianapolis: Bobbs-Merrill, 1946.

Braden, Charles S. *These Also Believe*. New York: Macmillan, 1949.

Graebner, Theodore T. *Spiritism*. St. Louis: Concordia Publishing House, 1919.

Hill, J. A. *Spiritualism: Its History, Phenomena and Doctrine*. New York: Doubleday, 1919.

Leaf, H. *What Is This Spiritualism?* New York: Doubleday, 1919.

The Spiritualist Manual. Washington, D.C.: National Spiritualist Association of the United States of America, 1944.

Swedenborgian (Churches of the New Jerusalem)

Barrett, B. F. *The Question, What Are the Doctrines of the New Church? Answered*. Germantown, Penna.: Swedenborg Publication Association, 1909.

Smythe, J. K. *Gist of Swedenborg*. Philadelphia: J. B. Lippincott Co., 1920.
Swedenborg, Emanuel. *Complete Works*. Boston: Houghton Mifflin, 1907.

Unitarian Universalist

Cassara, Ernest. *Hosea Ballou*. Boston: Beacon Press, 1961.
Chadwick, John W. *William Ellery Channing*. Boston: Houghton Mifflin, 1903.
Commager, Henry Steele. *Theodore Parker*. Boston: Little, Brown, 1936.
Howe, Daniel Walker. *The Unitarian Conscience*. Cambridge: Harvard University Press, 1970.
Hutchison, William R. *The Transcendentalist Ministers*. New Haven: Yale University Press, 1959.
Kring, Walter D. *Henry Whitney Bellows*. Boston: Skinner House, 1979.
Miller, Russell E. *The Larger Hope*. Boston: Unitarian Universalist Association, 1979.
Parke, David B., ed. *The Epic of Unitarianism*. Boston: Beacon Press, 1957.
Persons, Stow. *Free Religion*. New Haven: Yale University Press, 1947.
Wilbur, Earl Morse. *A History of Unitarianism in Transylvania, England, and America*. Cambridge: Harvard University Press, 1952.
Williams, George H. "American Universalism," *Journal of the Universalist Historical Society*. Vol. 10, 1971.
Wright, Conrad. *The Beginnings of Unitarianism in America*. Boston: Beacon Press, 1955.
———. *The Liberal Christians*. Boston: Beacon Press, 1970.
———, ed. *A Stream of Light*. Boston: Unitarian Universalist Association, 1975.

United Church of Christ

Atkins, G. G. *History of American Congregationalism*. Boston: Pilgrim Press, 1942.
Burton, C. E. *Manual of the Congregational and Christian Churches*. Boston: Pilgrim Press, 1936.
Horstman, J.H.E., and Wernecke, H. H. *Through Four Centuries*. St. Louis: Eden Publishing House, 1938.
Horton, Douglas. *The United Church of Christ*. New York: Thomas Nelson, 1962.
Rouner, Arthur A., Jr. *The Congregational Way of Life*. Englewood Cliffs, N.J.: Prentice-Hall, 1960.
Williams, D. D., and Shinn, R. L. *We Believe: An Interpretation of the United Church Statement of Faith*. New York: United Church Press, 1966.

Unity

Bach, Marcus. *The Unity Way*. Lee's Summit, Mo.: Unity Books, 1982.
Cady, H. Emilie. *Lessons in Truth*. Lee's Summit, Mo.: Unity Books, 1896.
D'Andrade, Hugh. *Herald of the New Age*. New York: Harper & Row, 1974.
Fillmore, Charles R. *Talks on Truth*. Lee's Summit, Mo.: Unity Books, 1926.
———. *Dynamics for Living*. Lee's Summit, Mo.: Unity Books, 1967.
Freeman, J. D. *The Story of Unity*. Lee's Summit, Mo.: Unity Books, 1972.

INDEX

INDEX

INDEX

INDEX

INDEX